KESHAB

JOHN A. STEVENS

Keshab

Bengal's Forgotten Prophet

HURST & COMPANY, LONDON

First published in the United Kingdom in 2018 by

C. Hurst & Co. (Publishers) Ltd.,
41 Great Russell Street, London, WC1B 3PL

Printed in India

A Cataloguing-in-Publication data record for this book
is available from the British Library.
ISBN 978-184904-901-6 *hardback*

www.hurstpublishers.com

CONTENTS

LIST OF ILLUSTRATIONS

ACKNOWLEDGEMENTS

I have received a great deal of help with all aspects of this book. My deepest thanks are due to Catherine Hall, who inspired me to pursue this project in the first place and has provided me with guidance, encouragement and kindness ever since. William Radice has given me invaluable support, and took me on an exciting journey from British history into South Asian history and the Bengali language. Arun Ghosh became my mentor in Kolkata out of sheer goodwill—I could not have wished for a more inspiring, knowledgeable and energetic guide to an unfamiliar city. I know he would have been delighted to see this book finally in print.

I am grateful for the financial assistance of the Leverhulme Trust, the Arts and Humanities Research Council, and the UCL Simeon Shoul scholarship, which have generously supported this project at various stages.

My thanks are due to Protima Dutt and Sahana Bajpaie, who have provided me with exemplary research assistance, as well as tuition in Bengali language. Hanne-Ruth Thompson has always spurred me on with her enthusiasm and help. The manuscript has been improved immeasurably by detailed comments I received from Christopher Bayly and Julius Lipner, as well as two anonymous peer reviewers. I am grateful also for suggestions from Clare Midgley, Antoinette Burton, Michael Collins, Sukanta Chaudhuri, Zoe Laidlaw, Axel Körner, Ana Jelnikar and Pradip Datta. Discussions with Stuart Hall, Pradip Basu and Keith McClelland have aided me in thinking through theoretical issues. My father Colin Stevens read an entire draft, and helped me to improve the language and style. Needless to say, any errors contained herein are my sole responsibility.

I have learnt a lot from the students of my course 'Modern Bengal', taught at SOAS, University of London. My thanks are due to Ben Murtagh, Rachel Dwyer and my other colleagues there. I have received valuable feedback at numerous conferences and seminars held at SOAS, UCL, the Institute of Historical Research, Cambridge University, the British Library, Scottish Church College, the Centre for the Study of Social Sciences, Jadavpur University, the Sadharan Brahmo Samaj and Presidency College. I am grateful to the librarians at the British Library, Colindale Newspaper Library, Harris Manchester College Library, the library of the Centre for the Study of Social Sciences, the National Library of India, the Ramakrishna Mission Institute of Culture Library, Kolkata, the library of the Sadharan Brahmo Samaj and the Bangiya Sahitya Parisad.

My work in Kolkata was aided significantly by the staff at the American Institute of Indian Studies. Indrani Bhattacharya and Prasenjit Dey provided me with many hours of valuable language tuition during my time there. My thanks are due to my fellow students for their friendship, and, in particular, for finding me medical assistance when I was knocked unconscious by a cat which fell from a tower block roof—one of the more surreal moments of my time researching this book.

I am deeply grateful to Bishan Samaddar, who welcomed me unreservedly into his family and circle of friends in Kolkata. It was through Bishan that I met many of the people who continue to make my time in India so enjoyable, including Rohini, Santanu, Sandip, Ludo, Candy and Rohit. Ludo and Candy (and Dobby) have looked after me on many occasions. I am thankful also to Nadia, Bijoy, Ananda and family for their generous hospitality in Bangladesh.

My interest in history has been inspired by numerous scholars and teachers with whom I have studied over the years, including Rebecca Spang, Peter Schröder, Karl Sampson, John Barnett and Mark Godowski. I am grateful to Michael Dwyer and the staff at Hurst for having faith in this project and for helping me to see it through to the end. I am lucky to have received a great deal of encouragement from my family and friends.

ACKNOWLEDGEMENTS

Finally, my thanks are due to my parents. They have always given me unqualified support in all my eccentric endeavours. This book is dedicated to them with love.

John Stevens
Tring
December 2017

A NOTE ON TERMINOLOGY

Although I have largely avoided inverted commas, I regard the categories of race, gender, class and civilisation as discursive—that is, as socially constructed concepts that have no essential referents. I have tended to retain inverted commas for the terms 'East', 'West', 'orthodox' and 'Hindu', to make it clear that I am referring to the ways in which these terms are being constructed at a particular historical moment. The phrase 'orthodox Hinduism' is used to denote historically specific constructions of what particular individuals and groups regarded as 'orthodox', and does not refer to an essential set of beliefs or practices—'Hinduism' is, as Julius Lipner has observed, a vast, varied and 'polycentric' cultural phenomenon.[1]

In rendering Bengali phrases and names, I have opted for consistency of spelling and ease of reading, and have avoided the use of diacritical marks. Inconsistencies occasionally arise where a term has been adopted widely in English. The spelling of Bengali names in the nineteenth century varied considerably (especially as rendered in English), and scholars of the present day differ in their spelling of the names of figures such as Ram Mohan Roy and Keshab Chandra Sen. I have aimed for consistency in my own text, but have retained original spellings in quotations and references. It is more natural to refer to prominent Bengalis of this period by their first name.

1

INTRODUCTION

In late 1883, Keshab Chandra Sen spent much of his time seated by a window in Lily Cottage, his large residence at number seventy-two, Upper Circular Road, Calcutta. He was watching workmen construct the 'New Sanctuary', a place of worship intended to provide a refuge for his family, his neighbours and his disciples. Immobilised by illness, Keshab was conscious that the construction of the sanctuary would be his last act. By now in straitened financial circumstances, he had directed that part of Lily Cottage be knocked down in order to provide the building materials, and had insisted that each Apostle of the New Dispensation put in some bricks and mortar. The consecration ceremony took place on 1 January 1884, at which point the building was still incomplete, and Keshab's health had worsened. He demanded to be carried into the unfinished hall to deliver his final prayer to an astonished congregation:

> My Mother is my health and prosperity, my peace and beauty, my life and immortality. I am happy amidst the agonies of my disease in the presence of my Mother, and may this happiness be yours also. I will not speak more, because I fear they will rebuke me if I do.[1]

Keshab died seven days later. At the foot of his tomb, alongside the combined symbols of the cross, crescent, trident and Vedic *omkar*, was inscribed an epitaph of his own creation: 'Long since has the little bird

"I" soared away from this sanctuary, I know not where, never to return again'.[2] This book is concerned primarily with what Keshab referred to as 'the little bird "I"'.

Keshab

Keshab Chandra Sen (1838–84) was one of the most prominent, powerful and controversial figures in nineteenth-century Bengal. He was a religious leader, whose distinctive, universalist interpretation of Hinduism found mass appeal in India, and generated considerable interest in Britain. He was a social reformer, who played an instrumental role in shaping Bengali society, particularly in the areas of education and the position of women. He was a renowned orator, who propounded novel and influential ideas regarding British rule in India, religion and spirituality, global history, universalism and modernity. He was wildly ambitious and intensely devout, and had a strong sense of his own historical importance. He was also sensitive, prone to depression and paranoia, and viewed his own life as a 'puzzle'.[3] He regarded himself as a proud Bengali and a patriotic Indian, who was determined to convey the value of his culture to Western audiences. He was also a colonial subject, whose material, social and psychic world was structured in fundamental ways by India's subjugated position within the British empire.

For Bengali readers, it might seem surprising that I have chosen to describe Keshab as Bengal's 'forgotten' prophet. Keshab's name is well known in West Bengal and he will appear in most general histories of the region. My regular journey by auto rickshaw from the library of the Bangiya Sahitya Parisad to M. G. Road metro station in Kolkata took me down a street which bears his name. However, Keshab has not received anything approaching the same degree of attention as other luminaries of Bengali culture such as Ram Mohan Roy or Rabindranath Tagore. He is a neglected figure in Bengali historiography.[4] Much of the literature that focuses on him specifically was written during his lifetime and in the forty years after his death. These works tend to be biased, written either by members of rival religious factions, Keshab's disciples, followers of Ramakrishna, Unitarians or Christian missionaries.[5] Keshab has proved to be a difficult figure to subsume into celebratory histories of Indian nationalism or Hindu reformism. He was a vehement critic of the abuses of British imperialism and an unquestionably patriotic apologist for Indian culture, and yet he stood firm in his conviction that Queen Victoria had been sent by God to rule India. He played a vital role in the development of Bengali Hinduism, and yet he was an ardent admirer of Jesus and argued in favour of the spread of Christianity in India. The figures he looked to for inspiration included Chaitanya, Ramakrishna, Theodore Parker, Charles Darwin and Thomas Carlyle. He had a resolutely internationalist outlook.

The vast majority of non-specialist readers from outside India will never have heard Keshab's name. Yet in the 1880s, we find the celebrated Orientalist scholar Max Müller claiming that Keshab's name 'has become almost a household word in England'.[6] Keshab's reputation among government officials, social reformers and Christian activists in Britain was considerable. His visit to England in 1870 transformed him into something of a celebrity: he lectured to a combined audience of over 40,000 people in the course of his stay, and his activities were reported in over fifty contemporary British newspapers and journals. The English Unitarians, who had been in contact with the Brahmos in Calcutta since the 1820s, became particularly enamoured of him, regarding him as a prophet of world-historical significance. They believed sincerely that his visit to the imperial metropole constituted a landmark in British religious history. Many Britons regarded him as a representative of all of India.

Keshab's ideas and actions caused a great deal of controversy during his own lifetime, and he remains a controversial and even confusing figure to this day. He was the subject of both extreme adulation and vehement criticism in India and in Britain. Accounts exist of large crowds prostrating themselves before him, believing him to be an avatar. His annual orations in Calcutta drew huge crowds. Yet he died with relatively few followers, his reputation in both India and Britain largely ruined. He was regarded by some as a prophet and a visionary, by others as a charlatan and a joke. A figure who self-consciously portrayed himself as a representative of India, Keshab became emblematic of a great variety of broad concerns regarding the relationship between India and the British empire. He was a polysemous figure, whose meaning was shaped in multiple and

3

divergent ways by the complex and contradictory character of the imperial world in which he lived.

The aim of this book is not to resolve the many contradictions and ambiguities that characterised Keshab's life and work, but rather to explore the historical forces out of which such contradictions and ambiguities arose. It aims to investigate the discourses through which Keshab understood the world and in terms of which he was understood. I am interested as much in what Keshab 'meant' as in what he 'did'. That is to say, an analysis of the ways in which Keshab was represented and imagined by a variety of historical actors in both India and Britain forms a major part of this study. In this sense, this book is not a work of biography. Rather, Keshab's experiences in London and Calcutta, along with accounts of him produced by a variety of observers in both metropole and colony, act as a lens through which to explore the construction and experience of subjectivity in a colonial context. As I am interested particularly in the ways in which Keshab's ideas and activities carried meaning for audiences in both Britain and India, I focus predominantly on the years between 1870 and 1884, as 1870 was the year in which Keshab visited England. This visit brought him into personal contact with a large number of Britons, and was followed by a sustained inter-cultural dialogue between Keshabite Brahmoism and British Unitarianism. My goal is to locate Keshab within an analysis which relates the transnational construction of identity in public discourses in multiple sites of empire to an analysis of the experience of colonial subjectivity at the level of friendship, emotion and self. I try to view Keshab, as he viewed himself, as both an 'Indian' and a 'man of the world'.[7]

Interconnected Histories

London and Calcutta were imperial cities that were profoundly interconnected. While Keshab's sphere of activity was confined largely to Bengal, his worldview was shaped by the cultural, intellectual and religious traditions of Britain and of India. His universalist project was directed not only at the transformation of India, but also the transformation of the 'West'. He had global ambitions and understood himself in terms of narratives of world history in which the 'East' and the 'West' were deeply enmeshed. Historians within the traditions of new imperial and transnational history have emphasised the manifold connections between the metropole and the colonies, and have drawn attention to the hybridity of imperial social formations. Recognition of the ways in which 'Britishness' was predicated on the representation and disavowal of colonial 'others' has served to challenge parochial understandings of Britain's 'island story'.[8] Keshab understood his Indian 'nationality' precisely through comparisons with the 'others' of the British empire, although from the perspective of his home in Calcutta, it was England that existed 'out there' in the empire as an imagined space of difference and familiarity that might be disavowed, but could also be claimed.

At times, Keshab adopted a binary view of the world, bifurcated by an imaginary line separating clearly the 'West' and the 'East'. Binary oppositions of West/East, coloniser/colonised, Britain/India, Hindu/ Christian, played a significant role in the ways in which Keshab conceptualised the world, and affected the ways in which he was interpreted by British audiences. However, stark divisions of this kind offer limited analytic value in understanding his worldview, which was hybrid, creative and changed over time.[9] Keshab was, to borrow Tony Ballantyne's term, 'entangled' in empire. He existed within 'dense webs of exchange fashioned by imperial activity [which] connected disparate points across the globe into new and highly uneven systems of interdependence, entangling previously disparate communities in new and often fraught relationships'.[10] This book draws on insights from transnational approaches to writing history that have rejected the nation-state as an adequate unit of analysis, and have instead studied the past across and beyond geopolitical borders, stressing intercultural connections and interactions.[11]

Histories of intercultural connections and interactions, however, do not have to be histories of collaboration and mutual understanding. It has been a long and difficult process for historians to begin to 'rewrite' black and South Asian people back into British domestic history.[12] While this enterprise is politically and intellectually crucial, it is important not to fall into a trap of reproducing a celebratory account of the 'imperial family' which emphasises collaboration and creativity without paying due attention to resistance, conflict and oppression.

Shruti Kapila has criticised the failure of global intellectual history to note 'significant ruptures in the meaning, content, and use of "European ideas," which, in the very act of dislocation from Europe, were significantly transformed'.[13] In examining Keshab's interaction with Britain, it is vital to be attentive to the limits of his influence, the extent of opposition to his ideas, and the ways in which his aims and intentions could be manipulated and misappropriated. Similarly, it must be emphasised that while Keshab might appear at times as an apologist for the imperial enterprise, his undoubted respect and admiration for 'Western' culture was fractured by abrupt ruptures with hegemonic imperial discourses, and by stringent critiques of colonial rule and 'Western' civilisation.

As Frederick Cooper has observed, a central feature of empire is that it 'reproduces differentiation and inequality among people it incorporates'.[14] Differentiation and inequality were sustained and reconfigured through a 'grammar of difference' which 'was continuously and vigilantly crafted as people in colonies refashioned and contested European claims to superiority'.[15] As Catherine Hall has contended, grammars of difference were elaborated 'across the axes of class, race and gender. These elaborations were the work of culture, for the categories were discursive, and their meanings historically contingent'.[16] Feminist historians have provided especially valuable insights into the ways in which masculinity, femininity and sexuality were imbricated in structures of imperial power that created and proliferated inequality and difference.[17] Insights from these traditions of scholarship are important to keep in mind when exploring Keshab's dialogue with Britain. This was a dialogue that was imbued with a rhetoric of inclusion and harmony, but was articulated within a political and ideological terrain that was structured fundamentally by exclusion and inequality.

Colonial Subjectivity

One goal of this book is to present a more nuanced, complex and plausible understanding of a figure who, along with many elite Bengalis of his generation, has been portrayed as existing in a state of 'perennial identity crisis', characterised by a series of sudden shifts in attitudes towards constitutionalism, social reform, women's emancipation and historical progress.[18] It is entirely understandable that questions of identity and even 'identity crisis' should arise in connection to the Bengali elite of Keshab's era, as these were figures who were English-educated and tied closely to the British administration, and yet participated, to varying degrees, in an assertive revival of Indian culture that would become an important basis for Indian nationalism. Keshab spoke openly of what he perceived to be 'Eastern' and 'Western' elements within his own personality, and was aware that these elements did not cohere harmoniously. However, as Michael Collins has observed, the notion of 'identity crisis' suggests some kind of 'psychological flaw; perhaps something inherent in the mind of the individual concerned', and thus 'misleadingly implies an empty centre to the mental world, which sees the individual mind lurch between extremes'.[19] The psychological category of 'identity crisis' also misleadingly locates broad historical shifts (which may or may not be regarded as 'crises') within the psychological make-up of individuals negotiating particular historical circumstances, and simplifies the complexities of colonial encounter into a negotiation of homogenised polar opposites.

Nevertheless, as Marc Bloch has written, 'historical facts are, in essence, psychological facts'; it is 'human consciousness' that is 'the subject matter of history'.[20] I share Catherine Hall's conviction that 'Emphasising the "voices within", the inner conflicts, the tensions at work within individuals, the successes and failures in resolving them, is as vital to historical understanding as what happens on the outside'.[21] While I do not resort to simplistic notions of 'identity crisis', I do place questions of identity and subjectivity at the heart of this book.[22] In *The Postcolonial Challenge*, Couze Venn draws attention to the tendency of scholarship concerning identity and subjectivity to define the two terms against one another.[23] Identity has been taken to refer to 'the relational aspects that qualify subjects in terms of categories such as race, gender, class, nation, sexuality, work and occupation, and thus in terms of acknowledged social relations and affiliations to groups'.[24] Subjectivity has been taken to refer to 'the substantive acting, thinking and feeling being'.[25] As Kathryn Woodward has contended, 'The concept of subjectivity allows for an exploration of the feelings which are brought and the personal investment which is made in positions of identity and of the reasons why we are attached to particular identities'.[26] If the term 'identity' refers to a possible subject-position within a historically specific symbolic and social order, then the term 'subjectivity' refers to the ways in which subjects identify with particular identities, why they do so, how they experience their sense of self, and how their sense of self may refer to, but also conflict with and exceed, this process of identification.

As the feminist theorist Judith Butler has argued, it is through the 'performance' and 'citation' of identity that subjects are both subjected to discourse and create new possibilities for ways of being in the world.[27] Butler's concepts of 'performativity' and 'citationality', which draw on J. L. Austin's linguistic theory of performative utterances, are useful aids when attempting to think about concepts of identity and subjectivity in tandem. In Butler's view, identities only exist through their performance by subjects, and performances of identity are only rendered meaningful as each performance will necessarily 'cite' a previous performance. While the concept of performativity continues to rely upon a dichotomy between subject-positions and the subjects who perform them, it does, at least, enable us to consider both the discursive and experiential aspects of identity and subjectivity.

In my view, the dichotomy between subjectivity and identity is really a false dichotomy, but one that it is difficult to think without. Humans make sense of themselves and their place in the world through an open-ended process of identification with a whole host of discourses, practices and symbols that are not of their own making. As becomes particularly clear in the context of imperial culture, this process of identification places people in profoundly unequal relations of power even as it renders their lives meaningful. While historical actors have no more control over the symbolic and discursive worlds into which they are born than they have over the geographic, political and material conditions in which they find themselves, they nonetheless attempt to shape their own history and to articulate their own identity.

The intellectual and religious histories of Bengal could be enriched by paying greater attention to the ways in which the genealogies of thought they trace were embodied in the cultural practices of the everyday. As C. A. Bayly has observed, 'powerful ideas persuade people to courses of action, but only in the context of their particular lived worlds'.[28] By paying close attention to the ways in which Keshab's ideas were embodied in his everyday practices and domestic life, we can gain insight into the important roles played by emotion, friendship, intimacy and the body in the exercise and experience of empire. As Burton and Ballantyne have demonstrated, the 'body' brings into focus 'the material effects of geopolitical systems in everyday spaces, family life, and on-the-ground cultural encounters'.[29] The body assumed particular significance when it became a 'spectacle', as was often the case when travellers from various sites of empire appeared in person in the metropole and became an object of fascination for metropolitan observers.[30] The particular importance of the body in the performance of religion—through manners of dress, modes of dramatic speech and presentation, repetitive performances of ritual practice and the adoption of postures—has been emphasised by numerous scholars within history, religious studies and anthropology.[31] Histories of representation, emotion and cultural practice provide a useful lens through which to address the question of how 'the outer world [was] taken in and the inner world projected into wider social practices and institutions'.[32] Ideas are not only thought, they are lived, and I aim in this book to emphasise the importance of the subjective and performative dimensions of Keshab's universalism.

Universalism

The nineteenth century was an era of grand narratives and globe-making projects, underpinned by a belief in historical progress. A central 'alibi' of empire, to use Karuna Mantena's term, was that, through rational means, it served to speed up the progress of subject populations towards the historical goal of (Western) 'modernity'.[33] A belief in the immutability, singularity and inevitability of historical progress, with a 'Western' model of modernity as its goal, became characteristic of what has been termed the 'Western historicist paradigm'.[34] Rational, ethical, scientific, religious and political intervention in the name of historical progress was one important way in which British imperialism was justified, at least in the first half of the nineteenth century. Grand narratives of liberalism, Christianity and science became intertwined in metropolitan visions of empire.

I approach these 'grand narratives' in this book as varieties of universalism, as they were narratives that purported to encompass the entirety of human history—to structure the full spectrum of human experience into a consistent whole. In his work on universalism in Meiji Japan, Michel Mohr defines a 'universalist' perspective as one that 'would supposedly be valid regardless of a specific time and place'.[35] New technologies of mass communication, combined with imperial political systems and transnational capitalist networks, provided the background for the emergence of grand universalist ideas which purported to have a global reach. The Enlightenment concept of 'universal reason' was one such idea, as was the concept of 'universal religion', which, in the nineteenth century, was regarded by a generation of religious reformers, including Keshab, as perfectly commensurable with rational and scientific perspectives.

Ideas that purported to be universal were, however, always mutable and plural. I agree with Mohr that concepts of universality are always '*colored* by innumerable cultural and individual filters'.[36] Rather than engaging in an abstract philosophical discussion of 'universals', I follow Tsing in adopting an historical approach that examines a 'practical, engaged universality' that 'can only be charged and enacted in the sticky materiality of practical encounters'.[37] As Tsing argues, 'actually existing universalisms are hybrid, transient, and involved in constant reformulation through dialogue'.[38] They are not politically neutral: universalist ideas are deeply imbricated in both the history of European colonialism and the history of anti-colonial resistance. Bose and Manjapra have drawn attention to the importance of the 'colonized world as a fount of different universalisms' that served to challenge Western claims to universality.[39] They have also explored South Asian involvement in a variety of alternative European universalisms, including literary modernism, communism and fascism.[40] Michel Mohr's work has explored the ways in which Japanese intellectuals, in dialogue with Unitarian interlocutors in the West, attempted both to redefine their sectarian identities and to recast their religion in universal terms.[41] Ayesha Jalal has examined the role of Islamic universalism in the global history of anti-colonial resistance.[42] As Tsing writes, 'Universals beckon to elite and excluded alike'.[43]

As Theodore Koditschek reminds us, universalist ideologies of history and progress were never monolithic, but were transformed and reconfigured as they 'assumed the form of concrete discourses, articulated by actual people, with specific motives, operating in circumscribed historical contexts'.[44] Universalist visions of history and of progress emerged from the colonial periphery as well as the metropolitan centre. These visions were often the product of dialogues between the metropole and the colonies, emerging in 'cosmopolitan thought zones created by passages across the Indian Ocean'.[45] The 'universalizing channels' that Mohr identifies as linking discourses of religious universalism in Japan and the West—Hegelian philosophy, Theosophy, Swedenborgianism, Unitarianism, new religious movements and liberal Christianity—were equally important in the South Asian context.[46] Keshab himself thought on a global scale, and is known for advancing a variety of universalism that became institutionalised, in the final years of his life, as the *Naba Bidhan* or New Dispensation. He developed this universalist vision in dialogue with reformers in India and the West. This book examines Keshab's universalism in relation to a variety of other forms of universalism, both religious and political, that were influential in nineteenth-century Britain and Bengal.

Firstly, this book explores Keshab's universalism in its interconnection with discourses and practices of liberalism. 'Liberalism' is, of course, a notoriously difficult concept to define, and it is more appropriate to think in terms of a variety of 'liberalisms', as the work of Karuna Mantena has demonstrated. Rather than defining liberalism in narrowly political terms, I follow Koditschek in viewing liberalism as 'a loose constellation, encompassing free trade, free labor, free association, free press, and formal equality'.[47] As C. A. Bayly has argued, in the Indian context, a loosely-defined liberalism included 'arguments, projects and sensibilities which the English-speaking intelligentsia believed would give Indians freedom from despotic government, superstitious religiosity, social tyranny and economic backwardness.... Indian liberalism also comprised a sustained series of attempts to build up a civil society (then called a "public") by promoting civic responsibility, morality, Indian political representation, progressive religion and a free press'.[48]

When liberalism is defined in this loose way, it is difficult to refute Uday Mehta's contention that the nineteenth century 'was an epoch of liberal triumph in Britain'.[49] The nineteenth century witnessed the abolition of slavery, the gradual extension of the franchise in Britain, increased tolerance of the Jewish and Catholic religions, and the emergence of free trade as the dominant—if still contested— economic perspective, all of which bear testament to what Mehta terms the 'deepening of liberal "culture" in Britain' in the nineteenth century.[50] Mehta's account of the rise of liberal culture points to the ways in which liberalism—a putatively universal and politically inclusionary ideology—involved, in practice, the systematic exclusion of various groups of people. In Mehta's view, the response of liberal theorists when they encountered unfamiliar experiences and peoples was to 'see those experiences, those life forms, as provisional'.[51] While people of other cultures may have been regarded as exhibiting the potential for political inclusion, they did not exhibit those capacities in the present, and were thus confined to what Dipesh Chakrabarty has termed 'an imaginary waiting room of history'.[52]

The liberal model of imperialism was the most prominent and powerful ethical justification for empire in the nineteenth century. As Sartori has argued, 'Liberalism has been plausibly implicated, with enormously varying degrees of necessity and contingency, in the conceptualization, institutionalization and legitimization of hierarchical practices of subordination on the basis of race, gender and other categories of difference'.[53] Interconnections between liberalism and empire are visible not only in the intellectual history of the nineteenth century, but also in the economic history of global capitalism. Through an analysis of agrarian relations in rural Bengal, Sartori has examined the role of property in the constitution of a liberal polity in which liberal norms were constitutively bound to practices of commodity exchange.[54] However, liberalism as a historical tradition was never monolithic, and it did not necessitate empire. Liberal critiques of empire were prominent in the late eighteenth century, and nineteenth-century projects motivated by liberal ideals took a variety of forms as they were implemented in different locations and circumstances. By the late nineteenth century, ethically orientated theories of imperial legitimacy—focused on the 'improvement' of 'native' societies—were challenged increasingly by 'scientific' and sociological understandings of empire which emphasised insurmountable racial barriers to 'native' improvement.[55] Following a series of mid-century rebellions, Britons began to question whether it was really possible for imperialism to civilise its subjects. During his visit to England in 1870, Keshab articulated a distinctive version of liberalism at the very moment that liberal visions of empire were being challenged by conservatism in Britain and by cultural (and political) nationalism in India.

The second variety of universalism with which this book is concerned is Christianity. The scholarly literature concerning the relationship between Christian universalism and British imperialism is vast, and has done much to further understanding of how liberal narratives of progress related to Christian discourses concerning the conversion and salvation of non-Christian peoples.[56] It became common among evangelicals of the early nineteenth century to emphasise the indissoluble bond between progress, civilisation and Christian belief, and many Christians throughout the nineteenth century argued that the Christianisation of colonial societies could serve to speed up the development of a race or nation through stages of civilisation. If liberal universalism included an exclusionary thrust that made possible the hierarchisation of people into those who were worthy of self-government and those who were not, then Christian universalism evinced a similar tendency to proclaim the fundamental equality of humanity (in spiritual terms) whilst simultaneously ordering people of different faiths according to complex grammars of difference.

However, the religious dimensions of empire cannot be reduced to a history of Christian universalism and evangelical missionary activity. Evangelical missionaries met with only very limited success in India, while creative interactions between prominent religious figures in Britain and India were sustained and diverse. In India, more than any other site of empire, there exists an alternative religious history of empire, one of inter-cultural dialogue, innovation and syncretism. As Arvind-Pal S. Mandair has demonstrated, discourses of religion in imperial India were themselves contingent on the emergence of the idea of 'religion' itself as a universal and translatable concept. Conceptual and experiential developments in religious discourses and practices remained tied deeply to imperial structures of power and knowledge, even as they gave rise to new forms of colonial subjectivity.[57] This is true of the emergent discourses of comparative religion in the nineteenth century, which, while purporting to transcend religious and cultural differences, must be viewed, as David Chidester has argued in relation to southern Africa, as a 'crucial index for imperial thinking'.[58] More than any other imperial science, Chidester claims, 'comparative religion dealt with the essential identities and differences entailed in the imperial encounter with the exotic East and savage Africa'.[59] It was the discourses and practices of comparative religion that constituted a key channel of interaction between Keshab and the British Unitarians, as they engaged in parallel attempts to discover 'universal' religious truths. This search for 'universal' truth was informed by imperial structures of knowledge and power.

On the fringes of British Christianity, Unitarian universalism—while largely, but not exclusively, Christian in orientation—exerted a powerful religious, intellectual and political influence. Unitarianism developed from the early nineteenth century in dialogue with Bengali Brahmo universalism, and engaged frequently with imperial questions. Unitarian respect for non-Christian religious faiths was such that many Unitarians in Britain came to regard Keshab, for a time, as a genuine 'prophet' of world-historical significance. It was Unitarian contacts, money and enthusiasm that lay behind much of the publicity which Keshab's visit to Britain generated. The closeness of the Brahmo-Unitarian connection raises some important and interesting questions. What motivated Unitarians to devote so much attention to the ideas and activities of a colonial subject from Bengal? How far was Keshab accepted as an equal in the Unitarian circles in which he moved in Britain? What were the grammars of difference which structured the Unitarians' encounter with Keshabite Brahmoism? What exclusionary thrusts, if any, lay within the most inclusionary religious ideologies of nineteenth-century Britain?

Lastly, this book attempts to understand Keshab's universalism in its interconnection with 'grand narratives' of scientific progress. The interconnections between science, religion and empire are profound and extremely complex.[60] Like many of their contemporaries, Keshab and his followers devoted an enormous amount of intellectual energy to the theme of science and religion, and to what they took to be their epistemological corollaries—reason and intuition (or faith). Keshab's universalism aimed not only to synthesise world religions into a coherent whole, but also to reconcile this synthesis with a 'scientific' worldview. This attempt to reconcile science and religion was of great interest to the English Unitarians, who were engaged in a parallel project to reinterpret religion according to scientific principles. Both the Brahmos and the Unitarians believed that is was necessary both to spiritualise rationality and to rationalise spirituality. They were deeply concerned that a 'religious' or 'spiritual' perspective on the world should not be lost in the face of the advancing power of scientific knowledge. This concern was reflected in British and Indian society more broadly.

These prodigious epistemological questions were intertwined with imperial concerns, not least because India was, by the mid-to-late nineteenth century, imagined increasingly as a repository of 'spiritual' knowledge from which Westerners might learn. Britons on the fringes of Christianity (and those involved in alternative forms of spirituality that were non-Christian) were beginning to look to India as a spiritual reference point.[61] The distinctively 'spiritual' character of Indian society was emphasised repeatedly by Indian nationalists. Keshab played a significant role in forging a vision of India as a place of spiritual power and non-rational insight. In doing so, he posed a challenge to some of the epistemological assumptions that underpinned British justifications for empire.

The Bengal Renaissance and the Bengali Elite

Keshab was a child of the Bengal renaissance, a period of intense cultural production and social reformation, centred in Calcutta in roughly the first half of the nineteenth century. He was a member of the *bhadralok*—a class of urban, English-educated, Hindu elites, who had come to prominence in the early nineteenth century as beneficiaries of a series of administrative, legal and land reforms, and had often taken up positions as interpreters, clerks and traders in the East India Company. Many historians have traced the beginnings of the Indian freedom movement back to the politicisation of the ideologies, societies and public sphere (newspapers, debates, public meetings, and so on) created by the *bhadralok* of the Bengal renaissance. According to this view, the professional intelligentsia turned to political activities some time in the 1870s in order to advance their own interests. Moderates initially prevailed, but the turn of the twentieth century saw the rise of political extremists or *swarajists*.[62] David Kopf's influential work on the Brahmo Samaj, a *bhadralok* society dedicated to religious and social reform, provides a nuanced and detailed account of the ways in which the Calcutta *bhadralok* profoundly influenced the rise of political consciousness and nationalism in India. The title of his book, *The Brahmo Samaj and the Shaping of the Modern Indian Mind*, effectively sums up a perspective on Bengali history that has become widespread: that Indian 'modernity' and nationhood were forged in the crucible of the Bengali encounter with the 'West', in which modern and progressive 'Western' values were combined with Hindu institutions and traditions.

The historical narrative of a Bengal renaissance led by a progressive *bhadralok* that sowed the seeds of Indian modernity and independence has been challenged from a variety of angles. For some historians, the Bengali *bhadralok* have appeared to be conservative, reactionary, and blind to the evils of colonial subjugation.[63] For others, they are best characterised as a comprador class, who collaborated with the British as they struggled for power within the limited opportunities for self-rule provided by the institutions of colonial government.[64] Scholars within postcolonial studies and subaltern studies have emphasised the extent to which the Bengali elite's worldview was 'colonised' through the inculcation of discourses derived from 'Western' systems of power-knowledge.[65] Rather than a golden age during which India first began to progress towards 'modernity', the Bengal renaissance was a time during which Bengali elites, partly through English education, became steeped in 'Western' discourses. Anti-colonialism drew its forms of social organisation and its rhetorical tropes from the discourses and forms of power which had formerly repressed colonial states. The 'imagined community' of India envisaged by elites was derived from 'Western' structures of power-knowledge, and thus failed to resonate with the majority of Indian subalterns.[66]

There can be no doubt that uncritical, celebratory and heroic accounts of a renaissance elite who led the Indian nation into 'modernity' are naïve at best. Historical critiques of the Bengali elite and the Bengal renaissance have refined understandings of concepts such as 'nation' and 'modernity', corrected—in part—the elitist bias of Indian historiography, provided valuable analyses of the discursive dimensions of imperial power, and pointed to the Eurocentrism of history writing itself. However, they have also served to reinscribe the binaries of 'East' and 'West' which they have purported to deconstruct, and, through focusing on the provenance of ideas (as either emanating from the 'West' or from pre-colonial forms of understanding), have encouraged a view of identity and colonial subjectivity which revolves around the question of the extent to which a particular individual's worldview can be shown to be 'authentic' or derived from colonial forms of knowledge. Within such a polarised historiography, Keshab can appear as a figure who must be either celebrated as a proto-nationalist (whether reformist or conservative), or maligned as an apologist for British imperialism. It is my view that he should simply be understood, as far as is possible, in all his complexity.

It is not possible to understand the ideas of a figure such as Keshab solely in terms of the extent to which they were 'derived' from 'European' or 'indigenous' concepts, even if the provenance and authenticity of ideas was something with which Keshab was often preoccupied. To approach history in this way is to flatten and homogenise the intellectual life of both 'Europe' and 'India'. As C. A. Bayly has argued, the 'rapidly developing connections between different human societies during the nineteenth century created many hybrid polities, mixed ideologies, and complex forms of global economic activity'.[67] I agree broadly with Andrew Sartori's contention that 'the history of a European concept's appropriation in Bengal should be analysed in the same manner as the history of the generation of that concept in Europe in the first place—in terms of the practical structures that render that concept a compelling lens through which to make sense of the world'.[68] For Keshab, an English-educated elite individual with close ties to the British administration, there can be no doubt that these 'practical structures' were shaped profoundly by the political, material and cultural power of British imperialism. But power did not only flow in one direction. Keshab contributed actively, critically and creatively to debates that were of great consequence to both Britons and Indians.

These debates were staged in a transnational public sphere in which the medium of communication was English. Of course, Keshab also lectured and wrote in Bengali, and appeared extensively in the Bengali-language press. Since the 1860s, Keshab had published newspapers in both English and Bengali; following the Cuch Bihar controversy in the 1870s, his detractors within the Sadharan Brahmo Samaj similarly established both English- and Bengali-language mouthpieces. Keshab's Bengali-language publication, *Dharmatattwa*, has been an important source for this book, as has the Sadharan Brahmo Samaj's *Tattwa Koumudi*, edited by Sivanath Sastri. However, the most important articles from both of these publications also appeared in translation in English-language Brahmo newspapers such as the *Indian Mirror*, *New Dispensation* and *Brahmo Public Opinion*. Similarly, reports on Brahmoism appearing in the British and Anglo-Indian press (as well as material appearing first in English-language Brahmo periodicals and newspapers) were translated and reprinted in the Bengali publications. Keshab's anniversary orations, which were by far the most widely publicised of his public lectures, were always conducted in English. Keshab's closest disciple, P. C. Majumdar, claims that Keshab's 'English lectures, tracts, and articles, contain in a most elaborate form his teachings'.[69] In general, I have not found significant discrepancies between Keshab's teachings as they appear in his English- and Bengali-language publications, although his private correspondence during his time in England, written in Bengali, does contain material which he did not express elsewhere.[70]

Keshab's mastery of the English language was, of course, crucial to the dissemination of his ideas to British audiences. As Antoinette Burton has argued, Victorian domestic ideology was 'staged neither in Britain nor India alone but in the transnational communities of colonial culture that imperial social formations generated, of which the press was a crucial discursive technology'.[71] While Keshab's activities were reported extensively in the national newspapers during his visit to England, for the most part the transnational community generating much of the material under consideration in this book was undoubtedly small: an urban, literate, English-educated Brahmo elite; an Anglo-Indian press tied closely to missionary enterprises and the colonial government; and a religiously marginalised, if politically influential, community of Unitarians in England. Among the Unitarians, it was Keshab's friend and correspondent Sophia Dobson Collet who did more than anyone to disseminate his ideas, publishing his lectures, collections of reports concerning his English visit, and editing her own *Brahmo Year Book*, which compiled a great variety of lectures, sermons and commentary produced in India and in Britain.[72] She also contributed material to the Unitarian journal *The Inquirer*, which followed Keshab's career closely from the late 1860s until his death.

Keshab moved in elite circles in both India and in Britain, and became part of a transnational religious community that existed, in many ways, outside the cultural mainstream. He was simultaneously a member of the Bengali elite and a colonial subaltern, exerting considerable influence from a position of power that was always fragile and anomalous. The scale of his ambition, combined with his close proximity to the British administration, has, at times, garnered him a reputation—in his own era and in the historiography—for egotism and even recklessness. He attempted boldly to forge a grand universalist synthesis from a great diversity of tradition, which, as Marx so memorably wrote, 'weighs like a nightmare on the brains of the living'.[73] This book is not a defence of Keshab, but aims to throw some light on the ways in which he experienced the imperial world, and the ways in which he carried meaning for his contemporaries.

2

KESHAB IN THE CONTEXT OF NINETEENTH-CENTURY BRITAIN AND BENGAL

On Sunday 14 October 1833, the mood in the South Place Chapel, Finsbury, London, was decidedly sombre. The assembled congregation of Christian Nonconformists and Unitarians had gathered to mourn the passing of the great Bengali social and religious reformer Ram Mohan Roy, who had died in Bristol two weeks previously. It is likely, although not certain, that Sophia Dobson Collet, aged eleven, was in attendance. She had met Ram Mohan recently, in person and in this very room, and he had left a deep impression on her and her family. The minister and future Member of Parliament William Johnson Fox began his sermon with a paean to the spirit of Orientalism, which, he believed, animated Ram Mohan and men of his stamp:

> Abraham was an Oriental; and whatever the nation of the individual, I apprehend that an Orientalism of nature and mental character belongs to this class of reformers. I mean by Orientalism, a tendency towards the spiritual, the remote, the vast, the undefined, as distinguished from the microscopic and grovelling intellect, which looks only upon earth, sees only in details, and comprises all philosophy in the calculations which most directly solve the questions, 'What shall we eat, what shall we drink, and wherewithal shall we be clothed?' The men whose monuments rise on the ascending path of human improvement, like 'towers along the steep,' beneath which the tide of time has hitherto beaten in vain, have always had loftier and wider views than these.[1]

The service concluded with a hymn written for the occasion by the celebrated social theorist and essayist Harriet Martineau. As the congregation of Londoners began to sing, their thoughts were focused on India.

Imperial Cities: London and Calcutta

By the middle of the eighteenth century, London was the largest city in the West. Throughout the nineteenth century, it was probably the most populous city in the world.[2] London was the centre of the biggest empire in history, an empire which, by the beginning of the twentieth century, held sway over approximately one quarter of the total population of the globe. By far the world's biggest food importer and consumer, London was home to huge processing industries—corn-mills, sugar refineries, distilleries and breweries. Although London's status as a manufacturing centre was to decline slowly in the nineteenth century, in 1871 it was still home to one sixth of all manufacturing workers in Britain.[3] Britain's nineteenth-century economic boom was fuelled not only by the industrial revolution, but also by the international finance of the City and the international trade of the Docks, facilitated by military and imperial expansion. London announced its status as the 'workshop of the world' in the Great Exhibition of 1851; the creation of the Greenwich Meridian in 1884 placed the metropolis at the centre of global time.[4]

London was a city suffused with empire. Vast quantities of goods from across the globe passed through the Docklands and into circulation in the metropolis. Imperial exhibitions such as the Colonial and Indian exhibition of 1886, the Stanley and African exhibition of 1890 and the Greater Britain Exhibition of 1899 attracted millions of visitors from Britain and abroad. Music halls, 'nigger minstrels' and pleasure gardens—with their ever-popular 'natives on show'—transformed empire into entertainment. Imperial themes were present in political discourse, the press, novels, plays, children's literature and advertising. At times, empire featured prominently in the English imagination—in the campaign for the abolition of slavery, in the aftermath of the Indian 'mutiny' in 1857 and the Morant Bay rebellion in Jamaica in 1865.[5] For the most part, however, empire existed as part of the important but unremarkable fabric of the everyday. Empire could easily find its way into what many regarded as its antithesis—the 'home'—which was itself a notion 'informed by tropes of material comfort associated with food, cleanliness, etc., themselves dependent upon imperial products'.[6] The most mundane of commodities would arrive in the capital as part of global, imperial circuits of production and distribution.

London was not only a place in which the material products of empire and the discourses and signs of imperialism circulated. It was also a place to which imperial subjects travelled, a place which became home to a variety of people from abroad. London's size and population grew enormously in the nineteenth century. This was partly the result of increasing birth rates and decreasing death rates, but was also the product of increasing immigration. Between 1841–51, 330,000 migrants arrived, forming 17 per cent of the total population of the city.[7] Many came from Ireland, fleeing famine; others arrived from the south east of England.[8] By 1900, London's population of six million included tens of thousands of residents who had been born in Czechoslovakia, Italy and Germany.[9] The metropolitan Irish population by this time had reached approximately 435,000.[10] Other residents included Australians, New Zealanders, Canadians and South Africans. From the mid-nineteenth century, Chinese immigrants—many arriving as sailors or ships' launderers—began to settle in Limehouse. Records exist of resident Madagascans, Malayans, Arabs, Turks and South Sea Islanders, many of whom arrived as lascars aboard ships.[11]

During the eighteenth century, London's Jewish population expanded. In 1850, there were approximately 20,000 Jews living in the capital; by the 1880s that figure had more than doubled.[12] By 1900 the Jewish population had increased to 130,000, partly due to an influx of Russian Poles fleeing pogroms.[13] Peter Fryer estimates that there were up to 20,000 Africans living in England by the end of the eighteenth century.[14] Burton contends that 'people of colour, slave and free, were everywhere to be seen on the streets, in the docks, and even on evangelical hustings…Refugees from Madagascar, "native converts" from China and Malaya, "coloured" visitors to the Great Exhibition, held in 1851, and the occasional tour of colonial royals represent some of the more spectacular evidence of colonial peoples that Britons might have witnessed before the 1870s'.[15]

Of all of the non-white peoples in London, Indians were, at least from the mid-to-late nineteenth century, perhaps the most visible and the best organised. Certainly in terms of archival material, Indian princes and students have left behind the most evidence for historians, as they moved in elite and middle-class public spaces and wrote accounts of their experiences.[16] Jonathan Schneer contests that, by the turn of the twentieth century, Indian anti-imperialists and nationalists in London were 'active, well-organized, well-connected, politically sophisticated'.[17] He estimates that the number of Indians resident in the metropolis in 1900 was approximately 1000.[18] Visram puts the figure a little lower, contending that from the mid-nineteenth century to 1914, several hundred Asians—most from the subcontinent—lived in Britain as a whole. However, hundreds of ayahs (nursemaids or nannies) and thousands of lascars (sailors or militiamen) passed through Britain each year.[19] Indian residents were diverse. Lascars tended to live in the slums of the East End, surviving on the margins of society. Visram has unearthed records of Indian tract-sellers, casual labourers, domestic servants, singers, musicians, vendors and snake-charmers.[20] Resident Indian princes and elite Indian visitors mingled with the upper-classes, dined with prime ministers and were presented to Queen Victoria. Professional residents were active in medicine, education, law, business, politics and the women's movement.[21]

In the mid-nineteenth century, Indian students began to arrive in the capital. Some came on government scholarships (established in 1868), others were funded privately. Education and training in England was essential to gain entry into the Indian Civil Service, and the Bar in Calcutta and Bombay. Although colonial students lived all over London, Bloomsbury was especially popular due to its proximity to the British Library, Temple Bar and the Inns of Court.[22] Visram contends that over 700 Indian students were resident in Britain by 1910, mostly studying in London, Oxford, Cambridge and Edinburgh.[23] Many Indians who were later to become prominent nationalist figures studied in London in the mid-to-late nineteenth century: both Gandhi and W. C. Bannerjee (later the first president of the Indian National Congress) studied in the metropolis.[24]

Societies designed to promote Indian issues, to encourage Indian-British contact, or to provide 'aid' of various kinds to visiting and resident Indians, had been in existence in London since the 1830s.[25] Such organisations increased in size and numbers throughout the nineteenth century, especially from the 1860s onwards. 1865 saw the formation of the first Indian society of any significant influence, the London Indian Society. The impetus for the society's establishment came from the future British MP Dadabhai Naoroji, W. C. Bannerjee, G. M. Tagore, B. Tyabji and a number of Indian students and businessmen in London.[26] The inaugural meeting was held in March at University Hall in Gordon Square. The purpose of the society was to discuss 'political, social and literary subjects relating to India with a view to promot[ing] the interests of the people of that country'.[27] In December 1866, the society was superseded by the East India Association, formed by a group of Indians including Naoroji, along with a number of sympathetic retired British officials. The London branch attracted a number of prominent Liberal and Radical MPs, many of whom were persuaded to raise issues concerning India in the House of Commons.[28] The association gained considerable influence through publications, meetings and deputations to Westminster. Its membership had grown to over 1000 by 1871.[29] However, by the 1880s, the organisation had become dominated by Anglo-Indians and had lost its political edge.

Of the other London-based societies, the most influential was the London India Society (as distinct from the London Indian Society). Cambridge student Ananda Mohan Bose, who had been converted to Brahmoism by Keshab in 1869 and would later play a leading role in the Indian National Congress, founded it in 1872. Naoroji also played a leading role in this organisation and became its president. The purpose of the society was to 'foster the spirit of nationalism among the Indian residents in Britain'.[30] Bose was a formidable speaker, and regularly delivered impassioned speeches concerning the wrongs of British rule in India.[31] The society continued to produce nationalist propaganda for over fifty years. Its activities drew the attention of the India Office, which sent spies to its meetings. A spy at a meeting of 28 December 1898 estimated that there were 150 Indians present.[32]

These organisations demonstrate that, whilst limited in numbers, colonial subjects—and, in particular, Indian subjects—did exert influence in the imperial metropole in the nineteenth century. London was suffused with what Mary Louise Pratt has termed 'contact zones', that is 'social spaces where cultures meet, clash, and grapple with each other, often in contexts of highly asymmetrical relations of power'.[33] These contact zones were, of course, of a limited and often fleeting nature. As Hall and Rose have observed, there were times when empire was 'simply there, not a subject of popular critical consciousness. At other times it was highly visible, and there was widespread awareness of matters imperial on the part of the public as well as those who were charged with governing it'.[34] Keshab's visit to Britain stimulated a considerable degree of interest in imperial matters within and outside the metropole, and brought many Britons into direct and sustained contact with a colonial subject. This encounter took place within the context of a city in which empire continually exerted a powerful, if uneven, influence.

While empire figured in metropolitan consciousness in London to an uneven degree, Calcutta was undoubtedly first and foremost an imperial city. The 'second city of the empire' and the British capital in India until 1911, Calcutta constituted the most important political and administrative centre of British power in India. Calcutta was also the most important commercial centre of the East India Company, acting as the trading hub for the opium, textile and jute industries. By 1856–7, Bengal contributed 44 per cent of the total British Indian revenue; in 1884–5 the figure remained as high as 25 per cent.[35] The degree of revenue generated by the region has led Pradip Sinha to characterise Bengal as 'the most exploited region in colonial India, with Calcutta as the nodal point of this process of exploitation'.[36] In the early nineteenth century, joint commercial enterprises between Europeans and the emergent Bengali *bhadralok* elite—who had prospered as monied purchasers of estates following the Permanent Settlement of 1793—led to the creation of business networks which brought colonisers and colonised into mutual collaboration.[37] The 1830s and 1840s have been characterised by Blair Kling as an 'Age of Enterprise', symbolised by Calcutta's largest business enterprise of the period, the Union Bank, which operated under joint European and Indian management with both European and Indian stockholders, and whose policy, until 1844, was essentially controlled by the zamindar (landowner), businessman and social leader Dwarkanath Tagore.[38] Commercial collaborations of this kind were, of course, restricted in general to Calcutta's rich and powerful elite.

While the trade and business connections between British and elite Bengali businessmen continued throughout the nineteenth century, the global financial crisis of 1848, which led to the collapse of the Union Bank and, ultimately, to the end of Calcutta as an independent centre of capital accumulation and investment, profoundly altered the nature of commercial relations between Britons and Bengali elites in the city. Post 1848, collaboration between Bengali and British businessmen became less common, capital investment came increasingly from Britain, and the economy of Eastern India was divided increasingly into an agrarian social order and a Calcutta-centred commercial world.[39] As Andrew Sartori has observed, 'The Calcutta-centred commercial world would be marked as constitutively white and Western by the marked exclusivity of European control and management of capital-based enterprise—in the sense of the profound subordination of the regional economy to the metropolitan capital market and in the sense of the racial exclusivity of the locally based business interests that were no longer dependent on native investment'.[40] By the 1870s, the commercial collaboration evident in the 1830s and 1840s had been fractured irrevocably along racial lines.

The racial divisions which became increasingly apparent in the commercial sphere from the mid-nineteenth century were evident earlier in the spatial division of Calcutta into a 'White Town', based around Chowringhee, and a 'Black Town', located in the north of the city. Sinha has contended that the 'White Town' and the 'Black Town' were separated to such a degree that the former exerted little impact, at a 'cognitive level', on the latter.[41] However, other historians have stressed the extent to which a variety of 'contact zones', facilitating interaction between Europeans and Calcuttans of all classes, emerged in the city in spite of the divisions between the two 'towns'.[42] Such contact, however, always took place within the context of fundamental inequalities of power immanent in the imperial relationship.

The economy and topography of Calcutta, along with its status as the centre of British administrative power in India, lent the city an overtly imperial character in comparison to other Indian urban centres. The impact of Western culture was also particularly pronounced. The

Calcutta *bhadralok* elite came to prominence not only as a result of economic opportunities generated by the Permanent Settlement, but also due to their access to English education, which facilitated their employment in a variety of lower-level Company and government positions. Calcutta was affected more than any other Indian city by the proliferation of institutions offering English education, which resulted from the triumph of the Anglicist camp in the Orientalist/Anglicist debates of the 1830s.[43] A vast literature exists exploring the effects of English education in Bengal, and the role which Indian exposure to 'Western' knowledge played in engendering the 'Bengal renaissance'. The extent to which the culture of the Calcutta elite was influenced or even dominated by imperial forms of knowledge and education remains controversial and problematic. However, there can be no doubt that the culture into which Keshab was born in 1838 was hybrid and entangled deeply in imperial relationships.

A Biographical Introduction to Keshab Chandra Sen

The only account of Keshab's early years is that left by P. C. Majumdar, a lifelong friend and disciple of Keshab, who published a biography of Keshab in 1887. Majumdar became acquainted with Keshab in early childhood, as he was a distant relative and was born in Garifa, the ancestral village of the Sens. Keshab was born in November 1838 in Calcutta. He made only infrequent visits to his ancestral village during his boyhood. Aged nine, Majumdar was taken to Calcutta to be educated and stayed in a house only a few feet from the residence of the Sens. From this time on the two boys, both of a similar age and part of the same family network, forged a close friendship which was to last throughout their lives.

According to Majumdar, Keshab was a direct descendent of the Sens of Garifa, an ancient dynasty who, 'with hoary antiquity on their heads', were 'semi-mythological potentates who ornamented the Hindu periods of the ancient history of India'.[44] The Sen dynasty included such illustrious figures as Ballal Sen and Lakshman Sen, who ruled in East Bengal during the thirteenth century. The Sens were by caste *vaidyas*, meaning 'versed in the science of medicine'; a caste which, according to Majumdar, was 'regal and high-placed', distinguished by the privilege of its members to acquire sacred knowledge of the Vedas and to act as gurus, and 'next to the traditional supremacy of the *Brahmans*, the caste that is most influential and intellectual in Bengal'.[45]

The prestige of this ancient lineage was augmented by the activities of Keshab's grandfather Ram Kamal Sen, who, in Majumdar's words, was 'the real architect of the wealth, honour, and reputation which the Sens of Garifa came to possess'.[46] Ram Kamal Sen was a contemporary of the celebrated religious and social reformer Ram Mohan Roy. He learnt English in Calcutta and began his career as an assistant typesetter in the Asiatic Society's press. Encouraged by the Orientalist scholar and East India Company surgeon H. H. Wilson, he rose through the ranks of the society, becoming a clerk and then a member of the council. He later became treasurer of the Calcutta Mint and went on to accept the Dewanship of the Bank of Bengal. A prominent and respected public figure with a handsome salary, he built a mansion in the centre of Calcutta and became actively involved in a range of charitable, governmental and educational institutions of the time. He took a deep interest in the Hindu College and School Book Society, helped fund Sanskrit College, and was a member of the District Charitable Society. He served on the committee of the Parental Academic Institution (a school for European and Eurasian children), he took an active part in the government Medical Education Committee, and, alongside close friend William Carey, jointly founded the Agricultural and Horticultural Society. In the 1830s he wrote and published a *Dictionary of the English and Bengalee Language*. In short, he established the Sens as a prominent and powerful *bhadralok* family in Calcutta, and forged many links with the British administration in the city. His considerable status as a public figure and the extent of his contacts with the British administration in India are evidenced by the fact that, apart from Ram Mohan Roy, he was the only Indian to be mentioned in the 1845 edition of Maunder's *Biographical Treasury; A Dictionary of Universal Biography*, published in England.[47]

Keshab's father held the post of bullion-keeper of the Calcutta Mint; beyond this, little more is known. He died when Keshab was a boy, but the wealth and status of the family was sufficient to ensure that Keshab did not suffer in material terms as a result. Keshab's early life was presided over by the head of the joint household, his uncle Hari Mohan

Sen.[48] Hari Mohan Sen took over the Dewanship of the Bank of Bengal upon his father's death; most of his siblings also held powerful positions in banking.[49] His family could be described as occupying the more 'conservative' end of the Calcutta Hindu spectrum: his grandfather was a charter member of the *Dharma Sabha* (a conservative Hindu religious society whose members opposed the abolition of *sati* or widow-burning) and was conservative in his views on family, caste and religion.[50] Keshab's mother, according to Majumdar, had married aged nine or ten and been 'trained up according to the strictest rules of Hindu seclusion'.[51] Keshab was educated in his early years in the vernacular by an elderly Bengali guru, but later went on to receive an English education at Hindu College, with a brief interim at Metropolitan College, where he took a particular interest in the study of mental and moral philosophy.

Majumdar's account of Keshab's life and teachings must be treated with caution, as it is imbued, to a degree, with unquestioning veneration, a characteristic of much of the material on Keshab written by his disciples. Nevertheless, a number of anecdotes Majumdar provides in relation to Keshab as a boy do provide valuable insight into the material circumstances of Keshab's youth and the high status occupied by his family. Majumdar recalls the esteem in which the Sens were held during their visits to the village of Garifa. He writes:

> The Sens…were so wealthy, distinguished, powerful in our little old-fashioned village that an unapproachable brilliance enveloped their old and young. The men appearing in the village at long intervals were treated like demigods, every one flattered them excessively; and the boys, fair, well-dressed, and inaccessible, seemed to have dropped out of the clouds…The Sens of Garifa were proud of their wealth, and fond of display. 'I was reared,' says Keshub, 'by a wealthy father and grandfather. Opulence and luxury surrounded my childhood, but as I grew up my mind began to show the spirit of natural poverty.'[52]

In his study of the Bengali social reformer Ishwar Chandra Vidyasagar, Brian Hatcher draws attention to the importance of Ram Mohan and Vidyasagar's status as *kulin brahmans* in engendering their strong dedication to educational and social reform.[53] This dedication, Hatcher writes, may be seen 'to be rooted in their conviction not only that as *brahmans* they had a special responsibility toward their community, but also that they spoke and acted from a position of awesome authority'.[54] Keshab was not a *brahman*, but it should be emphasised that the Sen family's financial wealth, its extensive connections in local philanthropic, educational and governmental institutions, and its high caste status—especially what the latter meant in terms of access to the Vedas and privileges to act as a guru—must have engendered in the young Keshab a strong sense of his own unusual and important status.

Following his marriage in 1856 to a girl of around nine years of age, Keshab is reported to have entered a state of depression, shunning the company of his wife and spending his time reading Christian sermons and books of philosophy. He began to associate with a number of Christian teachers from the Church Missionary Society and the American Unitarian Mission, including C. H. A. Dall, who introduced Keshab to the writings of Unitarian radicals such as Theodore Parker. Keshab received Bible instruction from the domestic chaplain to Bishop Cotton, Bishop of Calcutta.[55] Majumdar would later recall that it was during this time of depression and austerity that Keshab laid 'the rocky foundations of a pure character'.[56] He 'composed short exhortations and words of warning for passers-by, which he caused to be stuck on the house-walls in the neighbourhood'; he also staged a production of *Hamlet*, with himself in the lead.[57] Keshab would suffer bouts of depression throughout his life.

The Brahmo Samaj

In 1857, Keshab joined the Brahmo Samaj, a theistic organisation committed to religious and social reform, founded (as the Brahmo Sabha) in 1828 by Ram Mohan Roy. At the age of eighteen, Keshab experienced a 'clear revelation' in which 'God Himself' told him that 'he had a Heavenly Friend always near'.[58] The following year, a publication of the Calcutta Brahmo Samaj fell into his hands, and he found that Brahmoism 'corresponded exactly with the inner conviction of his heart'.[59] Keshab's deep connection with the Brahmo Samaj would continue until the end of his life, and the traditions of Brahmoism undoubtedly form the most important context in which Keshab's ideas should be understood.

The origins of Brahmoism may be traced, in part, to the growing influence of Christian missionaries in India in the early nineteenth century. Prior to 1813, it was the policy of the East India Company to prevent missionaries from operating in India, as it was feared that missionary interference in the religious and social practices of Indians could provoke a negative backlash, and thus destabilise the country. However, from the late eighteenth century, as the influence of evangelical Christianity—and in particular the influence of the powerful Clapham Sect—grew, considerable pressure was put on the British government to change this policy. When the East India Company Charter came up for renewal in 1813, it was agreed that Christian missionaries thenceforth would be able to operate.

The Baptist missionaries based in the Danish enclave of Serampore, led by William Carey, had, long before the change of policy in 1813, been writing about the abuses they perceived in 'orthodox' Hinduism. Lurid accounts of practices such as *sati* were arousing intense interest in Britain, and also began to circulate in Calcutta through missionary journals such as the Bengali journal *Samachar Darpan*, established by the Serampore missionaries in 1818. Although Governor-General Wellesley had introduced press regulations to limit the activities of the British press in India in 1799, under the administration of Marquis Hastings a more liberal attitude to the press was adopted, and this new stance towards the press, combined with the open policy towards missionary activity from 1813, led to a flourishing of newspapers and journals written by Christian missionaries. These journals acted as vehicles for Christian propaganda and were highly critical of what was termed 'orthodox Hinduism'. These accounts were in turn reprinted in the missionary journals in the metropole, and, through the widespread journalistic practice of extracting and reprinting articles, came to reach a much wider audience. Missionary accounts of the 'superstitions' of Hinduism, abuses against women, and the stultifying effects of the institution of caste, stimulated a variety of social reform movements calling for the social and religious regeneration of India— most notable among these was the campaign against *sati*.[60] This campaign drew the attention of many female social reformers in Britain, who attempted to win the support of privileged British Christian women for a cause that would help their suffering 'heathen sisters'.[61] Although British officials in India were often reluctant to intervene in matters of religious and social reform, it was becoming increasingly common for politicians and intellectuals in Britain to regard religious, as well as educational, reform as a central element in the imperial enterprise.

In the early nineteenth century, therefore, Hinduism was being challenged in Britain and, through the missionary press, in Calcutta. In a context in which missionaries were gaining influence in the fields of journalism, vernacular education, and social and religious reform, it was important for the Bengali elite that they should not be left by the wayside, that they should also have a voice in the debates fuelled by missionary activity, and that they should provide an alternative program of religious and social reform—one that would address the perceived 'abuses' of 'orthodox' Hinduism from within the Hindu tradition— which would curb the power of the missionaries and prevent the conversion to Christianity of their own descendants. Ram Mohan Roy was one such Bengali elite figure who entered the fray, and, more than any other, his views formed the foundation for the ideas and activities of subsequent generations of religious and social reformers in Bengal, including Keshab.

It is important to recognise Ram Mohan's wide-ranging universalism, as this affected Keshab deeply.[62] Ram Mohan's indebtedness to 'Western' thought has often been emphasised by scholars, but this emphasis gives a rather narrow impression of his background and outlook. Ram Mohan was, like many of the Bengali elite in Calcutta in the early nineteenth century, a supporter of British rule in India in so far as he regarded its policies as progressive. He worked in the East India Company for the British official John Digby, he learnt to speak and to write flawless English, he acquired a huge stock of learning on Western history, philosophy and religion, and, as is demonstrated by his oft-quoted letter to Lord Amherst concerning the founding of Sanskrit College, he was very much in favour of the spread of English education in Bengal.[63]

However, Ram Mohan also had access to the Sanskrit and Hindu and the Persian and Arabic heritages that were of interest to Orientalist scholars. His father and grandfather had served as officials in the court of the Nawabs of Bengal and thus knew Persian very well, and Ram

Mohan himself was sent to Patna to learn Arabic and Persian at the age of nine. One of his earliest works, the 'Gift to Monotheists', was written in Persian with an Arabic preface, as was his publication 'Discussions on Various Religions'.[64] Aged twelve, Ram Mohan was sent to Benares to learn Sanskrit and to study the Vedas; he also spent a number of years in Tibet and may have acquired some knowledge of Buddhism. He published the first translation into Bengali of the Upanishads and wrote an abridgement of the Vedanta. Ram Mohan's monotheism derived not only from his knowledge of Unitarianism, but also from his study of Islam and ancient Hindu texts.[65] Ram Mohan's access to the Islamic and Hindu heritage, and his tendency to justify his views on the basis of ancient texts from within these traditions, should therefore make us question his supposed indebtedness to the Western philosophical canon.

Ram Mohan made a very significant contribution to the creation of a public sphere of journalism in Calcutta. He founded a Bengali-language journal in 1821 and a Persian journal in 1822, hoping to provide a counterbalance to the burgeoning missionary literature. Following the introduction of a harsher press ordinance in 1823, Ram Mohan fought hard to persuade the government to relax the restrictions, and, although his efforts were unsuccessful, he was remembered by subsequent generations of Brahmos as a champion of the freedom of the press.[66] His extensive use of the press as a means of mobilising public opinion became a model for later social reformers in Bengal.

Ram Mohan's work in relation to *sati* should also be noted, as it was his writings protesting against the practice that formed much of the basis of his celebrity in Britain. Ram Mohan intervened in many debates concerning the position of women in Bengali society: he was in favour of the education of women, he opposed the practice of *kulin* polygamy, and he argued in favour of inheritance rights for women. However, his intervention in debates concerning *sati* was of particular importance. In the publications of missionaries in Bengal, and in the discourses surrounding Hinduism in Britain, the practice of *sati* had become emblematic of the supposed cruelty and 'backwardness' of orthodox Hinduism, and was used repeatedly as an argument in favour of the British government in India adopting a more interventionist approach to Indian religion and society.[67] Ram Mohan argued that legislation banning *sati* would be counter-productive, but that the practice of *sati* could be stamped out by changing public opinion through the publication of anti-*sati* tracts and newspapers. Governor-General Bentinck went against Ram Mohan's advice and, in 1829, initiated legislation that would ban *sati*.

Ram Mohan's status as founder of the Brahmo Samaj was not established until many decades after his death.[68] The Brahmo Sabha he instituted had no formal membership and no systematic theological or ideological basis. Ram Mohan left for England just ten months after the inauguration of the Brahmo Sabha, and there is little evidence to suggest that the organisation under his leadership exercised much influence in Calcutta society. David Kopf contends that, under both Ram Mohan and his successor, the Brahmo Sabha was simply one Hindu sect among many, distinguished by its universalist pretensions and Vedantic bias.[69] Nevertheless, there can be no doubt that Ram Mohan became of essential importance as a founding figure for all of the various branches of the Brahmo Samaj that came into existence in the nineteenth century. Ram Mohan's activities and principles—his commitment to universal theism; his commitment to social reform; his support for the education and rights of women; his use of journalism and publishing as a way of influencing public opinion; his use of reason as the ultimate standard through which to judge religion; his conviction that religious faith was purest in its most ancient forms; his inclusive attitude towards other faiths on the grounds that all religions ultimately worship the same, single Deity; his conviction that progress in India should involve both the technologies and ideologies of Western civilisation, and also the ancient traditions of Hindu and Muslim civilisations—all of these principles remained central to Brahmoism throughout the nineteenth century.

After Ram Mohan's death, the Brahmo Samaj fell into decline. He was succeeded as leader by Ram Chandra Vidyabagish, who continued to hold weekly services, but the Samaj for the next decade really functioned as a small church. The organisation was revitalised by Debendranath Tagore, who took over leadership in 1843.[70] The father of the famous poet Rabindranath Tagore and the son of the influential businessman Dwarkanath Tagore, Debendranath had, in 1839, founded the Tattwabodhini Sabha, an organisation whose object was the diffusion of knowledge of the Upanishads, and which was established to counter the influence of Christian missionary Alexander Duff, who was enjoying some success in converting English-educated Bengalis to Calvinist Trinitarian Christianity. Debendranath's Tattwabodhini Sabha tried to counter Christian missionary influence through its newspaper (the *Tattwabodhini Patrika*, established in 1843), the Tattwabodhini School (established 1840) and the Tattwabodhini printing press. The first texts to emerge from the printing press were republications of the works of Ram Mohan. The Tattwabodhini Sabha, and its newspaper, became the central vehicle for the propagation of Brahmo ideals. The Sabha, upon inception, had just nine members; by 1856 it had a membership of seven hundred.[71]

The Tattwabodhini Sabha merged with the Brahmo Samaj in 1843, and Debendranath and twenty others took an oath that bound them to the tenets and practices of the Brahmo religion, as set out in a newly elaborated version of Ram Mohan's Brahmo Samaj trust deed. The principles espoused in the new document were defended as being those of 'real Hinduism'—a return to a pure faith which had been corrupted by later generations. The return to the earliest texts to provide a secure footing for reform became characteristic of many Hindu reform movements, and Debendranath's use of such texts arguably reflected Orientalist notions that Indian civilisation had once been great but had fallen into decline, and, therefore, that indigenous texts should be privileged in accordance with their antiquity.[72] According to the covenant of the newly-constituted Brahmo Samaj, the most privileged text of all was the Vedanta, which was—as Ram Mohan had argued— the true source of Hindu faith. As well as elevating the Vedanta to the status of the scriptural basis of Brahmoism, Debendranath's covenant also repudiated idolatry, questioned the need for Hindu rituals, emphasised the importance of doing good and expressed the solidarity of the Brahmo community.[73]

In Debendranath's Samaj, Ram Mohan's paradigm of rational theism was largely adhered to. However, there were some influential figures within the Samaj who expounded a form of humanism. Akkhoy Kumar Dutt (1820–86) was deeply influenced by Western positivism, deism, science and rationalism. He combined his scientism and deism by arguing that God's 'scripture' lay not in texts, but in the harmonious workings of the universe, which were to be 'read' through the study of science. Dutt persuaded Debendranath to give up the Vedanta as the 'book' of the Brahmos in 1851, from which time Brahmos did not regard any sacred text as infallible.[74] Another influential humanist, affiliated to the Samaj through the Tattwabodhini Sabha, was Ishwar Chandra Vidyasagar, principal of Sanskrit College from 1851. Vidyasagar, like Ram Mohan, returned to the earliest Hindu sacred texts in order to interpret them rationally. Vidyasagar was an atheist, but was convinced that social reform would be most effective if pursued from within the Hindu tradition. Along with his work in education, Vidyasagar is most often remembered as a champion of the rights of women—his leadership of the campaign to enable widows to remarry resulted in the Widow Remarriage Bill of 1856, which incorporated many of his ideas on social reform.[75] Keshab's entrance into the Brahmo Samaj in 1857 thus brought him into contact with a religious and intellectual milieu in which not only universal theism, but also qualified humanism, a focus on science, education and the rights of women were important strands.

Keshab's entry into the Brahmo Samaj resulted in alienation from his family, although matters were eventually resolved when Keshab suffered a period of illness. Indeed, in subsequent years, Keshab's mother became a member of the Brahmo Samaj of India. However, the time of his entry into the Brahmo Samaj was one of great stress and loneliness. Debendranath was a great source of support, and accompanied Keshab on a sea voyage to Ceylon (Sri Lanka) in 1859.[76] Following the family tradition, Keshab had been employed as a clerk in the Bank of Bengal, but he resigned in June 1861 to become a Brahmo missionary.[77] From now on, Keshab averred, he would rely only on Providence for his income, although he did receive 20,000 rupees from his share of the paternal property in 1862.[78]

Debendranath Tagore recognised Keshab's considerable talents, and Keshab rose rapidly through the ranks of the Brahmo Samaj, becoming a minister in 1862. He lectured extensively in the Brahmo School in the 1860s, published numerous tracts on the philosophical basis of Brahmoism, engaged in religious controversies with Christian missionaries in Calcutta, established the *Indian Mirror* (with a view to influencing the Hindu community on religious and educational

Fig. i   Keshab Chandra Sen in 1859.

matters), and embarked, in 1864, on an extensive missionary tour of India. His *Tracts for the Times*, published from June 1860, stressed the intuitive basis of Brahmoism, included no references to Hinduism, and used many biblical illustrations. Tracts eight and nine were anthologies of Keshab's favourite extracts from philosophy through the ages, and thus provide a valuable insight into his intellectual development.

Extracts were provided from Aristotle, Hallam, Locke, Morell, Hamilton, Shaftesbury, Buffier, Hume, Reid, Beattie, Jacobi, Ancillon, Coleridge, Dugald Stewart, Thomas Brown, Abercrombie, Cousin, M'Cosh, and John Tulloch. Meredith Borthwick rightly perceives that the extracts included show 'the extent of Keshub's familiarity with Western thought and philosophy, and his lack of similar roots in the Indian tradition'.[79] The fact that English education had a considerable intellectual impact on the young Keshab is beyond question.

In the early 1860s, Keshab began to correspond with theists in other parts of the world, including, in England, F. W. Newman and Frances Power Cobbe. Keshab became dissatisfied increasingly with Debendranath's gradualist approach to social reform and attempts to close the gap between Brahmoism and 'orthodox' Hinduism. He began to rally support among a younger generation of Brahmos for his reformist and universalist ideas, and stressed the importance of 'liberal social reform', which would mean the extension of aid to victims of famine, disease and floods; the establishment of institutions for female education; and increased activity to support widow remarriage and end *kulin* polygamy. Conservative Brahmos denounced Keshab's emphasis on universalism over national culture, and accused Keshab and his followers of denationalising the intelligentsia. Keshab's faction responded by claiming that the older generation of Brahmos, while paying lip service to a liberal, rational religion and ethics, were guilty of practicing idolatrous Hindu rites in their own homes. Keshabite Brahmos also attacked Debendranath's authoritarian leadership of the Samaj, arguing in favour of democratic decision-making and a Brahmo constitution.[80]

Whereas Debendranath always stressed the 'Hindu' character of Brahmoism, Keshab's religious attitude was more universalist. Conservative Brahmos criticised the younger generation, who looked to Keshab as their guide, for threatening the cultural integrity of Hinduism. The *National Paper*, established by the conservative Brahmos in 1865, sought to win over theistic Hindus to Brahmoism as a counterbalance to Keshab's youthful progressives. Dwijendranath Tagore was a major contributor, and published articles that denounced the adoption of European dress and manners, equated progress with national identity, and attacked Keshabite universalism as 'a masquerade for European Christianity'.[81] Debendranath reportedly called for

Keshab's expulsion from the Brahmo Samaj in January 1865.[82] A formal schism took place between the conservative and the Keshabite camp in 1866, and the Brahmo Samaj split into two organisations: the Adi (or original) Brahmo Samaj, headed by Debendranath, and the Brahmo Samaj of India, headed by Keshab.

Fig. ii   Universalist architecture. The Brahmo Samaj of India Mandir.

One of the greatest achievements of the Brahmo Samaj of India was to greatly increase the mass appeal of Brahmoism. An effort to expand the influence of Brahmoism beyond the narrow elite circles of Calcutta was initiated by Keshab in the 1860s. The Vaishnava Bijoy Krishna Goswami became an influential figure in the Samaj's missionary efforts, and he persuaded Keshab that the fusion of popular forms of the Vaishnava and *bhakti* traditions would increase the mass appeal of Brahmoism. Members of Keshab's Samaj who embraced Vaishnavism formed a group of ascetic missionary Brahmos who were institutionalised as the Sri Durbar in 1870. Members of the Durbar tended to be non-Westernised, lower middle-class Vaishnava converts. They enjoyed considerable success in their mission activities.[83]

The status of Keshab's Brahmo Samaj of India as a powerful and independent religious movement was given material form with the establishment of a permanent place of worship in Calcutta in 1869, which proclaimed the universalism and eclecticism of the faith by mixing the architectural forms of Hindu temples, Christian churches, and mosques, and attracted some attention in the British press (Fig. ii).[84]

British Religious Nonconformity and The English Unitarians

Although Keshab excited interest in Britain beyond the sphere of religion, there can be no doubt that it was religious groups, and, in particular, Nonconformist religious groups, for which he held the greatest appeal. The mid-to-late Victorian period marked a high point for Nonconformist Christianity, both in terms of the numbers in attendance at Nonconformist chapels and in terms of their degree of political influence.[85] We know from the religious census of 1851 that Nonconformist attendance exceeded Anglican attendance in twenty-one out of twenty-nine towns designated as chief manufacturing districts, and constituted 28 per cent of church attendance in the counties.[86]

The term 'Nonconformist' encompassed a wide variety of distinctive groups, including a range of Methodist churches, Congregationalists (also known as Independents), Baptists, Presbyterians, Quakers and Unitarians. While all of these groups had their distinctive theological and organisational characteristics, it is possible to make a few generalisations about Nonconformity. The majority of Nonconformists were aligned politically with the Liberal party, which had inherited the Whig principles of civil and religious liberty. Largely made up of middle-class worshippers, Nonconformists enjoyed considerable voting power in the period between the Reform Act of 1867 and the Franchise Act of 1918, as the former Act allowed organised groups to exert considerable electoral power at a time when a considerable proportion of the working classes (those who were not 'respectable' householders) were excluded from the franchise.[87]

Nonconformists took a marked interest in political and social matters, as political and social injustices tended to be regarded as instances of 'sin', and thus of direct religious significance. In the mid-to-late nineteenth century, Nonconformist chapels took an active role in campaigning on a range of issues, including temperance, Home Rule, anti-Catholicism, urban overcrowding, agitation against the Contagious Diseases Acts, and protests against the toleration of idolatry in India. With the exception of Quakers and Unitarians, Nonconformists were generally evangelical in tone: they aimed to eradicate social evils in order to save people from sin. It was evangelical participation in the anti-slavery movement—on the basis that slavery was sinful and thus could not be tolerated by Christians—which formed the blueprint for subsequent Nonconformist agitation on a variety of issues.[88] The extent to which religion and politics were intertwined in what Bebbington terms the 'Nonconformist Conscience' is demonstrated by the variety of content in the journal *The Christian World*, which included a digest of the activities of all of the major Nonconformist groups in Britain, along with a range of articles on political and social issues in Britain and across the empire.[89] It devoted considerable space to Keshab's ideas and activities following his visit to Britain.

Undoubtedly, the group of Britons who paid the greatest attention to Keshab, and who did the most to popularise his ideas and to publicise his activities, were the Unitarians, who resided on the outermost fringes of British Nonconformity. The early history of Unitarianism is beyond the scope of this book, but it is necessary to elucidate some of Unitarianism's distinctive features, in order to provide some context for the Unitarians' fascination with Keshab.[90] The movement emerged chiefly out of Protestant dissent in Britain in the eighteenth century.[91]

As Ruth Watts has suggested, the 'Unitarians' of the eighteenth century might more accurately be described as 'rational dissenters', united by their agreement that 'humanity and its environment were best understood by reason, experience and experiment'.[92] Rational criticism of the Bible—a cornerstone for all dissenters—was central to most Unitarians' rejection of the divinity of Jesus (and thus the Trinity), and the doctrines of atonement and eternal punishment. This emphasis on scholarly biblical criticism should be viewed within the context of the reorientation of biblical studies, which gathered pace from the early nineteenth century as the Bible became a legitimate object of study for historical criticism, philology, and later anthropology and comparative religion.[93] An emphasis on the use of reason to arrive at one's own judgement, and a fusion of religion with philosophy and science, were characteristic of the more liberal dissenting academies of the eighteenth and nineteenth centuries, out of which many Unitarians emerged.[94] Joseph Priestley attended one such academy in Daventry in the mid-eighteenth century, and went on to teach at Warrington.[95]

Priestley is remembered most often for his important work in chemistry and radical political theory, but his contributions to metaphysics and theology were crucial to the creation of a Unitarian Christianity which denied the Trinity and atonement and upheld Jesus as an example of moral perfection. Although not all Unitarians were Priestleyans, Priestley's mode of theological argument exemplified Unitarianism's impulse to interpret religion scientifically and rationally. His argument against the divinity of Jesus was based, in part, on a philosophy of matter which posited a material origin of consciousness and thus undermined the theory of the pre-existence of Christ. His necessarianism (a theory that everything has a cause traceable to a first cause or God) was based on the physician and psychologist David Hartley's theory of nerve vibrations. His assertion that Unitarianism was a form of Christianity rested on the emphasis the faith gave to Jesus as a model of human perfection, and the central place accorded to a (critically-interpreted) Bible.[96]

However, Unitarians were distinctive not just because of their agreement on certain points of theology, and in their fusion of religion, philosophy and science, but moreover because of the wide variety of beliefs which could be encompassed under the umbrella term

'Unitarian'. As William J. Fox observed in 1830: 'Let sects enforce uniformity, and chain the mouths and the minds of their members—it is for Unitarians to cherish independence of thought by the free expression of individual opinions'.[97] This focus on tolerance and the celebration of individual opinion has led Lynn Zastoupil to characterise Unitarianism as 'Christianity's permeable boundary zone, a religious space that individuals holding divergent beliefs might briefly enter or permanently occupy while claiming a Christian identity, however contested that identity might be'.[98] It is certainly true that Unitarians' celebration of heterodoxy within their own congregations made the movement particularly receptive to religious ideas from other parts of the world, and that this receptiveness was crucial to the entrance of Ram Mohan and Keshab into Unitarian circles.

Alongside Unitarian anti-Trinitarian theology and non-sectarian inclusiveness, it is important to note Unitarians' strong commitment to social reform, particularly with regard to education and the social position of women. Unitarians' concern with social reform stemmed partly from the marginalised status of their religion, which only became legalised in 1813 after a long battle.[99] The Unitarian commitment to religious tolerance, meritocracy and social equality led to considerable Unitarian involvement in a range of reform issues, including municipal reform, Catholic Emancipation and the 1832 Reform Act.[100]

The relationship between Unitarianism and early feminism has been demonstrated by Kathryn Gleadle and Ruth Watts.[101] While Unitarians generally subscribed to the ideology of 'separate spheres', which, as Hall and Davidoff have demonstrated, formed a crucial ideological component in the making of the English middle class, they placed considerable emphasis on the necessity of women to receive the same education as men, if only to be able to better manage the domestic sphere.[102] In practice, many Unitarian women left the boundaries of domesticity and entered the predominantly male public sphere of the nineteenth century, notably Harriet Martineau (who published a series of works on political economy), Frances Power Cobbe (whose *Essay on the Theory of Intuitive Morals* appeared in 1855) and Sophia Dobson Collet (who wrote extensively on Brahmoism).[103] Cobbe and Collet were frequently held up for praise by the Brahmos in Calcutta, and their efforts to raise money for the Brahmo Samaj were acknowledged with gratitude.[104] Collet, in particular, was treated in the Brahmo press as a serious interlocutor and expert theologian, who had 'enormously facilitated the Brahmo Samaj to flourish'.[105]

It must be stressed that, while Unitarians exerted considerable social influence, their numbers were small and they occupied a marginalised place in English religious life. The religious census of 1851 suggests that there were only around 50,000 Unitarians in England and Wales in the mid-nineteenth century.[106] This compared to 490,000 Methodists and 165,000 Congregationalists (Independents).[107] However, despite their small numbers, Unitarians possessed considerable economic power.[108] Unitarians were drawn largely from the middle-class and artisan sections of society, and included many merchant 'princes' and wealthier industrialists of commercial and textile manufacturing centres.[109] The disdain and fear with which the majority of Christians regarded Unitarian communities (many Christians were concerned that Unitarianism amounted to, or would lead to, atheism) led Unitarians to create their own networks of religious and financial connections, in an age in which the raising of capital often took place on a personal or local basis. As Ruth Watts has observed, 'The continuing fear of Unitarians among the orthodox was often a bar to social intimacy and thus stimulated the Unitarians' extraordinary familial networks which gave both financial and cultural support to those within them and to the liberal causes they supported'.[110] These strong financial and familial networks were augmented by the Unitarians' influential political connections: many were elected to national and local political office, and, as Zastoupil has argued, they did much to help forge the alliance between dissenters and Whig reformers that would become a foundation of the Liberal Party.[111]

The Celebrity of Ram Mohan Roy

It was the Unitarians' high degree of access to the press, their political connections and their access to a variety of groups promoting liberal causes, coupled with their extensive financial resources, that facilitated the transformation of Ram Mohan Roy into a 'celebrity Unitarian' during his visit to England, 1830–33. As Spencer Lavan has demonstrated, the Unitarians had a long history of contact with India, including, somewhat surprisingly, a degree of missionary interest.[112] The Unitarians became aware of Ram Mohan in the 1810s, and, following the publication of his 'The Precepts of Jesus' in 1820, became deeply interested in his religious teaching and social reformism, which they felt corresponded with their own ideas.[113] The Unitarian journal *The Monthly Repository* republished many of Ram Mohan's exchanges with the missionary Joshua Marshman, which appeared in the English-language journal of the Serampore missionaries, *The Friend of India*, during the 1820s.[114] Ram Mohan was attractive to the Unitarians not only because his ideas in many respects corresponded closely with their own, but because he offered the possibility of a religious reformation in India which would move in the direction of the rational monotheism favoured by Unitarians, as opposed to the evangelical Trinitarianism of the majority of missionaries.

Ram Mohan's visit to England caused something of a sensation both in Britain and in India. Ram Mohan timed his visit carefully—he wanted to intervene in debates concerning the appeal against the abolition of *sati*; he wished to observe the progress of electoral reform in Britain; he also wanted to be present for the renewal of the East India Company Charter that was due to take place in 1833. The debates concerning the renewal of the Charter Act, in which Ram Mohan participated, led to considerable changes in British policy in India. Under the terms of the Act, the Governor-General of India became responsible for the civil and military administration of the totality of India, and provisions were made for the free settlement of British nationals in India, who could invest freely in the colonial economy.[115] The Act also removed the East India Company's remaining trade monopolies in China—thus inaugurating an era of complete free trade—and resulted in a massive increase in exports of raw materials from India to Britain, as well as an increase in exports of manufactured goods from Britain to India.[116] The Act was passed during the Governorship of William Bentinck (1828–35), which witnessed the planning and implementation of numerous reform schemes in India in the areas of law, education and infrastructure.[117] Ram Mohan's visit thus occurred at a time when the future direction of British rule in India was a subject of considerable political and public interest.

Ram Mohan's activities in England were widely reported upon in the British press, he met many of the most prominent political and intellectual figures of the time, he delivered countless speeches, sermons and addresses, and he submitted papers to the parliamentary select committee on the affairs of the East India Company. There is some evidence to suggest that he considered the possibility of becoming an MP.[118] Ram Mohan's visit to England is important to the present study in a number of respects. Firstly, Ram Mohan was the first high-caste Indian to visit Britain, and the first in a line of Bengali visitors to achieve celebrity in Europe and America in the nineteenth century. The deep impression Ram Mohan left on the public imagination led his memory to figure as an important element in the ways in which Britons responded to later prominent visitors to the West, including Keshab, Swami Vivekananda (who made a sensational impression at the World Parliament of Religions in Chicago in 1893) and, of course, Rabindranath Tagore.[119]

Secondly, Ram Mohan's visit is significant because many of those who organised Keshab's activities in England had either met Ram Mohan personally, had relatives who had done so, or had taken a deep interest in his life. This was certainly the case with Mary Carpenter, whose own efforts at educational and social reform received great inspiration from Ram Mohan's example, and who published an account of Ram Mohan's visit to England in 1866—four years before Keshab arrived.[120] It was Mary's father Lant Carpenter who had done so much to promote Ram Mohan in the 1830s.[121] Sophia Dobson Collet was affected deeply by her childhood encounter with Ram Mohan at South Place Chapel, London, and her fascination with him continued to the end of her life.[122] The Martineau family also took a great interest in Ram Mohan's activities and ideas.[123] There was, therefore, a great deal of overlap between the strong familial, financial, religious and political networks which enabled both Ram Mohan and Keshab to enter the British public sphere.

Thirdly, Ram Mohan's visit is significant because of the way in which it has been dealt with in the historiography. Hagiographical accounts of Ram Mohan tend to accord his 'triumphant' visit to England a prominent place in his mythology as the first 'modern' Indian.[124] The historical narrative which places Ram Mohan at the fountainhead of 'Indian modernity' has a wide currency, and is lent a powerful visual force in the exhibition halls of the museum to Ram Mohan which has opened in his former residence in Kolkata. Lynn Zastoupil's account of Ram Mohan's visit to England offers a balanced account of his encounter with Christianity, but nevertheless exaggerates greatly the impact he exerted on British society. There can be no doubt that Ram Mohan achieved celebrity status in Britain (he was, after all, the inspiration for Harriet Martineau's critique of 'literary lionism'), but Zastoupil's contentions that he exerted a significant impact on the course of early Victorian feminism, and that he enabled Britons to 'imagine a multiethnic House of Commons', surely overstate Ram Mohan's degree of influence and popularity.[125]

While Ram Mohan was often praised by British commentators for his intelligence, his knowledge of Western philosophy and politics, and his 'manly' independence, these virtues were taken most often to signify the extent to which he was *unlike* the majority of Indians. Sutherland's account of Ram Mohan—one of the most widely circulating in the period—presented Ram Mohan as noteworthy because he 'surpassed the generality of his countrymen in his personal appearance almost as much as in his mental powers'.[126] Many accounts of Ram Mohan which represented him as a 'Christian convert' located the origin of his exemplary character in the civilising qualities of the Christian faith.[127] Ram Mohan's submissions to parliament, while imploring the government to employ 'natives' in the highest official positions, also recommended (or were, at least, interpreted by many as recommending) the Europeanisation and even Christianisation of India.[128] Ram Mohan's visit to England may well have served to reinforce, rather than challenge, interventionist and racist attitudes towards India. The misrepresentation of Ram Mohan's influence in Britain in much of the historiography acts as an important reminder that, in examining Keshab's interaction with Britain, one must never fail to pay attention to the limits of his influence and the extent of opposition to his ideas.

One final point as regards Ram Mohan concerns his memorialisation and status as an 'originary' figure. Ram Mohan's position as the 'founder' of Brahmoism only became cemented in the decades after his death—his status as the originator of 'modern Hinduism' was a construct which emerged through a process of 'reiterative imagining' on the part of numerous generations.[129] As we shall see, the need to trace an intellectual and religious lineage to Ram Mohan—to 'claim' him—was evident in the activities of numerous branches of Brahmoism as the movement fractured into various factions. The Unitarians' continued memorialisation of Ram Mohan evinced a similar desire to 'claim' Ram Mohan for a particular tradition—in the case of the Unitarians, the tradition of the 'great reformer'. Ram Mohan visited Britain at the height of the age of reform, an age in which the memorialisation of the exemplary lives of great reformers contributed to a sense of British national and imperial identity. The interventionism and reformism characteristic of British policy towards India from the 1830s was diluted considerably following the uprising of 1857–8. In the 1870s, the memory of Ram Mohan provided the Unitarians with an important bridge back to an era in which the religious transformation of India had been a serious concern not only of British and Indian reformers, but also of the British government. Ram Mohan occupied an originary position in Brahmo thought as the 'founder' of the Brahmo Samaj, and an originary position in Unitarian thought as the 'father' of the connection between religious and social reform in England and India. As Maurice Halbwachs has noted, commemoration is an important means through which members of social groups create collective memory: it was the collective memory of Ram Mohan which provided a key basis for the sense of inter-cultural connection between Brahmos and Unitarians in the 1870s.[130]

The 'Two Schools' of Unitarianism

Unitarians were distinguished by their readiness to tolerate heterodoxy within their own congregations; nevertheless, it should be noted that strong divisions existed within the Unitarian movement. The spectrum of Unitarian beliefs evident in the mid-to-late nineteenth century can be summarised through a consideration of the position occupied by the prominent Unitarian journal *The Inquirer*—the journal which did most to publicise Keshab's activities in Britain. The objective of *The Inquirer*, as stated by its longstanding editor and minister of London's Stamford Street Chapel, Thomas Lethbridge Marshall (1825–1915), was to mediate between what were known as the 'old' and 'new' schools of Unitarianism.[131] *The Christian Reformer*, founded in 1815 by Robert

Aspland, occupied the conservative end of the Unitarian spectrum of belief, upholding the scriptural basis of faith and propounding the determinist philosophy of Belsham.[132] *The National Review*, first published in June 1855, and including frequent contributions from James Martineau and Matthew Arnold, laid less emphasis on scripture as the basis for Unitarianism, and focused upon the teachings of Jesus as opposed to debates concerning his divinity. *The Christian Reformer* and *The National Review* ceased publication in 1863 and 1864, respectively, and the two schools of Unitarianism came to be represented by *Christian Life*—a conservative journal with a scriptural emphasis, first published in May 1876 under the editorship of Robert Spears—and *The Inquirer*, which, despite the intention of its editor to act as mediator, leaned increasingly in the mid-to-late nineteenth century towards the anti-supernaturalism of James Martineau.[133]

Divisions within Unitarianism widened as the century progressed, not least because of the so-called 'Parker controversy' of the mid-1870s, which was stimulated by the proposal of the British and Foreign Unitarian Association to publish the works of the American Transcendentalist Theodore Parker.[134] *The Inquirer* presented the 'Parker controversy' as exemplifying the division between Unitarians who regarded the Bible as the authority, if not a revelation, for all theological belief (and were thus opposed to the publication) and Unitarians who regarded scriptures as fallible and based their theological belief on 'the intuitions of the soul' (and were thus in favour).[135] In the Bengali context, it was the work of Parker (whom Keshab greatly admired) that formed part of the basis of theological disagreement between the so-called 'progressive' and 'conservative' wings of the Brahmo Samaj in the 1860s.[136] Keshab's pronouncements on subjects such as inspiration, the role of prophets, the nature of eclecticism, and the necessity of both 'inner' and 'outer' forms of faith were of particular interest to *The Inquirer*, because they engaged with many of the same issues that arose in debates concerning the Transcendentalist influence on English Unitarianism.

The Transcendentalist influence on Brahmoism had come about through the activities of Charles Dall, who had ensured that thousands of copies of the works of Channing, Emerson and Parker were circulated among the Brahmos from the late 1850s.[137] These works were imbued with eclecticism and romantic idealism, and emphasised self-reliance, self-development and self-transcendence as a route to spiritual enlightenment. In viewing the individual psyche as a direct point of access to the metaphysical, Transcendentalist philosophy contributed to a 'psychologisation' of religion, which the historian of esotericism W. J. Hanegraaf has identified as characteristic of a broader secularising impulse within new age religion and occultism.[138] Transcendentalism provided Brahmos and Unitarians with a bridge back to older forms of esotericism, in particular the traditions of thought associated with reformation spiritualism, which emphasised an interconnection between knowledge of self and knowledge of God.[139] These traditions existed within an even broader epistemological framework of 'mysticism', which encompassed a diverse range of movements in Western and Eastern theology that promoted an individualistic and subjective consciousness of salvation.[140]

Unitarianism and Brahmoism thus drew on a long history of shared traditions. It was not simply the case that Unitarianism influenced Brahmoism, or vice versa. Their theological affinity arose from their parallel engagement with spiritual traditions which emphasised subjective and/or scientific routes to enlightenment.[141] These traditions were drawn upon by a wide variety of radical movements in the mid-to-late nineteenth century, including Theosophy, Spiritualism, mesmerism and freemasonry, many of which looked to India as a source of inspiration.[142] To some extent, both the Unitarians and the Brahmos engaged with or participated in these movements.[143] It was no coincidence that Keshab and the English Unitarians, particularly those of the 'new' school, were engaged in parallel debates concerning the value of intuitive and scriptural insight, prophetic and rational religion.

The Shifting Landscape of British Policy in India from 1857

It should be emphasised that the continuing concern of a variety of religious groups in Britain with converting the religious beliefs and transforming the social environments of colonial subjects was, from the mid-nineteenth century, largely out of step with government policy in India. In the years following the Indian 'Mutiny' of 1857–8, the question at the heart of debates surrounding India was the following: to what extent had British social reform and religious innovation produced discontent that had contributed to the uprising? Conservatives argued that social and religious interference had contributed greatly to popular discontent; supporters of the government insisted that the causes of rebellion lay elsewhere. Nevertheless, there was widespread agreement that the government should no longer attempt to reform Indian customs or to evangelise in India. Even evangelicals such as Lord Lawrence admitted that a 'Christian policy' could not be pursued against the wishes of the native community.[144] The Queen's Proclamation of 1858 assuming the government of India for the Crown declared that the role of the government should be limited to keeping the peace, and that the reform of Indian religious beliefs and social customs was no longer to be sought. The transformation of India along Western lines would now depend on the slow spread of education and enlightenment in Indian society, not on legislative interference.[145] The 1860s thus saw very few attempts to legislate against customs that were perceived by the British as injurious. British officials and members of the English-educated Indian elite agreed that, while the eradication of 'backward' practices was desirable, direct government intervention should be kept to a minimum.

A more cautious attitude towards religious and social interference went hand in hand with attempts to create a stronger, more paternalist form of British rule in India. The so-called 'Mutiny' had proven to the British that ultimately they held India by force, not consent. The 'Mutiny' led to a hardening of racial attitudes in Britain towards Indians, as accounts of the rebellion in the British press had focused on the perpetration by Indians of atrocities against Britons and, in particular, British women.[146] A growing perception that Indians required firm imperial control led to a drastic increase in the number of British troops in India, and the number of Indians serving in the British army was reduced. By the time of Keshab's arrival in 1870, the number of British troops in India was double what it had been in 1857.[147] Lawrence and Mayo (who served as Viceroy 1864–9 and 1869–72, respectively) both regarded the reconstruction of government machinery, the strengthening of executive power and the maintenance of law and order as central objectives.[148]

Central to debates concerning the restoration of British supremacy in India was the question of how to create a stronger alliance between the British government and key sections of the Indian population. Canning (who served as Governor-General and Viceroy prior to Lawrence) regarded the Indian landed aristocracy as the most reliable bulwarks of British rule, and attempted to draw them into the administrative system through the employment of *taluqdars* (secondary landowners) and *zamindars* as honorary magistrates. Relations between the races could also be improved through the incorporation of 'natives' into the Legislative Council, and through the granting of greater powers to local governments, which would, Mayo argued: 'afford opportunities for the development of self-government, for strengthening municipal institutions, and for the association of Natives and Europeans to a greater extent than heretofore in the administration of affairs'.[149] The Legislative Council Act of 1861 stripped the Council of its pseudo-parliamentary procedures introduced by Governor-General Dalhousie, and allocated half of the additional seats to non-official members, both Indian and European. The Act fell short of the demands of the British Indian Association (who wanted to see much greater Indian representation in the Council) and was, in essence, a further attempt to secure the loyalty of the aristocratic and princely classes. Most of those selected for the Councils were conservative members of these classes, although the Bengal Legislative Council did contain a few English-educated Bengalis. Nevertheless, Mayo's Resolution of December 1870 did grant a much greater degree of financial and administrative independence to the local governments. It is noteworthy that Lawrence was opposed wholeheartedly to any such moves towards decentralisation, and attempted unsuccessfully to abolish the Bengal Legislative Council during his time as Viceroy.

The extent to which Indians should participate in the administration of government was also debated in relation to the Indian Civil Service (ICS). Indians had participated in the uncovenanted ICS since the time of Hastings, and T. B. Macaulay was one among many liberals who had strongly supported the values of equal employment opportunities for all as proclaimed in the Charter Act of 1833.[150] However, in reality, Indians had been confined to positions of little influence within the uncovenanted Service, and barred entirely from entering the more powerful and prestigious covenanted Service. The covenanted Service was opened to Indians in 1853, but the requirement that the entry exam be taken in London rendered this development all but meaningless in practice—the first Indian to pass the exam, Satyendranath Tagore, did so in 1864.[151]

By the 1860s, the government was forced to consider opening up the ICS to a greater degree, in the face of growing pressure from the English-educated Indian elite.[152] The Bengali *bhadralok* in Calcutta were especially keen that the ICS should be opened up through competitive examinations in India. As members of a community that had long been under the influence of English education, they had the most to gain in terms of employment opportunities, power and prestige. Various proposals were considered in the course of the 1860s, but the strength of opposition from local governments and the central government of India, as well as from self-interested members of the ICS, led countless schemes proposing wider participation to be rejected. The India Act of 1870 gave the government of India the power to appoint 'natives' to all offices (including the covenanted ICS), and also the power to decide how Indians would be selected for these posts. In 1879, the rules of selection were finally clarified: up to 20 per cent of the civilians employed each year would be Indians; these Indians would be handpicked by local governments on the basis of family and social position, as well as education and ability. The 1870 Act was thus rendered symbolic rather than practical, and the government of India continued to employ only those Indians who met with its standards of loyalty and 'character'. Aristocrats well-disposed to British rule were generally chosen; the English-educated Bengalis of Calcutta tended to be excluded.[153]

Although the government kept its interference in social and religious reform to a minimum, attempts were made in the post-'Mutiny' period to expand the scope of education in India, as the spread of English education was generally agreed not to have contributed to the discontent which led to the 'Mutiny'. Although the number of grants-in-aid to missionary schools was reduced considerably, grants were made available on a wider scale to schools organised by the Indian community, most of which used English as the medium of instruction. As government intervention in social and religious matters was regarded increasingly as dangerous, so education became the primary means through which the level of 'civilisation' in India would be raised.

The tendency of reformers in Britain and Bengal to link the level of 'civilisation' in India to the condition of Indian women led a number of Indian and British reformers to lay particular stress on the need for women's education in India. Education for women was sought by a number of members of the Calcutta *bhadralok*, most notably Vidyasagar, who was involved in Bethune's school for women between 1849 and 1869. The British social reformer Mary Carpenter engaged in numerous attempts to foster women's education in India in the 1860s and 1870s.[154] As we shall see, the condition of women in India was of major concern to Keshab, who strongly advocated female education as well as the reform of marriage customs.

Conclusion

When Keshab arrived in London in 1870, he entered a society in which many of the issues central to his own concerns in India were being discussed. Keshab intervened in debates concerning education, the position of women, social and religious reform, and the extent of Indian participation in the machinery of government. The social, political, cultural, financial and familial networks of Unitarianism provided the basis for Keshab's entrance into the British public sphere; these networks had, from the early nineteenth century, extended to Bengal through the connections between Brahmoism and Unitarianism. These connections had a deep emotional significance for Unitarians, in large part due to their memorialisation of Ram Mohan Roy. In journeying from Calcutta to London, Keshab was performing an act which, for both Keshab and the Unitarians, was laden with associations of the journey Ram Mohan had performed some forty years earlier. The following chapter focuses on the arguments Keshab made to British audiences, and examines the ways in which his experiences in the metropole affected his conceptions of the British-Indian relationship, and of his own place in the imperial world.

3

'TRUTH IS NOT EUROPEAN'

KESHAB ON HISTORY, EMPIRE, OTHER, SELF

On Monday evening, 12 September 1870, the Hanover Square Rooms in London were crowded on the invitation of the Committee of the British and Foreign Unitarian Association. The occasion was a soirée to bid farewell to Keshab Chandra Sen, prior to his departure for India. Eleven denominations of Christians were present at the meeting, and a representative of each took turns to express their enthusiasm for Keshab's endeavours and god-speed for his safe return. Encouraged by a suggestion that he provide the assembled audience with his impressions of England, Keshab took to the platform and declared proudly:

> On the banks of the Thames, as on the banks of the Ganges, I have opened the secrets of my aspiration and prayers to the one loving and holy God, and He has heard me here as He did there... I am now, thank God, a man of the world, and can say that England is as much my Father's house as India... From Her Majesty down to the poorest peasant in the kingdom, I have received sympathy and kindness...

> ...I have been in official circles, and from the authorities I have received emphatic assurances that earnest efforts will be made in order to do justice to India... I was always a faithful and loyal subject of Her Majesty Queen Victoria, but since my interview with her, my attachment to her has been deeper than ever...

…From England I go away, but my heart will always be with you, and England will always be in my heart. Farewell, dear England; 'with all thy faults I love thee still.' Farewell, country of Shakespeare and Newton, land of liberty and of charity. Farewell, temporary home where I realized, and tasted, and enjoyed the sweetness of brotherly and sisterly love. Farewell, my Father's Western House.[1]

Keshab in England

By the time he made this speech, Keshab, aged thirty-two, had been in England for almost seven months. He had delivered speeches at over sixty public engagements, he had been escorted around London by the former Viceroy Lord Lawrence, conversed with prominent individuals such as John Stuart Mill, Max Müller, J. R. Seeley, James Martineau and John Bright, been presented to Queen Victoria at Osborne House and exchanged words at breakfast with Prime Minister Gladstone. He had delivered sermons and lectures to a combined audience of over 40,000 people, in London and in a range of provincial cities and towns in England and Scotland. His activities had been reported in over fifty contemporary newspapers and journals in England, Wales, Scotland and Ireland, and news of his visit had spread to many European countries and across the Atlantic to America. P. C. Majumdar claimed later that 'English cities sometimes take strange fancies to…certain individuals for a season, and London specially suffers from such fits of sporadic hero-worship… [Keshab] became the rage of the day. There was no newspaper that did not chronicle his doings, and there was no English town to which his fame did not spread'.[2] In 1884, the famous Orientalist Max Müller, reminiscing about Keshab, remarked: 'I have been struck, when lecturing in different places, to find that the mere mention of Keshub Chunder Sen's name elicited applause for which I was hardly prepared'.[3]

Keshab visited England for three primary reasons: first, to study English culture and society in general and, more specifically, to gather information on English philanthropic institutions that he could employ in his own efforts at social reform in Calcutta; second, to inform the English public of defects within the British administration in India, and to do everything he could to ensure these defects were remedied; third, to promote the faith of the Brahmo Samaj of India and, although he did not achieve this, to establish a Brahmo Church in England. He was accompanied by five other members of the Brahmo Samaj—including Ananda Mohan Bose (who would proceed to Cambridge University to study, returning to India in 1874) and P. K. Sen (a Brahmo missionary, who would later write a biography of Keshab).[4] In London he was met by Bihari Lal Gupta and Romesh Chandra Dutt, both of whom had arrived in England in 1868 to study for upper-service positions in India. Keshab and his companions lodged for some time with Krishna Govind Gupta, who was studying for the open examination for the ICS at University College London. It is notable that very few of the numerous articles written on Keshab in the British press make any mention of his Bengali companions.

While Keshab was greeted in London by a network of Bengali associates, his itinerary was organised meticulously by the British and Foreign Unitarian Association. As his diary reveals, he spent the vast majority of his time speaking at engagements that they had arranged. The milieu of dissenting, and, in particular, Unitarian social reformers of which Keshab became a part shared a common interest in the alleviation of poverty, the spread of education (especially among women), and the promotion of interdenominational religious discussion both in England and in India. These were the primary topics upon which Keshab spoke during his addresses in a variety of Unitarian and Baptist chapels, peace societies, societies for the promotion of women's education and temperance societies. In addition to these contacts with religious organisations, Keshab had access to the highest official circles through his association with the former Viceroy of India, Lord Lawrence. Lawrence accompanied Keshab personally to an endless stream of official dinners, gatherings at the India Office, concerts at the Crystal Palace and 'At Home' soirées, in the course of which Keshab was introduced to a host of England's most prominent literary, religious and political figures. It was on these occasions that Keshab took the opportunity to express his views regarding the governance of India.

Keshab's reputation for spectacular oratory, his standing as the supposed 'Apostle of the East', his mastery of English, and his status as an exotic 'Eastern other' made him an obvious choice for chapels and meeting halls that wished to attract large audiences. Religious revivalism had been gathering fresh momentum in England since the 1850s, and grand religious spectacles, staged in large halls or open fields, were highly popular. Each denomination had its own 'oratorical stars', and 'sermon-tasting' (that is, attending sermons delivered by renowned speakers of different denominations) was a favourite pastime of the devout.[5] Keshab was so much in demand that he had to decline invitations to over forty towns, and suffered a physical breakdown mid-way through his visit. As he wrote home to his wife in April 1870, 'I have met with very many important men here—usually I receive an invitation every day...it is not possible to rest'.[6]

Keshab's Two Narratives of History

Keshab was publicly critical of many aspects of British rule in India, but he framed his criticisms within a broader view of the history of British imperialism which was largely positive. His English listeners would have been familiar with one narrative of history he expounded, as it reproduced what David Arnold has described as the 'Orientalist triptych', an historical paradigm which organises Indian history by 'contrasting the achievements of ancient Hindu civilisation with the destruction and stagnation of the Muslim Middle Ages and the enlightened rule and scientific progress of the colonial modern age'.[7] In Keshab's view, the greatness of India lay in a past when the ancient Hindus possessed a 'better literature, better scientific ideas, and better and purer social and domestic customs and manners' than the 'West', which was sunk in 'ignorance and barbarism'.[8]

The demise of India had been engendered by two primary agencies: first, the 'oppressive and tyrannical' rule of the Muslim era; second, the subsequent dominance of Hindu 'crafty priests', who had spread idolatry and superstition, encouraged child marriage and polygamy, and fortified caste divisions through religious sanctions.[9] It was the British nation that had been sent by God to rescue India from this decline:

> [When India] lay sunk in the mire of idolatry and superstition, when Mahometan oppression and misrule had almost extinguished the last spark of hope in the native Indian mind, when Hinduism, once a pure system of Monotheism, had degenerated into a most horrid and abominable system of idolatry and polytheism, when the priests were exceedingly powerful, and were reveling in their triumphs over down-trodden humanity, the Lord in His mercy sent out the British nation to rescue India. (Cheers).[10]

However, although Keshab subscribed clearly to a stadial view of history which placed contemporary British society at the apex of civilisation, this view existed alongside another conception of historical progress which was holistic rather than linear, and which accrued to India a special place within the scale of nations. The liberal imperial 'narrative of progress'—according to which civilisations were placed at different points in time, and in which it was the burden of the more advanced nations to speed up the passage to modernity of the less advanced—was, in Keshab's hands, transformed into a narrative in which India played a vital role. Keshab took India and England to represent 'East' and 'West', respectively. He divided the world into two halves, making very few references to societies, forms of knowledge or systems of belief other than those he associated with India and England. Keshab believed that the people of the 'East' and the 'West' possessed distinctly different qualities. He almost always elucidated the uniqueness of the Indian 'nation' (a term he used frequently) and the Indian 'mind' through contrast with his perceptions of the English. His sense of Indian 'national' identity, however complex and protean, was predicated on comparisons with the English 'other'. In his address entitled 'My Impressions of England', the theme Keshab took up first was English commerce and activity:

> The first thing that struck me and dazzled my eyes in London was the brilliancy and splendour of your shops...their number bewildered me... East, west, north, south, everywhere was handbills and advertisements...the Englishman's activity troubled me very much... He works and works and cannot live for anything like contemplation or thought. He is a machine made for work, eternal and everlasting work, and he does not like rest.[11]

The qualities Keshab ascribed to India in his parting words at Southampton were in stark contrast:

> When I turn to my country and the East, I find—warmth of heart, solitary contemplation on her hills and mountains, deep communion with the indwelling and omniscient spirit of the One Supreme God; I see a voluntary and deliberate withdrawing of the heart from all anxieties and cares of the world.[12]

What English civilisation lacked, Indian civilisation could provide. Just as 'commodities' were exchanged through 'mutual traffic', so 'in the spiritual traffic going on in this world we are beginning to recognise the principle of exchange'.[13] The English could offer 'earnestness and firmness of purpose', 'force of will', 'strength of character', 'conscientious strictness, noble charity, practical duty'.[14] The Indians, in return, would provide 'warmth of heart', 'contemplation', 'deep communion', 'sweetness of temper, meekness, and resignation unto God'.[15] England and India embodied entirely different yet complementary qualities. Neither 'nation' could progress towards truth or God without the other: 'I see there [India] the heart of man, and in England the mind of man,—there the soul, here the will, and as it is our duty to love God with all our heart and soul and mind and strength, it is necessary that all these four elements of character should be united'.[16]

The association of India with the spiritual and the emotional, and of England with the material and the rational, had been a trope of British Orientalism and Utilitarianism for generations. Indeed, discourses of Indian 'spirituality' in European thought date back to at least the sixteenth century. As Ronald Inden has argued, in the eighteenth and nineteenth century, this trope was promulgated both by 'positivists'— who tended to denigrate India's 'spiritual' heritage as embodying 'superstition'—and by 'romantics' (especially the 'neo-Orientalists' of the mid-to-late nineteenth century), who placed high value on the myths or symbolic forms which the positivists denigrated or ignored.[17] In Inden's view, both 'romantic' and 'positivist' approaches to Indian history participated in the construction of India as a 'spiritual' place: 'the romantics insist that India embodies a private realm of the imagination and the religious which modern, western man lacks but needs. They, therefore, like the positivists, but for just the opposite reason, have a vested interest in seeing that the Orientalist view of India as "spiritual," "mysterious," and "exotic" is perpetuated'.[18]

While Keshab's bifurcation of the world into a spiritualised 'East' and a materialist 'West' drew, in part, on Orientalist, Utilitarian and Romantic notions of India, the epistemological framework in which he conceptualised the interaction of 'East' and 'West' was quite distinctive. Liberal imperialist progress narratives of the nineteenth century (what Dipesh Chakrabarty refers to more generally as the 'Western historicist paradigm') were based epistemologically on an assumption that 'Western' rational, scientific and objective knowledge occupied a privileged position in relation to the knowledge that people from outside the 'West' had of themselves, which often seemed irrational, unscientific and subjective.[19] The vast morass of human experiences in a continent the size of India could only be understood by an observer outside those experiences, an observer who possessed the superior 'Western' knowledge which enabled him to explain what the Indian, caught up in a subjective, localised experience and devoid of 'Western' rationality, could not explain for himself. Edward Said refers to this attitude as a '*textual* attitude', an attitude which allows that a text could acquire a 'greater authority, and use, even than the actuality it describes'.[20] The reality of the knower thus transcends the reality of the known. Such a view began to predominate in British intellectual and political circles in the 1820s and 1830s, and found perhaps its most systematic expression in James Mill's totalising *History of British India*.[21] As Mehta has argued, elements of Indian culture and society which defied explanation were, in Mill's account, regarded as not amenable to rational analysis because of their innately irrational character—this is what Mehta describes as Mill's 'strategy of inscrutability'.[22]

In contrast to this view of history—in which all knowledge can be subsumed within a single system of representation, other than that which is, by its nature, 'inscrutable'—Keshab's view of history and of 'truth' emphasised the subjective nature of knowledge and experience. This is particularly evident in Keshab's characterisation of Christianity:

> Christ has come to India in a foreign and repulsive form… There is no reason why Christianity should in the present day be presented to the Indian population in any other than an Oriental and Asiatic aspect… Do we not find there [in the Bible] imageries and precepts of an Asiatic and Oriental stamp?… Do we not feel that the *spirit* of Christianity comes to us as something very natural, congenial to our hearts, something with which, by the very peculiar constitution of the Indian mind, we are bound to sympathize.[23]

The 'spirit' of Christianity transcended national boundaries, its truth could not be comprehended fully by any single nation, and every nation contributed to an understanding of its truth by perceiving it from a unique angle: '[Christianity is] a many-sided religion, and every individual and nation takes in a small portion of this many-sided thing'.[24]

According to this perspective, the many-sided nature of truth demands that it is regarded subjectively; increased comprehension of truth requires the exchange of subjective conceptions of its nature. While Keshab was convinced that British rule in India was sanctioned by God, and that Indian progress depended to a great extent on the spread of Western customs and values, he argued also that progress required different civilisations to interact and to learn from each other. In Keshab's view, just as the 'East' could not progress without the influence of the 'West', so the 'West' could not progress without the influence of the 'East'. In the scale of nations, India may occupy a lower position than England, but on the broader scale of universal progress—conceptualised holistically as the gradual union of 'East' and 'West', rather than linearly, as the gradual transformation of the 'East' into the 'West'—India and England occupied positions of equal value. Although this model of progress contains all of human experience and history, the object towards which the model progresses—universal religion, God and truth—cannot be contained, Keshab argued, within a single system of representation. Civilisations, according to Keshab, did not, in fact, all pass through the same stages; rather they progressed along different, although related, paths.

It was this way of viewing God, truth and progress which enabled Keshab to see the histories of India and England, of 'East' and 'West', as closely intertwined, while never giving up his belief in the distinctiveness and value of the Indian 'nation' and the Indian 'mind'. The unique qualities of the Indian 'mind' allowed Indians to provide a unique perspective on truth and God that was not available to those in the 'West'. The Westernisation of Indians would result in nothing less than the loss of a perspective on truth which was peculiarly 'Eastern', and which was of equal value to perspectives offered by the 'West'. As Keshab put it to the congregation of the Union Chapel in Islington, 'Truth is not European'.[25]

Keshab on British rule in India: Gender, Reform and Civilisation

Keshab's holistic philosophy of history bolstered his conviction that Indians not only had much to learn, but much to teach. Part of the purpose of his mission to England was to teach the English about what they were doing wrong in the administration of India. He delivered his first lengthy discourse on the subject—'England's Duties to India'—at the Metropolitan Tabernacle in London (a grand meeting hall on the revivalist model, owned by the prominent Baptist Joseph Spurgeon) on 24 May 1870. He began by echoing the sentiments of Lord Lawrence, who was chairing the event: 'I fully agree with the noble lord who sits in the chair, that to India the British Government has been the best that India could possibly have'.[26] Nevertheless, 'there still are certain blots on the administration of that country which ought to be obliterated.'[27] Faults in the administration of India could be highlighted within a broader framework in which the Providential and beneficent character of British rule was acknowledged. However, as God Himself had invested the British with the power to rule in India, they therefore had a duty to do so responsibly and in the best interests of the Indian people:

> It is my humble conviction that you Englishmen stand there in India merely as trustees. You hold India on trust, and you have no right to say that you will use its property, its riches, or its resources, or any of the power which God has given you, for the purpose of your own selfish aggrandizement and enjoyment.[28]

In what was perhaps a coded reference to the Indian 'Mutiny' of 1857–8, Keshab stated in Leicester: 'The days when Englishmen believed they could trifle with that country with impunity were gone by, and now he [Keshab] hoped that every Englishman believed that if grave injustice was done to India it would recoil tremendously on England. (Hear, hear)'.[29]

Keshab urged the government to employ more 'natives' in the administrative machinery, declaring that, 'the natives, if properly trained, are not unfit to hold the highest offices in the State'.[30] However, while he undoubtedly believed in the equal capacity of Indians and Britons to hold high office, Keshab at no point during his visit enunciated a demand for Indians to participate in representative government. He grounded his appeal for greater Indian participation in the machinery of government in an argument which stressed the improvement which such participation would engender in the 'character' of those employed—Indians who occupied high positions would receive 'practical training and discipline which is so integral to integrity, honesty, and probity'.[31] As Keshab emphasised later in the speech, he had come to England to 'implore your sympathy and aid towards the moral and social reformation of India'.[32] He had not come to make political demands. Keshab's bifurcation of the English and Indian 'minds' in terms of a difference between 'material' and 'spiritual' qualities made Indians particularly suited to the role of promoting spiritual, moral and social health, which would contribute further to the elevation of 'character'.

A desire for the regeneration of 'character' also lay behind Keshab's appeals for 'a better, a more honourable set of Englishmen' to be sent to India.[33] As Keshab lamented, 'The bad influence of immoral men neutralizes the influences of genuine Englishmen, whose number is unfortunately not very large in India'.[34] Of particular concern were Englishmen who inflicted violence upon the 'helpless Hindu'—one example he employed frequently, and which found echoes in Rabindranath Tagore's novel *Gora*, was that of a man who was crushed to death under the wheels of a steam-engine, only to be mocked by Europeans nearby.[35] These criticisms of violent Englishmen were, of course, mitigated by Keshab's conviction that those who acted in such a manner did not constitute 'genuine Englishmen'. The erratic and un-English behaviour of the English abroad was due, in part, to environmental factors: the physical and social atmosphere of India demanded a great deal of 'Christian patience', as, in India, the English would see 'many things which are calculated to excite your bitterness, and to make you haughty, impatient, angry and fretful'.[36] This could result in Europeans being 'driven by anger to deeds of violence and murder'.[37] However, the misdeeds of Europeans abroad should not colour Indians' view of the British character in general: 'I wish I could take with me...hundreds of the good souls of England into my country...and say to my countrymen and women, "Here are truly British hearts—generous and magnanimous hearts"'.[38] The 'true' British 'heart', Keshab avowed, was to be found in the metropole, not in the empire.

Questions concerning the violent behaviour of Europeans abroad, and, more generally, concerning the 'proper' manner in which Englishmen should behave towards 'subject' populations, were very much in the English public imagination at the time of Keshab's visit. Attempts by the Jamaica Committee to prosecute Governor Eyre on criminal charges following his brutal suppression of the uprising in Morant Bay in Jamaica in 1865 had, by 1868, proved a failure; however, the civil case that followed was concluded finally in June 1870, with a ruling that generated considerable public interest.[39] As Hall, Rendall and McClelland have argued, debates surrounding the attempted prosecution of Eyre were interlinked with domestic British discourses concerning the passage of the Reform Bill.[40] Concerns over the threat posed by subject populations in Jamaica to civil order were articulated alongside fears that the extension of the franchise in Britain would result in anarchy. India, too, figured in these debates: the events of 1857–8 were invoked frequently as examples of the mayhem that could ensue when subject populations were not properly controlled.[41] This constellation of fears surrounding the control of subject populations formed the backdrop for debates concerning the India Act of 1870, which granted the government of India the right, in theory, to appoint 'natives' to all government offices, including the covenanted Indian Civil Service.

Questions concerning the 'character' of English, Jamaican and Indian men were of central importance to all of these debates. As Catherine Hall has argued, the Eyre controversy, and the prominence achieved by the Jamaica Committee and the Eyre Defence Committee in the British public sphere as a result of it, led to the sustained public enunciation of two conceptions of manliness, articulated most forcefully by John Stuart Mill and Thomas Carlyle.[42] For Mill and the Jamaica Committee, blacks, Indians and women were formally equal, and should be encouraged by rational and liberal Englishmen to achieve full equality with white men from the development of their full potential through the civilising power of education. For Carlyle and the Eyre Defence Committee, differences of race and of class were grounded in hierarchies predicated on natural law—hierarchies which should be preserved by the vigorous maintenance of order by passionate, decisive and heroic manly leaders. As Hall observes, 'While Carlyle clung to a notion of hierarchy and order with white Englishmen as the ultimate arbiters in the interests of all, Mill dreamed of a more egalitarian society in the future in which all individuals, whether black or white, male or female, would have achieved civilization'.[43] The capacity or incapacity of Indian men to achieve the levels of civilisation envisaged by Mill was a key question in debates concerning the ability of Indians to occupy high government posts. As Metcalf has suggested, the essential qualities of an administrator were regarded as lying in his 'character' as opposed to his ability to pass exams.[44] The views of George Campbell, who believed that, in order to occupy high government posts, Indians would need to 'become so completely Europeanized as to be really and practically on the footing and imbued with the character of an English highly educated gentleman', were still widely held in 1870, and the capacity of Indians to achieve such Europeanisation was a subject of major concern to those drafting the India Act.[45]

Keshab promulgated a very different vision of the 'character' of Indian masculinity to British audiences than the conceptions of manliness articulated by Mill and Carlyle. The regeneration of Indian masculinity would not involve the transformation of Indians into Englishmen envisaged by Mill, nor would it be limited by the racial thinking of Carlyle. Rather, Keshab imagined an Indian manliness built on both the preservation of 'Indian' difference (the national characteristics of the Indian 'mind') and on a moral and social regeneration effected by a truly liberal exchange of ideas between men of the 'East' and the 'West'. Theodore Koditschek has argued that, in stressing the special capacities of Indian men to promote spiritual health, Keshab drew parallels with British feminists' claims to a separate sphere of moral regeneration: 'Let British men keep the spheres of militarism, business, and politics, he avowed. Bhadralok men and British women would share the moral and spiritual spheres among themselves'.[46] However, I have found no evidence to suggest that Keshab drew such parallels explicitly. Rather than aligning Indian masculinity with British femininity, Keshab promulgated a vision of spiritualised Indian manliness which, through the liberal exchange of ideas, would, in time, engender a more spiritualised form of manliness in the 'West'. If participation in government would improve the 'character' of 'natives', then contact with Indians would also improve the 'character' of liberal British men. The power of Indian spiritualised manliness to influence European masculinity would, in Keshab's view, have a direct effect on the ways in which British rule in India was conducted, rather than merely influencing a sphere that was external to politics.

Alongside his vision of Indian masculinity, Keshab promulgated ideas about Indian femininity. Keshab harked back to a golden classical age of femininity in which Indian women had 'freely mixed with each other in society in India...celebrated ladies solved mathematical problems, and evinced the deepest interest in mathematics and science generally'.[47] These arguments drew, no doubt, on the ideas of Ram Mohan, who had also claimed that, in ancient India, women had been treated as in no way inferior to men. In particular, Ram Mohan had pointed to the independence of women in antiquity, evidenced by the equal share in property awarded by ancient lawgivers to a mother and her son following the death of her husband.[48] In Keshab's view, the practices of polygamy and early marriage, and the introduction of laws preventing widow remarriage, had degraded the condition of Indian women, with the result that women in India tended now to 'conserve all the traditions, all the errors and prejudices, and all the injurious institutions that exist in the country'.[49] In particular, Indian women prevented Indian men from achieving their full potential: 'Many [husbands] would come to England, many would break through caste distinctions, many would stand forward as heroes in matters of social and religious reformation, but they cannot do so, simply because they are kept down by their wives'.[50] The education of women in India was of critical importance, as it would result in 'intelligent and happy homes', which would serve to 'purify and regenerate the nation'.[51] Keshab identified a close relationship between the wife, the home and the nation—a relationship that Chatterjee and Sarkar have shown to be characteristic of early Indian nationalist iconography.[52]

The model of an 'intelligent and happy home', in Keshab's view, was to be found in England, and he implored his audiences to help in 'obtaining for my land...English homes'.[53] He also encouraged British women to write to and visit their 'Indian sisters', as this would 'do a great deal towards exercising a high moral and intellectual influence upon them... It will help them to attain not merely knowledge, but also that discipline of life, that softness of disposition, and that righteousness of outward life and inward life, which are essential to true refinement'.[54] Nevertheless, while Keshab often held up the English household and English femininity as a model for Indians to emulate, he also objected to attempts to Westernise Indian women by encouraging them to adopt the 'external refinements' of civilisation: 'There are some not only in India but in England, who think that if native women don't wear crinoline, speak French, and play on the piano, they are past redemption'.[55] What was needed was 'solid education' in the vernacular for 'native' women who, Keshab assured his audience, were 'quite as lively as their English sisters'.[56]

The worries Keshab expressed with regard to the Westernisation of women were part of wider concerns he articulated in relation to 'ideas and projects of denationalizing the Indian nation'.[57] He spoke of a 'patriotic fire running through my heart' before making the following appeal:

> Proud of our nationality, we shall ask you to give us all the good things you have in England, but not your corruptions. Let the stream of enlightenment and knowledge which you send forth to my country promote morality and religion without sweeping away Indian nationality. You are as much responsible as we are for the jealous and careful preservation of everything that is good and ennobling in Indian society.[58]

The elements of Indian society that Keshab wished to see preserved were to be found in the 'quiet little villages in the provinces', where one could see 'homely Hindu life' in its 'original and primitive simplicity'.[59] Clearly the English household was not the only model of domesticity which was of value—Keshab's admiration for urban English family life existed in tension with a deep respect for the rural 'Hindu' household. As will become evident, Keshab's views on Indian femininity and domesticity would shift considerably in the course of the 1870s.

While Keshab placed particular emphasis on the education of women, he was, in general, a strong advocate for mass education in India. Keshab certainly shared the British liberal faith in the power of education to promote 'civilisation', and argued that mass education was the 'first great duty' of the British government in India.[60] He hoped that the 1870 Education Act in Britain would be extended, in some measure, to India, and was optimistic that the Indian Council might recommend such an extension.[61] English education was a panacea that would lead to the reform of 'backward' customs and the dissolution of caste:

> Her [India's] great curse is caste; but English education has already proved a tremendous power in levelling the injurious distinctions of the system.

The Indian who has received a liberal English education finds it impossible
to retain his allegiance to caste... The customs of premature marriage, and
the practice of polygamy, had long been acting banefully in India; but the
influence of English education has tended to operate most powerfully in
turning away public opinion from these baneful customs.[62]

However, while Keshab emphasised the ability of English education
to remove corruptions from Indian society, he looked to the Hindu
tradition to provide the positive content that would act as the
foundation for subsequent development. This content was to be found
'in the early books and institutions of the Hindus, [where] there is a
substratum for future reforms as strong and firm as a rock'.[63] The need
to return to ancient Hindu texts as a basis for reform had been
enunciated powerfully by Ram Mohan, and was central to
Debendranath's theological vision. It also formed the basis for Keshab's
reformist program for India.

However, Keshab's desire to use ancient Hindu texts as a basis for
reform existed in tandem with his belief in the power of the Bible to
regenerate India. Christianity, he informed his British audiences, 'went
to work in the very heart of the nation', and was effecting the 'moral
and religious reformation of the country'.[64] While Hindu texts were of
great value, the Bible was indispensable: 'However proud we may be of
our own religious books...it is a fact which must be admitted by all
candid men that India cannot do without the spirit of the Bible.
(Cheers.)'.[65] While Keshab's positive attitude towards Christianity was
frequently attacked in India by writers in the *National Paper* (and
distinguished the theology of the Brahmo Samaj of India from that of
the Adi Brahmo Samaj), Keshab represented Christianity as a religion
which, like Hinduism, had originated in the 'East' and thus already
constituted a part of Indian 'national' culture—it was not a Western
importation. He stressed the need for Christianity in India to assume
an 'Oriental and Asiatic aspect', and, building on arguments advanced
by Ram Mohan, emphasised the 'Oriental' character of Christ.[66]

In Keshab's view, it was the failure of missionaries to acknowledge
the 'Eastern Aspect' of Christianity which had led the majority of
Indians to reject the religion. Indeed, 'professing Christians' in India
were exerting a 'baneful influence'.[67] Missionaries emphasised doctrine
over practice, and all emphasised different doctrines to each other.[68]

Keshab saw missionary sectarianism as an effect of the 'materialistic' character of British Christianity, in which 'Every sect is like a small shop where a peculiar kind of Christianity is offered for sale...no Christian sect puts forth the genuine and full Christ as he was and is'.[69] London life had taught him that 'there is an attempt in every Christian sect to follow both God and mammon'.[70] Christianity in England was, in general, 'too muscular and hard...more materialistic and outward than spiritual and inward'.[71] There was undue emphasis on 'cold intellectualism' and 'dreary systems'.[72] The result, as Keshab expressed it in recognisably Carlylean rhetoric, was that 'men's hearts have become dry...our hearts are sunk in worldliness... We are lost amidst the charms and allurements of the world'.[73] Keshab would not have agreed with Carlyle's racism, but he certainly concurred with Carlyle's critique of the mechanised character of industrial Britain, and of the ways in which industrialisation had led men to regard reason as more valuable than passion, emotion and religious feeling.[74] Keshab later told an audience in Bombay that he had seen in England 'a mutilated Christianity and a mutilated Christ... I saw Christ's hand in England, but I did not see Christ's heart and soul'.[75] He lamented that 'England is still as far from the Kingdom of Heaven as you and I are. In England there is still much that you would see of bigotry and superstition,— there are sects far more numerous than I ever thought'.[76] Keshab's experience of Christianity in the metropole had convinced him that England was no more advanced, in terms of religious thought and practice, than India.

Keshab's attacks on the materialistic and mechanical character of English Christianity formed part of a broader critique of 'Western' civilisation, towards which his attitude was ambivalent and complex. While Keshab referred to the power of education to engender civilisation, and often extolled the virtues of 'civilised' English women, he also used the term 'civilisation' to denote an excessive concern with material objects and physical pleasures. In an address to the United Kingdom Alliance of May 1870, he spoke with evident passion about the 'ravages of so-called civilization' that were obliterating a simpler, purer form of life. The picture he paints is of an India under threat, of an older, purer society being killed off by the 'creeping' vices of modernity:

Go into the quiet little villages in the provinces, and you there see homely Hindu life in its purity and charming simplicity, such as has not been surpassed in any other portion of the globe. But where is that simplicity and purity now? It is fast dying out amid the ravages of so-called civilization…We do not see Hindu society in its original state of purity. All these modern vices are fast creeping into Indian society, and depriving it of its original and primitive simplicity.[77]

Chief among the 'modern vices' of 'so-called civilization' was alcohol. Keshab addressed numerous temperance societies, and was at his most vitriolic on such occasions: '[My countrymen] see clearly that the British Government is actuated by motives of filthy lucre; and for the sake of a few million pounds is really doing prodigious mischief… Famines and epidemics have often desolated India and carried off thousands in a few hours; but they are, in comparison, not such gigantic evils as intemperance is'.[78] Keshab chastised the British administration for placing before young Indian men a dangerous cocktail of new ideas and alcoholic liquors. He narrated a story of 'an ignorant Indian' who, through English education, became a 'fine-looking, educated man', only to drink himself to death with 'English books on one side…the dangerous bottle of brandy on the other side'.[79] It was England's greatest gift—education—which was unsettling minds and paving the way for the evil of intemperance: 'people sometimes compute the results of English education by the number of deaths that actually take place every month and year through intemperance!'.[80] Education without spiritual guidance would result in denationalisation, excess and an undue regard for the 'external refinements' and bodily pleasures of materialistic civilisation.

While Keshab was critical of the 'materialism' of 'so-called civilization' in the 'West', he was not generally critical of capitalism or of the imperial economy—in fact, quite the opposite. As we have seen, Keshab argued that the 'principle of exchange' through which 'spiritual traffic' changed hands was the same principle according to which 'commodities' were exchanged and distributed across the world. Keshab rarely referred to economics (except in metaphorical terms), but it may be the case that his use of the free exchange of material commodities as a model for the free exchange of spiritual commodities drew on the economic ideas of Ram Mohan, who, as Bayly points out, was 'an economic liberal' who 'argued for free trade as vehemently as contemporary English liberals'.[81] However, while Ram Mohan's advocacy of free trade was grounded in his hope that it would destroy the corruption of the East India Company, Keshab's advocacy of the free exchange of spiritual ideas was grounded in his hope that, through inter-cultural dialogue, humanity could achieve moral and spiritual regeneration. While Keshab was well aware that Britain occupied a pre-eminent place in the global material economy, and was responsible for the manufacture of a vast quantity of the commodities circulating within it, he argued that it was India which held a near monopoly over the global spiritual economy—both in terms of the production of spiritual knowledge that was to be exchanged, and in terms of the dissemination of that knowledge across the world.

Keshab on England and the English

Keshab spoke candidly to his audiences about his impressions of the positive and negative aspects of life in England. He praised the 'happy English home', which he felt combined 'warmth' and 'affection' with the 'highest moral and religious restraint and discipline'.[82] He extolled the virtues of English philanthropy and pointed to the 'power of English public opinion' as a force for reform—a force he believed was absent from Calcutta.[83] Keshab was clear about which elements of English society he wanted to take back to India: 'I can ask for nothing better than the co-operation of Englishmen in obtaining for my native land English charity, English homes, and English public opinion'.[84] Keshab was not simply flattering his English audiences. Upon his return to India, he delivered speeches in which he reiterated the positive aspects of English life that he had pointed out to his audiences in England. [85]

However, there were certain aspects of English life for which Keshab was unprepared, which shocked him profoundly, and of which he was deeply critical. Chief among these was the degree of poverty he witnessed. He lamented the ubiquitous presence of poverty in a number of his public lectures in England, and frequently characterised English society as benighted by caste: 'Your rich people are really Brahmins, and your poor people are Sudras. (Hear hear.) I thought caste was peculiar to India; certainly in a religious sense it is, but as a social institution it perpetuates prodigious havoc in this country'.[86] In a later address to an Indian audience, he criticised poverty in stronger terms: 'There are the worst men in England, as there are the best everywhere. The worst, the lowest, the most wicked are to be found in it. Destitution,—poverty in its worst and frightful phases is found in the streets of London—ignorance, frightful and appalling, pervading the masses of the people'.[87] In a private letter to his wife, Keshab drew parallels between poverty in Calcutta and London, and wrote of impoverished women on the streets of London in a disdainful tone: 'As in our country poor beggars sing on the street for money, so here too the same thing can be seen from time to time; occasionally we give money to those of them who live in our neighbourhood... In various places on the street lower-class wretched women sell fruit and all kinds of things'.[88] Keshab's experiences in England had taught him that it was not only India that needed to be raised in the scale of nations.

Keshab's criticisms of the English 'caste system' are significant, as it was precisely 'caste' that had been identified in Orientalist and Utilitarian accounts of India as a hypostasised force that had robbed Indians of agency.[89] As Nicholas Dirks has argued, the events of 1857–8 stimulated a renewed interest in the production of ethnographies of caste that, with the aim of furthering British knowledge of Indian 'tradition' in order to avoid political interventions that would stimulate revolt, attempted to catalogue the 'characteristics' of particular castes. This anthropologisation of colonial knowledge served to reinforce earlier assumptions about caste as a barrier to individual agency and national self-determination.[90] As Maria Brun has argued, the Female Infanticide Act of 1870 and the Criminal Tribes Act of 1871 both utilised notions of unchanging 'caste characteristics' as the basis for legislation.[91] In drawing attention to caste as a 'social institution' in Britain and India, Keshab was both distancing the genesis of caste-systems from the doctrines of Hinduism, and was identifying both working-class Britons and low-caste Indians as similarly benighted by the prejudices of social hierarchy.

In addition to deploring the condition of the English poor, Keshab was also critical of the manners of the English elite. His perspective on English table manners caused a great deal of amusement among his audience:

An English dinner party…is a hunting party (laughter)…They always go armed with spoons and forks and knives, in order to attack the fowls of the air, the beasts of the wilderness, and the fishes of the sea that are gathered on the table. (Continued laughter.) It troubled me very much, may I say it frightened me, when I saw birds and beasts on the table almost ready to start into existence again… My flesh creeps on my bones when I see a huge piece of roast English beef on the table. (Renewed laughter).[92]

Although Keshab was clearly enjoying himself, his criticisms of English table manners are of more serious significance. Persuading 'native' populations to eat with 'spoons and forks and knives' had been a major concern of the imperial civilising mission. Norbert Elias, in *The Civilizing Process*, has uncovered a deep connection between notions of civility and table manners in the West since at least the thirteenth century.[93] Missionaries, in particular, in various parts of the empire, treated instruction in the use of cutlery as an essential part of 'raising' the condition of the 'natives'.[94] Keshab's criticism of 'roast English beef' may have been motivated by his vegetarianism, but he could hardly have chosen a more potent gastronomic symbol of English liberty than this staple food of 'John Bull'.[95]

Keshab's remarks on female dress on the same occasion led to a flurry of comment in numerous sections of the British press, and earned him a cartoon in *Punch*:

The Girl of the Period is really a peculiar creature. I hope she will never make her appearance in India. There are two things in particular which I object to—the head and the tail. (Much laughter.) In these days of 'women's rights,' may I not seriously suggest that women ought not to occupy more ground than men. (Laughter.) It is a fact that a civilized and refined lady of the West occupies five times as much space as a gentleman. The fair sex ought to be fair. (Renewed laughter.) And as regards the head…I am told there is a secret inside that huge protuberance at the back of the head, which would not bear criticism. (Continued laughter.) I hope educated and sensible ladies of the present day will give better proof in future of the fertility of their brains. (Laughter and applause).[96]

'Native dress', of course, was another major concern for those wishing to 'civilise natives' across the empire. Descriptions of naked children as 'in a state of nature' proliferate in travel accounts written by English visitors to the colonies in the nineteenth century and earlier. Inadequate or indecent dress was taken to be a direct, visible sign of a lack of civilisation. 'Inadequate' women's dress, in particular, was believed to signify a degraded moral and intellectual state of 'native' womanhood, which functioned in turn as a sign of a degraded civilisation in general.[97] Keshab's remark that he wished to see more proof of the fertility of English women's brains than the 'protuberance at the back of the head' should be read in the context of his general disdain for the 'external refinements' of civilisation, his complaints against the denationalisation of Indian women through the adoption of Western manners, his belief that Indian and English women were equally matched in their capacity for education, and his conviction that external appearances did not provide a valid guide to inner nature.

Keshab's general dislike of the 'external refinements' of civilisation is clearly perceptible in much of his private writing composed in England. Of the food on the boat to England he remarks in his diary: 'Civilization does not satisfy our belly as much as it makes outward *dhoom dham* [display]'; having attended a small private party after a series of official dinners he records: 'How I hate large dinners—how I love these small friendly gatherings'.[98] Although he was impressed by the technology on display at the Crystal Palace, he was not moved by the gigantic musical performance: 'the treat is grand if not sweet; I admire it though I do not enjoy it. Its scientific character is really astonishing'.[99] His dislike of outward show is apparent in his disdain for excessive speech: he found a sermon delivered by the influential theologian Henry Liddon at St. James' Church, Piccadilly, to be 'a little tedious'; the remarks of the philosophers at the Metaphysical Society, including James Martineau, were, in his opinion, 'rather rambling and "not to the point"'; in a letter to his wife he wrote of Mary Carpenter: 'She...has many good qualities, but her propensity to talk is quite fearful. She can talk so much that people cannot help getting annoyed with her'.[100] He summed up his impressions early on in a letter to a friend in Calcutta: 'People do not put their heart into their beliefs, they just throw arguments around'.[101] Keshab saw his philosophy of history, in which the 'East' represented the 'inner' and the 'West' the 'external', confirmed wherever he looked.

Keshab on Himself

How did Keshab represent himself to the numerous sections of the British public to which he had access? First and foremost, he expected the English to take him, and the country he was claiming to represent, seriously. Keshab had a strong sense of the role of 'great men' in history, which was interlinked with his view of Divine Providence, and, certainly later in life, came to see himself as one such 'great man'.[102] At his welcome soirée, he intimated that a Divine hand lay behind his visit: 'I have not come to England for the sake of business or pleasure; it is not to satisfy idle curiosity, or make money, that I am amongst you. A most sacred duty brings me here: I have an important mission to fulfil. I come from India to tell you English men and women what you have done in my country'.[103] His mastery of the English language was complete, and he was determined that what he said should be internalised and acted upon by the English men and women to whom he spoke. Speaking in Bath, he alerted his listeners to the importance of the matters he was bringing to the attention of the English public: 'I hope you have not come merely to hear how a native of Bengal can speak the English language. I hope you have not assembled merely to satisfy your curiosity, but that you have come for a higher and nobler purpose'.[104] Keshab introduced himself to his audiences on numerous occasions as the 'humble representative of the people of India'.[105] He raised himself above different regional, religious or ethnic groups, declaring, 'I stand on the platform as one who desires to represent the wants and wishes of all sects of the Indian community, so far as it is possible'.[106] He was confident that he spoke from a position of great authority.

Keshab criticised English attitudes to India as ill informed and parochial. He told his audiences in no uncertain terms that 'the English people are profoundly ignorant of the actual state of things in India'.[107] He insisted that India was no 'dream-land', but a 'real land, and a great country'.[108] It deserved a greater degree of attention in parliament, and should not be treated 'as though it were a country peopled by savages'.[109] The parochial English should not talk about India in a 'patronizing way', as the Thames 'is a little stream compared with the mighty Ganges, and your mountains are mole-hills in comparison with the Himalayas'.[110] Keshab aggregated to himself the ability to represent India in its entirety; an ability that so many English observers had previously aggregated to themselves. His comments concerning the mediocrity of the English mountains and rivers in comparison to those of India may be read as an early example of an attempt to provincialise Europe.

In his final speech to the British and Foreign Unitarian Association in 1870, Keshab declared proudly: 'The result of my visit to England is that as I came here an Indian, I go back a confirmed Indian; I came here a Theist, I return a confirmed Theist.... I have not accepted one single new doctrine that God has not put into my mind before'.[111] Keshab emphasised his capacity for independent judgement—a quality that was absolutely central to English conceptions of male civic virtue from the Scottish enlightenment onwards.[112] He represented himself, in part, as a product of English education—'I must myself own what a wonderful effect English education has had upon me'—but he stressed that his religious belief did not emanate from the West.[113] His biography, as he narrated it to a number of audiences, ran along the following lines: he 'was a Hindu, and as such believed in his early days in all the superstitions and idolatries of his unfortunate motherland'; he 'placed himself under the influence of a liberal English education, which taught him that idolatry and caste were false' (he made it clear that this change in belief was *not* the result of contact with Christian missionaries); 'English education unsettled his mind, and left a void; he had given up idolatry, but had received no positive system of faith to replace it'.[114] Faith came later through revelation: it was 'Providence' which 'reveal[ed] the light of truth to me in a most mysterious manner'.[115] English education, therefore, had altered Keshab's beliefs in relation to idolatry and caste, but had not engendered faith in God. Keshab's faith in God had come from within, from direct communion, not from the West. He insisted that his view of Christ was a personal, 'Indian' view of Christ: 'If each sect in Christendom accepted, as it were, a part of Christ, might not he, an Indian, accept him in his own humble way, and which he believed was the right way? He would allow no Christian sect whatever to interfere in his own independent judgement'.[116]

The uniqueness and value that Keshab saw in Indian culture and society undoubtedly formed a critical element in his sense of identity. A member of one half of the circle of human progress, Keshab—as an 'Indian'—could address his English audiences on equal terms, he could tell them about their faults as well as their good qualities, and he could stand firm in his own convictions as to which doctrines he would and would not accept. However, alongside Keshab's sense of 'Indian-ness' was his universalism. He frequently referred to himself during speeches in England as being both an 'Indian' and a 'Man of the World'.[117] He presented his own biography, as well as the history of the Brahmo Samaj, as an example in miniature of the process of synthesis described in his holistic philosophy of history. He placed the Brahmo Samaj at the centre of reform in India, claiming that it effected reform from 'within' by uniting the best attributes of 'East' and 'West': 'It [the Brahmo Samaj] may be described as the product of English enlightenment... [but] will present to your eyes all the good influences which are found in Hindu books and in Hindu institutions...[it] unites the good things of the two nations, and forms them into one harmonious whole'.[118] Keshab viewed his own 'mind' as similar to that of Ram Mohan, who 'tried to unite the East and the West, for in his own mind the results of English education and Vedic training had harmonized, and he could not be unfaithful or untrue to either'.[119]

Keshab's sense of himself as both 'Eastern' and 'Western', along with his universalist religious beliefs, allowed him to feel quite at home in a foreign land. Indeed, he referred often to England as his 'temporary home'.[120] He had a strong sense that English culture was a part of his own culture. It belonged to India and was not simply a foreign imposition: 'Shakspeare, Milton, and Newton...in some measure... have become our own.... Your philosophy and science are ours'. [121] This accorded with his view of truth as many-sided. He was surprised and delighted by the reception he had received from his English 'beloved brothers and sisters', and regarded himself as surrounded by 'my best and most intimate friends'.[122] In Calcutta, he had drawn great comfort from receiving letters from England, at times when 'my brethren in my own country were wanting in sympathy, and were ready to persecute me'.[123] His visit to England had convinced him that 'there are thousands of Englishmen and English women who, from the bottom of their hearts have assured me of their sympathy'.[124] Thus, he felt that 'Though I am in a foreign land, I almost forget the place where I am...I forget your country, I forget the external differences of nationality and colour; I find that I am on God's earth, and that there are brethren around me'.[125] Keshab had a strong sense that he belonged to a loving imperial family.

Keshab was the subject of a number of photographic portraits during his visit to England (Fig. iii and Fig. iv). British reactions to Keshab's physical appearance will be considered in some detail in the following chapter; at present, it is enough to note that Keshab's attire while in England did not differ significantly from the clothes he wore in Calcutta. According to Frances Power Cobbe, he was always dressed in the manner depicted in the photographs.[126] He certainly did not imitate English gentlemanly fashion by wearing a suit, in the manner of so many later Indian arrivals in England.[127] In the portraits his clothes appear dignified and plain. In some images in circulation, his finger marks a page in a book, indicative of his learning.

Fig. iii   Photographic portrait of Keshab Chandra Sen in England, 1870.

Fig. iv   Photographic portrait
of Keshab Chandra Sen
in England, 1870.

Keshab was lionised by many sections of the British public, his speeches were attended by many thousands of people, and the speeches of introduction he received on such occasions were often eulogistic in the extreme. He was deeply grateful for the respect and admiration with which he was treated, but was clearly bemused by the extraordinary level of attention he received. Describing his reception in Glasgow, he wrote to his wife:

Around four thousand people were present, all displaying intense enthusiasm. After the lecture, everyone began to crowd around, pushing and shoving in an attempt to see me and to touch my hand. There was such a crowd, grabbing hold of my hands and pulling this way and that. You would not be able to believe what a famous person I have become. I am honoured here as a King, there is no doubt that had you been here with me you would have been treated as a Queen!! What respect there is for your Keshab!![128]

Keshab was keen to reassure his wife that he had not been affected adversely by the attention he was receiving. By July he had tired of repeated rapturous receptions, and reaffirmed his 'Bengali-ness' through evocations of simple food eaten by hand:

Everybody has treated me with such reverence that it is now difficult to bear. Those with whom I have mixed have raised me up to the status of a great man. Perhaps you have thought that I have become conceited, but that is not at all the case. I am still the same little Keshab, eating rice, potatoes, dhal and milk!! The same rice-eating [bheto] Bengali!![129]

Although Keshab signs off one letter to his wife 'your "British friend"', when he describes himself in his private writings it is most often in a way that refers affectionately to his 'Bengali-ness'. His diary indicates the deep sense of relief he found in the quiet services he and his Bengali companions conducted each evening in their mother tongue.[130] In his autobiography or 'Life Scriptures', he emphasised his dislike of 'places where I behold the grandeur of wealth and honour' and his sense of awkwardness when in the company of 'the rich, the famous, and the learned'.[131] When meeting with such men, 'the thought comes into my mind "O when will this meeting end, when shall I go back to my familiar company, to my humble friends! When shall I return home and feel that ease that my simple nature craves for? Shyness makes me miserable"'.[132] It seems that shyness may have been a later development in Keshab's character; at least, he makes no reference to it in his private writings whilst in England. On the contrary, he appears confident and regards himself as on an equal footing with even the most esteemed of the people he meets (when John Stuart Mill came to call unannounced, Keshab made him wait outside until he had finished writing his correspondence).[133] Nevertheless, Keshab disliked the pomp and ceremony he saw in English culture, and sought solace in the company of his Bengali companions.

Keshab's confidence derived from his religious convictions, his belief in the value of a unique 'Indian-ness', his conversance with educated English culture, his sense of himself as an example of his holistic philosophy of history in miniature, and the genuine value he attached to what he describes as his Bengali 'simplicity'—a quality which could shield him from the 'external refinements' of civilisation. The universal, the metropolitan, the national and the regional all figured in his sense of self. That these elements did not cohere harmoniously would become evident in the course of his life. However, in 1870 at least, lying in the parks of Hampton Court, Keshab seemed at ease with a sense of self that was both metropolitan and colonial:

> I enjoy the breeze, stretched *ala Bengali* on the ground under a shady tree, and read the interesting messages received this day from home. For the first time in my life I see tapestry on the walls of the court.[134]

Conclusion

When we consider Keshab's faith in the civilising capacity of education, his notion that British rule was the best possible form of rule in India, his belief in the equality of different races and sexes (even if they exhibited unique qualities), and his firm conviction that historical 'progress' was occurring (and that the British empire was exercising an indispensable role in furthering this 'progress'), it seems fair to conclude that he shared many of the convictions associated with liberal models of imperialism in the mid-nineteenth century. Indeed, Keshab's desire to see sustained and widespread government intervention in religious and social customs, his plea for mass education in India, and his conviction that the spread of knowledge of the Bible would contribute to the moral and social regeneration of the country, have much more in common with the British liberal imperialist impulse of the Bentinck era, than with the more cautious, paternal and non-interventionist politics of the post-'Mutiny' period.

However, this apparent accommodation with liberal imperialist thought masks some abrupt ruptures. The 'narrative of progress' Keshab presented to British audiences was driven not only by the spread of English liberty and education across the world, but also by a dialectic between 'East' and 'West' which would lead to the regeneration of both Britain and India. This dialectic was conceptualised within an epistemology that stressed the value of subjective experience, and challenged assumptions that the 'West' held a monopoly on 'truth'. The Providential nature of the British empire did not serve as proof of the superiority of British culture and society. The West did not occupy a uniquely central position in the unfolding of history, and modern Anglo-Saxon man did not represent the apex of civilisation. Keshab's idealist vision of history, while theological in its presentation, served to covertly rupture imperial political hierarchies by pointing to their fundamental immorality. This was political theology, which took aim at 'Western civilisation' even as it valorised empire as Providential.

Keshab's attitude towards 'Western civilisation' was ambivalent: on the one hand, 'civilisation' stood for education and the spread of freedom from superstition, prejudice and error; on the other hand, 'civilisation' stood for servitude to material goods and superficial refinements. While the knowledge of the 'West' could engender negative freedom by liberating India from the errors of ages, it was the knowledge of the Indian 'mind' and 'nation' that would provide the positive content for freedom in the future. This was a 'nation' united by unique qualities intrinsic to the Indian 'mind'; it was not dependent on political independence for its realisation. The future Keshab imagined for Britain and India was one of increased collaboration and interaction, not of independence from one another—his narrative of progress was dependent on the crossing of 'national' boundaries. The continuance and strengthening of the British-Indian connection would not result in the transformation of Indians into Englishmen; rather, it would transfigure both Indians and Englishmen into men of the world. In representing himself to British audiences as a 'man of the world'—as an example of his holistic philosophy of history in miniature—Keshab was representing himself as an embodiment of this ideal.

4

SPECTACLE, DIFFERENCE, FEAR AND FANTASY

REPRESENTATIONS OF KESHAB IN VICTORIAN ENGLAND

On 25 June 1870, the London newspaper *The Graphic* emerged from the printing presses with a large portrait of Keshab Chandra Sen emblazoned on its pages (Fig. v). The accompanying article spoke excitedly of the arrival of 'Baboo Keshub Chunder Sen':

> It is surely a significant sign that at a time when the Church of England is disquieted by the dissensions of Ritualist and Rationalist, and when the Roman Church is forging her thunderbolt-anathemas to hurl at all who doubt her infallibility, there should come a man from heathen India, the cradle of mythology, the land of caste, the home of superstition and fanaticism, to teach enlightened Europe the virtue of toleration, the beauty of morality, the unity of truth, and the brotherhood of humanity. The religious reformer whose name appears at the head of this article is certainly one of the most remarkable men of his age...

> It may be regarded as a proof of the genuineness of his modesty as well as of his general good sense, that when he observed that the eloquence of the preachers and the length of the services, resulted in a species of ecstasy in the congregations, he thought proper to caution them against the extremity of religious emotion, recommending them to exercise self-control lest they should become mere spiritual voluptuaries. Were it his ambition to be regarded as a demi-god, his plain course would have been to encourage, rather than check, this tendency in his followers.[1]

Fig. v   'Baboo Keshub Chunder Sen'. Portrait in *The Graphic*,
25 June 1870.

Representations of Keshab

In his history of the Brahmo Samaj, the Bengali Brahmo Sivanath Sastri remarked that, after Keshab's initial reception in the Hanover Square rooms, 'the career of Mr. Sen in England was something like a triumphal march'.[2] Keshab's disciples certainly regarded his visit as a triumph, and this favourable view has been reproduced by scholars who have relied on Sophia Dobson Collet's collection of sources, all of which reinforce the view that Keshab was received with unqualified enthusiasm. It is true that Keshab's visit generated a great deal of favourable publicity, that he spoke to rooms filled to overflowing with interested spectators, and that he, at times, received a level of adulation that he himself found bewildering. The first questions that must be asked, therefore, are: why did Keshab become so popular? What made Keshab such a fitting candidate for 'lionisation'? Why did Lord Lawrence, once the iron man of the Punjab, accompany him personally to so many official and semi-official events? Why did representatives of almost every religious denomination gather to hear him speak? Why did the Unitarian journal *The Inquirer* describe his visit as 'a landmark in our religious history'?[3]

That said, a consultation of the broader British press reveals that the sources collected by Sophia Dobson Collet, and the accounts by Keshab's disciples, paint a very biased picture of Keshab's reception in England. Keshab did not, in fact, receive unqualified support during his sojourn. On the contrary, many regarded him with deep suspicion and even outright hostility. He was represented variously as a threat to Christianity, as a dupe of the Unitarians, as a joke, as an upstart, as superficial and spurious—an ersatz gentleman. Many poured scorn on those who supported him, denouncing their adulation as irrational and hysterical. Keshab's lectures and speeches received many poor reviews—his thinking was criticised as woolly, his philosophy half-learned. Controversies raged in many of the editorial columns and letters pages of the religious and secular press. Should Keshab be welcomed or rejected? Should he be allowed to preach or should he be made to listen? Should religious organisations extend a warm welcome to a man who had come so far from 'Hindu superstition', or should they reject this blasphemous, deluded, false prophet? The spectacle of a colonial subject speaking from platforms in the heart of the empire was, for many, a cause for celebration; for others, it was a cause for deep concern.

Representations of Keshab in England were multiple and diverse. An extraordinary range of commentators entered into a contest over the meaning of Keshab's appearance in England—a contest in which an attempt to elucidate precisely the limits and aetiologies of Keshab's differences from and similarities to the English was a central concern. Through an examination of these representations, we can investigate the ways in which a diverse range of actors responded to a colonial subject, and analyse the strategies through which those who encountered or described Keshab ordered his colonial subjectivity in relation to a range of intersecting discourses. In what ways could Keshab carry meaning in England in 1870? How were these meanings generated, and for whom?

Imperial Spectacle

The Christian World, a digest of the activities of all the major branches of Nonconformity, described the interest Keshab generated thus: 'No one who has ever landed on our shores has created more interest in himself and his work amongst all classes of religionists in this country than our Hindoo visitor… At more than one of our May meetings his reception has been—I can use no other words—a perfect ovation'.[4] The radical newspaper the Daily News commented that 'to see a Brahmin… cordially welcomed here by eminent representatives of almost every Church, is indeed a spectacle to excite more than an idle and transitory wonderment'.[5]

Keshab on the platform was certainly a 'spectacle'. He appeared by and large in Nonconformist venues, which played host regularly to religious rallies and 'indignation meetings'. Such occasions, writes Bebbington, were 'designed for enjoyment and excitement. Resolutions were carried, but people came for the speeches. Rallies were a suitably moral substitute for the theatre among those who, by and large, would still refuse to see any play'.[6] Keshab's appearances were well advertised in the religious and secular press; punters were enjoined to snap up tickets quickly before they sold out. His ability to fill large venues put him much in demand, and organisations clamoured to secure from him an appearance.

What did people come to see? Undoubtedly, the greatest draw for audiences was the fact that Keshab was from the 'East': he was an 'Oriental other', and thus an object of immediate fascination. In his essay on 'The Spectacle of the "Other"', Stuart Hall links the recognition of a variety of 'differences' to the production of 'spectacle': 'In representation, one sort of difference seems to attract others—adding up to a "spectacle" of otherness'.[7] What aroused such excitement among Keshab's audiences, however, was not only his 'difference', but also his 'similarity'. The Liberal *Pall Mall Budget* commented that 'His features are well cut, and combine a certain sweetness with an expression of marked decision'; the Conservative weekly *The Saturday Review* reported that he exhibited a 'manly straight-forwardness and a manly warmth'; Lord Lawrence, speaking at the Metropolitan Tabernacle, referred to his 'friend' as an 'educated, civilized, and intelligent man of the world'.[8]

Central to Keshab's manliness were his physical appearance, his independence, his earnestness and his capacity for rational thought. Physical strength assumed a particular importance in the mid-to-late nineteenth century in the discourses of masculinity related to 'muscular Christianity', associated with, among others, the Anglican Charles Kingsley. For Kingsley, 'a central, even defining characteristic of muscular Christianity [was] an association between physical strength, religious certainty, and the ability to shape and control the world around oneself'.[9] Myths of Indian physical weakness were commonly invoked to justify continued political subjugation—Mark Singleton has shown how discourses of physical and national culture worked to engender 'the British conviction of the physical, moral, and spiritual inferiority of Indians, as judged against the idealized masculine body and perfect conduct of the English gentleman'.[10] It is in this context that comments on Keshab's physical appearance—in particular, the frequent references to his tallness and the squareness of his jaw—become significant.[11]

While notions of bodily strength as a prerequisite for manliness were of particular importance in the discourses of 'muscular Christianity', conceptions of strength of will and earnestness of purpose as defining characteristics of masculinity had a much wider currency. The freeborn Englishman was to have autonomy of the self in relations to others, to enjoy freedom of action; in contrast, Indians were often characterised as slaves to superstition, as fitted for foreign rule. As important as the ability to exercise one's will was the ability to direct one's will on the basis of reason.[12] A strong association between rationality and masculinity was common throughout the nineteenth century, but it held a particular importance among dissenting Christians, especially Unitarians. The influential Unitarian W. E. Channing had regarded reason as the key to understanding religion; James Martineau and his ministerial friends 'steered Unitarians towards basing their religion on reason and conscience rather than the Bible'.[13] The biographer of the great Baptist preacher C. H. Spurgeon argues that Spurgeon 'clearly saw standing steadfastly for "the truth"—and doing so alone, if necessary—as a criterion by which both a man's godliness and his manliness could be measured'.[14] This belief enabled him to view Luther as the epitome of a godly man, even though he was more inclined to agree with the doctrines of Calvin.

In this context, what was most crucial to Keshab's manliness was not that he professed a wholehearted Christian belief (which he did not), but that he expressed his beliefs sincerely. Having witnessed Keshab preach, the Nonconformist digest *The Christian World* drew attention to 'the earnestness of his appeal'; the conservative Anglican journal *The Record*, while highly critical of Keshab's beliefs, admitted that he spoke in 'earnest and expressive terms'.[15] In the large portrait of Keshab printed by *The Graphic*—accompanied by text describing him as 'one of the most remarkable men of the age'—Keshab's 'expression of marked decision' is clearly in evidence: Keshab is a man to be taken seriously.[16]

How had Keshab become so 'manly'? What Keshab had acquired above all was an English education, and what was taken to signify this most clearly was his voice. Almost every single article written about Keshab mentions his voice. Detractors and supporters alike were astonished by his ability to speak extempore, with hardly a trace of an accent. The *Pall Mall Budget*'s comments were echoed throughout much of the press: 'Keshub Chunder Sen talks as good English as any Englishman, and very much better English than the majority of those who undertake the duty of weekly admonition in religious matters. There is a slight trace, but nothing more than a slight trace, of foreign accent, and he speaks with perfect fluency, with complete grammatical accuracy, and apparently even without the use of a note'.[17]

It was the imperial mission, rather than Keshab's own endeavour, that was applauded as the source of Keshab's eloquence and familiarity with 'English ideas'. *The Saturday Review* represented Keshab as an 'effect' of imperialism, which had made him both intelligent and earnest: 'Keshub Chunder Sen is an example of what Western, and especially English, civilization is making of native gentlemen in Bengal. He has thrown himself into the study of English religion and English books'.[18] *The Telegraph* described him as 'the living and visible result of

Western education on the Eastern mind'.[19] Lord Lawrence, who declared that he had been 'in some degree instrumental' in inducing Keshab to visit England, attributed Keshab's abandonment of idolatry to the influence of his English education, and believed that the influence of the Brahmo Samaj would have 'a leavening effect over whole masses of the Hindus'.[20]

The Unitarian James Martineau also drew a causal connection between Keshab's English education and his abandonment of idolatry. He identified India as a 'victim' of 'her keen intellect and flexible imagination', and argued that it was the latter quality that had led to Indian polytheism.[21] Rational as opposed to imaginative speech had led Keshab to religious truth, much in the same way as it had steered Martineau and his colleagues towards their own critical and reasoning Unitarian faith. Other commentators reversed the causality, and regarded religion as opposed to reason as the fountainhead of Keshab's transformation. The *English Independent* commented that English missionaries 'have originated and quickened new influences which... have radiated suddenly in light over the whole Indian Empire.... This fact is brought conspicuously before our view in the presence of Keshub Chunder Sen'.[22] Whichever way round the causality, the origin of Keshab's manliness was located firmly in the 'West'.

Lord Lawrence's friendship with Keshab is somewhat curious. The details of how they came to know one another are unclear, and it seems surprising that Lawrence, (in)famous for his strong-handed suppression of the 1857 uprising in the Punjab, and accused of beating his Indian servants, should have gone to such great lengths in introducing and entertaining Keshab during his visit to England. Of course, it may well have been the case that the two men genuinely enjoyed each other's company, but Lawrence's official correspondence during his time as Viceroy suggests that he had more practical motives in maintaining good relations. He wrote to Lord Cranborne that he associated with 'leading natives' in India as 'I...never miss an opportunity of gaining information when it is likely to be of any value'; he also expressed concerns that 'the gulf between the two classes [the English in India and the 'natives'] is very wide.... I look on this as the great danger to which our rule in India is exposed.... The educated Bengallees are sensitive and irritable and dislike the bearing of the English towards them'.[23]

Associating with Keshab would enable him to gain information and to improve relations between the colonisers and the colonised, both of which would help to protect British rule. It was acknowledged frequently in the press that, as a representative of his country and an insider, Keshab would be able to aid the British in governing India. *The Inquirer* asserted that 'He is the voice of his country reminding us of our national obligations'; many newspapers that were otherwise ambivalent in their attitudes to Keshab agreed that he 'would be able to say something as to the best mode of governing India'.[24]

However, Keshab did not just have value as a guide to more effective government. Keshab's visit to England also presented an opportunity to advertise to English audiences the beneficial effects of an improving British imperialism on a country which, just over a decade earlier, had revolted against colonial rule. Lawrence presented Keshab to the public as the very embodiment of the benefits which English knowledge and rule were bringing to India—benefits that outweighed any mistakes of government that may have been made: 'I feel certain that whatever may be the shortcomings of my countrymen in India, what English education can do and has done among the natives of India has been most satisfactorily exemplified in his own case. (Cheers.)'.[25] Here Keshab's agency disappears altogether: he 'is' what English education has 'done'. *The Saturday Review* explained Keshab's aetiology using the same straightforward causality, and regarded him similarly as a justification for imperialism: 'whatever may be said against our rule in India, types of character like this are the direct product of it'.[26] A product of colonial rule, Keshab was a valuable commodity in that he could be exhibited as an advertisement for the imperial system out of which he had been produced. By emphasising to audiences the simple, one-way causality of Keshab's production, Lawrence and others ensured that the labour that had gone into Keshab's making was never occluded in the spectacle of Keshab on the platform. Keshab was speaking with an English voice imparted through English education: this commodity did not 'evolv[e] out of its wooden brain grotesque ideas' of its own, or 'begin dancing of its own free will'.[27]

If Lawrence was keen to emphasise the imperial influence on Keshab, he also regarded Keshab as a man who, now properly educated, could engender through his own activity widespread reform in India.

An overwhelming majority of representations of Keshab agreed that his impact on India would be considerable and its effects favourable. His impact would encompass both religious and social change. Keshab's project would entail 'abolishing idolatry, breaking down caste, and diffusing a higher moral and intellectual life amongst the people'.[28] This elision of social and religious reform is unsurprising—we have seen how closely education and religion were tied together in the comments of Lawrence and Martineau, and it was a longstanding trope in British representations of India that the 'natives' were the victims of the twin agencies of Hinduism and caste, and that the destruction of one agency would effect the destruction of the other.

Although some missionary organisations regarded Keshab as an obstacle to the progress of Christianity in India, the most common way in which the religion of the Brahmo Samaj was characterised was, in the words of Sir Bartle Frere, as 'a half-way house to Christianity' and thus 'a decided step in the right direction'.[29] Many echoed the comments of the Baptist Rev. Samuel Cox, who declared that 'I strongly suspect that Mr. Sen is much more distinctly Christian than as yet he knows himself to be'.[30] While the more conservative sections of the Anglican Church condemned Keshab for his divergence from doctrinal orthodoxy, the Dean of Westminster saw the Brahmo Samaj as evidence of the 'heavenly origin of our religion', a religion that, having sprung from the 'East' and conquered the 'West', was now returning 'to win back unto itself the higher intelligences of the remoter East'.[31] A man committed to a 'comprehensive' view of Christianity, who invited preachers of many denominations to preach at Westminster Abbey, Dean Stanley was prepared to accept that the Christianity of India might be different in form, if not essence, to that of England: 'in the same way as Roman Christianity planted itself in the Latin race, and Teutonic Christianity in the race of England, Germany, and America, so there would arise some native form of Indian Christianity. (Cheers.)'.[32]

Much of the secular press, as well as those sections of the religious press that did not regard doctrinal orthodoxy as fundamental, agreed that Keshab would be more effective than European missionaries in winning converts. His criticisms of missionaries in India met with widespread support, and it was acknowledged often that his 'native' status would give him access to areas of India inaccessible to Europeans.

Keshab's focus on the 'essential spirit' of Christianity would hold a wider appeal than the missionaries' attempts to instil confusing and contradictory doctrines.[33] Of course, it is unsurprising that everyone who supported Keshab as the 'Apostle of India' (as he was dubbed by Frances Power Cobbe) did so on the basis that the God he followed was, in essence, the God of Christianity.[34] However, what is surprising is the extraordinary ease with which ministers from almost every denomination assumed that Keshab was either already fully Christian or was well on the way to being so, despite Keshab's repeated and emphatic protestations that he was a Brahmo (or, sometimes, 'Hindu'). Keshab did come under attack for his religious beliefs from those committed to doctrinal orthodoxy, but his supporters always interpreted his religious progress in terms of an overall narrative of an overarching Christian God. If Keshab was manly, educated and pious—in short, civilised— then he simply must be already or potentially Christian.

An embodiment of the benefits of English thought and religion, a template for the future of India, a proselyte, imperial agent and diligent pupil, the spectacle of Keshab enabled viewers to see for themselves what imperialism had done, and what it could do in the future. If Keshab was, as *The Inquirer* claimed, the 'voice of India', this was the 'voice' of a transformed India of the future, a voice that had been imparted to India through the enterprise of imperialism, a voice that spoke in unison with the civilising mission, and which justified its continuance.

The Value of Otherness

In his controversial study *Ornamentalism*, David Cannadine argues that class and status, as opposed to race, were the central categories through which the British imperial system was organised.[35] If, as has been argued above, representational strategies that produced an image of Keshab as 'imperial spectacle' tended to emphasise his 'English manliness', then it might appear that Keshab's racial otherness was deemed to be of lesser importance than his education, piety, appearance and manners. If Keshab was accepted because he behaved and spoke like an 'English gentleman', then perhaps class and status, as opposed to race, were the central categories through which he was interpreted and assessed. Occasionally, Keshab's manliness was represented as the product of his class and status.

Frances Power Cobbe wrote that Keshab was 'In a word...a gentleman'; he had 'a pedigree as long as that of any Norman noble'; his features bore 'the marks of good blood and gentle breeding'; his manners exhibited 'the easy inborn dignity of a well-bred man of high European birth'.[36] However, this account of Keshab is exceptional. Indeed, not everyone was aware of Keshab's wealth and status (*The Graphic* claimed that he had 'sprung out of the Bankside slums').[37] It was far more common for commentators to view Keshab's manliness as remarkable precisely *because* of his racial difference. Keshab's supporters and detractors alike never lost sight of the 'fact' of Keshab's undeniable otherness.

It would be a mistake to overemphasise the extent to which Keshab was imagined to embody an 'English' form of manliness. Keshab's manners, eloquence and learning may have signified the transformative capacity of the imperial mission, and thus implied that the boundaries of racial difference were not entirely fixed, but Keshab was never represented entirely as an 'effect' of imperialism. He was never taken to embody fully Thomas Macaulay's dream of the 'Indian in blood and colour, but English in taste, in opinions, in morals, and in intellect'.[38] Rather, there were aspects of Keshab's character that were represented as definitively and distinctly 'Oriental'.

Descriptions of Keshab's 'English manliness' almost always included references to qualities that were taken to signify his 'Eastern' otherness. The *Pall Mall Budget*'s description of him as combining 'a certain sweetness' with 'marked decision' was echoed repeatedly—Keshab appeared to combine the qualities of an effeminised 'East' and a masculine 'West'.[39] Of course, 'sweetness' was not imagined to be the exclusive preserve of women or of men of the 'Orient'. Norman Vance has demonstrated that Christ and St. Paul were often held up as paradigms of Christian masculinity because they combined the virtues of both sexes in their energy and gentleness.[40] However, the evidence suggests strongly that commentators did indeed link Keshab's supposed sweetness and simplicity specifically to his Indian-ness, as opposed to his 'Christian' religiosity or chivalry. For example, in a letter to the Rev. Charles Wicksteed, James Martineau described Keshab as 'not perhaps strikingly intellectual, but of singular strength and sweetness of character,—simple, pure, and high-minded...I believe I have something in me which responds to the Indian temperament'.[41]

As we have seen, Keshab's effectiveness as a proselyte in his own country, and his value as a guide to effective British rule in India, were acknowledged frequently. For some commentators, Keshab's position as an outsider also endowed him with a special capacity to observe and assess England. The *Leicester Chronicle* welcomed Keshab in his role as a critic of English society: 'Coming to us from India to tell Englishmen of their shortcomings, is truly "turning the tables" upon us; while we in our national self-complacency, are apt to think we may "lecture" the whole world with a perfect consciousness of our moral and spiritual authority'.[42] Keshab's critiques of English sectarianism were particularly popular, and he was often congratulated for bringing together representatives of diverse religious denominations.[43] The *Daily News* enjoined its readership to listen to his opinions with care: 'Western religionists may in Mr. Sen's speeches see themselves as others see them, and we may see how Western religion looks to a pair of the most intelligent Eastern eyes which have ever looked upon it'.[44] Keshab's 'otherness' combined with his intellect made him an ideal critic of 'Western religion'.

However, the value that was ascribed to Keshab's 'otherness' amounted to more than just an ability to provide the colonial government with information and to offer a novel perspective on English society. Keshab's supporters (and some of his detractors) associated him with qualities such as simplicity, purity, innocence and tenderness—virtues that were associated broadly with notions of the 'spirit' or of the 'heart'. *The Asiatic*, a scholarly journal which was later highly critical of Keshab, praised his 'tender and lowly heart'; *The Inquirer* commented that 'he speaks to the heart'; Frances Power Cobbe observed that 'Probably there is something in his Eastern simplicity and absence of all self-consciousness which makes it more possible for him than for a European to allow his hearers to see into his heart'.[45] For Cobbe, it was precisely Keshab's 'otherness' that gave him special value as a teacher: 'His greatness lies in quite a different direction from that of our teachers and thinkers, whose powers would probably prove comparatively useless to do the Indian reformer's proper work in his own land. It is not in the region of the intellect…but in the realm of religious sentiment itself that Keshub is so highly gifted'.[46]

Representations of Keshab which associated him with notions of the 'spirit' or of the 'heart' were related to a broad range of discourses concerning the value of 'spiritual' insight and religious faith which occupied an important place in Victorian intellectual culture. The elevation of faith, conversion and Christian living over theological study and biblical criticism was characteristic of evangelicalism, a movement that Mark Pattison, writing in 1863, portrayed as 'the insurrection of the heart and conscience of man against an arid orthodoxy'.[47] A subordination of reason to emotion was also characteristic of the new 'romanticism' that, from the 1830s, 'had swept Europe with its emphatic preference for intuitive truth, imagination, lyricism and the mysterious in religion rather than reason, facts and science'.[48] Romantic epistemology, with its distrust of the 'meddling intellect' and its cult of the 'heart'—the organ of intuitive insight—was a major influence on the prophet of spiritual and emotional life, and critic of Utilitarianism, Thomas Carlyle. Carlyle, an elderly man by 1870, had, in 1836, described the age as 'at once destitute of faith and terrified at scepticism'—a scepticism which might lead to 'social disintegration or outright revolution if religion were abandoned, or by the appalling vision of a mechanistic universe devoid of spiritual life or moral value'.[49] Carlyle was a figure to whom Keshab was sometimes compared.[50]

Epistemological debates concerning the value and limitations of rational and intuitive knowledge structured much of British philosophical discourse in the mid-to-late nineteenth century, and had profound theological dimensions. Two of the most important philosophical influences in mid-Victorian Britain were John Stuart Mill and Sir William Hamilton, and Mill's famous critique of Hamilton's philosophy was published in 1865.[51] Mill's critique centred on his claim that Hamilton, while professing to restrict all knowledge to the knowledge of phenomena, in truth claimed that authentic, unconditioned knowledge could be accessed through 'belief' or 'faith'. Linda Raeder sees this critique as emblematic of much broader theological debates, and argues that the 'vast majority' of 'religious thinkers' in mid-to-late Victorian Britain 'defended theological morality on the grounds of intuition'.[52] Mill's positivist and materialist philosophy rejected the validity of 'intuitive or innate knowledge of any sort, whether respecting God, morals, politics, cosmology, mathematics, science, or any other area of human speculation'.[53] This view garnered him criticism from the Brahmos in Calcutta, who claimed that Mill's 'sole dependence on external scientific methods' had led him to attempt to 'overpower God'.[54] The rejection of a priori knowledge in toto had profound theological implications, as it left no foundation for concepts such as 'belief' and 'faith'. Philosophers, theologians and ministers of a variety of stamps produced stringent defences of 'faith' as a response to the increasing influence of materialism and positivism. Such defences could be based on an idealist vindication of intuitive knowledge, or, as in the case of the Oxford don and Anglican priest Henry Longueville Mansel, on a rigorous theological orthodoxy that stressed the literal truth and infallibility of the scriptures.[55]

Debates of this kind led Walter Houghton, in his classic study of the 'Victorian frame of mind', to argue that a tension between a 'critical spirit' and a 'will to believe' was characteristic of Victorian British intellectual culture in general.[56] Houghton sees evidence of a 'tension between the emancipated head and the traditional heart' in such personalities as Tennyson, Charles Kingsley, Matthew Arnold, John Stuart Mill and Beatrice Webb. [57] This bifurcation of intellectual culture is, of course, somewhat reductive, but it does point in a general way to an important series of enduring and disquieting tensions that characterised the mid-to-late Victorian era. A tension between reason and faith is undoubtedly evident in the writings of many of those in the middle-class, educated, Nonconformist and Unitarian circles in which Keshab moved.

It might seem surprising that a religion of the 'heart' should have become an important current in Unitarianism—it was, after all, a religion in which reason was held in greater esteem than the Bible, and whose seminal exponent, Priestley, had supplied Jeremy Bentham with his most famous dictum.[58] However, although Unitarianism remained undoubtedly a religion which stressed the virtues of the intellect, from the 1830s onwards the influence of W. E. Channing led many Unitarians to combine Priestleyan intellectualism with an emphasis on affection, principles and the capacity of 'rising' by their own free will to God. Ruth Watts suggests that the influence of Channing 'helped soften and spiritualize an intellectual religion'.[59] This emphasis on the 'spiritual' was given further importance by William J. Fox, who appealed to

Unitarians looking for a more spiritual and 'loving' faith, and, later, by Mary and Lant Carpenter, both of whom were influenced by evangelicalism, and stressed the loving side of Jesus and the importance of compassion. James Martineau certainly recognised a link between a desire to question and a desire to believe when he observed in 1840 'a simultaneous increase, in the very same class of minds, of theological doubt and devotional affection'.[60]

Concerns over the loss of the 'spiritual' in the face of the 'material' figured prominently in a long article devoted to Keshab published in April 1870 in *The Spectator*, a liberal publication co-edited by the Unitarian and former student of James Martineau, Richard Holt Hutton. The article was ambivalent and at times even mocking, but it was serious in its central conjecture that there was a dangerous imbalance between the 'spiritual' and the 'material' in favour of the latter, and that Keshab may be the person to restore equilibrium.[61] The author advised Keshab to study Christian life as well as Christian doctrine, in order to avoid 'the same calamity from which we are now suffering in England—a divorce between its intellect and its faith'.[62]

Commentators who were, in other respects, wary of Keshab also expressed hope that he could restore something of the 'essential spirit' of Christianity to a civilisation in which it had been lost. *The Asiatic*, which was often highly critical of Keshab, admitted that 'many among our clergy and laity might well learn a useful lesson from...this preacher from the far East', namely that 'the life and soul of all religion' is 'heartfelt belief in the guidance of an overruling Providence, not mere dry intellectual assent in the same'.[63] The notion that dogmatic doctrinal divisions had been engrafted upon a purer, ancient Christianity (in an analogous manner to the way in which the 'superstitions' of Hindu priests had corrupted a prior monotheism) was expressed frequently by those who used Keshab as a way to criticise sectarianism at home and dogmatic divisions between missionaries abroad. Keshab seemed, to some observers, to embody an ancient spiritual purity. As one commentator wrote of his appearance in Liverpool: when 'India's greatest native apostle' was present, 'The old days of the wandering apostles seemed to be revived'.[64]

Nowhere was Keshab's religious significance acknowledged more sincerely than in Unitarian chapels and in the Unitarian press. In order to explain why this was so, it is worth quoting at some length a passage from James Martineau's welcome speech to Keshab, which encapsulated many of the reasons why Unitarians regarded Keshab as such a sensational, praiseworthy and important figure:

> The European mind had a certain hardness in it, in virtue of which intellectual force was gained at the expense of spiritual depth; and the larger the scientific universe became, the more did it shut us up in a materialist prison... It seemed in our own time as if there was to be again an apparent hostility between Science and Religion. With the Indian genius he believed it would be otherwise...if their Eastern friends could restore to them something of that tender mind, and of that sweet affectionate humanity of which they had an example present that evening...they would be returning perpetual good for transitory ill; and, by redeeming their Western brethren from the European hardness, would give them the best form of forgiveness for the offences of a Clive and a Hastings, and the truest gratitude for the benevolent justice of a Bentinck and a Lawrence. (Loud Cheers).[65]

Martineau's views on Brahmoism, the 'West' and the 'East' were remarkably close to the perspectives Keshab expressed during his own speeches in England. Both men identified the 'West' primarily with hardness, materialism, intellect and science, and the 'East' with tenderness and spirituality; they regarded the 'East' as offering qualities lacked by the 'West' and yet central to its proper development; they saw progress in terms of a union of these contrasting but complementary qualities; and they regarded Brahmoism as an example in miniature of this process of union.

It is undoubtedly the case that the warmth that existed between Keshab and the Unitarians was engendered, in part, by the extraordinary affinity that existed between their ideas. Unitarians interpreted the fact that such similar attitudes to religion had arisen independently in India and in England as a proof of the truth of their beliefs. However, Keshab was significant not just because he offered a proof of Unitarianism, but because he symbolised the possibility of a resolution of Unitarianism's contradictory impulses. The two major currents of thought within Unitarianism in the mid-nineteenth century—Priestleyan intellectualism and the emphasis on affection promulgated by Channing and the Carpenters—brought into sharp relief within the Unitarian church the broader 'hostility between Science and Religion' to which Martineau refers. We can recall that Martineau himself observed in 1840 'a simultaneous increase…of theological doubt and devotional affection'. The Unitarians were affected most keenly by the conflict between 'the critical spirit' and the 'will to believe', and it was Keshab who had come to symbolise the possibility that the conflict could be resolved.

There is a final notion expressed by Martineau that helps to explain why the Unitarians were so enamoured of Keshab: the notion of 'forgiveness'. Bebbington argues that a defining feature of the 'Nonconformist conscience' in the 1870s and 1880s was 'a conviction that there is no strict boundary between religion and politics'.[66] Mass political activity among evangelicals had emerged during the anti-slavery campaigns, when slavery was identified as sinful and thus a fitting religious concern. This preoccupation with sin persisted in the activities of Nonconformists in the 1870s and 1880s.[67] *The Inquirer* was in no doubt that Keshab had been 'raised up by Providence…to restore to us a purer Christianity'; Martineau's words suggest that the purification was to be not only religious, but also moral and political.[68] Martineau portrays Keshab as embodying qualities associated with the 'East' that, if given to the 'West', would redeem Europeans from their 'hardness' and free them from the 'materialist prison' of industrial modernity. In 'returning perpetual good for transitory ill', the 'East' would offer 'the best form of forgiveness' for the actions of Lord Clive and Warren Hastings, and the 'truest gratitude for the benevolent justice' of William Bentinck and Lord Lawrence. The giving of the 'gift' of the 'East', embodied in the person of Keshab, would expiate the imperial sins of the past, and offer confirmation that the empire of the present was just, and not sinful. Understood within the context of a Unitarian church in which it was widely believed that Keshab had been 'raised up by Providence', and within a 'Nonconformist conscience' for which 'religious' matters of 'sin' and 'forgiveness' had a direct political significance, it would not just be the colonised that would be forgiving the colonisers through the giving of the gift—it would be God. Keshab symbolised the Providential transmission of a spiritual gift from 'East' to 'West', which would redeem England from its imperial sins, purify its politics and its religion, and confirm that its present imperial rule was just and benevolent in the eyes of God.

The symbolic significance that Keshab acquired in the eyes of many Unitarians helps to explain the adulation with which he was received, and the extraordinary level of excitement with which his doings were chronicled in *The Inquirer* throughout 1870. *The Inquirer* claimed that Keshab's appearance in pulpits imparted to them 'a kind of consecration' and declared that 'his visit to England will be a new landmark in our religious history'.[69] These sentiments should be understood in terms of broader concerns over the spiritual health of Western civilisation, and the particular relationship of Unitarianism and Nonconformity to these concerns. That many of those who travelled to see Keshab did so in order to receive spiritual rejuvenation was a fact not lost on *The Asiatic*, which described Keshab's audiences disparagingly as 'refreshing their wearied souls with draughts of "Asiatic Christianity"'.[70] James Martineau certainly regarded Keshab as a source of spiritual regeneration, and claimed that Keshab 'so moved our hearts, so elevated our souls, as to give us a new revelation of what can be the dignity and the nobleness of a pure and simple and devout religious life.[71] The portraits of Keshab advertised throughout 1870 in *The Inquirer* were perhaps hung in English Unitarian households as symbols of the 'religious life' Martineau described, and reminders of the spiritual 'gift' of the 'East' and the redemption it would offer. The commodification of Keshab in material form had enabled, ironically, one to purchase a portion of the 'spiritual' for one shilling (Fig. vi).

The Unitarians regarded Keshab as a man of extraordinary importance—a prophet, a landmark in religious history. However, this conviction did not, in fact, destabilise a discursive binary opposition of coloniser and colonised, nor the unequal power relation that inhered in the binary, which continued to structure fundamentally the ways in which they responded to him. While the Unitarians took Keshab's criticisms of empire seriously, they applied his critique to the empire of the past, and represented Keshab in a way that served to justify a reformed empire of the present. While Keshab's religious importance was acknowledged, his Theism was contained within a frame of reference that was Christian. Keshab's Theism was interpreted as Unitarian Christianity (which, admittedly, many in England would not have regarded as Christian at all): he was a living proof of the truth of beliefs that the Unitarians already held. Furthermore, while the

Fig. vi　Keshab as a commodity. Advertisement in *The Inquirer*, 2 July 1870.

Unitarians recognised in Keshab much of what they held to be valuable in 'Eastern' civilisation, this recognition did not undermine an underlying belief in the paternal relationship of England to India. Frances Power Cobbe claimed that many people, having seen Keshab, said they could 'better understand Christ's child-like confidence in God'.[72] *The Inquirer* argued that the creed of the Brahmo Samaj could succeed in India (and among the working classes in England) as it was a 'simple child-like faith'.[73] This was praise, not criticism, but it was praise that served to infantilise Keshab even as it found value in his 'simplicity'.

A letter from Mary Carpenter to Keshab, written shortly after his departure, demonstrates the tendency of his admirers both to valorise him and to place him in a position of subordination. Carpenter writes that Keshab evinces a 'true Christian spirit' and assures him that 'I love India as a mother does her child, and...I have a true friendship for you, her honoured son'.[74] Keshab later recalled Carpenter's infantilising behaviour towards him in conversations with Majumdar, according to whom: '[Carpenter] gave him incessant directions about the usages and etiquette of English society. Her restless spirit of reform criticized his dress, his diet, even the manner of combing his hair'.[75] Even Keshab's most ardent admirers responded to him in a way that contained his meaning within a symbolic order in which the unequal power relations between colonial masters and colonised subjects remained firmly in place.

The Dangers of Otherness

The Unitarians were exceptional in acknowledging Keshab as a true religious teacher. While a number of religious and secular publications deemed it acceptable to point out the value of Keshab's focus on the essential spirit rather than the dogma of Christianity, most did so with the caveat that there was much in Keshab's philosophy that should be regarded with 'very mingled feelings'.[76] Indeed, as Keshab's confidence in expressing his religious beliefs grew, so did hostility to his preaching. There was considerable disagreement over the proper sphere of Keshab's activities and the standards according to which he should be judged. The *English Independent* argued that Keshab did not have 'any specific Christian truth to teach our Churches', but had a 'spiritual truth' to impart to rationalists in India and Unitarians at home.[77] The *Birmingham Daily Post* applauded Keshab's 'social reforms' in India but railed against his propagation of 'Deism'.[78] Keshab's status as a 'social reformer' was often acknowledged and his status as a 'religious reformer' refused.

Although there were exceptions (most notably Dean Stanley), Keshab was received, in general, much more favourably by Nonconformists than by Anglicans or Presbyterians. The main publications of the conservative wing of the Church of England—*The Rock* and *The Record*—greeted Keshab with enthusiasm initially, but later became resolutely opposed to his activities. Certain sectors of the dissenting churches—most notably Baptists, for whom doctrinal definition held a particular importance—were also ambivalent in their attitudes to Keshab. Keshab received favourable publicity in the Nonconformist digest *The Christian World* during the first half of his visit, but he all but disappeared from the mainstream Nonconformist press during the latter part of his stay. Attitudes in the secular press varied widely, and the letters columns of many newspapers contained heated debates on the propriety of welcoming Keshab to England.

Unsurprisingly, much of the hostility towards Keshab stemmed from the fact that he was not a Christian. Keshab's visits to Leeds and Birmingham excited considerable controversy in the leaders and letters pages of the respective local presses. The central question was whether welcoming a man who was not a Christian would be improper and even sinful.[79] *The Rock* and *The Record* initially welcomed Keshab as someone who was on the road to full Christian belief (i.e. the acceptance of the divinity of Christ) and who would lead India in the same direction. However, both *The Rock* and *The Record* performed complete about-turns in their attitudes to Keshab upon the publication of his *Four Lectures*, edited by Sophia Dobson Collet, in mid-1870. *The Rock* now referred to him as the 'so-called Indian Reformer' and 'the recognized leader of the Theistic Church of India, of which the most essential doctrine is the denial of the divinity of our LORD'.[80] Most scandalous was Keshab's attitude to Christ: 'he…[classifies] the Blessed REDEEMER, reforming Judaism, with the Hindoo prophet CHAITANYA, who reformed the religion of Hindostan'.[81] Keshab's comparison between Christ and Chaitanya appeared to place the work of both reformers on the same level, a subversion of power relations that *The Rock* was unable to accept.

Keshab's elevation to the platform, lecturing English audiences, was an uncomfortable reversal of the proper relations between colonial teachers and colonised learners. Opposition to Keshab assuming the position of a religious teacher stemmed, in part, from the view that he had misunderstood Christianity. He was represented often as an unfortunate, impressionable character who, in his state of incomplete learning, had failed to understand the doctrines he attempted to teach, and had fallen into the 'bad company' of Unitarians. *The Record* described him as 'half-awakened and half-instructed', and pointed to his 'theological confusion'.[82] Rationalism and 'destructive criticism' were particularly dangerous influences in India considering the 'intellectual sagacity of the Hindoo', and they provided the 'educated Hindoo' with a 'ready foil against the earnest call of the missionary'.[83] 'Intellectual sagacity' was a pernicious quality among a people who were 'half-awakened'.[84] The work of the civilising mission in India was not yet complete, and for those who were but half-civilised to assume the position of teacher would undoubtedly result in their pupils being led in the wrong direction.

Reports from various branches of the Church Missionary Society suggest that they too feared Keshab's influence in India.[85] However, the extent to which Keshab's influence was taken seriously varied among missionaries. While *The Record* feared that 'Brahmoism, instead of preparing the way to Christianity, may become its substitute', the Rev. Bruce, at the annual meeting of the London Missionary Society, reassured his audience that Keshab would become, in his religious convictions, 'altogether as we are', and return to India to 'become one of many who will preach in better terms than the Europeans to his own people… I cannot think that the opposite will be the result—I cannot think that he will convert us to his position of Theism'.[86] While many feared that Keshab would succeed in steering 'half-awakened Hindoos' away from the path of religious truth, most agreed that his influence on those who were 'fully awake' would be negligible. The principles of a 'half-learnt philosophy' could only influence the minds of those who were 'half-awakened'—the English would not be deceived.

However, some commentators did, in fact, express concern that Keshab would not only disrupt the religious progress of India, but would also have a damaging effect on Christianity in England. The Presbyterian minister John Thomson became convinced that Keshab was influencing Christian ministers in England to a greater extent than they were influencing him. He portrayed Keshab as part of a wider conspiracy of 'Rationalism, Naturalism, Advanced Unitarianism, Deism, Infidelity, Unbelief' and warned that 'As to winning him, it is to be feared that the winning has been on the other side…Christian ministers have been ensnared into saying things and applauding sentiments which they, it is to be hoped, now regret'.[87] The warm welcome extended to Keshab would soon be extended to other Deists, and the 'health' of English Christianity would be damaged, if not ruined altogether, by 'exposure to an infected atmosphere'.[88] The infection was stemming, in part, from enemies within (the most inimical of whom were the Unitarians), but was more generally the result of England coming into contact with the ideas and peoples of other nations: 'Japan and Uganda will soon become part of Christendom. There are tides, and currents…'.[89]

Thomson's views would doubtless have appeared somewhat hysterical to many English observers, but his fears of 'infection' resulting from 'exposure' to Keshab's ideas did echo broader concerns, albeit in a hyperbolic form. Many commentators expressed anxiety that Keshab would succeed in 'infecting' the minds of 'Hindoos', and the adamant refusal of many, though not all, members of the Church of England to accept him as a religious teacher suggests a desire to keep the circles of religious instruction 'pure'. The elevation of Keshab to the position of teacher could undermine the close association between Protestantism and English national identity: 'natives' might safely be welcomed into the folds of Christianity as learners, but if they began to teach, then the purity of the Church of England as 'English' could be undermined.

Discourses on the 'manliness' of Keshab were undercut by representations of him that branded this 'manliness' counterfeit—mere appearance and show. Mrinalini Sinha, in her excellent study of colonial masculinity, has drawn attention to the ways in which discourses on the superficiality of educated, middle-class Indians served to reinforce earlier notions concerning the effeminacy of Indians, and particularly of Bengalis, that went back to the earliest days of colonial rule.[90] In the 1770s, Richard Orme had commented upon the 'effeminacy of character' of all 'natives', and the particular weakness and enervation of Bengalis.[91] These sentiments were echoed by T. B. Macaulay in the 1830s, and by Lord Lawrence in the 1860s.[92] Effeminacy was associated, in particular, with English-educated Indians, a large majority of whom were Bengali Hindus. As Sinha has argued, the association of English-educated Bengalis with effeminacy reflected a shift in British colonial attitudes towards English-educated Indians, from mediators between the colonial administration and the rest of the population to an unrepresentative and artificial minority representing nothing but the anomaly of their own situation.[93]

This shift, I would argue, was related also to a more general 'hardening' of racial attitudes in Britain towards colonial subjects across the empire in the wake of the uprisings in India in 1857–8 and in Morant Bay in Jamaica in 1865. Representations of the superficiality of English-educated Indian manliness should be read in the context of an increasing preponderance of biological rather than cultural explanations of racial difference. If Indians' biological racial difference prevented them from fulfilling Macaulay's dream of their becoming Englishmen, then the apparent 'Westernisation' exhibited by the Indian English-educated middle-classes was to be explained as mere show—a cultural exterior which had failed to alter a fixed internal racial otherness. From the 1880s, as the power of organisations such as the Indian National Congress increased, English-educated Indians who demanded greater equality for India in its relations with the imperial government were often branded *babus*, a term which had come to denote men possessed of a superficial and deceptive learning that hid an internal effeminacy.[94]

As we have seen, the way in which Keshab spoke was a central concern for those who supported him. His speech could be taken to signify a triumph of English education, or to signify a particularly 'Oriental' simplicity that was valuable in that it spoke to the 'heart'. The analysis of speech was significant in the interpretation of racial difference throughout the nineteenth century, particularly in relation to India. In the wake of the visit to England of several delegates from the Indian National Congress (INC) in 1885, the press characterised the group as 'gushing' and 'vaporing'.[95] The INC was referred to as the 'Indian talking shop' and delegates as 'persons of considerable imitative powers'.[96] These discourses, Burton argues, had an older pedigree:

'Since Macaulay, and perhaps before, Indian men had been seen not as incapable of speech, like Africans or slaves, but capable only of inexactitudes, of speech that mimicked and approximated English but never actually succeeded in *being* English'.[97]

Some commentators regarded Keshab as dangerous precisely because he was in control of what he said. As one outraged writer to the *Birmingham Daily Post* put it, Keshab was a 'dangerous heretic' because he 'is a man who is not a savage or barbarian convert...He embraces Theism as the result of deep thought and great study'.[98] However, Keshab's detractors more often presented him as deceived by his own speech, as incapable of saying what he meant. *The Spectator* noted that 'Gentlemen of his race are noted for possessing a fatal fluency on platforms'.[99] *The Christian World* agreed that, in the hands of a Hindu, fluency in English could lead to misunderstanding.[100] While Frances Power Cobbe was astonished and delighted by the spectacle of perfect English flowing from the mouth of a Hindu, for some observers Keshab's fluency signified a loss of control, an inability to say what he meant. It was a flow of speech in which the meanings of words were perverted in the moment of their utterance. As *The Asiatic* commented, this was a danger of 'superficial English education' in general, which 'does more harm than we can imagine' to a 'mind that is just now in a transitional stage'.[101] Fluency in English was a dangerous capacity for someone who was not, in fact, English.

For some observers, Keshab had been deceived by his own speech; for others, he was using speech as a means to deceive. Thomson had no doubt that the intentions of Keshab were iniquitous: 'Why does Mr. SEN adopt the language of doctrines which he repudiates? Because the whole world are going after Christ; so that His bitterest enemies must wear the garb of His friends if they are to succeed in their nefarious designs'.[102] A missionary writer to the *Church Missionary Intelligencer*, in a letter that was reprinted in many newspapers, warned readers of Keshab's capacity to deceive: 'He can talk and preach like an angel of light; his manners captivate, and his speech may deceive the very elect. But depend on it he is, under all that pleasing exterior, "an enemy to the Gospel of Christ"'.[103] *The Saturday Review* reasoned that Keshab's deceptiveness was unsurprising considering his background: 'Nobody takes the posture you want like a Bengali'.[104]

However, despite the occasional hyperbolic outburst, most commentators did not feel that it was Keshab's deliberate intention to undermine Christianity. Rather, he was a victim of his own success. *The Asiatic* bemoaned that the 'blaze of enthusiasm, which flares up at the mere novelty of a Hindoo addressing a Christian assembly, is but a fitful exhalation; and immoderate applause…is unwholesome both to giver and receiver'.[105] Keshab, 'himself a modest, and…retiring young man…cannot but suffer more or less from the overbearing attentions of strong-minded women and effervescing enthusiasts'.[106] The *English Independent* was relieved that Keshab had left England 'rather less spoiled than might have been expected after the lionising he endured and the foolish manner in which Unitarians followed him about with extravagant adulation'.[107] Those who opposed Keshab invariably classified his supporters as either female or as men guided by emotion rather than reason. *The Asiatic* claimed that, in offering 'gingerbread honour' to Keshab, 'English gullibility has outstripped itself'.[108] Keshab had been made 'an idol of the chapels and the lion of the drawing room' by 'enthusiastic religionists, and impressionable females! But… the fever heat of gullibility has to some extent subsided, and rational minds are beginning to measure the apostolic Baboo by the rules of common-sense'.[109] He had been 'encircled by petticoats and beleaguered by chignons; his words…"hung upon" by greedy listeners, and possibly wept over by weak enthusiasts who, like the old Scotchwoman who sobbed because the preacher had said "Mesopotamia" in his sermon, were affected by the unintelligible'.[110] Keshab appeared to be both the perpetrator and the victim of a veritable orgy of misunderstanding and irrational hysteria.

The note of ridicule in the words of *The Asiatic* was echoed in other articles in the secular and satirical press. Keshab was often portrayed as a mysterious joke, a plaything of irrational women and effervescing men. One writer in *The Saturday Review*, in an article entitled 'Lions and Lion-Hunters', saw Keshab as one 'lion' among many, a 'performing animal' who was paraded for the pleasure of 'Miss Progress alone', who 'watches the scene from her sofa, fat, forty, and impassible'.[111] Keshab's ideas, it was implied, would hold no sway among an audience of rational men. Rather, 'Conundrum Baboo' (or '*leo hereticus*' as he was also branded) appealed only to irrational, bored and complacent women.[112] *Punch*, in an oft-quoted piece of doggerel, portrayed Keshab as an idle pursuit rather than a man to be taken seriously: 'Let's beard this "lion" in his den—This BABOO KESHUB CHUNDER SEN. So, come to tea and muffins, then, With BABOO KESHUB CHUNDER SEN'.[113] That Keshab was merely a passing fad, a momentary distraction, was an idea expressed too by *The Asiatic*, which declared triumphantly in August 1870 that 'the irrational excitement produced among Unitarians, strong-minded females, and a few earnest but weak enthusiasts, has already died away, and if rumour does not lie, Brahmoism has found a formidable rival in— croquet!'.[114] The comparison between Keshab and croquet reduced him to mere entertainment—a game. In fact, the mainstream Nonconformist press had all but ceased to report on Keshab's activities by August (four months into his six-month visit), and did indeed include a remarkable number of articles pointing out the symbiotic relationship between Christianity and croquet.[115]

However, there is something in the writings of those who represented Keshab and his supporters as a 'joke' which suggests that deeper fears lay beneath the surface of ridicule. These fears were expressed, in part, through hints that the relations between Keshab and his champions had become so close that they bordered on indecency. *The Asiatic* protested against Keshab's 'unseemly exhibition' and the 'heady and unnatural atmosphere of excitable females' in which he had been forced to preach.[116] *The Record* printed a letter condemning the way in which Keshab was 'exhibiting himself'.[117] *The Saturday Review* commented on Keshab's method of administering the 'shock' of his heretical views with a 'gentle titillation'.[118] Keshab's remarks on the appearance of English women were among his most widely publicised in the British press; the *Punch* cartoon which they inspired depicted him seated in close proximity to a white female.[119] The young woman seems distracted as her hair blows in Keshab's face, and Keshab takes the opportunity to peer over her shoulder and flash a smile and cocked eyebrow at the reader (Fig. vii). If not actually regarded as indecent, the 'fanfaronade' surrounding Keshab indicated at least a loss of propriety and self-control.[120] The Presbyterian Minister Thomson saw evil forces at work in Keshab's apparent ability to reduce normally rational men to irrational behaviour. Such behaviour, he argued, might well be expected from Unitarians (and, many others would have added, from women), who were inclined to "gad about' after celebrities', but that 'evangelical men should have joined in giving this ovation...proves the truth of Paul's proverb: "Evil communications corrupt good manners"'.[121]

Fig. vii   'A Baboo on Beauty'. Cartoon in *Punch*, 24 September 1870.

Representations of Keshab that portrayed him as a 'performing animal', as providing 'gentle titillation' and as inducing irrationality in the normally rational, bear close resemblance to representations of him that (often in praise) focused on the disjuncture between the 'English manliness' exhibited by his voice and the racial otherness evident in his appearance. The link here is 'Carnival'. Stallybrass and White, in *The Politics and Poetics of Transgression*, draw on Bakhtin's notion of 'Carnival' to argue that practices of 'transgression' occupy a central place in the formation and transformation of European culture.[122] They define 'transgression' as "'symbolic inversion"...any act of behaviour which inverts, contradicts, abrogates, or in some fashion presents an alternative to commonly held cultural codes, be they linguistic, literary or artistic, religious, social and political'.[123] Commentators who denigrated Keshab's supporters as irrational, or represented him as a 'joke', did not fail to notice that Keshab's appearance on platforms entailed a number of significant symbolic inversions: the colonised subject was teaching the colonial master; the Indian subject had the capacity of rational speech, while his English audiences had become irrational; the Indian subject appeared as a paradigm of 'English manliness', while the previously rational men of England were reduced to 'effeminate' displays of irrational emotion; the Indian subject from the 'land of idol-worship' was being worshipped as an idol in the land of Christianity. In addition to these reversals, both those who supported and those who opposed Keshab during his visit tended to notice that he was not what he appeared. Frances Power Cobbe was astounded at the discrepancy between Keshab's 'native' appearance and 'English voice'; criticisms of Keshab often focused on the notion that his appearance was deceptive—that he was wearing a mask.

The fears expressed concerning Keshab's capacity to engender symbolic inversions suggest that there were limits to the extent to which the 'spectacle' of his 'otherness' could be contained within discourses which placed him within an unequal binary opposition of 'coloniser' and 'colonised'. As we have seen, representations of Keshab which valorised his apparently 'English manliness' located the source of his manliness in the 'West': in these discourses, the transformation of a colonial subject into a model of 'English' masculinity did not threaten the masculinity of English men. However, the description of Keshab as a 'performing animal' is rather more complex. In one sense, it suggests that Keshab's apparent 'English' manliness is mere show—a performance in which the spectacle of his unexpectedly civilised behaviour occludes (in the minds of his irrational audiences) his inherently uncivilised nature. However, in 'performing' the role of the coloniser, Keshab, the former colonial 'other', was reducing the English to the behaviour of the colonised and conjuring up spirits of 'otherness' that inhered in their 'English' selves. Thomson's claim that something 'Evil' lay behind Keshab's ability to corrupt English 'good manners' suggested that Keshab was imbued with a peculiar sorcery, that his mask of civility could reduce the normally rational to improper behaviour in his presence. However, while deep fears concerning the inversion of norms of behaviour of coloniser and colonised may have underlain satirical accounts of Keshab, it must be remembered that these fears were contained within the assumption that Keshab's celebrity was temporary—that he was only a passing fad. The carnival of activity surrounding the spectacle of Keshab on the platform would, commentators agreed, subside, and normality would soon be restored.

Conclusion

The ways in which Keshab was represented as a 'colonial subject' in the metropole were extraordinarily diverse. The press coverage that Keshab received transformed him into a celebrity figure, and made him a focal point for debates within a wide range of discourses concerning imperial rule, Christianity, missionary activity, the relationship between Britain and India, the balance between the 'spiritual' and 'material', and the precise differences and similarities between Indians and Britons. Commentators diverged significantly in the ways in which they placed Keshab within these intersecting discourses, and he became the object of both great adulation and deep criticism. However, it was overwhelmingly the case that Keshab's supporters and opponents alike interpreted him in a way that reinforced rather than undermined a fundamental binary opposition between coloniser and colonised.

Representations of Keshab that drew attention to his 'English manliness' almost always pointed to English civilisation as the source of his transformation. The fundamental inequality of power between coloniser and colonised was emphasised even as the progress of the latter towards the former was acknowledged. If Keshab was represented as able to exercise considerable agency in India, he was envisioned as doing so on behalf of the civilising imperial project. Representations of Keshab that found value in his 'otherness' reflected deep-seated concerns in Victorian society regarding the loss of the 'spiritual' in the face of the 'material'. However, the 'Eastern' virtues of simplicity, emotion, spirit and purity with which Keshab was identified were associated also with women and children, both of whom occupied subordinate positions to adult men. Even the Unitarians, who regarded Keshab as a man of great significance, infantilised him even as they praised him. They took him to confirm beliefs that they already held, and interpreted the 'gift' of his teaching as a blessing for the continuance of a benevolent imperialism. Representations of Keshab as an enemy of Christianity emphasised an immutable racialised 'core' that lay behind his external refinements of civilisation. When commentators feared that Keshab's 'performance' on the platforms was inverting norms of behaviour, these fears were contained within the assumption that order would swiftly be restored.

The manner in which representations of Keshab produced multiple versions of what he 'meant', without ever letting these meanings undermine the unequal power relation between Britain and India, should remind us of the enduring importance of Edward Said's comments on 'Orientalism', which, he writes, 'depends for its strategy on [a] flexible *positional* superiority, which puts the Westerner in a whole series of possible relationships with the Orient without ever losing him the upper hand'.[124] Keshab was entangled in the empire in complex ways and through diverse networks, he exercised considerable agency and influence, and he carried a plethora of meanings for British audiences. However, this plethora of meanings never undermined (except, perhaps, in the realm of fantasy) the fundamental, racialised and unequal symbolic binary of coloniser and colonised.

5

TENSIONS AND TRANSITIONS: 1870–77

In March 1875, the great Bengali mystic and yogi Sri Ramakrishna Paramahamsa came with his nephew, Hriday, to visit Keshab Chandra Sen at his garden house in Belgharia, five miles north of Calcutta. By this time, Ramakrishna had been the head priest at the Dakshineswar Kali Temple on the eastern banks of the Hooghly for almost twenty years. On being introduced to Keshab, he said, 'Babu, I am told that you people have seen God. I have come to hear what you have seen'.[1] Ramakrishna himself had been striving to see God by means of intense spiritual endeavours at Dakshineswar. He would later recount a summary of these endeavours to a disciple:

> God made me pass through the disciplines of various paths. First according to the Purana, then according to the Tantra. I also followed the disciplines of the Vedas. At first I practised sadhana in the Panchavati. I made a grove of tulsi-plants and used to sit inside it and meditate. Sometimes I cried with a longing Heart, 'Mother! Mother!' Or I again, 'Rāma! Rāma!'

> While repeating the name of Rāma, I sometimes assumed the attitude of Hanuman and fixed a tail to the lower end of my backbone. I was in a God-intoxicated state. At that time I used to put on a silk robe and worship the Deity. What joy I experienced in that worship!

> I practised the discipline of the Tantra under the bel-tree. At that time I could see no distinction between the sacred tulsi and any other plant. In that state I sometimes ate the leavings from a jackal's meal, food that had

115

been exposed the whole night, part of which might have been eaten by snakes or other creatures. Yes, I ate that stuff. Sometimes I rode on a dog and fed him with luchi, also eating part of the bread myself. I realized that the whole world was filled with God alone. One cannot have spiritual realization without destroying ignorance; so I would assume the attitude of a tiger and devour ignorance.

While practising the disciplines of the Vedas, I became a sannyasi. I used to lie down in the chandni and say to Hriday: 'I am a sannyasi. I shall take my meals here.'

I vowed to the Divine Mother that I would kill myself if I did not see God.[2]

Ramakrishna, Liberalism and Culturalism

Ramakrishna Paramahamsa (1836–86) is widely revered in Bengal to this day. Born into a poor Vaishnava family in rural Bengal, Ramakrishna was the first of a new brand of 'traditional' gurus who emerged in Bengal in the later nineteenth century and found favour with many of the urban English-educated elite. Keshab was instrumental in bringing Ramakrishna to the attention of the Calcutta public through a number of articles in his English-language paper the *Indian Mirror*, and the Bengali-language *Dharmatattwa* and *Sulabh Samachar*.[3] Keshab and Ramakrishna developed an intense friendship, and Keshab encouraged many members of the Brahmo Samaj to visit Ramakrishna and to learn from this remarkable man and spiritual master. Keshab and his followers regarded Ramakrishna as one of their most 'important supporters' throughout the 1870s and 1880s.[4]

Even as a child, Ramakrishna experienced frequent visions and spiritual ecstasies. His parents both had similar experiences. His mother believed she had been impregnated by the light of God around a year before Ramakrishna's birth.[5] Eccentric, brilliant and rebellious, the young Ramakrishna is reported to have 'enjoyed acting and staying with women, wearing female dress and ornaments so well he was mistaken for a female. At the age of seven, he fell into a trance at the sight of cranes'.[6] At the age of nineteen he was appointed head priest at the Kali temple at Dakshineswar, a large temple complex built between 1847 and 1855 by the philanthropist Rani Rashmoni, who embarked on the project having experienced a vision of the Divine Mother in the form of the goddess Kali.

Today, Ramakrishna's legacy is institutionalised in the form of the Ramakrishna Mission, a vast organisation founded in 1897 by Ramakrishna's chief disciple Swami Vivekananda. With hundreds of centres all over the world, the Ramakrishna Mission remains devoted to social service, education and charity, and expounds the principles of Vedanta and religious toleration. However, as a variety of scholars of religion have pointed out, the rather austere Vedantic character of the present-day Ramakrishna Mission does something to obscure Ramakrishna's own multifaceted spiritual endeavours.[7] Ramakrishna performed many varieties of spiritual practice, although he is most often described by historians of religion (although not in the Ramakrishna Mission literature) as a Tantric devotee of Kali.[8] June McDaniel characterises him as embodying the 'singular dedication of devotion to a deity and the universalism of Vedānta, combined with yoga and tantra', and places him within the Sakta tradition, which contains elements from tantric Buddhism, Vaishnava devotion, yogic practice, shamanism and worship of village deities.[9] Ramakrishna's religious practice was certainly universalist and eclectic: he believed all religions to be true, and he acted on this belief through religious practice and devotion, rather than by attempting to combine different faiths into a higher intellectual synthesis.

What one would not appreciate by visiting the solemn buildings of the Ramakrishna Mission's global headquarters at Belur Math is that Ramakrishna's devotions could sometimes take rather extreme forms. There are accounts of him losing consciousness at the touch of metal or coins, falling to the floor in a state of paralysis and rubbing his face into the ground, throwing money and earth into the Ganges, and cleaning outhouses with his hands and eating the excrement of others.[10] His style of conversation was entertaining, unpredictable and rustic, far removed from the formal dialogues conducted by the Brahmos. In a highly controversial study, Jeffrey Kripal points to strongly sexual elements in his teachings, arguing that Ramakrishna's mystical experiences can be seen, in part, as the result of sublimated homoerotic desires.[11]

I mention this not in an attempt to sensationalise a figure who is much revered in Bengal, but to emphasise the degree of cultural separation between Ramakrishna and the Brahmos. What was it about Ramakrishna that so entranced Keshab and many of his fellow devotees? There must certainly be some truth in Andrew Sartori's contention that part of the appeal of the new generation of 'traditional' gurus lay in 'their rural-folk idiom and their lack of formal Western-style education', particularly when one considers that Western-educated *babus* could often be the targets of satire and ridicule.[12] Timothy Dobe has demonstrated that the figure of the Indian 'saint' or 'holy man' was resignified in the mid-to-late nineteenth century, coming to function as a sign of India's spiritual superiority as opposed to degeneration. The forms of ascetic practice adopted by these 'saints' served to embody religion in a way that was often suited to public performance.[13] However, as Amiya Sen has suggested, there was also something in Ramakrishna's evidently genuine mystical experiences which spoke further to 'unresolved' and 'unfulfilled' aspects of the social experience of many members of elite Calcutta society.[14] His criticism of the '(Brahmo) obsession with "guilt" and sin, his belief in the centrality of God and God-vision...the precedence of faith over reason and ritual'—all had an 'electrifying effect' on Bengalis 'for whom a rational view of state and society was probably belied by their actual state of being'.[15] Ramakrishna offered Keshab a way of rekindling a relationship with an 'authentic' and 'ancient' culture from which he feared he had become disconnected, and an ecstatic and subjective path towards enlightenment which stood in stark contrast to the dreary dogmatism he had experienced in England.

It is important to understand that Keshab and Ramakrishna's first meeting took place during a period that has been identified by historians as a time of tension and transition in Bengali culture as a whole. Many scholars have noted that elite Bengali discourses of liberal reform that were preponderant in the early nineteenth century were challenged in the mid-to-late nineteenth century by the increasingly influential ideas and practices of movements that have been described variously as neo-Hindu, revivalist, revitalist, and proto-nationalist.[16] Historians including Andrew Sartori and Tapan Raychaudhuri have pointed to the 1870s and 1880s as decades in which the Bengali elite moved away from the liberalism they had expressed previously, and began to articulate a different set of ideas which contributed to the growth of 'nationalist' consciousness.

In Partha Chatterjee's view, the period of 'social reform' in India comprised two distinct phases: in the first, Indian reformers attempted to reform traditional institutions and customs through collaborations with the colonial authorities; in the second, state interference was resisted in matters which related to the 'spiritual domain'.[17] Nationalism transformed the 'spiritual domain' in the areas of language (with mid-century 'modern Bengali'), education (with the mid-century effort to establish secondary schools led by the Bengali elite, outside state control) and family (with the creation of a new patriarchy, the 'new women' and resistance to state interference in family matters).[18] Chatterjee contends that spaces of interracial commingling, in which 'nonofficial Europeans, Eurasians, and members of the new Indian elite' had exchanged liberal ideas, had all but disappeared by the 1830s due to the growing power of racism and theories of civilisational difference.[19] As a result, Indians ceased largely to propound abstract theories of liberalism of the sort advanced by Ram Mohan and other elite Bengalis of his generation. In contrast, C. A. Bayly has pointed to the persistence of liberal modes of thought in the articulation of Indian nationalism.[20]

Chatterjee's periodisation of Bengali history is reflected in Sartori's contention that the history of nineteenth-century Bengal might be divided into two ages: the Age of Liberalism and the Age of Culture.[21] Initially, culture was associated with the liberal reformism of figures such as Ram Mohan Roy. Culturalism in the form of antiliberalism arose in Bengal after 1848, when a global financial crisis led to the collapse of the Union Bank and, ultimately, to the end of Calcutta as an independent centre of capital accumulation and investment. In Sartori's view, as capital spread across the globe in the eighteenth and nineteenth centuries, debates over concepts of culture emerged around the world in response. In the Bengali context, Sartori regards the changing thought of the Bengali writer Bankimchandra Chatterjee (1838–94) as emblematic of a shift from 'liberalism' to 'culturalism', as, during the 1870s and 1880s, Bankimchandra gradually moved away from his advocacy of radical liberal reform and became one of the chief exponents of neo-Hinduism.

These are broad and problematic arguments, underpinned by a vast and varied historiography concerning the emergence of nationalism in Bengal. Of course, dividing nineteenth-century Bengal into two distinct 'ages' will inevitably result in reductionism. Human history has a way of resisting neat periodisation of any kind. Nevertheless, there can be no doubt that significant shifts were taking place in Bengali culture and society in the 1870s and 1880s. These shifts are reflected in Rabindranath Tagore's great novel *Gora*, published in 1910, in which the characters struggle to negotiate the competing forces of colonialism and nationalism, liberalism and revivalism. Keshab's friendship with Ramakrishna must be understood in the context of these competing forces. Keshab's changing 'modes of life' and 'modes of thought' in the 1870s reflected broader social and cultural changes, but in complex and personal ways. If the 1870s was indeed a period of tensions and transitions, how were these tensions and transitions lived?

Liberal Social Reform: 1870–72

Keshab arrived back in India on 15 October 1870 in a triumphant mood, and delivered an optimistic speech to a large audience gathered at a Welcome Soirée in Bombay, organised in his honour by the Prarthana Brahmo Samaj. The results of his visit to England, he declared, had been 'cheering and encouraging in the extreme'.[22] He had not swerved from telling the English 'honest truths' and 'Thousands of hands were raised on all sides indicating hearty appreciation of what I said; all stood up sometimes in order to show that dishonesty, oppression and injustice must be put down'.[23] Keshab criticised English Christianity; he placed India and England on an equal footing when he declared that India had as much to teach England in terms of 'devotion, faith and prayer' as England had to teach India in terms of 'practical righteousness'; he reiterated his firm belief in the Providential character of British rule in India; he assured his audience that 'the whole of the civilised world through England has assured me of Western sympathy with Eastern nations'.[24] Keshab felt strongly that the English had treated him with respect, and that they would treat Indians in general as equals. He was greeted in Calcutta by thousands of cheering admirers, and even those sections of the Calcutta press that were usually hostile to the Brahmo Samaj agreed that his visit had been triumphant.[25] The writers in *Dharmatattwa* expressed their gratitude to the English Unitarians, and their delight that 'an eternal bridge of friendship between the East and the West has…been established'.[26] Keshab received a steady stream of visitors to whom he exhibited the gifts he had received from Queen

Victoria, and his first address at the Brahmo Mandir since his return to India was attended by large crowds.[27]

Had Keshab's visit to England led him to realise, as a number of historians have claimed, that he had 'taken too literally the claims made on behalf of modern Christian civilization'?[28] He had certainly been shocked by the extent of poverty in England, and dismayed by Christian sectarianism, and there can be no doubt that, by the mid-1870s, Keshab had departed, in part, from the liberal social reformism of a figure such as Ram Mohan Roy. However, from 1870 to 1872, Keshab threw himself into a series of enterprises that aimed to recreate in India the social reform institutions he had observed during his visit to England. He had been impressed by the extent of English philanthropy, by the range of educational institutions he had visited (especially for women), by the power of newspapers such as *The Times* and the *Echo* to shape public opinion, and by the felicitous domestic arrangements of the 'well-regulated English family'.[29] Far from turning away from rationalist reform on the English philanthropic model, Keshab used his prominent public position to implement precisely such a program. The years 1870 to 1872 saw Keshab pursuing liberal social reform with more vigour than ever.

In cooperation with Mary Carpenter, Keshab had established the Bristol Indian Association in September 1870, which had among its objectives the education of the Indian 'masses', the 'improvement of women' and the promotion of 'friendly intercourse' between Britons and Indians.[30] The parallel organisation Keshab established in Calcutta in November 1870—the Indian Reform Association—had as its aim nothing less than 'the social and moral reformation of the Natives of India'.[31] This objective would be achieved through the establishment of institutions which aimed at practical activity, with the religious element kept to a minimum: 'In order to accomplish the object effectively it is proposed to avoid, as far as possible, mere theories and speculations, and to aim chiefly at *action*'.[32]

The association was divided into five sections: charity, temperance, women's improvement, mass education and cheap literature. From November 1870, the cheap literature section published a weekly newspaper in Bengali—the *Sulabh Samachar*—which was designed to appeal to ordinary Bengalis and to improve the condition of the poor through cultivating moral discipline, self-reliance and basic education.[33] It sold 281,149 copies in its first fourteen months and remained relatively popular—in 1879, 190,000 copies were sold.[34] The mass education section established an Industrial School for instruction in technical arts, a night school for peasants and a Working Man's Institution for the elementary education of the poor. A Brahman boys' school came under the control of the association under the name of the Calcutta School, and was later raised to the level of a second-grade college. The women's improvement section established a Normal School for Ladies with the financial aid of Mary Carpenter, which aimed to provide instruction for young girls and adults in a range of disciplines including Bengali and English literature, grammar, geography, natural science and Indian and European history, and to train up a new generation of Bengali female teachers.[35] The temperance section organised lectures and meetings, attempted to reduce the import of whisky from England, and published a monthly journal *Mad na Garal?* (Wine or Poison?). The charity section organised a social service committee to assist the distressed during natural catastrophes, and distributed alms and medicine to the poor.

Following negotiations with the government of Bengal, Keshab was able to obtain a grant-in-aid of Rs. 2,000 for the Female Normal School, once the authorities had been forced to acknowledge that their own institution for female education had proved to be a failure.[36] Keshab's willingness to seek government aid in his social reform efforts distinguished his Indian Reform Association from rival organisations such as the British Indian Association (founded in 1851 under the presidency of the conservative Radhakanta Deb) which, in 1865, had written to the government of Bengal stating that 'the government should be the last resource of the community to put down any social abuse or promote any religious or moral reform'.[37] Keshab, in contrast, actively sought government support and was delighted to publicise a letter from the Queen's private secretary that expressed Queen Victoria's 'satisfaction at the success which has attended the efforts of…the Indian Reform Association'.[38] Keshab's educational schemes accorded well with the post-1857 government policy of encouraging 'native institutions' through grants-in-aid, which was intended to place a renewed emphasis on education without provoking an Indian backlash against perceived government interference.[39] The annual prize-giving ceremonies of the Female Normal School were conducted on a number of occasions by the Viceroy Lord Northbrook and members of the viceregal court.

Keshab's close connections with the British government aided his attempts to alter government policy to promote temperance, and abetted his most important reform of the early 1870s: the 1872 Marriage Act. Keshab had established close contact with temperance societies in Britain during his visit, and the Viceroy requested him to provide information on the topic. A circular was issued by the Indian Reform Association to English and Bengali temperance leaders, English physicians and Christian missionaries, which elicited many responses advocating the limiting of the sale of alcohol in Bengal. Keshab published an open letter to the Viceroy in the *Gazette of India* and presented a petition signed by 16,200 residents of Bengal to the government in 1873.[40] The agitation led directly to increases in import duty and to revisions in the Bengal excise system restricting the sale and consumption of alcohol in 1875 and 1876.[41] Direct action of this kind—utilising international contacts and connections with the highest-level government officials, and employing the press as a means to influence and mobilise public opinion—was characteristic of the methods of the Indian Reform Association in the early 1870s.

Undoubtedly the most important and controversial reform for which Keshab and his organisation campaigned in the early 1870s was the Marriage Act of 1872. For a Hindu marriage to be recognised by the British government in India as legal, it had to conform to certain specified rites and procedures. As members of the Brahmo Samaj of India had rejected many of these rites, their marriages were no longer recognised legally. A Brahmo marriage bill had been introduced into the Governor-General's Council at Simla in 1868 when Keshab was invited there by Lord Lawrence. Sir Henry Maine had proposed the bill on the grounds that 'it was not the policy of the Queen's Government to refuse the power of marriage to any of Her Majesty's subjects' and had recommended, in effect, a civil marriage law which would be open to any 'natives' who were neither Christians nor subscribed to any of the recognised 'native religions'.[42] Keshab had attempted to garner support for a marriage bill during his visit to England in 1870, and the progress of his campaign was watched closely by Anglo-Indian publications in Calcutta and attracted considerable interest in the press in England.

The proposed marriage bill generated intense opposition from the orthodox communities in Bengal, who argued that a civil marriage act would allow marriages to take place according to whatever rites the marrying parties wished, and would thus undermine fundamentally the integrity of marriage as a religious institution. A revised bill was proposed in 1871, which confined the legislation to Brahmo marriages alone, but this proposal was argued against vociferously by the Adi Brahmo Samaj, who complained that their marriage rites were already perfectly legal according to Hindu law, and that a specific Brahmo marriage act would render previous Brahmo marriages invalid and imply that Brahmo marriages were not Hindu. A public statement from the Adi Brahmo Samaj stressed the Brahmo Samaj's 'essentially Hindoo features' and objected that 'the Brahmo marriage bill determines that the Brahmos as a body are distinct from the general body of Hindoos, whereas in fact the Brahmos now form an integral portion of that community'.[43]

The bill was finally passed in March 1872 as the Native Marriage Act, after a clause was introduced which would prevent the new legislation affecting any previous marriages undertaken outside its provisions. The key effect of the Act with regard to Keshab's Samaj was that it required the marrying parties to confirm that they were not Hindu, and thus could not be married under existing Hindu law. The Act thus formalised in law the schism that had occurred between the Brahmo Samaj of India and Debendranath Tagore's Adi Brahmo Samaj in 1866, and established the Brahmo Samaj of India as an organisation that was legally outside the Hindu community.

The depth of feeling against the Marriage Act in Calcutta was considerable. Representatives of the Adi Brahmo Samaj wrote to *The Friend of India* explaining that it was Debendranath Tagore who represented the Brahmoism of Ram Mohan Roy, and that Keshab was known to have 'inaugurated a new system of Christianity in India'.[44] Attacks on Keshab's Christianisation were complemented by denunciations of his Westernised habits, his egotism, his desire to please the European community in Calcutta and his proximity to Queen Victoria. The Indian Reform Association was accused of wasting money 'on carpeting the steps and floor of the Female Normal School on the occasion of the visit of Lady Napier' and 'doling out ice cream…to the English visitors'; Keshab, it was alleged, 'delights in writing congratulatory letters to the Queen and publishing them to the world, and has not time to think of a poor brother, who dies in a hospital'.[45] Keshab's desire for 'fuss' and 'noise' was dated to 'the return of our minister from England'; Keshab's head had been turned by the adulation he received in Britain, and his main concern now lay with courting favour with the British, as opposed to serving the people of Calcutta.[46]

However, the Anglo-Indian press in Calcutta, the missionary presses and the press in England uniformly declared themselves in favour of the proposed marriage bill, as it would prohibit bigamy and polygamy, sanction inter-caste and widow marriages, and prohibit 'child marriage' by setting a minimum marriageable age of fourteen for males and eighteen for females. *The Times* declared the bill to be one of the government's 'cleverest hits in law-making' and 'one of the most important Bills ever framed with relation to India'.[47] Its importance lay in the reformation of a marriage system that, in India, constituted 'the pivot round which revolves the entire, gigantic, social system'.[48] The *Pall Mall Gazette* advocated strongly in favour of the bill, chiefly on the grounds that it would abolish 'the curse and disgrace of Hinduism… infant marriages'.[49] It was confident that the desire for 'religious reform' and 'purer morality' that motivated the marriage reform agitation were 'all the fruit and creation of British influence upon India'.[50] Reports on the Marriage Act in the British press placed Keshab firmly at the centre of progressive liberal social reform in India in the imagination of the English public, and he was championed widely as an advocate of female improvement in India and a loyal British subject.[51]

Keshab used the Indian Reform Association to apply, in an Indian context, the social reform methods he had observed in England by establishing institutions aimed at the reformation of conditions in the 'external world'. These activities drew on a Unitarian social gospel that focused on the practical reformation of society, which would in turn have beneficial spiritual and religious effects. The Indian Reform Association was intended to bring to Calcutta some of the 'practical activity' and 'philanthropy' that Keshab regarded as impressive and distinctive features of people living in the 'West'. However, the qualities Keshab associated with the 'West' comprised only half of the qualities necessary for the continuance of human progress. The Indian Reform Association had focussed only on activities aimed at the external, objective world. From 1872, Keshab would direct more attention towards the internal, subjective aspects of religion.

Primitive Faith and Spiritual Life

Sartori claims that a distinctive feature of 'Culturalism' was that it 'articulated a claim about the fundamental "underdeterminedness" of human subjectivity—the freedom of subjectivity from determinations of objective necessity such as biology, nature, economy, or society'.[52] The distinction between the subjective and the objective was of primary concern to Keshab, and he articulated it in his anniversary oration of 1872 as a distinction coterminous with the difference between the primitive and the modern:

> we find that primitive faith is more of a subjective character; it has reference more to the facts of our religious consciousness than to outward objects... In modern times religion is evidently more objective; it kills the spiritual yearning of the soul instead of encouraging and satisfying it; it turns man's attention not so much to actual enlightenment and purification of the soul as to the men and the things in the external world capable of producing such effects.[53]

As Keshab explained in a later lecture, the difference between subjective and objective realities was so great that the two constituted separate 'worlds':

> There is a spirit-world just as there is a matter world. Now in the heart of man must be created a little world complete in all its parts... The whole thing is complete, a world perfect in itself, and satisfying all the needs of the higher spirit, as completely as this world satisfies the needs of the flesh.[54]

The 'heart of man' provided an inner space in which to satisfy the 'needs of the higher spirit' in contradistinction to the needs satisfied by the external world. However, the aim was not to cultivate the inner self in opposition to external reality, but rather to harmonise inwardly-directed and outwardly-directed activity in a single character: 'In extolling devotion and contemplation, I do not mean to ignore or to under-value work... The fullest measure of meditation must be combined with the fullest measure of activity and work... The intellect, the emotions, prayer and work, all must harmonize to complete the circle of true religious life'.[55]

A 'culturalist' attempt to articulate a conception of subjectivity that was free from the determinations of objective necessity became common in proto-nationalist Bengali elite discourse from the 1870s onwards.[56] However, it should be noted that the need to achieve a balance between inward spiritual development and outwardly directed activity was also a preoccupation of Ram Mohan in the early nineteenth century. Ram Mohan's notion of the 'godly householder' occupied pride of place in his theological vision, and was central also to the ideas and activities of Debendranath Tagore. The 'godly householder' would be able to pursue spiritual elevation by remaining in touch with ultimate reality whilst also engaging in 'worldly' pursuits such as employment and property ownership. As Brian Hatcher has contended, the concept of the 'godly householder' was important to *bhadralok* men of the 1830s, as they attempted to reconcile their religious lives with their new bourgeois status: 'these men shared a set of values regarding the proper way to harmonize the spiritual life with a desire to succeed and prosper in their urban colonial environment. The 1830s were a time of optimism and aspiration for Bengali Hindu elites, who were moving into a wide variety of successful private and public roles'.[57] Keshab undoubtedly laid greater stress on the 'subjective' aspects of religion from the mid-1870s, but this constituted a shift in emphasis, not a wholesale rejection of his previous commitment to social reform.

Following in the footsteps of Ram Mohan and Debendranath, Keshab and his co-religionists turned to the Hindu tradition as a repository from which to draw the means to cultivate the subjective aspects of religion. As the distinction between the subjective and the objective was perceived by Keshab to be coterminous not only with the distinction between the 'primitive' and the 'modern', but also with the distinction between the 'East' and the 'West', it made sense to look to 'Eastern' culture for the means of cultivating qualities broadly associated with a notion of the 'spirit'. This would also provide a way for the Keshabite Brahmos to reconnect with the Hindu name they had renounced in order that the 1872 Marriage Act could be passed. While Keshab regarded the Act as the 'greatest triumph of his career as a reformer', he was distressed deeply that it had forced him to break formally from Hinduism.[58] Social progress had come at a high religious price. Accordingly, Keshab 'meant to cover the disadvantage of renouncing the name by an abundance of the true Hindu spirit and life'.[59]

Modes of Life: The Domestic Sphere

Keshab's changing domestic arrangements in the 1870s demonstrate that adopting a 'true Hindu spirit and life' did not, for Keshab and his followers, entail the rejection of foreign influences in favour of a supposedly pure and authentically 'Indian' way of life. In 1872, Keshab established the *Bharat Ashram*, a religious boarding house in which approximately twenty-five families lived together, participating in communal meals, studies and religious devotions. Sivanath Sastri—a resident for some years—claimed that Keshab wished to instil in the inhabitants of the ashram the English religious habits of order, neatness, punctuality, and daily domestic devotions.[60] Social intercourse between men and women was promoted through common meals and prayers.[61] The core members of the *Bharat Ashram* were the Brahmo missionaries who had been associated with Keshab since the 1860s.

The inculcation of positive aspects of the domestic life Keshab had observed in England was balanced by the pursuit of practices Keshab associated with 'Hindu' and 'primitive' culture. In 1875, Keshab began to advocate *vairagya* (asceticism) as a key element of life in the ashram. A libel case of the previous year, which had brought the ashram into disrepute in the Calcutta press, was perhaps the motivating cause, but the call for asceticism also stemmed, no doubt, from Keshab's ongoing fears about the proper balance between worldly and spiritual occupations. Symptoms of depression, which plagued Keshab throughout his life, took hold once again in 1875, and Keshab admonished the missionaries at the centre of the ashram to devote themselves to solitary contemplation and to cook their own meals. As Majumdar recalls, 'He felt an intenser course of spiritual life was necessary for the community. The cry for *Vairagya*, renunciation, detachment of worldliness of every kind, thus arose'.[62] Keshab had retired to live in his garden house in Belgharia in late 1873, and the missionaries were encouraged to join him in what he termed the 'Forest of Asceticism', where they would engage in solitary devotions and meditation. In 1876, Keshab purchased another garden, the *Sadhan Kanan*, and most of the missionaries joined him there in the middle of the year. In the *Sadhan Kanan*, the missionaries were encouraged to live in a 'perfectly primitive style': religious conversation and devotion alternated with food preparation, gardening and other manual work; activities were conducted 'squatting on grass mats, pieces of rough woolen stuff, and tiger skins'.[63]

A new emphasis on renunciation was complemented by an attempt to restructure the Brahmo Samaj along the lines of the ancient division of Hindu spiritual culture into the four ways of liberation: *jnana* (union with God through knowledge), *karma* (union with God through service to fellow men; this was termed *sheba*, but the content remained the same), *bhakti* (union with God through intense love) and *yoga* (union with God through contemplation and introspection).[64] Keshab invoked the Vedas to legitimise the step, and encouraged the study of 'the four Vedas of humanity, the four books of universal scripture of mankind'.[65] A renewed emphasis on *bhakti* found expression in fervent displays of devotion through singing, dancing, crying and chanting the names of God. Majumdar claims that Keshab began to express 'the greatest contempt for the intellect in regulating the relations between the devotee and his God... All the excesses of oriental piety...gradually found their embodiment in him'.[66]

Bengali Vaishnavism had been an important element in the activities of the Brahmo Samaj of India since the 1860s, in part due to the influence of the Vaishnava Bijoy Krishna Goswami. The adoption of Vaishnava devotional forms was part of an attempt to broaden the appeal of Brahmoism through popular forms of worship that would resonate with poorer inhabitants of rural Bengal. It also reflected Keshab's desire to emphasise the emotional and devotional aspects of faith. Particular stress was placed on the use of the *ektara*, a single-stringed musical instrument which Keshab identified with primitive simplicity, and which often appears in photographs of Keshab as leader of the New Dispensation (Fig. viii). From time to time, Keshab had his head shaved and adopted the dress of a Hindu mendicant. From 1875 onwards, with the exception of his anniversary orations, he began to lecture almost exclusively in Bengali.[67]

Fig. viii   Photograph taken at Simla, north India, in 1883. Keshab poses
with an animal skin and an *ektara*.

Keshab's attempts to refashion Brahmo modes of life in line with notions of 'primitive' and 'Hindu' practices always existed in tension with his role as a prominent public figure who was expected to engage in gentlemanly social intercourse with British officials. The demands of ascetic renunciation and contemplation sat uneasily alongside the strong sense of social duty Keshab felt towards the inhabitants of Calcutta. The problem of how to achieve a balance between a worldly and an ascetic lifestyle was one that Keshab discussed eagerly with Ramakrishna. If one figure above all others embodied for Keshab the spirit and value of 'primitive' asceticism, it was Ramakrishna. An article in the *Indian Mirror*, published in 1875 shortly after Keshab and Ramakrishna first met, described how Keshab had been charmed by Ramakrishna's 'depth, penetration and simplicity of...spirit. The never-ceasing metaphors and analogies in which he indulged are, most of them, as apt as they are beautiful... Hinduism must have in it a deep source of beauty, truth and goodness to inspire such men as these'.[68]

The record of Ramakrishna's teachings, the *Kathamrita*, documents many of the interactions that took place between Keshab and Ramakrishna from 1875 until the end of Keshab's life. Keshab and his fellow Brahmo devotees were clearly concerned that their worldly duties would impede their spiritual progress. On a boat trip organised by Keshab in 1882, one Brahmo anxiously enquired, 'Sir, can't we realize God without complete renunciation?'.[69] Ramakrishna responded reassuringly: 'Why should you renounce everything? You are alright as you are, following the middle path'.[70] However, sometimes the response was not so accommodating. While visiting Keshab's house in April 1882, Ramakrishna was suddenly struck with fear that 'Keshab might belong to someone else, that is to say, that he might become a worldly person'.[71] He sang a song directly to Keshab, the meaning of which he explained in the following way: 'renounce everything and call on God. He alone is real; all else is illusory. Without the realization of God everything is futile. This is the great secret'.[72]

Keshab's attempts to balance the subjective and objective demands of religious life—the need to cultivate the inner self and the duty to perform good works in the external world—resulted in him leading, in effect, a 'double life' during the 1870s. It was during the period of adopting a 'primitive' mode of life in the *Sadhan Kanan* that Keshab was simultaneously attempting to generate funds to open the Albert Hall in Calcutta, a venue he hoped would function as a 'meeting place to develop friendly relations between the English administrators and the local gentle class'.[73] According to Majumdar, he 'hewed wood, drew water, and ate scanty meals' and then 'returned to society with a well-oiled and well-combed head, with flowing robes, and cheerful looks to mix with the highest in the land'.[74] In October 1877, when Keshab moved to a new place of residence in Calcutta, Lily Cottage, he first converted one of the rooms into a domestic sanctuary, before furnishing 'a drawing room for the reception of his many visitors, both European and Indian. He planned his library and sitting room, extended his gardens and tank, but in the midst of it all, set up a little straw-thatched hut, where he might practice solitary devotions and self-discipline'.[75] In attempting to perform the ideal of a harmonious spiritualised masculinity that he had advocated in Britain, Keshab ended up performing two roles, and created two distinct spaces in his own household in which he could perform them. His intellectual bifurcation of the world into a spiritual 'East' and a material 'West' was mirrored by a bifurcation of his home, his daily life and even his dress.

Modes of Life: Spiritualised Femininity

Concepts of femininity were accorded a special position in attempts to reconnect Brahmoism with an 'authentic' and ancient Hinduism. In the course of the 1870s, the ideal of femininity that Keshab propounded became centred increasingly on virtues associated with 'primitive Hinduism'. This ideal of femininity departed markedly from views Keshab had expressed during his visit to England. Keshab had argued against the denationalisation of women during his lectures in England, but he had been a staunch advocate of an 'unsectarian, liberal, sound and useful education' for Indian females, and had held up 'civilised' English women as models for emulation.[76] He had claimed that the education of women was important precisely because Indian women of the present tended to 'conserve all the traditions, all the errors and prejudices, and all the injurious institutions that exist in the country'.[77] It was in ancient India that evidence could be found of independent, rational and intellectual women.

From the mid-1870s, Keshab placed less emphasis on the intellectual capacities of classical Indian women, and constructed, instead, an ideal of classical Indian femininity that stressed their 'primitive' virtues of simplicity and closeness to nature. He had his wife photographed as a yogi, holding an *ektara*, and as a 'primitive Aryan devotee', with wild flowers in her hair.[78] As Majumdar recalls, he became opposed to the university education of women, advocated the retirement of women, and became critical of 'the idea of an artificial, conventional, strong-mannered or strong-minded womanhood'.[79] Annette Akroyd, an Englishwoman who responded to Keshab's appeal to English women in 1870 to come to India, was outraged to find on her arrival that Keshab had apparently regressed from his former liberal stance on women's education.[80] Akroyd wrote incensed letters to a variety of newspapers and to Keshab himself, although it was her own 'dreadful behaviour' and 'awful fury' that was criticised in the Anglophone newspapers and periodicals.[81] Sivanath Sastri, a member of the rationalist progressive faction within the Samaj, clashed with Keshab over the extent to which females should receive training in subjects such as logic, metaphysics and geometry—subjects which Keshab felt were unnecessary for the improvement of women.[82] As Keshab increasingly associated women with the values of the subjective aspect of religion, the education of women became less of a priority than a celebration of spiritual feminine virtues.[83]

The prevalence of discourses of 'spiritualised' women in the articulation of early nationalism has been the focus of a great deal of scholarly interest. While questions of female 'emancipation' had occupied a central place in the activities of reformers such as Ram Mohan, Vidyasagar and, as we have seen, Keshab, such questions became of less importance in the later nineteenth century. Ghulam Murshid has contended that mid-nineteenth century attempts to 'modernise' the condition of women were stalled by nationalist politics, which glorified India's past, defended traditional values and opposed attempts to change customs and lifestyles, particularly within the family.[84] Other historians have adopted a different view, pointing to a fundamental social conservatism with regard to women in the ideas of even the most radical of reformers, and arguing that reformers were always highly selective in their acceptance of liberal values. Nationalist attitudes to women, therefore, merely continued the social conservatism of an earlier generation.[85] Partha Chatterjee, in contrast, has pointed to the critical role played by changing concepts of femininity in nationalist articulations of the 'spiritual domain'. In Chatterjee's view, the 'spiritual domain' came to be associated with the space of the 'home' (in contrast to the 'world'), a space in which females could help to preserve the essential marks of 'inner' culture. The reason for the disappearance of the question of 'female emancipation' in the later nineteenth century lay in 'the refusal of nationalism to make the women's question an issue of political negotiation with the colonial state'.[86] The 'nation' was already 'sovereign' in the 'home'; the political struggle would take place in the 'external world'.[87]

There can be no doubt that, from 1872 onwards, Keshab came to associate Indian femininity with a pure form of spirituality embodied in the women of ancient India and in his own wife. He also became increasingly resolute in his opposition to the 'Westernisation' of women through education that focused too closely on rational and scientific subjects. However, in the same period in which Keshab ascribed increasing importance to the spirituality of the 'Hindu' home and family—represented pre-eminently by the figure of the Indian wife and mother—he also attributed increasing spiritual significance to the imperial family.

In the mid-1870s, Keshab began to refer freqently to the motherhood of God. In the same period, he began to lay emphasis on the motherhood of Queen Victoria. In his lecture 'Philosophy and Madness in Religion', Keshab drew a comparison between the 'Hindu' household and the imperial family: 'The Hindu householder loves the father as the head of the house…so he loves his sovereign as the father of the state… That the sovereign is father and mother of the subject population is essentially a Hindu idea'.[88] Loyalty to Victoria stemmed, not from 'the presence of purely secular feelings', but from 'a strong religious sentiment'.[89] Keshab reiterated these ideas in the 1880s. In the first edition of the *New Dispensation*, he referred to Victoria as 'our Queen-Mother' and 'India's mother', and argued that 'A man who hates his sovereign is morally as culpable as he who abhors or maltreats his father or mother'.[90] Keshab may have attempted to create a 'spiritual domain' within his own home (albeit alongside a European drawing room), but it was not only the home and the immediate family that were spiritualised. The 'spiritual domain', for Keshab, was also the domain of 'politics' and the 'state'. The figure of the spiritualised 'mother' was embodied equally by Indian wives, by God and by Queen Victoria. The 'family' referred both to the domestic household and to the imperial family. The 'world', in this respect, was also the 'home'. Keshab undoubedly contributed to the popularisation of the idea that 'spirituality' was fundamental to Indian 'national' identity. However, concepts of both the domestic and the imperial family were deeply imbricated in his construction of spiritualised femininity.

Modes of Thought: Inspiration

Keshab had spoken of inspiration before he met Ramakrishna, but it is likely that Ramakrishna's insistence on the necessity of direct communion with God as the basis for preaching, and the moving spectacle of Ramakrishna in a state of *samadhi* (which Keshab witnessed frequently in his own house—see Fig. ix), made a strong impression on Keshab, and convinced him further of the special value of inspiration as a mode of thought.[91] Keshab and Ramakrishna discussed the relative merits of rational enquiry and inspirational experience as bases for religious preaching on many occasions. Keshab had engaged in similar discussions in England, where his supporters had often praised his style of preaching for its passion, emotion and appeal to the 'heart'. Ramakrishna was insistent on the qualities necessary for a religious teacher: 'A man can only teach if God reveals himself and gives the command...it won't do if a man only imagines himself that he has God's command. God does reveal himself to man and speak. Only then may one receive His command. How forceful are the words of such a teacher!... But mere lectures? People will listen to them for a few days and then forget them'.[92] Worldly activity, like teaching, was only possible through God's power: 'You people speak of doing good to the world. Is the world such a small thing? And who are you, pray, to do good to the world? First realize God, see Him by the means of spiritual discipline. If He imparts power, then you can do good to others; otherwise not'.[93]

Keshab devoted his anniversary lecture of January 1873 to the subject of inspiration. Prophets and martyrs of 'ancient times', he explained, had enjoyed many opportunities for attaining true inspiration from God.[94] The main obstacle that modernity created for access to inspiration was 'a massive and materialistic civilization' which 'has so affected us that we cannot rise into the higher regions of the spirit-world'.[95] However, inspiration in modern times was still a possibility:

Fig. ix   Photograph of Ramakrishna in *samadhi* at the house of
Keshab Chandra Sen, taken on 21 September 1879.
His nephew Hriday stands behind him.

'With all the lusts of the flesh and carnal humanity within us, and the new dangers of modern materialism around us, we have reason to hope that at least the same means and opportunities of attaining inspiration and grace will be vouchsafed to us as were enjoyed in the earlier epochs of society'.[96] These means and opportunities would not be afforded, however, if inspiration continued to be approached in the terms of modern materialist societies: 'Inspiration is treated, in this degenerate age, as a commodity which can be purchased in books'.[97]

This contrast between inspiration and the commodity-form is significant. We can recall that, in his speeches in England, Keshab drew a direct comparison between the exchange of commodities in the free market of material goods and the exchange of spiritual insights in the free market of ideas. By 1873, he was invoking the commodity as a form that was utterly incomparable to the spiritual idea of inspiration. Inspiration, he avowed, could never be contained or exchanged within a capitalist marketplace. Furthermore, inspiration could not be found in books, but could only be experienced directly through communion with God.

According to neo-Marxist interpretations of Bengali history, a fundamental contradiction of the position of the Bengali elite in the mid-to-late nineteenth century lay in the fact that the philosophy of liberalism they espoused had its basis in a system of capitalist exchange from which they were increasingly excluded. As a result, from the 1870s onwards, members of the Bengali elite began to articulate conceptions of subjectivity that were not rooted in liberal understandings of the free, rational individual pursuing self-interest in civil society. Sartori interprets Bankimchandra Chatterjee's shift from liberal politics to 'neo-Hinduism' in the 1880s as emblematic of this broader shift in thought: 'Where the practices of (Western) commercial society presented only a travesty of independence, indigeneity might provide an alternative path of authentic self-realization...one that turned on a language of sacrifice rather than happiness, worldly renunciation rather than the pursuit of self-interest, and India's cultural rather than Europe's material civilization'.[98] Sartori refers to this as Bankim's 'revivalist turn'.[99]

Keshab's rejection of the capitalist exchange of commodities as a model for the exchange of spiritual ideas, his insistence on India's special capacity for accessing inspirational knowledge that overly materialist societies were unable to comprehend, and his attempts to reconnect with 'Hindu' modes of life and thought, may lead us to detect a similar 'revivalist turn' in his thought in the 1870s. Keshab's advocacy of *vairagya* and his frequent calls for his inner circle of adherents to live off public alms certainly suggest an attempt to remove himself and his organisation from the commercial capitalist sphere.

However, a stark periodisation of nineteenth-century Bengal in terms of a shift from 'liberalism' to 'culturalism' cannot really capture Keshab's (or Bankim's) position.[100] Many of Bankim's 'revivalist' ideas were anticipated by Keshab: the emphasis on devotion and direct communion with God as the highest human faculties; the use of a language of 'motherhood' as a way of imagining the 'nation'; the argument that religious insight constituted science's higher principle.[101] However, 'Eastern' spirituality, for Keshab, never served as a completely 'external' standpoint for the critique of Western civil society, as it did in Bankim's 'culturalism'.[102] Keshab's identification of both a 'spiritual world' and a 'material world' allowed him to invoke inspiration as a means of criticising 'Western' materialism from the external standpoint of the 'spiritual world', but the 'spiritual' and 'material' worlds both remained internal to Keshab's broader conception of a Providentially guided holistic narrative of human progress in which the two 'worlds' would be harmonised.

Just as discourses of 'liberalism' could take many forms, so discourses of 'culturalism' were varied and complex. They emerged not only in response to the spread of capitalism, but also in response to a range of other factors, and took on different dimensions in metropolitan and colonial contexts. Concerns over the need to retain a spiritual life in the face of a materialist world lay behind many Victorian Britons' acceptance of Keshab during his visit to England. The Unitarians were particularly susceptible to tensions between the 'critical spirit' (reason) and the 'will to believe' (faith). These tensions were experienced more broadly in Victorian society with the growth and professionalisation of science and the reinterpretation of religious belief.[103] While Keshab's advocacy of *vairagya* might be interpreted as a negative response to the spread of global capital, this interpretation is problematised by the fact that Keshab maintained his firm belief in the superiority and necessity of 'Western' technology, enterprise and material progress.

Keshab did not simply shift from a 'liberal' to a 'cultural' view of subjectivity. Rather, he held both views simultaneously. His intellectual bifurcation of the 'world' into material and spiritual domains, and his physical bifurcation of his home along parallel lines, enabled him to advocate both the pursuit of a subjectivity grounded in the inner cultivation of spirituality through direct communion with God, and also the pursuit of a subjectivity grounded in the realisation of social aims within civil society. Keshab was, first and foremost, a universalist: while he laid greater emphasis, in the 1870s, on modes of life and thought which he regarded as authentically 'indigenous', he always attempted to reconcile them with modes of life and thought which he regarded as 'Western'. Bifurcating nineteenth-century Bengal into an 'age of liberalism' and an 'age of culturalism' obscures this powerful universalist tendency in Bengali (and, indeed, British) intellectual life in the mid-nineteenth century.

Modes of Thought: Reason, Madness and Science

In Keshab's view, inspiration was not opposed to the dictates of reason and science. In his anniversary lecture on inspiration, Keshab was keen to convince his audience that he could provide 'corroborative testimony' as evidence for inspiration—this evidence could be found in history, experience and natural instincts.[104] Keshab preached that God intervened directly in response to prayer, but this did not require God to 'break or suspend His laws'.[105] The spiritual world and the material world operated in accordance with separate, but related, laws. Far from being contrary to scientific views on the physical universe, inspiration was profoundly scientific: 'As you go and study other sciences, go and study the science of inspiration, and as you investigate the laws of the physical universe, investigate likewise…the laws which govern the spiritual world'.[106]

Although Keshab spoke often of science in modern times as one of religion's 'sworn enemies', he fully believed that the conflict between science and religion could be resolved.[107] With regard to the science of physics, which had 'peopled God's universe with godless laws and

Godless forces', all that was necessary was to recognise the 'Living Person' of God, a person distinct from mind and matter yet immanent in both.[108] A 'well-balanced mind' would discern in all of the physical sciences not merely 'Wisdom, but a wise and beneficent Will'.[109] This argument is reminiscent of the combination of scientism and deism propounded by the Brahmo Akkhoy Kumar Dutt, who argued that God's 'scripture' lay not in texts, but in the harmonious workings of the universe, which were to be 'read' through the study of science.

However, the ways in which Keshab attempted to resolve the conflict he perceived between religion and science were not so straightforward as those proposed by a rationalist like Dutt. In 1877, Keshab preached his anniversary lecture 'Philosophy and Madness in Religion'. The lecture was predicated on a fundamental opposition between philosophy and madness that corresponded to a long series of further antitheses: 'Four thousand years ago the burden of India's song was Meditation. To-day the war-cry of educated India, is Civilization. The cry of the first century was Madness; but the watchword of modern Christian Europe is Philosophy'.[110] He continued, 'The difference between philosophy and madness is the difference between science and faith, between cold dialectics and fiery earnestness, between the logical deductions of the human understanding and the living force of inspiration'.[111]

Keshab used the lecture to provide an alternative discourse to the discourse of 'reason' that he identified as characteristic of Christian European civilisation, and to argue for the value of madness, the 'song' of ancient India.[112] The lecture thus constituted an attempt to expand on the ideas he had expressed in England of 'truth' as 'many-sided', by elucidating the nature of the perspective on 'truth' that Indians had to offer. The lecture took the form of an imaginary court-case—a 'long-pending suit—Madness versus Philosophy'; Keshab proposed that only 'rational discussion' of 'both sides of the controversy' could 'arrange and settle the mutual differences of the two parties'.[113] It was by the rational standards of philosophy that the 'suit' between philosophy and madness would be judged.

The power of madness was that it converted philosophical belief into actual perception. The unseen Reality which philosophy could only encounter through speculation (and which thus remained resistant to the empirical observation of sense-experience) was, through madness, rendered directly seen and experienced, and thus became amenable to observation and experiment. With regard to the study of the Divine, madness was thus eminently more philosophical than philosophy: 'while philosophy is satisfied with only believing that God is not less real than matter and self, madness converts this intellectual belief into a vivid perception'.[114] Keshab presented the mediums of sense-perception through which madness observed the spirit-world (meditation and inspiration) as equivalent to the mediums of sense-perception through which philosophy observed the matter-world. Philosophy and madness existed in unity, not opposition.

However, while madness and philosophy shared the same empirical method of observing and experimenting upon objects of sense-perception, madness—viewed on a world-historical scale—would allow humans to progress further towards perfection than philosophy. Keshab illustrated the superiority of madness to philosophy by combining a description of the threefold nature of reality (which divided reality into matter, mind and the Absolute) with an interpretation of Darwinian evolution—'the cry of modern scientists'.[115] The threefold nature of reality corresponded with four stages of evolution. Nature had transformed inorganic matter into animality (evolutionary states which corresponded to the reality of 'matter'). Philosophy and reason had enabled humans to evolve out of animality into humanity (an evolutionary state which corresponded to the reality of 'mind'). However, philosophy could not enable humanity to evolve beyond the reality of 'mind' towards the Absolute reality of the Divine. Only madness, Keshab averred, 'drags you to that higher stage…where Divinity speaks and rules in man'.[116] Man should not only conquer animality, but should 'himself be conquered by Divinity… To put on this "new man" is to be mad with the inspiration of the Holy Spirit'.[117] Madness thus ultimately exceeded the philosophical method in its capacity to further human progress. This 'scientific fact' was proved by the eminently philosophical doctrine of evolution itself: 'The same law, the same science of evolution which has enabled you to conquer matter and animality, will yet enable you to conquer humanity and attain Divine life'.[118]

Raina and Habib have drawn attention to attempts by the Calcutta *bhadralok*, between 1897 and 1913, to reinterpret evolutionary theory in a way which 'preserv[ed] the theological cosmos of the Indians, while simultaneously rendering modern secular science commensurate with it'.[119] Keshab's attempt to reconcile a philosophy of madness with Darwinian evolutionary theory clearly predates the timescale they suggest. The importance of Darwin's theory of evolution with respect to the origins of humans only became fully manifest in the 1870s, with the publication of *The Descent of Man* in 1871 and *The Expression of the Emotions in Man and Animals* in 1872. Both of these works emphasised relentlessly the animality of humanity, whilst also contending that humans were all part of the same species. As is well known, they elicited many responses from religious thinkers, including the Unitarians, which attempted to reconcile Darwin's insights with theological traditions.[120] Darwin's ideas had been a subject of discussion in *Dharmatattwa* since 1874.[121]

The effects of Darwinian thought on ideologies of progress and racial difference were, of course, profound, although notions of racial evolution were often articulated in opposition to Darwin's ideas.[122] As Koditschek has observed, a key effect of Darwinian thought on imperial understandings of race was to decrease the 'velocity' of narratives of 'progress'.[123] The process of 'civilisation' would now take place over the *longue durée*: 'bio-social evolutionary theory…could endorse the superiority of Anglo-Saxon civilization in a more formidable "scientific" manner and reaffirm the civilizing possibilities for lesser peoples, albeit in gradual, imperially directed ways'.[124] Keshab's narrative of progress—from animality to humanity to divinity—operated on a timescale that, in its breadth, was commensurable with the *longue durée* approach demanded by biological understandings of human evolution. Indeed, Keshab broadened the timescale still further, looking beyond the present age of 'humanity' into a distant future of the Divinely-conquered 'new man'. If it was the 'Western philosophy' of 'reason' that had enabled man to evolve out of his animality, then it was 'Eastern' 'madness' that would enable humans to evolve still further. The *longue durée* history of the past may have been dominated by 'Western' forms of knowledge, but the *longue durée* history of the future would be written according to 'Eastern' modes of perception. Epistemologically at least, in the future it would be Westerners who would be confined to the waiting room of history.

These developments are significant when we consider that the advent of a new, incremental and evolutionary perspective on racial development coincided with a series of colonial crises between 1857 and 1886, which were, as Koditschek has observed, 'leading metropolitan liberals to doubt whether Greater Britain's racial others could easily be transformed into darker versions of themselves'.[125] The hardening of racial attitudes engendered by the coincidence of colonial crises with the emergence of evolutionary racial thinking would certainly have been felt on the ground in Calcutta from the mid-1870s. Open hostility towards Indians on the part of British officials increased markedly with the appointment of Lord Lytton as Viceroy in 1876, who was notorious, in particular, for his disregard of the 'Westernised' Indian elite.[126]

The language of 'madness' in which Keshab couched his challenge to the 'Western' discourse of 'reason' may appear unusual to many readers, but it drew on a long tradition of ecstatic religion in Bengal. In fact, the concept of 'Divine madness' is not unique to Bengal or even to India, but has found expression in a variety of traditions, including Eastern Orthodox and Western Christianity (particularly the Catholic mystical tradition), Hasidism, Sufism and a variety of practices of possession and trance around the world.[127] Ecstatic experiences, such as powers or visions arising during meditation, form an important part of the history of yoga.[128] However, discourses of madness have a particular resonance in the religious traditions of Bengal. Many Bengali saints are called 'madmen' by their devotees and biographers.[129] The life of the great Vaishnava saint Chaitanya, whom Keshab revered, was a long series of ecstatic states, and madness and ecstasy (both ritual and spontaneous) remained crucial to the Vaishnava tradition. It is important to note that religious madness and clinical madness are viewed as quite distinct in the Bengali ecstatic tradition. Ramakrishna himself was subjected to Ayurvedic treatment amid fears that he was clinically insane, but it was declared eventually by a conference of scholars that his madness was religious in nature, and that he was a saint or avatar, or even himself divine.[130]

Discourses of madness take on a particular significance in the context of British imperialism. Partha Chatterjee has drawn attention to attempts by a number of Bengali public figures in the later nineteenth century to escape from what he has termed a 'prisonhouse of Reason'.[131] Bankimchandra Chatterjee, a rationalist essayist, and Bhudeb Mukhopadyay, a rationalist defender of 'orthodox' tradition, both turned to writing imaginary and utopian histories that aimed to escape from rational Western teleology.[132] For the colonised middle-class mind, 'the discourse of Reason was not unequivocally liberating. The invariable implication it carried of the historical necessity of colonial rule and its condemnation of indigenous culture as the storehouse of unreason…made the discourse of Reason oppressive'.[133] English education might have brought new opportunities to the Hindu elite, but its epistemological and historical assumptions could constitute an intellectual and spiritual prison.

For Keshab, however, madness was not strictly an 'escape' from reason. In Keshab's view, madness conformed to the dictates of rationality and the latest scientific theories, and, in its ability to perceive the Absolute, exceeded the philosophical method in its empiricism and rationality. Keshab's advocacy of madness challenged British imperial denigrations of Indian irrationality by arguing against the condemnation of unreason itself. His identification of madness with ancient India was clearly distinct from constructions of the Indian past propounded in the earlier nineteenth century by figures such as Ram Mohan, which had, at their core, assertions of the evidence in antiquity of rationality, citizenship, justice, property and independence. However, if Keshab found the discourse of reason oppressive, he did not link this experience of intellectual and spiritual oppression to the concrete reality of British political domination in India. His arguments against reason, while often made in tandem with arguments against 'Western' materialism, never became arguments against the historical necessity of British rule. On the contrary, Keshab used the concept of madness precisely to advocate the continuance of British rule in India. While it was rational philosophy that allowed for the 'recognition of abstract law and justice', it was madness that dealt with the 'sentiment' as opposed to the 'principle' of 'loyalty'.[134]

Responses in London and Calcutta

Keshab's attempts to combine a 'primitive' ascetic lifestyle with his continued role as a public figure were the subject of frequent derision in the Anglo-Indian press in Calcutta, and were generally regarded as extremely eccentric. An article in the Methodist *Lucknow Witness*, reprinted in *The Friend of India* in Calcutta, suggested that if Keshab wished to be treated seriously as a religious reformer, he should stop 'wearing articles of gold in prominent relief about his person' and dress instead in 'a strip of bark' and 'feed on bulbs'.[135] This was presumably intended as a joke, but clearly struck a nerve with one of Keshab's admirers, who assured the readers of the newspaper that Keshab wore a 'simple black *choga*', travelled third class on the train, and could not wear 'bark' in the company of the 'ladies and gentleman whom the requirements of his position oblige him to see'.[136] Indeed, to adopt such habits would remove him from 'the field of rational life'.[137] A pamphlet circulating in 1879 pointed to the hypocrisy of Keshab's professed 'asceticism', listing his 'abstinences' as including 'living amid the luxuries of a lord'.[138]

Keshab's 'Westernised' habits of living also drew opprobrium from his Bengali contemporaries. It is likely that Keshab himself was the subject of one of Bankimchandra Chatterjee's many satires on the Westernised *babu*, a creature that was full of universal aspirations and self-regard but condemned to a life of insignificance.[139] Accusations of 'Westernisation' were never levelled against Ram Mohan Roy or reformers of his generation, although they may have been accused of 'innovation' and 'worldliness'.[140] From the 1870s, however, a new generation of proto-nationalist critics began to regard the 'Westernised' activities and manners of the reformist *bhadralok* as indicative of an unreflective and debilitating imitation of the English, which led to a resurgence of the stereotype of the subservient and effeminate *babu*.[141]

Keshab's efforts to reconnect the Brahmo Samaj of India with an 'authentic' form of Hinduism led to British missionary support for his organisation falling away. As we have seen, while Keshab was in England many missionary organisations expressed a hope that Keshab would prove to be a valuable ally in moving his countrymen along the path towards Christianity. The most common way that Brahmoism was represented in the British press was as a 'half-way house' between Hinduism and Christianity, and the majority of ministers who met or wrote about Keshab believed him to be almost, if not already, Christian. The enduring power of this conviction was demonstrated by the widespread reporting of a (false) claim, made by the Wesleyan Methodists in 1871, that Keshab had been baptised and was now functioning as a Methodist preacher. This claim was reproduced in most of the leading newspapers in London and the provinces, and the lack of comment or surprise it elicited suggests that the lasting impression Keshab left upon the British public was of a man who was progressing fast towards Christianity.[142]

However, by late 1873, the vast majority of missionary organisations had turned against Keshab. The immediate cause may have been the initiation ceremony of the Unitarian Charles Dall into the Brahmo Samaj, in the course of which Keshab made it clear that Brahmos were '*pure* and not...*Christian* theist[s]'.[143] Many members of the Brahmo Samaj in Calcutta subsequently echoed this claim of 'pure' as opposed to 'Christian' Theism. The *Illustrated Missionary News* in London expressed considerable shock that 'Christ' had been 'deliberately rejected' and lamented that the Brahmos' 'glory has departed'.[144] Having failed to accept the 'life-giving element' of the Godhead of Christ and the atonement for sin, 'THE BRAHMIST MOVEMENT, which for a while seemed so hopeful in its tendency towards Christianity, appears now to have reached its climax and to be receding towards Hindooism again'.[145] The monthly journal of the Baptist Missionary Society, the *Missionary Herald*, agreed that Brahmoism would prove 'a nine days wonder' and that 'Hinduism will tend more and more to become a mere cloak for the absence of all religion'.[146] One could move either forwards or backwards along the path to Christian religion, and the lack of full acceptance of Christianity would result in retrogression towards Hinduism or atheism.

The London Missionary Society concurred that either 'full acceptance' or 'retrogression' were the only two options for those on the path to religious truth.[147] Religious intercourse between Brahmos and English Theists had led the Brahmos to believe that individual 'intuition' (a term which the British press used interchangeably with 'inspiration') was 'the great source of religious knowledge'.[148] A reliance on intuition was an inevitable consequence of the use of the 'Eclectic principle': 'this implies a power in the individual to discriminate between the true and the false...if an individual is possessed of this power, it seems a very natural and easy inference to make, that he himself may have an intuitive knowledge of truth and goodness'.[149]

While religious intuition was a principle central to the Christianity propounded by the missionaries (in the sense that individuals possess an intuitive sense of God's moral law), intuition should be tempered by 'something more stable' otherwise 'it is simply identical with the uncontrolled imagination of the individual'.[150] The Brahmos had 'passed into mysticism', and there was every chance that Brahmoism would 'split upon the rock of individualism' (with each member asserting the truth of his own intuition) or would be 'degraded into the worship of some leader of the movement'.[151] In the eyes of the missionaries, Keshab had retreated from the principles of scriptural authority and reason that were essential to 'stable' religion, and there appeared to be little chance that he would return to the Christian fold. While Ram Mohan had adhered to reason and propounded Christian teachings as 'the supreme guide to life eternal', Keshab's 'comprehensive' approach had abandoned Ram Mohan's principles, either as a result of 'moral cowardice', 'national prejudice' or misguided 'sincere conviction'.[152]

The *Calcutta Review*, an Anglo-Indian paper with a pronounced Christian orientation aimed at the English-educated Bengali middle-classes, offered a different interpretation of Keshab's relation to Ram Mohan.[153] Keshab's pronouncements on the importance of inspiration were interpreted as a clear step forward from Ram Mohan's belief that the Vedas were an 'authority'.[154] Ram Mohan's Brahmoism had failed because, as a religion of the 'intellect', it could not become an effective 'moral force'.[155] A religion of the intellect, as opposed to a religion that exercised 'subjective power' and pressed on the 'individual conscience', would tend towards authoritarianism, and made 'a comfortable esoteric doctrine for those who are tempted to assume superiority over their fellows'.[156] Intuition could act as a guard against authoritarianism, but only on the assumption that what was intuited was Christianity: 'Intuitionalism, as it is called by the Brahmas, but in reality Christianity, has given them a Father in Heaven'.[157] Keshab's refusal to acknowledge his debt to Christianity was leading Brahmos to exalt their religion as the 'only truth', but they would be forced in time to acknowledge that 'Brahmism is not the goal'.[158] While the London Missionary Society and the *Calcutta Review* differed in their views on the relationship between intuition and authoritarianism, they agreed that intuition was valuable only insofar as it conformed to Christian principles.

The Friend of India, the journal of the Baptist missionaries at Serampore until 1875, when it was acquired by the dissident imperial critic Robert Knight, followed the activities of the Brahmo Samaj of India closely throughout the 1870s and 1880s. It was the most important source of information on Keshab's activities for British audiences, as its articles were reproduced frequently in newspapers such as the *Pall Mall Gazette* and *Birmingham Daily Post*. [159] *The Friend of India* was generally supportive of Keshab in the early 1870s—it applauded the activities of the Indian Reform Association, and praised Keshab's lecture on 'Primitive Faith and Modern Speculations' for propounding 'a great key principle of religion…which cannot fail to spread, and spread for good'. [160] However, it was intensely critical of Keshab if he appeared to claim authority as a teacher of Christians in the West, or to introduce innovations into Christian practices. An article in the *Indian Mirror* that claimed that 'the principles of Keshub Chunder Sen are spreading in England' was dismissed as 'utterly puerile' and 'an exquisite joke'. [161] The Brahmo search for 'truth and moral purity…deserves respect… But it does not comprehend Christianity as known in the West'. [162] The practice of cutting out references to the divinity of Christ from Christian hymns was roundly condemned as 'BRAHMO HYMNICIDE'—the 'mutilation of noble hymns' tampered with 'men's convictions in connection with the most sacred subjects in the world'. [163] Keshab was expected to learn from Western Christianity, not to innovate.

Keshab's activities received considerable press coverage in Britain in the years immediately following his visit and during the agitation for the Marriage Act of 1872, but press attention subsided subsequently. Although Keshab was not an object of sustained attention after 1872, he continued to be referred to in passing, and the casual nature of the references—without background information concerning his identity and activities—suggests that he remained a well-known figure among the educated British public. [164] Once reporting on the Marriage Act had ended, the next article concerning Keshab to be widely reproduced in the press in Britain was a long piece from *The Friend of India* of 13 May 1876, which provided the British public with a portrait of Keshab which differed significantly from the image of him as India's pre-eminent 'liberal reformer' that had preponderated in previous British coverage. [165]

The history of the Brahmo Samaj had become, according to the article, the 'history of the mind of Baboo Keshub Chunder Sen'.[166] Keshab was Brahmoism's 'prophet', and it was as such that 'his name is well known in Europe and America and at the English antipodes'.[167] Within the movement (and thus within the 'mind' of its leader), there were 'great apparent forces now struggling': 'the effort to Hindooise the Christian doctrines it has embraced, and the effort to modernise and rationalise (some might prefer to say spiritualise), the old Hindoo doctrines and practices'.[168] This attempt to strike a balance between two religions was taken as proof that 'the religious school…is not fitted to endure'.[169] It was Brahmoism's Christian leanings that had secured 'its position in the eyes of the world', but 'of late the leaning back towards Hindooism has been as marked as the leaning forward towards Christianity formerly was'.[170] Keshab's eclecticism was 'more apparent than real', and amounted to a 'morbid' endeavour to 'find a Hindu phrase for a notion formerly expressed by a Christian one'.[171] Brahmoism would gravitate 'towards one or other system whose integrity is greater than its own…[and] it is no longer in danger of being swallowed up by Christianity'.[172] The place of Hinduism and Christianity on the scale of religious progress was quite clear; Keshab's alternative vision, which placed Hinduism and Christianity on an equal footing, was roundly rejected.

Sophia Dobson Collet was more amenable to Keshab's attempts at eclecticism. In *The Brahmo Year Book*, she provided detailed accounts of developments in the Brahmo Samaj of India, and she corresponded regularly with Keshab and other writers in the *Indian Mirror*. While she reserved most of her praise for the secular efforts of the Indian Reform Association, she also found much to admire in the *bhakti* movement, which she interpreted as fostering the 'Augustinian side of religion,—the strong sense of sin, the need of regenerate life, the passionate thirst for God as Saviour and Comforter'.[173] Indeed, *bhakti* constituted a significant advance on the Brahmoism of Ram Mohan and Debendranath Tagore, as it 'unlocked the deepest fountains of religious life'.[174] Similarly, the *vairagya* or ascetic movement would prove fruitful providing it 'keeps clear of the well-known abuses of earlier times' and emphasised attachment to God as opposed to detachment from the world.[175]

Collet wrote to the *Indian Mirror* expressing her concern that asceticism should be moderated by religious activity directed at social reform, and she found Keshab's letter of response to be 'reassuring'. [176] Keshab promised her that 'The amount of ascetic self-mortification actually existing amongst us has been greatly exaggerated... Energy, philanthropy, meditation, work, self-sacrifice, intellectual culture, domestic and social love, all these are united in *my* asceticism'. [177] Nevertheless, Collet remained concerned that the emotional side of religion should be kept in check by a commitment to Brahmoism as a social gospel. An excess of 'emotion', she opined, could prove dangerously attractive to members of 'so susceptible a race'. [178] While Keshab's supposedly racial predisposition towards emotion had made him attractive to Unitarians during his visit to England, this quality could prove dangerous if not held in check by more reasonable minds.

Although Collet was amenable to Keshab's ascetic practices, she could not accept his restructuring of Brahmoism in accordance with the ancient divisions of *jnana*, *sheba*, *yoga* and *bhakti*. *Jnana* (knowledge) and *sheba* (service) were, in her view, valid distinctions, equivalent to the distinction between philosophy and philanthropy in the West, but the distinction between *yoga* (communion with God) and *bhakti* (love of God)—and particularly the creation of a 'saintly class' devoted to these practices—was dangerous. [179] It instituted a false distinction between what people '*do*' and what people '*are*', and could lead those respected as a '*siddha yoga*' or a '*siddha bhakta*' to believe that they had accomplished their religious purpose and 'completed the work of cultivation'. [180] Collet's constant interventions demonstrate her desire to manage the religious development of Keshab and his followers, and to prevent them from being carried away by their own ideas. Her maternal attitude towards Brahmoism is suggestive of the more general ways in which Unitarianism's inclusionary and exclusionary impulses could operate side by side. It was the simplicity and emotional purity of Indians that rendered their ideas worthy of inclusion, even emulation, by Unitarians, but these same qualities excluded Indians from the ability to control fully their religious development.

Although Collet was to turn against Keshab following the Cuch Bihar marriage and would argue vehemently against Keshab's concept of *adesh* (discussed in the following chapter), *The Brahmo Year Book* series prior to 1878 includes no criticisms of his increasing reliance on inspiration as the basis for religious teaching. Collet had defended Keshab's doctrines of inspiration and 'Great Men' in an article of 1870, in which she identified his beliefs as in consonance with 'the spiritual Theism of England and America, as represented by Francis Newman, Theodore Parker, and Miss [Frances Power] Cobbe'.[181] Keshab was a great admirer of Parker's ideas (he later dedicated a 'Pilgrimages to Saints' to him), and there can be no doubt that Keshab's use of the concept of inspiration shared a great affinity with the teachings of American Transcendentalism. Both Parker and Keshab propounded the ideas that the laws of the human spirit were analogous to the laws of matter, that obedience to spiritual law constituted Divine inspiration, that Divine inspiration was universal, and that the more closely one was able to obey spiritual laws, the more one took on the qualities of God.[182]

It certainly seems that the Transcendentalist philosophy of Parker was the primary intellectual schema through which Frances Power Cobbe (herself a follower of Parker) interpreted Keshab's doctrine of inspiration. What united the creeds of Keshab and Parker, in her view, was that they: 'make no pretension whatever to authority or special privileges of any kind, but…merely appeal to the hearts and intellects of their followers, and encourage them to trust to reason and conscience, instead of to the voice of priests or prophets'.[183] Unlike Swedenborgianists and Spiritualists, who believed that 'the visions of their teachers' were 'veritable occurrences', Brahmos and Transcendentalists did not entertain the belief that one member of their church had 'entered into unique relations with the Almighty'.[184] Instead, they both claimed inspiration to be universal, and preached a democratic creed that rejected authoritarianism and placed each individual in a personal relationship with God.

The close affinity between the teachings of Keshab and Parker rendered Keshabite Brahmoism comprehensible to left-leaning Unitarians. While the British press and the evangelical missionaries regarded Keshab's claims to inspirational knowledge as indicative of regression into mysticism, the Unitarians continued to view Keshab's ideas as in accord with those of the most progressive Unitarian thinkers in Britain and America. The Unitarians shared Keshab's desire to achieve a proper balance between 'spiritual' and 'material' aspects of life, and believed firmly in the power of alternative modes of understanding to 'reason'. They did not reject wholesale his critique of rational thinking. In 1877, *The Inquirer* declared that the Brahmo Samaj of India still represented 'The best hope of the future of religion in India'.[185]

Conclusion

Considering the starkness of the way in which Keshab's thought bifurcated the world into a spiritual 'East' and a material 'West', it is not surprising that his attempts to 'live out' his ideas resulted in him living, in effect, a double life during the 1870s. The changes in his views in the 1870s cannot be described adequately in terms of a comprehensive shift in outlook from 'liberalism' to 'culturalism'. While Keshab articulated a discourse of madness as an alternative to the discourse of reason, he took pains to establish that madness conformed to rational standards. While he accorded concepts of motherhood, femininity and the home a particular 'spiritual' importance, he also spiritualised his conception of the imperial family. His attempt to reconcile discourses of liberalism and culturalism within an overarching framework of holistic human progress (occurring over the *longue durée*) suggests that, rather than shifting from liberalism to culturalism, Keshab merely reconfigured his universalism in a way that placed greater emphasis on the subjective dimensions of religious experience.

It may be that the difficulty of subsuming Keshab into conventional periodisations of Bengali history stems from the simple fact that, while broad shifts in thought may be discerned at a regional or global level, concrete historical experience differs at the local and personal level. As Tapan Raychaudhuri has noted with reference to the ideas and activities of Bhudeb Mukhopadhyay, Bankimchandra Chatterjee and Swami Vivekananda, differences in their approach 'reflect the diversity in life experiences and personalities, an important dimension of the concrete historical experience which has not been adequately emphasized in the literature on colonial or pre-colonial India'.[186] Although I do not intend to conduct an investigation into Keshab's psychology, I will suggest that, while the shifts in emphasis apparent in his thought in the 1870s reflected broader shifts in Bengali elite discourse, his changing ideas also stemmed from a deeply personal internal struggle.

The evidence suggests strongly that, in the course of the 1870s and 1880s, Keshab came increasingly to sense that he might be, uniquely, Divinely inspired. At one level, Keshab's advocacy of inspiration and madness can be regarded as building upon the ideas of truth as 'many-sided' that he had propounded in Britain. His belief in the validity of alternative modes of perception to 'reason' was not foreign to Hinduism, Brahmoism, Christianity or Unitarianism. However, at another level, Keshab's advocacy of 'inspiration' served not only to challenge 'Western' epistemological supremacy, but also to convince Keshab of his own special importance in the unfolding of world history.

In his anniversary oration of 1875, Keshab encouraged his audience to disregard his teaching and to seek truth from God, but he claimed also that what he taught was true precisely because it was 'no theory of my own invention'.[187] His teachings, he claimed, were the result of 'spoken' inspiration received directly from God, and bore 'the stamp of the Divine seal'.[188] Indeed, Keshab declared that 'I possess the highest credentials and can cite the very authority of Heaven'.[189] It was this circular argument (which may be summarised crudely as 'I should not be regarded as a prophet because the doctrine I preach has come directly from God') that Keshab would employ to defend himself in his lecture 'Am I an Inspired Prophet?', delivered in 1879 in the aftermath of the Cuch Bihar controversy.[190]

Keshab's charismatic and authoritarian leadership of the New Dispensation in the 1880s, grounded in the doctrine of *adesh*, has most often been interpreted by historians as a cynical attempt to gain followers in the aftermath of the Cuch Bihar controversy, although some scholars have regarded Keshab's behaviour in later life as symptomatic of a nervous breakdown.[191] I find neither of these explanations to be adequate. It is plausible, although speculative, to suggest that Keshab's struggle to lead a double life in the 1870s was resolved ultimately through a subjective transcendence of the bifurcated categories of 'East' and 'West', made possible by the experience of a direct and constant communion with the Divine. There can be no doubt that Keshab's continued search for universal religion in the 1880s would involve his own personal transformation: from reformer, to prophet.

6

THE CUCH BIHAR CRISIS AND THE SEARCH FOR UNIVERSAL RELIGION

In January 1878, Keshab wrote with extraordinary candour in his 'devotional' column in the *Sunday Indian Mirror*. As was his custom in this column, he addressed his words directly to God. His subject on this occasion was Divine inspiration. His words indicate a deep concern that he was coming to believe that his own ideas were of a uniquely Divine origin, and that this belief was a delusion:

> I have strangely got into the habit, O my God, of crediting Thee with all my ideas and plans. I, as Thy servant, ought to follow only Thy commandments, forsaking all that pleases me and adopting whatsoever is agreeable to Thee. But instead of doing this, I strive to follow my own plans and schemes and then ascribe to Thee their authorship. Having come so far in the path of religion, I feel it a humiliation to believe that I am carrying out my own wishes. I would fain believe that in all my doings I only follow Thy leading, and I feel glad when people give me credit for obeying Thy will and sacrificing my own. But as self-sacrifice is a hard thing, and I am carried away by my own ideas, feelings, and tastes, all that I can do is to make myself and others believe that everything I do is the Lord's doing, and that all my purposes are divine purposes. Thus errors and vices in my life become sacred in my estimation in the course of time with the imaginary imprimatur of Thy seal. Lord, deliver me from this delusion.[1]

Shortly after this was published, Keshab announced that his daughter was to be married to the Maharajah of Cuch Bihar. His daughter, Suniti Devi, was thirteen years of age; the Maharajah was fifteen.

The Cuch Bihar Crisis

The controversy surrounding the Cuch Bihar marriage is well documented, and has been the subject of impassioned and lengthy debates conducted by Brahmos and scholars ever since it took place.[2] While commentators have taken a variety of positions regarding the purpose and consequences of the marriage, all have agreed with the view of Keshab's closest disciple, P. C. Majumdar, that the Cuch Bihar marriage 'formed the great turning point of Keshub Chunder Sen's career'.[3] As David Kopf has observed, scholarly accounts of the controversy have tended to 'treat the marriage as a disaster from every point of view'.[4] In Kopf's opinion, while the marriage damaged Keshab's reputation and led to a decrease in membership of the Brahmo Samaj of India, it served to strengthen Keshab's position in a region hitherto outside of his sphere of influence. This line is also taken by Koditschek, who contends that the marriage was a 'strategic concession designed to enhance…[Keshab's] influence in India's more backward, less westernized, native states'.[5] In her study of marriage and modernity in colonial Bengal, Rochona Majumdar treats the Cuch Bihar marriage as an instance of a recurrent tension between secularist marriage reform legislation and the resilience of ritual observances in Hindu weddings.[6] Keshab's Brahmo contemporaries, for the most part, regarded the Cuch Bihar marriage as a fundamental betrayal of Brahmo values and an instance of hypocrisy on the part of Keshab. The fact that Keshab has been relatively neglected in Bengali historiography seems to stem, in part, from the irrevocable damage the marriage controversy did to his reputation.

The initial impetus for the marriage came from the British government, which first approached Keshab with its proposal in August 1877. The British were attempting to strengthen their influence in Cuch Bihar, a princely state that had been subject to British suzerainty since the late eighteenth century, and had fallen under government control since the Maharajah had ascended to the throne at the age of ten months. As the work of Barbara Ramusack and others has shown, while the British eschewed the annexation of princely states, interference in their internal politics was commonplace, ranging from the deposition of rulers, to advice about policies and appointments and to more subtle forms of social engineering.[7] At the behest of the colonial government, the Maharajah had been educated by an English tutor and was to finish his education in England. His marriage to the daughter of a loyal subject of British rule, with close ties to the administration, would secure British influence in a strategically important region, which was at risk from Bhutanese incursions.[8]

Once the marriage had been agreed, the royal household of Cuch Bihar was quick to stipulate that the ceremony should be conducted in accordance with their preferred rites of Hindu 'orthodoxy', as opposed to Brahmo practice. A Hindu marriage was the only condition on which the matriarchs of the family would agree to the government's plans to send the Maharajah to England. As Angma Dey Jhala has demonstrated, royal marriages in the later nineteenth century brokered by the colonial government often resulted in officials becoming 'engaged in a political tug-o-war of compromise with the matriarchs of the zenana'.[9] Suniti Devi's own recollections of the marriage bear witness to the intense pressure under which Keshab was placed by the British negotiators, who frequently made assurances on behalf of the Cuch Bihar household which were not honoured.[10] Keshab submitted numerous conditions in an attempt to secure the conformity of the marriage rites as far as possible to Brahmo practices. In the event, these conditions were not met, and the Brahmo newspaper the *Sunday Indian Mirror* was forced to admit that idols had been present at the marriage and that the *hom* ceremony had been performed in defiance of Keshab's strictures.[11] The official Administration Report of the Cuch Bihar State and the Report on the Administration of Bengal both stated that, despite some concessions to Keshab's party, the marriage was 'recognized by the Hindus as orthodox'.[12]

It is significant that the event that created the greatest controversy in Keshab's entire career was one that revolved around the question of the proper regulation of his daughter's sexuality. The treatment of women had long functioned as a yardstick by which to judge the civilisational status of peoples—a striking example is the way in which the violent treatment of women and the break up of domestic order in the West Indies became central themes in debates concerning the abolition of slavery.[13] Incidences of practices perceived to be particularly cruel towards women—for example, the practice of foot-binding in China, of veiling and clitoridectomy in the Arab world and North Africa, and, in British India, the practice of *sati*—came to function as emblematic of the general 'barbarity' of peoples in a variety of colonial contexts.[14] The reputation of Ram Mohan among reformers in Britain (especially posthumously) was built in large part on his involvement with campaigns against *sati*; much of the reformist enthusiasm for Keshab stemmed from his stance towards polygamy, child marriage and female education. He himself regarded the Marriage Act of 1872 as his greatest achievement, and this piece of legislation garnered a great deal of support in the British press.

In this context, the fact that the Cuch Bihar marriage created so little opposition in the mainstream British press, even though it directly contravened the provisions of the 1872 Act, is worth exploring. The British press, when it devoted any space to the Cuch Bihar marriage, tended to react favourably, accepting, for the most part, the line taken by the government—that the marriage would secure British rule through an enlightened, English-educated Maharajah guided by rational and Theistic principles. Reports tended to sideline (or frequently ignore) the fact that the marriage was underage according to the 1872 Act and had been recognised as 'orthodox'.

From the perspective of the British government, it was crucial that the marriage should take place according to conventions that were recognisably 'orthodox'. Assurances of orthodoxy were required in order to secure the consent of the royal household in Cuch Bihar; also, as the 1872 Act did not apply outside British India, a Brahmo marriage in Cuch Bihar would not have had legal validity.[15] Furthermore, an orthodox marriage would appear to align with post-1857 official policy towards India in general. Following the events of 1857–8, Queen Victoria proclaimed publicly a policy of non-intervention in religious and social practices. Efforts to ameliorate social and moral conditions would now operate through the spread of education, encouraged through the wider availability of government grants to schools organised by Indian communities.

However, as a growing body of scholarship is demonstrating, social and religious intervention on the part of the colonial government did, in fact, persist post-1857, particularly in the area of marriage.[16] As Rachel Sturman writes, 'the customs of marriage formed the grounds for a highly politicized fashioning of intimate life, linked at once to the material and symbolic reproduction of society and to questions of colonial governance'.[17] By arranging an 'orthodox' Hindu marriage between a native prince and the daughter of a well-known, English-educated social reformer, the government could further British interests through dynastic match-making while appearing to adhere to a policy of non-intervention in matters of religious and social practice. Their claim that the marriage would promote the moral uplift of Indians by placing them in the care of an 'emancipated' ruler served to occlude the fact that they were engineering a marriage that contravened the government's own law of 1872 concerning legal marriageable age.

In general, the British press accepted this occlusion. While the *Pall Mall Gazette* expressed opposition to the marriage on the grounds that it was underage, and claimed that the Maharajah was likely to 'indulge in a plurality of wives hereafter', the view of *The Examiner*, which stressed the value of the opportunity presented to conduct an 'experiment of a Hindu ruler emancipated from the narrow superstitions of Hinduism', was more commonly taken.[18] The *Bristol Mercury*, which devoted sustained coverage to Keshab during his visit to England in 1870, frequently citing him as a champion of the abolition of early marriage, declared that the government was 'worthy of all honour' and that the marriage would 'mark an epoch in the social history of India'.[19] The age of the marrying parties was bypassed altogether, suggesting that, in this instance, the extension of British rule and the wider social good that would result was of greater import than a single early marriage. Notices of a telegram expressing Queen Victoria's congratulations to Keshab on the occasion of the marriage were widely circulated.[20]

The bride herself was notable by her absence from reports on the marriage, which focused instead on the involvement of eminent members of government, the favourable response of the Queen, and the good characters of the Maharajah and Keshab. The *Bristol Mercury*'s announcement of the marriage reads as if the only two parties involved in the 'alliance'—'proposed' and 'sanctioned' by the government—are

Keshab and Prince Nripendra Narayan, both of whom can be relied upon as men of good character: 'He [the Maharajah] is an eminently amiable and teachable person, and it is fairly to be anticipated that his alliance with a man like Keshub Chunder Sen will tend immensely to the enlightenment and moral improvement of his country'.[21] Any anxiety concerning the age of the marrying parties is alleviated—or, indeed, eclipsed—by the knowledge that Keshab is a civilised man of reputation, and that the young Maharajah is also a subject who is, or can become, civilised and respectable. Representations of Keshab circulating widely during his visit in 1870, which portrayed him as embodying a very 'English' form of 'manliness', clearly had left a lasting impression. What was not noted was that Keshab's 'manly' image in 1870 had rested in large part upon admiration for his 'enlightened' principles regarding women and Hindu 'orthodoxy', principles which were now compromised by the very same marriage the image was being used to justify.

The importance of Keshab's reputation as a 'civilised' subject in gaining support for the marriage in the British press is made apparent further when the response to Cuch Bihar is considered alongside the sensational and highly-publicised scandals concerning early marriage that were to occupy the attention of the British press in the 1880s. Of these scandals, the case to generate the greatest degree of public interest and disapproval was the trial of Rukhmabai, which has been viewed by historians of Indian culture and society as one of the precursors to the Age of Consent Act of 1891—legislation that raised the age of consent for girls (including married girls) from ten to twelve.[22] In 1884, Dadaji Bhikaji petitioned the Bombay High Court to direct that his wife Rukhmabai, who had married him as a child but had lived apart from him for over a decade, take up residence with him. The case was initially dismissed in 1885, but was later taken up again, culminating in 1887 when the courts ruled in favour of Dadaji, ordering Rukhmabai to move into his house or face six months imprisonment.[23] The case caused a storm of controversy in India and in Britain, partly because the Matrimonial Causes Act had removed such penal provisions for English spouses in 1884.[24]

Antoinette Burton, in her persuasive study of the Rukhmabai trial, argues that the late Victorian press 'made public' the body of an Indian woman as evidence of the necessity of British imperial rule at the same time that the Indian National Congress emerged as an expression of Indian political will in the metropolitan public eye. Burton contends that 'Implicit in this public display of the Hindu child bride was the argument that by virtue of their incapacity to protect—or manage—a recalcitrant wife, Indian men were as yet unfit for self-government'.[25] Dadaji became subject to intense personal attacks in the British press, being characterised variously as 'vulgar', 'idle' and an 'ignorant and degraded peasant', despite his protestations that he was, in fact, a man of considerable property and education.[26] If Rukhmabai came to function as emblematic of the oppressed condition of women in India in general, then Dadaji symbolised the ineffective and uncivilised nature of Indian men. In contrast, Keshab's image as respectable, educated and pious—a model 'civilised subject'—allowed the early marriage in which he had participated to function as symbolic of the possibility of the moral uplift of Indians, as opposed to emblematic of the limits of their transformative capacity. While child marriages were commonly understood at this time to contribute to the enervation and degradation of the Indian 'race' (and, by extension, the strength of the British empire), the Cuch Bihar marriage—understood as an 'alliance' between two respectable men, brokered by the government—could signify the possibilities of Indian amelioration as opposed to degradation.

While the memory of the respectable image Keshab created in 1870 was no doubt important in garnering the support of most of the British press for the Cuch Bihar marriage, it would be wrong to suggest that the images of respectable Keshab and 'vulgar' Dadaji were all that differentiated the two cases. The political and dynastic character of the Cuch Bihar marriage was, of course, a critical factor in garnering public support, particularly considering that royal marriages often involved a degree of religious and cultural compromise in the interests of building alliances. Furthermore, the degree of public sympathy generated for Rukhmabai was also due to the fact that early marriage gained much greater recognition as a 'problem' worthy of British public interest in the 1880s than in the 1870s. This was due to the coincidence of the Rukhmabai trial with a number of metropolitan cases which generated a moral panic concerning the regulation of female sexuality—the "Maiden Tribute of Modern Babylon" series concerning child prostitution in Britain published in the *Pall Mall Gazette* in 1885, the highly-publicised divorce proceedings of Sir Charles Dilke's alleged mistress, the repeal of the Contagious Diseases Acts in 1886 following the successful campaign led by Josephine Butler, and the implementation of the Criminal Law Amendment Act of 1885, which raised the age of consent for females in Britain from thirteen to sixteen.[27] As Philippa Levine has demonstrated, imperial concerns contributed to anxiety about prostitution and venereal disease in many of these cases, due to the high incidence of venereal disease among soldiers in the empire.[28]

However, while it would take the confluence of these metropolitan cases with the sensational Rukhmabai trial to make early marriage in India a subject of national public interest in Britain, child marriage had long been a concern of the reformist, Nonconformist and Unitarian circles with whom Keshab was in contact. For them, the Cuch Bihar marriage was nothing less than a sensation and an outrage. British social reformers had long regarded early marriage as a source of cultural stagnation in India and thus as an appropriate site of imperial intervention.[29] It was Mary Carpenter who was responsible largely for generating interest in the issue among Victorian feminists from the late 1860s onwards with the publication of her hugely successful *Six Months in India*. [30] This referred frequently to the 'degraded' condition of Indian women, articulated the Orientalist equation between 'heathen' religion and early marriage, and numbered among the consequences of early marriage a lack of opportunities for education and an inability to provide adequate maternal care for children.[31] As Burton has argued, Carpenter's 'determination to improve Indian women's status was bound up with a desire to manage the bodies of Indian girls by diverting them from immediate marriage into professional occupations—a route toward improvement and "uplift" that brought them, from the 1870s onward, under the discipline of professional, Western female-supervised teacher training and that had as its ultimate goal the preservation of Indian women's procreative capacities inside the ideal of adult companionate marriage'.[32] For Carpenter, and for many others within the Nonconformist, Unitarian and reformist circles who followed Keshab's activities, the issue of early marriage thus brought together a number of key concerns: the 'problem' of women in India, the deplorable effects of Hinduism, the health of the Indian 'race' and the necessity for Western intervention.

Carpenter died a year before the Cuch Bihar marriage, but it seems safe to assume that her views on the event would have aligned broadly with those of Keshab's closest ally in Britain, Sophia Dobson Collet. Collet, more than any other figure, had been responsible for introducing Keshab to the British public before and during his visit to England, and had remained one of his most ardent champions throughout the 1870s. She was deeply shocked to hear of the 1878 marriage, and regarded it as a dreadful betrayal by a close friend. Collet had tried to encourage equilibrium between the cultivation of the objective and subjective aspects of religion in the Brahmo Samaj, but the marriage proved to her that this attempt had failed. Her concern had arisen 'two or three years ago', when 'Mr. Sen's increasing absorption in religious meditation began to draw away his attention and sympathy from other departments of Brahmic life'.[33] She pointed out that Majumdar, writing in 1877, had warned of the disastrous effect that would result if 'the valuable agencies of life, thought, and feeling imparted from the West...are suffered to grow feeble and inoperative...there is not much doubt that this result will follow, unless we combine the spirit of the East and the West in all our endeavours'.[34] In Collet's view, it was the spirit of the 'East' that had come to preponderate, and 'alas! the reactionary wave has carried away even the thinker who uttered the warning'.[35]

The decline of the Samaj's educational institutions and the discontinuance of the government grant-in-aid to the Brahmo Normal School in 1878 were evidence that 'the once energetic and enterprising "Brahmo Somaj of India" gradually declined from its original position, both in theory and practice'.[36] Collet castigated Keshab for his hypocrisy in sanctioning an early and 'heathen' marriage, and accused him of '*ignoring reality*' in the course he took—this total ignoring of reality perhaps the final consequence of an increasingly inwardly directed spiritual quest.[37] Collet rejected the self-effacing arguments Keshab advanced in 1879 in his lecture 'Am I an Inspired Prophet?', and described him in *The Brahmo Year Book* of 1879 as tending 'more and more towards the consolidation of a spiritual autocracy'.[38] As we shall see, Collet opposed Keshab vociferously throughout the 1880s, regarding him as an autocrat, a blasphemer and, ultimately, a madman.

However, the shock of Keshab's defection from the Unitarian social gospel and apparent embrace of autocratic spiritual mysticism did not in any way shake Collet's belief in the bright future that lay ahead for the 'Brahmo Samaj' (by which she now meant the Sadharan Brahmo Samaj—see below). The commitment of the Sadharan Brahmos to constitutional church government, liberal social reform and female education aligned directly with Collet's belief in a liberal Unitarian social gospel. Collet disassociated Keshab from the Brahmo movement as a whole, which, in her eyes, had never swerved from the path of progress: 'That the Brahmo Samaj was expanding and advancing, while Mr. Sen was standing still or going backward, has been evident to me for the last two or three years'.[39] Collet lamented that Keshab had suffered the decline that often befalls 'once-brilliant public men', and stated that 'I mourn his retrogression from his former self'.[40] The 'Keshab' of 1870—'his former self'—was the Keshab that Collet regarded as the 'real' Keshab; it was this 'Keshab' that she had attempted to protect from the dangers of asceticism and spiritual intoxication. But the 'former self' had proved too fragile to walk the delicate line between the spiritual and the material aspects of religion.

The Inquirer was less hasty in its condemnation of Keshab than Collet, preferring to reserve judgement on Keshab's actions until he produced a defence of them. When the *Indian Mirror* published a defence in May 1878 (albeit not authored by Keshab) that justified the marriage primarily on the grounds that it was the product of Divine command or *adesh*, *The Inquirer* declared itself immediately to be 'entirely converted' to the views of Collet.[41] The editorial focused on the defence of the marriage on irrational grounds, as opposed to the actual marriage, as the greatest source of outrage, and suggested that Keshab's invocation of *adesh* was insincere: 'Mr. Sen is much too able a man to deceive himself with this sort of cant. When a person of unimpeachable character does something that is particularly indefensible…. [they] in unctuous tones assert that "all is ordered by Providence."…we had thought that Mr. Sen occupied an infinitely higher plane'.[42] It was Keshab's justification of the marriage on the grounds of *adesh* that also generated the greatest degree of consternation among other elements of the religious press in Britain. Echoing comments made by the conservative Anglican publication *The*

Record, The Free Church of Scotland Monthly Record proclaimed that Brahmoism had been claiming for itself a higher authority than the Gospel, and had thus become an 'inflated bladder' that would 'burst by-and-by'.[43] The 'glory of having a royal son-in-law' had led Keshab to 'act cruelly towards his daughter' and to 'violate both the law of society and his own conscience'.[44] There was no doubt that the Samaj's influence was 'destroyed'.[45]

In the Calcutta press, the marriage created a storm of controversy. Child marriage, practiced by the higher castes in India since the Christian era, had become widespread in the nineteenth century, and its reform became the subject of debate among Indian reformers as they responded to missionary criticisms of the custom in the early nineteenth century. Many of these debates concerned the question of whether evidence of its sanction in sacred law was outweighed by descriptions of adult marriages in the Vedas.[46] Attempts to reform legislation in order to abolish the custom began in the 1850s with Vidyasagar, whose efforts led the government to include an age of consent provision in the Penal Code of 1860, making sexual intercourse with a girl under ten qualify as rape.[47] The custom of early marriage had, by the 1870s, become a characteristic concern among a variety of nationalists, who, as Burton has argued, 'critiqued the Hindu marriage system…even as they placed it at the heart of their socio-cultural struggle against Western values and influences'.[48] Early marriage was thus an issue of intense interest among reformers and nationalists of a variety of stamps in the 1870s, and arguably no one had done more to stimulate this interest than Keshab himself, with his successful (if limited) reform of the custom in 1872.

As Keshab's reputation in Calcutta was inextricably linked with his efforts to improve the condition of women and to reform marriage customs, it is unsurprising that the Cuch Bihar marriage caused a sensation, and a certain degree of disbelief. According to the vast majority of commentators, Keshab had placed himself in a position of patent and indefensible hypocrisy. According to Collet, the *Indian Daily News*, *Indian Church Gazette*, *Indian Tribune*, the *East*, the *Dacca Prakash* and the *Subodha Patrika* all formed part of the 'almost unanimous consensus of opinion against Mr. Sen, both as to the marriage itself, and the plea of *Adesh*…set up in its defence'.[49] *The Friend of India* initially withheld judgement, but subsequently stated vigorously its opposition to the fact that the marriage had been underage, and that Keshab had defended it on the grounds of *adesh*: 'The Brahmo leader…appears to have reached that unfortunate stage in the history of some prophets, when they receive special revelations to sanction their own irregularities; and the marriage itself affords less ground for questioning his fitness to remain at the head of the community than the very dangerous doctrine he has advanced in his defence'.[50] Suniti Devi later recalled that 'most of my father's followers had raised objections to the marriage…some of them even went so far as to threaten to kill him'.[51]

Opposition to the marriage was led by members of the *Samadarshi* faction, who had been opposed throughout the 1870s to Keshab's increasingly authoritarian style of leadership, his doctrine of *adesh* and his reverence for 'Great Men'. They broke formally with the Brahmo Samaj of India as a consequence of the marriage, and instituted the Sadharan Brahmo Samaj on 15 May 1878. The *Samalachak* and *Brahmo Public Opinion*, both established in early 1878, published a stream of articles condemning the marriage. Keshab was criticised for sanctioning a marriage that was underage and idolatrous, and for defending it on the basis of *adesh*—a defence that confirmed his pretensions to spiritual autocracy.[52] *Brahmo Public Opinion* claimed that God could not have countenanced the marriage, as it was idolatrous, and that Keshab's claim of *adesh* was thus 'either deluded or deceitful'.[53] While Brahmos accepted a doctrine of *adesh* which also recognised *nishedh* (the prohibition of certain forms of conduct), *adesh* without *nishedh* was a doctrine 'invented only very recently, to justify the conduct of Babu K. C. Sen'.[54] This distinction between the two forms of the doctrine was drawn in a statement issued by the Sadharan Brahmo Samaj following a public meeting in May 1878: 'We consider it a blasphemy…to claim Divine inspiration for any act opposed to the dictates of reason, truth, and morality'.[55] Inspiration without reason was contrary to moral law, and tended towards 'uncontrolled authority by a single individual'; when this individual was looked upon as 'a link between God and Man', the principles of Theism were violated.[56] Keshab's 'intermediary doctrine' and pretensions to be a 'special kind of man' were denigrated in the *Tattwabodhini Patrika* and *Tattwa Koumudi*, and the 'blind faith' of his remaining followers was denounced as an 'utter embarrassment'.[57]

The Sadharan Brahmo Samaj was set up on a constitutional basis and emphasised the need for liberal social reform and rational religion.

In sanctioning the Cuch Bihar marriage, Keshab effectively contradicted many of his strongest beliefs as expressed throughout the 1860s and 1870s, contravened his greatest legislative achievement as a reformer (the 1872 Act), and betrayed—in the eyes of many—the fundamental principles of progressive Brahmoism. His reputation among the vast majority of like-minded religious and social reformers in Britain was ruined, and the membership of the Brahmo Samaj of India was reduced considerably. Reportedly, fifty provincial Samajes sided with the Sadharan Brahmo Samaj in opposition to his actions.[58] According to *Tattwa Koumudi*, all of Keshab's committee members, with the exception of P. C. Majumdar and Narendranath Sen, deserted his organisation.[59] The schism was bitter and the actions of both parties— including the publication of numerous scurrilous pamphlets criticising the moral character of Brahmo leaders on both sides, anonymous letters written to the government accusing Keshab of misappropriating the funds of the Cuch Bihar treasury, and a physical confrontation at the Brahmo Mandir which ended with the police being called—made the usually respectable and earnest Brahmos the objects of considerable public derision.[60] As Majumdar recalls, the controversy caused Keshab to fall into a deep depression: he refused to answer the calls or read the protests of those demanding an explanation for his actions; he became increasingly paranoid and 'talked wildly of the dangers to his Church, the bitter animosities and ill-treatment which dogged him'.[61] In Meredith Borthwick's opinion, Keshab suffered a 'nervous breakdown'.[62]

Why did Keshab agree to a marriage that caused him so much public and personal distress? In her study of women and law in colonial India, Janaki Nair suggests that Keshab's agreement to the marriage can be seen as an instance of 'the gap between public (political) and private positions of reformers such as Roy, Sen or Ranade, [which] was one of the persistent ironies of the process of social reform, and was an expression of the contradictions inherent in the colonial social order'.[63] According to this reading, Keshab agreed to the marriage because his private attitude towards child marriage was distinctly less 'reformist' than the views he expressed publicly, and he chose, in this instance, to follow his private as opposed to his public convictions. While there can be no doubt that Keshab's private attitudes towards women were in a process of transition in the 1870s, the evidence suggests that he did not eschew his public duties in favour of his private beliefs, but, in fact, did quite the opposite.

In my view, Keshab's willingness to agree to the marriage stemmed from the intense pressure under which he was placed by the British government, and from his unswerving faith in the Providential nature of British rule in India. As Majumdar recalls, 'He fervently believed… that the representatives of the British Government could never deceive him'.[64] Keshab wrote later to Max Müller that his agreement to the marriage had stemmed from a combination of his conviction that the marriage was Providential, and his duty to place public good before individual interests: 'I saw the finger of God in all the arrangements, trials and struggles in connection with the marriage… A whole kingdom was to be reformed, and all my individual interests were absorbed in the vastness of God's saving economy, or in what people would call public good'.[65] In a letter to Frances Power Cobbe of 29 April 1878, Keshab acknowledged that, in deciding whether to sanction the marriage, he was forced to choose between his 'private' and 'public' selves:

> I never sought a Raja. I never coveted filthy lucre. As a private man I should not probably have acted as I have done. But I was acting all along as a public man… [The proposal would] help forward the good work so gloriously begun in that State by our benevolent rulers in the interests of millions of the subject population… You have justly said that a grave responsibility would have rested upon me if I had refused the overtures of the Government…I have acted as a public man under the imperative call of a public duty. All other considerations were subordinated to this sacred duty. All other considerations were subordinated to this sacred call, this Divine injunction.[66]

Surprisingly, Keshab's letter to Cobbe was the only 'public' (in that he intended it to be published for English audiences) defence he made of the marriage in the 1870s. The evidence does not provide any clear explanation as to why he refused to defend himself publicly in Calcutta or to write to any journals or newspapers himself in Britain, but chose instead to write only to an Englishwoman he had met briefly during his time in Britain. Keshab knew, perhaps, that Cobbe would be sympathetic—she wrote a defence of him in *Christian Life*, March 1878, arguing that he had been forced to compromise his principles in the interest of the wider social good. The motivations behind Keshab's public silence on the Cuch Bihar marriage, considering the scale of the controversy, remain something of a mystery.

The defence Keshab puts forward in the letter draws upon familiar tropes among religious and social reformers of the period of personal sacrifice in the name of duty. Keshab had sacrificed his private beliefs in order to further the public good. What is striking is the elision of the 'public' and the 'sacred': as the British government was guided by Providence, so its requests become Divine injunctions. Nair may be right to suggest that the difference between public and private positions of Indian reformers expressed contradictions inherent in the colonial social order—as we have seen, in his domestic life, Keshab struggled to resolve his roles as a 'native gentleman' and an urban guru. However, in the Cuch Bihar case, it was Keshab's private position that remained the more 'reformist' (at least according to what 'reformist' meant for progressive Brahmos and Keshab's Nonconformist and Unitarian allies in Britain) and his public position (necessitated by his relationship to the colonial authorities) that appeared 'conservative'. Nair's formulation suggests that the opposite was usually the case.

Keshab's elision of the public and the sacred complicates accounts of Indian nationalism which regard nationalism as first forging a domestic, 'spiritual domain', before entering the realms of the political. For Keshab, the political was precisely the 'spiritual'—the unfolding of history, and the crucial role played in it by the Providentially sanctioned British empire, constituted an expression of God's will. The great difficulty for Keshab, was that his private beliefs (and his 'inner' spiritual development) and his public duties (to the external world) were both sacred. In the 1860s and 1870s, Keshab's commitment and approach to the amelioration of women in India had been applauded by the government and at times directly furthered through legislation; the direct alignment between the reformist goals of the Brahmo Samaj of India and the desire of the British authorities and people had been confirmed, in Keshab's eyes, during his visit in 1870. By 1878, on the key principle of early marriage, the progressive Brahmo and British government positions were in direct opposition. Keshab had to conform to government requests as they had Divine sanction, but the requests contradicted the reformist and religious principles he held on the basis of rational enquiry. Keshab could not find a rational argument that would synthesise this opposition. Already experiencing severe tension between opposing modes of thought and modes of life in the 1870s, and turning increasingly to inspiration to resolve them, Keshab was faced in 1878 with the starkest possible choice between his private and public lives, his position as an 'Indian' and as a 'man of the world', his reputation as an Indian reformer and a loyal British subject. In the end it was *adesh* rather than reason to which he turned in order to make the choice.

As we have seen, Suniti Devi herself remained absent from reports on the marriage in the British press. However, she would go on to write her own memoir in 1921—the first published by an Indian woman in English. The memoir demonstrates that Suniti was keenly aware, at least in retrospect, of the government's machinations in attempting to secure Keshab's agreement to the marriage. She recalls that the negotiators were 'clever enough to understand that they must discover my father's weak point and work upon it'.[67] Keshab had refused the advances of the government officials repeatedly, going so far as to insist that Suniti was 'neither very pretty nor highly educated'.[68] It was the government's assurance that the marriage would enable Keshab to bring social and religious reform to Cuch Bihar, along with their insistence that the marriage would merely constitute a 'betrothal', that eventually persuaded Keshab to agree. His agreement was obtained, however, under intense pressure. He was warned, in a letter of January 1878, that the alliance would take place 'now or never'.[69]

Throughout all of the negotiations, Suniti was kept in the dark. She was informed that she was to be married to a Maharajah just hours before she was introduced to Mr Dalton, a British official acting as the Maharajah's advisor, who had come to assess in person whether or not she would make a suitable bride. Upon hearing the news, she recalls that she 'became quite red in the face' and hid in her pillow, after which she was prescribed a strong dose of quinine.[70] In order to assess her suitability, she was instructed to perform a piano solo for a number of officials in the family drawing room, all the while subject to Mr Dalton's 'kind but critical' gaze.[71] Angma Dey Jhala has noted how this encounter 'reveals the growing presence of colonial officials in arranging the political marriages of courtly Indian families during the nineteenth and twentieth centuries as part of a larger expansionist project of "civilizing", reforming and "anglicizing" Indian princes'.[72] Suniti became intensely aware of the political and cultural responsibilities entailed by her marriage, reflecting that 'it was left for me to prove the success or failure of the first Indian marriage which had defied traditional custom'.[73]

While Suniti was aware of the political and dynastic character of the marriage, she does not recall the event in her memoir in terms of expansionist alliances forged between the colonial government and a princely state. For her, she insists, the Maharajah was simply 'the fairy prince in my romance'.[74] Surrounded by noise, crowds and music during her journey to the royal household, she admits to having felt like 'a very scared miserable little girl'.[75] However, she was uplifted when she heard the 'gentle whistle' of the Maharajah approaching, which reminded her that 'in the darkness there was a cheery companion who loved me and wanted my love'.[76] Her brief period residing at the royal residence was a trying time, as she was subjected incessantly to the palace ladies' injunctions to become a Hindu. However, the Maharajah soon departed for England and she returned home, where she 'fell to wondering whether the past few weeks had been a dream or not'.[77] She recollects her married life as a blissful one, living in unity with a 'perfect husband', and taking pleasure in the extensive travels and social occasions necessitated by her royal position.[78] She enjoyed sitting for photographic portraits (Fig. x). Her sister, Sucharu, would marry the Maharajah of Mayurbhanj in 1904, and in later generations numerous women in the Sen family would marry into a variety of royal households.[79]

Undoubtedly, the Cuch Bihar marriage was very much a public and political affair, and was in many respects characteristic of increasing British attempts to intervene in courtly Indian affairs in the later nineteenth century. Public and private relations between the Cuch Bihar household and the British royal family remained close, with Queen Victoria stepping in to become the godmother of Suniti Devi's son in 1888.[80] A Brahmo Mandir was established in the capital of Cuch Bihar, although not until 1886.[81] However, while the demands of public duty and social reform had been at the forefront of Keshab's mind when he

Fig. x   Photographic portrait of Suniti Devi, Maharani of
Cuch Bihar, 1893.

agreed to the marriage, the Cuch Bihar alliance did not, in fact, lead
Keshab to eschew the cultivation of the subjective side of religion and
launch once more into a program of social reform. Rather, the opposite
was the case. The marriage had led to a significant decrease in the
membership of the Brahmo Samaj of India, with most of the educated
middle-class members leaving the organisation. Keshab's public
reputation was severely damaged and his influence greatly reduced. This
reduction in membership led the core of Keshab's Brahmo Samaj to
assume increasingly the form of a close-knit community of devoted
followers, with Keshab functioning as the central charismatic leader.[82]

Shortly before the marriage, Keshab had purchased Lily Cottage, a large mansion that became his residence from November 1877. In early 1878, a project was initiated to provide the Brahmo missionaries and their families with homes on the Cottage grounds. This neighbourhood was consecrated as *Mangal Bari* (Abode of Welfare) in January 1879. The missionaries were Keshab's most loyal followers (with the exception of Bijoy Krishna Goswami, they all sided with him in 1878) and they formed the nucleus of adherents to the New Dispensation, an organisation over which Keshab would assume an increasingly authoritarian control.[83]

The New Dispensation

During the period following the marriage until the end of his life, Keshab devoted himself to giving theological, practical and institutional form to a new kind of eclectic faith, known as the *Naba Bidhan* or Church of the New Dispensation. While Keshab did not formally announce the inauguration of the New Dispensation until 1881 (thus breaking finally with the Brahmo name), he began to use the term frequently in his orations after the Cuch Bihar controversy. Majumdar notes that Keshab had used the term 'New Dispensation' in sermons in 1874 and 1875; however, the idea of the New Dispensation as a comprehensive and distinct religion was not promulgated extensively until after Cuch Bihar. In Majumdar's view, the marriage controversy acted as a catalyst for Keshab to announce his views with greater radicalism and force, without fear of offending Brahmo opinion: 'He threw off every reserve, and boldly differentiated. He announced the New Dispensation with deliberate formalism and sacramental solemnity'.[84] Keshab recognised that he had been changed deeply by the events of 1878, asking in one of his conversations with God in October 1879 the question as to whether he was a Christian, a Hindu or a Brahmo, and receiving the reply: *'Thou art none of these… Those who knew thee yesterday know thee not today'*.[85] The Cuch Bihar marriage had forced Keshab to compromise or to contradict many of the principles that were central to progressive Brahmoism. As his reputation had been so irrevocably damaged as a consequence, he needed to reinvent himself, and to propose a decidedly 'new' vision which would enable him to establish the 'grand universal cathedral' he had envisioned in 1870.[86]

In discussing the New Dispensation, it is neither my intention to provide an exhaustive history of the movement, nor to cover comprehensively the extraordinary variety of theological, practical, ceremonial and philosophical innovations that took place during its short history under Keshab's leadership.[87] My aim, rather, is to examine some of its most striking aspects, and to relate these to broader social, cultural and political developments in Bengal and Britain in the period. In addition, I wish to lay particular emphasis on the ways in which the New Dispensation enabled Keshab and his adherents to 'perform'— subjectively, symbolically and theatrically—an ideal of unity of 'East' and 'West' which was dislocated increasingly from the social and political realities of Calcutta. Through his 'performance' of an ideal of unity, Keshab adopted a number of new and striking modes of self-representation that reveal the extent to which he no longer felt 'at home' in either Britain or India. We will approach the New Dispensation by considering in turn the three main purposes of the organisation as described by its adherents: that it was to be a 'universal religion', a 'national religion' and an 'apostolical religion'.[88]

The New Dispensation as 'Universal Religion'

The universalism of the New Dispensation differed from the universalism of prior forms of Brahmoism in that it constituted an attempt not only to discover the essential truths common to all religions (as had been a central objective of Ram Mohan), but also to create a system of faith that unified and superseded all prior religious 'dispensations'. While Brahmoism had attempted previously to strip away the additions and corruptions which had obscured the 'pure' monotheism of early Hinduism (and of religions in general), the New Dispensation was an attempt to create something new—to bring all faiths into creative synthesis through the establishment of a new religion.[89] Keshab was keen to impress the public with the notion that the New Dispensation was a religion of world-historical significance, of equal or greater significance to all prior faiths. He presented it as 'a Divine dispensation…fully entitled to take its place among the various dispensations of the world', and argued that the events in which he was taking a lead would 'be written and embodied in history'.[90] He described the new religion as an 'evolution' of previous faiths, each of which had necessitated the next. It was the 'logical' next step in an evolutionary sequence of Christ, Moses and Paul, and constituted the 'fulfilment of Moses', and 'Christ's prophecy fulfilled'.[91] The universalism of the New Dispensation was based on 'harmony': it constituted 'science and faith harmonized'; it effected 'the harmony of all scriptures and prophets and dispensations. It is not an isolated creed, but the science which binds and explains and harmonizes all religions'.[92] It was not merely another religion that would co-exist with the other religions of the world; rather, it synthesised and thus transcended all prior world religions.

This emphasis on synthesis and transcendence shows clearly the influence of American Transcendentalism on Keshab's new religious project. We can recall that Keshab's friend Charles Dall had ensured that thousands of copies of the works of Channing, Emerson and Parker were circulated among the Brahmos from the late 1850s. There can be no doubt that Keshab's belief in a new faith that would synthesise and transcend all others had much in common with the ideas and hopes of the American Transcendentalists. As Arthur Versluis has written of American Transcendentalists as a whole, 'All believed in the intuitive human ability to grasp the essences of all the world's religions, and all…believed that humanity was on the verge of a new religious understanding, one that could make sense of all traditions at once, an "age of the Spirit"'.[93] For both Keshab and the Transcendentalists, this age of the spirit would be the result of a modern, progressive and scientific religious 'evolution' stimulated by comparative religious scholarship and individual intuitional insight.

The language of 'dispensations', while originating in Quakerism, may also have reached Keshab through American influences. As Edward Cutler has noted, most mid-nineteenth century Spiritualist publications announced the advent of '"modern manifestations," a "new era," or a "new dispensation"'; this language signalled a sense of 'immanence' and 'historical culmination' which Keshab certainly embraced.[94] However, there is nothing to suggest that Keshab shared the Spiritualist interest in contacting the dead via mediums, although the Theosophist

H. P. Blavatsky did compare Keshab to a Spiritualist medium in her Theosophical journal, and claimed that Spiritualists themselves had made such comparisons.[95]

The universalism of the New Dispensation was characterised by a renewed emphasis on the need to draw upon religious influences outside the Hindu and Christian traditions. If a major part of the project of the Brahmo Samaj of India had been to bring into a productive relationship 'Western' Christianity and the 'Hindu' tradition (this was certainly how Keshab presented it to British audiences in 1870), then the New Dispensation aimed not only to reconcile and transcend Hinduism and Christianity, but to bring all world religions into harmony, and to produce humans who were truly 'men of the world'. Keshab had utilised texts from religions other than Hinduism and Christianity previously— indeed, his willingness to look outside Hinduism for religious inspiration was a major factor in the break between the Brahmo Samaj of India and the more 'nativist' Brahmoism of Debendranath Tagore and Rajnarain Bose in 1866. Nevertheless, it is worth emphasising that, in the context of an increasingly powerful 'Hindu revivalist' sentiment in Bengal that was evident from the 1870s, the New Dispensation constituted a bold restatement of universalist principles.

In his work on the New Dispensation, Brian Hatcher goes to great lengths to establish the fact that Keshab's universalist methodology during the 1880s was 'eclectic' as opposed to 'syncretic'. In Hatcher's view, 'syncretism names a historical process, while eclecticism names a method of interpretation and appropriation'.[96] As Julius Lipner has pointed out, this distinction is not unproblematic, as 'surely "syncretic" processes of historical religious change are constituted, in various circumstances, by conscious selection and appropriation, namely, by eclectic agency'.[97] Hatcher's point, however, is that all religions are 'syncretic': religions are culturally constructed and derive their content from a variety of precedents. A given religion will have emerged through a syncretic historical process of change, but this religion may then be actively and consciously reconstructed and changed through the 'method' of eclecticism. While eclecticism and syncretism both operate through processes of selection, what distinguishes syncretism is 'the additional feature of reconciliation… Syncretism involves blending, synthesizing, or harmonizing'.[98]

It is true that Keshab often referred to the 'eclecticism' of the New Dispensation, but he invoked equally often the language of 'blending, synthesizing, or harmonizing' that Hatcher associates with 'syncretism'.[99] Keshab's religious efforts in the 1880s cannot, in fact, be defined exclusively by the terms 'eclecticism' or 'syncretism'. They were directed both towards the 'conscious selection' of elements from diverse orthodoxies that provided alternative perspectives on truth, and also the 'synthesis' of these elements to forge a distinctive and new faith which harmonised and superseded the elements out of which it was forged. As we shall see, the New Dispensation aimed at both the eradication and preservation of difference.

Panikkar's distinction between 'democratic' and 'aristocratic' eclecticism, which Hatcher also employs, is a useful tool in understanding the methods of the New Dispensation. 'Democratic' eclecticism operates through the discovery of truths that are common to all of the orthodoxies: this method is characteristic of Ram Mohan, Brahmoism prior to Keshab, and Unitarianism.[100] Panikkar labels this variety of eclecticism 'minimalist'—that is, it is a variety of eclecticism which operates through subtraction: the aim is to strip away disagreements between orthodoxies and to find the points on which all religions agree according to the principles of reason. 'Aristocratic' eclecticism, by contrast, may be regarded as 'maximalist'—that is, it operates through addition: as there is truth in all religions, the aim is not to eradicate the differences between faiths in order to discover points of agreement, but to find in divergent orthodoxies a variety of perspectives which illuminate religious experience in multiform ways.[101] This form of eclecticism can be seen as characteristic of the Vedantic version of modern Hindu eclecticism, represented pre-eminently by Vivekananda and Radhakrishnan.[102]

Although they did not employ the terminology, the Unitarians in England certainly regarded the difference between 'democratic' and 'aristocratic' eclecticism as the key difference between their own beliefs and those of the New Dispensation. Keshab's pronouncements on eclecticism prompted *The Inquirer* to print a leading article on the subject, defined as 'one great need of the present age'.[103] For the Unitarians, the principle of eclecticism was based upon an ability to discriminate rationally between various forms of religious doctrine, recognising both points of agreement on 'underlying principle', and also points of divergence in matters of 'dogma'.[104] *The Inquirer* rejected the alternative principle of eclecticism propounded by the New Dispensation, which stated that 'Our position is not that there are truths in all religions, but that all the established religions of the world are true'.[105] For the Unitarians, the latter principle contradicted clearly the principles of reason, without which there was no criterion according to which the 'truth' of religion could be established.

In adopting an 'aristocratic' approach to religious universalism through the New Dispensation, Keshab departed significantly from the views he had expressed during his visit to England. In England, Keshab had adopted the position of Ram Mohan in arguing that both Christianity and Hinduism had once existed in a 'pure' monotheistic form. This original monotheism had later been corrupted by a polytheism evidenced in Hinduism by the prevalence of idolatry and in Christianity by the doctrine of the Trinity. Keshab attacked the prevalence of idolatry in Hinduism and the practices of baptism and the Eucharist in Christianity.[106] In contrast, idolatry, baptism, the Eucharist and the doctrine of the Trinity were all embraced by the New Dispensation. Embraced, that is, in a symbolic and radically altered form. Idolatry, for instance, was reinterpreted not as indicative of polytheism, but as symbolic of 'millions of broken fragments of God'— as a way of apprehending the one God's many-sided reality and living presence.[107] The Trinity was conceived in historical as opposed to theological terms: the kingdom of the 'Father' had been established through Ram Mohan's protest against idolatry; the kingdom of the 'Son' had been established in 1866, when Keshab broke with the Adi Brahmo Samaj, which refused to honour Jesus and Christianity; the kingdom of the 'Holy Ghost' had been established through the doctrine of Divine inspiration.[108] Keshab claimed repeatedly that his extensive use of ritual, and his profession of the utility of idolatry and the doctrine of the Trinity, did not represent a change in his fundamental belief in a single and monotheistic faith. However, there can be no doubt that they constituted a radical departure from his beliefs of 1870, and are indicative of a transition from 'democratic' to 'aristocratic' eclecticism.

Keshab's use of ritual also demonstrates what I have termed a desire both to 'preserve' and to 'eradicate' difference. The New Dispensation's baptism ceremony was justified on the basis of both Christian practice and Vedic precedent, and was conducted with 'no vulgar or mechanical imitation of Europeanism', but according to the 'Hindu festival' of '*Snan Jatra*'.[109] The Eucharist was administered in a manner amenable to 'Hindu life' in the form of rice and water as opposed to bread and wine.[110] The symbol of the crucifix was reinterpreted as Christ adopting a yogic posture.[111] In all of these instances, we can discern both a desire to find a single, common truth expressed by symbols or ceremonies from different orthodoxies (and thus to eradicate religious difference) and a desire to stress the 'national' form in which the symbols or ceremonies are 'performed' (and thus to preserve national difference). In stressing the 'national' form of the New Dispensation's rituals, and, indeed, in promoting the use of ritual in general, Keshab was continuing in his longstanding attempts to broaden the appeal of Brahmoism through 'popular' forms of worship.[112] He was also responding to a social and political climate in Bengal in which a burgeoning sense of national identity expressed through a defence of 'Hindu culture' had led many to find the criticism of ritual unacceptable.[113] Keshab's 'aristocratic' universalism allowed him to celebrate 'national' (Hindu) religious practices which 'democratic' universalists would be compelled to denigrate. One did not have to discard either 'European' or 'Asiatic' practices at the points at which they came into conflict; rather, one could have it both ways, and be, as Keshab put it, 'Asiatic and European, Hindu and Christian'.[114]

The New Dispensation as 'National Religion'

In discussing the New Dispensation as 'Universal Religion', we have already encountered Keshab's desire to present 'universal truths' in a 'national' form. While Keshab was never a 'revivalist'—he never proclaimed the superiority of Hinduism—he did, at times, proclaim the superiority of 'Asiatic' modes of perception over the 'philosophy' of the 'West'. The methodology of the New Dispensation may be regarded as an attempt to put the arguments Keshab advanced in 'Philosophy and Madness in Religion' (discussed in the previous chapter) into practice. Through the adoption of self-professedly 'Asiatic' practices, of which the 'Pilgrimages to Saints' was emblematic, followers of the New Dispensation attempted to arrive at a conception of universal religion through means that were quite distinct from the methods of comparative religion as pursued in the West. Through a methodology of 'madness', the New Dispensation would attempt to challenge the dominance of Western neo-Orientalist understandings of world religions.

The study of comparative religion had long formed an important part of the universalist project of the Brahmo Samaj of India, and also formed part of the universalist project of Ram Mohan. Keshab had used texts from outside the Hindu and Christian traditions since at least 1866, when, following the split with Debendranath's Brahmo Samaj, the Brahmo Samaj of India published a collection of sacred texts drawn from all religious scriptures.[115] The comparative study of sacred texts was pursued by members of the Brahmo Samaj of India throughout the 1870s and continued under the New Dispensation. One notable result of this enterprise was the first Bengali translation of the Koran, produced between 1881 and 1886 by Girish Chandra Sen.

While the example of Ram Mohan no doubt stimulated Keshab's interest in the study of comparative religion, the comparative project pursued within the New Dispensation was also influenced by the work of Keshab's contemporary and correspondent Max Müller, whose *Introduction to the Science of Religion* was a set text at the Brahmo Theological School.[116] Müller, as Girardot has argued, was one of the most influential figures associated with the 'institutionalized emergence of the "science of religion" or "comparative religions" during the last quarter of the nineteenth century'.[117] Müller's promotion of the comparative method played an important role in the revitalisation and professionalisation of neo-Orientalist scholarship within British humanistic sciences, in recognition of which the Second Congress of Orientalists was held in London in 1874.[118] Echoing Said's classic analysis of the 'textual attitude' of Orientalists of the late eighteenth and early nineteenth century, Girardot emphasises the 'relentless textuality' of Müller's approach, which focused on written scriptures as opposed to oral traditions, and privileged texts in accordance with their antiquity.[119] In Girardot's view, Müller's insistence on the 'written down textuality of the Rig Veda...really did violence to the Brahmanical insistence on the oral nature of Vedic tradition'.[120] As William Graham has argued, the textual approach of Müller's influential *Sacred Books* series played a significant role in sanctioning the notion that Oriental texts functioned as 'scriptures in ways analogous to the Hebrew and Christian bible'.[121] Müller's normalisation of text as the privileged form of religious expression—in particular, his turning of the Veda into a 'written book'—has been described by Wilfred Cantwell Smith as 'an entrancing instance of nineteenth-century cultural imperialism, here quietly imposing the Western sense of "scripture"'.[122]

While the translation and study of religious texts continued to be pursued by members of the New Dispensation, a new mode of comparison—which did not utilise textual sources—was instituted from 1880 known as the 'Pilgrimages to Saints'. The Pilgrimages were historical pageants devoted to a diverse range of 'great men' or 'prophets'—including Moses, Socrates, Sakya, the *rishis*, Christ, Mohammed, Chaitanya, Galileo, Newton, Keplar, Faraday, Sushruta, Emerson, Dean Stanley and Thomas Carlyle—who were taken to exemplify particular aspects of human religious and scientific insight and genius, and, by extension, to encourage the apprehension of the many-sided nature of the Divine. The Pilgrimages, as Borthwick has noted, drew on the contemporary activities of the Freethinking churches and the English positivists, who also organised large pilgrimages to the houses and tombs of great historical figures.[123] However, the Pilgrimages should also be seen as closely related to the project of comparative religion pursued in the Brahmo Theological School and, by extension, to the comparative religion of Max Müller. The 'Pilgrimages to Saints' constituted, in my view, an attempt to pursue Müller's comparative project through peculiarly 'Indian' means.

The 'Pilgrimages to Saints' exemplify one of the most important aspects of the New Dispensation, which Keshab described as follows: 'It is subjective. It aims at synthesis and it aims at subjectivity. It endeavours to convert outward facts and characters into facts of consciousness'.[124] With Christ, as with other 'saints', the aim was to transform an apprehension of his objective reality into a subjective absorption of his Divine qualities—to move from the 'dead Christ of religion and dogma' to Christ as 'an indwelling power, a living spirit, a fact of consciousness. It is this philosophy of subjectivity which underlies the Pilgrimages to Saints'.[125] As we have seen, Keshab saw in 'madness' an ability to transform perception into reality, and presented the mediums of sense-perception through which madness observed the spirit-world (meditation and inspiration) as equivalent to the mediums of sense-perception through which philosophy observed the matter-world. Keshab had argued throughout the 1870s that a capacity for communion through meditation and inspiration constituted a distinctive and valuable quality of Indian 'genius'. The purpose of the Pilgrimages was not only to 'perceive' saints through inspiration, but also to absorb, emotionally and subjectively, 'the spirit of…[each individual saint] in our lives, by means of a deep and profound communion'.[126] Whilst it was open to Western scholars to attempt to establish the unity of 'dead' religious texts through a comparative methodology based on reason, the Indian 'genius' for meditation and communion would allow them to establish the unity of 'living' religious 'saints' through a comparative methodology based on experience.

For Keshab, the Müllerian rational comparison of sacred texts and the inspirational comparison of Divine attributes through communion with saints were thus two sides of the same coin.[127] However, the 'Indian' method, Keshab claimed, was superior as it worked through comparison to 'unity' with greater alacrity:

> Without learning, without philosophy, without erudition, Asia jumped under a sort of natural impulse into the unsectarian eclecticism of faith… What Asia has done intuitively, Europe will do reflectively. The West will have to verify theologically what the East has realized in religious consciousness. The great scholars will be called upon to vindicate and verify, upon philosophical ground, the scientific unity of all the great religions which Asia has founded and shaped with all the simplicity and freshness of natural inspiration.[128]

The superiority of the approach of 'Asia' to comparative religion proclaimed in this statement can be read as an attempt by Keshab to steal some of Max Müller's thunder: Müller's task—as one of the 'great scholars' of the 'West'—is reduced to merely verifying what 'Asia' has already established.

Asia's unique capacity for 'natural inspiration' was a theme to which Keshab returned frequently in the 1880s, going so far as to proclaim in 1881 that 'Hindus are specially endowed with, and distinguished for, the yoga faculty, which is nothing but this power of spiritual communion and absorption'.[129] Keshab and his wife practised yoga for weeks at a time, and Keshab left an unfinished text on the subject when he died.[130] In her history of modern yoga, Elizabeth De Michelis argues that Keshab's 'most momentous, indeed paradigmatic shift must be seen to be in the epistemological domain: from [Debendranath] Tagore's "selective" intuition of revelation based on Hindu canonical (if no longer infallible) texts Sen progresses to a Transcendentalism-inspired concept of experiential revelation defined psychologically as a "state of mind"'.[131] I would qualify this argument somewhat: firstly, religious texts remained central to the New Dispensation's scholarly study of comparative religion; secondly, Transcendentalism was only one of many influences on Keshab's search for experiential revelation as a 'state of mind'. However, De Michelis is quite right to emphasise that the importance of an epistemological shift towards experiential revelation lay in a 'transfer of religious authority from "outer" sources (metaphysical, but socially upheld and validated) to "inner" ones (individually induced and validated)'.[132] I would argue further that this epistemological shift had a political purpose: to aggregate to Indians a spiritual power that could be used to challenge aspects of British imperial rule.

The 'Universal' and the 'National' in Social and Political Context

While Keshab insisted that the New Dispensation presented 'universal' truths in a 'national' form, it must be stressed that he continued to support British rule in India, and that 'Loyalty to sovereign' was stated explicitly in the New Dispensation's 'creed'.[133] However, Keshab's criticisms of British rule in India became increasingly vitriolic in the 1880s. 'Asia's Message to Europe', the most politically charged of all Keshab's public addresses, which he delivered before a vast audience of Bengalis and Europeans in January 1883, opened with a long and electrifying depiction of British brutality in India:

> Whence this plaintive and mournful cry, which so profoundly distresses the patriot's breast? It seems that a whole continent is writhing beneath the lash of oppression, and sending forth from the depths of its heart a deep wail of woe... It is India that weeps. Nay, not India alone; all Asia cries... Many there are in Europe who hold that Asia is a vile woman, full

of impurity and uncleanness. Her scriptures tell lies; her prophets are all impostors; her people…are all untruthful and deceitful… Europe…has perpetrated frightful havoc among the nations of the East… Europe, why do thy eyes still roll in wild fury and insatiate antagonism, as if bent upon Asia's total annihilation? …Before the formidable artillery of Europe's aggressive civilization the scriptures and prophets, the language and literature, of the East, nay her customs and manners, her social and domestic institutions, and her very industries have undergone a cruel slaughter. The rivers that flow eastward and the rivers that flow westward are crimson with Asiatic gore.[134]

When one considers the startling imagery of this address—evoking 'the lash' of the oppressors of slaves, cruelty towards women, the destruction of Indian religion and culture, the ruination of the Indian economy, the possibility of Asia's annihilation and the colonialist's monstrous and insatiate appetite for Asiatic 'gore'—it is easy to see why scholars and contemporaries have found in Keshab's thought the seeds of nationalism. However, Keshab follows on from depictions of British brutality to offer a 'flag of truce and reconciliation', to deliver characteristic paeans to British scientific achievements and Indian spiritual depth, and to issue a plea that the distinctive qualities of 'East' and 'West' should be both preserved and unified.[135] Significantly, his chosen metaphors to illustrate the 'perfection of consolidated fellowship' are the British 'state', the 'House of Commons' and a 'Government…synonymous with the most thorough-going and comprehensive representation'.[136] However, while Keshab encourages the British to continue their tendency of 'extending the franchise' (echoing his calls in 1870 for the British to increase the level of participation of Indians in government), he ultimately pulls back from demanding explicitly any political concessions from the British, saying of Asia: 'Any secular reconciliation or political treaty she would altogether repudiate'.[137] Instead, he proposes a 'spiritual alliance', effected through a 'double and perfect atonement' in which the unification of fallen humanity with Christ is mirrored by the unification of 'Asia' and 'Europe'.[138] After entreating Asia and Europe to 'shake hands with each other with the utmost cordiality', he reiterates his belief in the Providential character of Queen Victoria.[139]

Keshab thus encompasses an anti-colonial emphasis on British brutality and economic exploitation, a revivalist emphasis on the value of India's native faiths, a democratic and constitutional plea for the extension of the franchise, a universalist vision of 'East' and 'West' united and a statement of the Providential nature of the Monarchy. That Keshab could at once criticise the 'cruel slaughter' of Indian people and culture and also offer a eulogy to the Providential character of British rule appears, at first, paradoxical. However, one must bear in mind that what David Arnold has called the 'Orientalist Triptych' (a view of Indian history in which a golden classical Hindu age had been destroyed by a tyrannical Muslim rule which had Providentially given way to British regeneration) was an idea expressed not only by earlier universalists such as Ram Mohan, but also by contemporary nationalists such as Bankimchandra Chatterjee, Bipin Chandra Pal and writers in the *National Paper*.[140] Many of Keshab's contemporaries criticised British rule and demanded increased Indian participation in government without calling for the end of British rule in toto— indeed, this was initially the position of the Indian National Congress.[141]

Nevertheless, Keshab's repudiation of 'secular' or 'political' treaties in favour of a 'spiritual alliance' would, no doubt, have seemed hopelessly inadequate in the context of 1880s Calcutta. In 1870, it seemed possible that Keshab's call for Indians to occupy the highest posts in the British administration would be answered—the India Act of the same year granted the government of India the power to appoint natives to all offices (including the covenanted Indian Civil Service) and also the power to decide how Indians would be selected for these posts. However, by 1879, when the rules of selection were finally clarified after years of wrangling, it became clear that the government's apparently good intentions of 1870 had been rendered symbolic rather than practical: a maximum of 20 per cent of civilians employed each year would be Indians; these Indians would be handpicked by local governments on the basis of family and social position, as well as education and ability. Aristocrats well disposed to British rule were generally chosen; the English-educated Bengalis of Calcutta tended to be excluded.[142] From the late 1870s onwards, the *Indian Mirror* itself contains numerous articles condemning the sharp rise in unemployment among educated natives and the open racial discrimination by the British against Indians occupying 'high positions' in the administration.[143]

The hardening of racial attitudes and increasingly open parade of racial arrogance which preponderated among British officials and members of the Anglo-Indian community from the late 1870s was demonstrated through highly-publicised incidents such as the contempt case against Surendranath Bannerjee (which resulted from the publication in the *Bengalee*—which Bannerjee edited—of an attack on a High Court Judge), and found full expression during the Ilbert Bill controversy, which began the month after Keshab's speech was delivered.[144] The Bill, which proposed to allow Indian judges and magistrates to try British offenders at the District level, revealed the depth of racial antipathy of the Anglo-Indian community and engendered what Hirschmann has called a 'white mutiny', with much of the racist vitriol directed precisely at the English-educated class of Bengalis of which Brahmos were a part.[145] It was clear in this context that neither British officials nor the Anglo-Indian community were willing to 'shake hands' with 'Asia' as Keshab desired, and that 'symbolic' gestures of unity (as the 1870 India Act had been revealed to be) were of little practical consequence.

That practical as opposed to symbolic change was necessary had been recognised by the Sadharan Brahmo Samaj, which laid increasing stress not only on spiritual regeneration, but also social and political freedom. Sivanath Sastri and a number of other Sadharan Samaj Brahmos had taken a vow not to participate in government service in 1876. In the same year, the Indian Association, which was dominated by Sadharan Samaj Brahmos, was founded. Historians have regarded this organisation as a precursor of the Indian National Congress.[146] By the 1880s, the political activities of members such as Ananda Mohan Bose (secretary of the Indian Association and later senior leader in the Indian National Congress) had led the Sadharan Samaj to fuse their liberal, rational religion with a liberal, rational politics. Meanwhile, the Adi Brahmo Samaj continued to denounce Keshab's universalism in the *National Paper*, promoting instead a vigorous defence of Hindu 'national' culture in the face of British imperialism.[147] The fact that Keshab's ideal of a universalist 'spiritual alliance' failed to hold much appeal for the majority of Bengalis living in the reality of an increasingly racially divided and politically charged India is demonstrated by the small numbers of adherents to the New Dispensation in comparison to either Adi or Sadharan Samaj Brahmoism. As David Kopf has summarised the situation, 'The alarming increase of yellow dog racism and cultural imperialism ultimately made a mockery of Brahmo universalism'.[148] The discrepancy between Keshab's universalist rhetoric and the social and political reality of Bengal rendered his ideal of a 'spiritual alliance' illusory.

The New Dispensation as 'Apostolical Religion'

The fractured political stance of the New Dispensation appeared equally inadequate to Bengalis attempting to provide a defence of 'Hindu' culture and to Bengalis aiming to reform the British administration through direct political action. As the ideals of the New Dispensation appeared increasingly unobtainable in the reality of 1880s Calcutta, so Keshab focused on the realisation of its ideals on an apostolical scale. The movement became a project of self-realisation as opposed to national transformation, and, ultimately, became a vehicle through which Keshab could theatrically and symbolically 'perform' ideals of unity that were no longer possible to achieve in reality.

As we have seen, the Cuch Bihar controversy greatly reduced Keshab's prestige and influence, and led to a significant decrease in the membership of the Brahmo Samaj of India. That said, Keshab continued to be the subject of considerable press attention in Calcutta (much of it negative) and his anniversary orations were attended by large crowds. The Reverend Bickersteth calculated attendance at Keshab's anniversary oration of 1881 to exceed 3500; Charles Dall estimated that 'two thousand natives' were present for Keshab's anniversary oration of 1883, along with several British missionaries, General Walker of the Asiatic Society and numerous government officials.[149] It was Keshab's ability to draw substantial audiences that led *The Friend of India* (one of the few Anglo-Indian publications to support Keshab during the 1880s) to declare in January 1882 that 'When Keshub speaks, the world listens'.[150] The audiences were drawn in part, no doubt, by Keshab's fiery oratory and predilection for sensational announcements. Government officials had good reason to attend: Majumdar claims that a 'high government official' confided after Keshab's death that Keshab had the capacity to 'excite the thousands', and that his professions of loyalty as opposed to 'political discontent' were valued highly by the British.[151]

Nevertheless, while Keshab was still able to attract large crowds to his public speeches, he was well aware of the isolated position of the New Dispensation, and became concerned increasingly about the unity and fidelity of its remaining members. He wrote to a friend: 'This thing built by my hands, this thing of my heart...will it be broken to pieces? ...If to disbelieve in me is to reject the Dispensation of God, it troubles me to think what will become of men.... I fear infidelity very much'.[152] With the resources and readership of the New Dispensation press diminishing, Keshab was fighting a losing battle against the continuing attacks by the Sadharan Brahmo Samaj and Adi Brahmo Samaj newspapers.[153] The public scorn of the writers in *Tattwa Koumudi* was relentless: there was 'nothing new' in the New Dispensation; the Pilgrimages to Saints were an 'absolute joke'; the whole organisation functioned as a narcissistic vehicle through which Keshab could establish his own 'immortal fame'.[154] As his public support dwindled, Keshab increasingly focused his efforts on his closest allies—the missionaries, many of whom were ordained as Apostles in a ceremony of March 1881.[155] This inner circle of devotees lived together as a close community, depending upon public alms for their subsistence (Fig. xi). As is evident in his public lectures, Keshab regarded the mission of the Apostles as central to the development of the New Dispensation: God was in India, he had gathered around him 'a vast army...marching under his guidance to the promised land', at the 'forefront' of which were the 'band of apostles', 'the ordained few', working tirelessly 'under Divine command'.[156]

Keshab exerted an increasingly authoritarian control over his inner circle of followers. While he denied in his 1879 anniversary oration that he was an 'inspired prophet', in reality the New Dispensation was centred precisely around his own special status as a prophetic figure. As even his most loyal admirer Majumdar was forced to admit, Keshab's claims to 'magisterial' authority (through universal Divine inspiration) for every member of his church were, in reality, 'practically applied... to him alone', and the subjects on which he declared he must be implicitly and absolutely followed 'gradually widened, until they embraced almost every duty of life'.[157] Keshab was regarded by his

Fig. xi   Photograph of the Apostles of the New Dispensation, circa 1881.
As charismatic leader, Keshab sits in the centre, holding an *ektara*.
The flag reads *Naba Bidhan* (New Dispensation).

domestic servants as a 'demigod'; when he opened the trap door
installed between Lily Cottage and the missionary abodes, 'women
would pour in with their babies', calling him '*Karta* (Doer) or Master',
and believing that in seeing him their troubles would be resolved.[158]
When one considers Keshab's logic concerning Christ's divinity (that
Christ was Divine in the sense that his will harmonised perfectly with
the will of God), it is not impossible that he came to regard himself as
a Christ-like figure. Bijoy Krishna Goswami certainly feared this to be
the case, claiming in a public letter that Keshab had told him personally:
'You need to have a distinct idea about what I really am. The ones who
are *mukto* [free], are in league with the Almighty, and are sent to the
world by Him...I consider myself to be the kindred soul of Christ and
Chaitanya'.[159] Unitarian concerns that Keshab's personality had
undergone a transformation since the Cuch Bihar controversy and that
he was attempting to establish a 'theocracy' through the New
Dispensation were not unfounded.[160]
    As Majumdar recalls, 'the further Keshub felt his alienation from
Brahmos in general, the more compact he tried to make the small

apostolic body immediately around him, and consequently the greater was his dread to discover its elements more and more irreconcilable'.[161] Despite Keshab's attempts to establish harmony among his Apostles, disharmony increasingly prevailed. As the faculty of Divine inspiration was believed to be universal, so 'Whenever any rule or discipline was found unpleasant, or irksome, the plea of inspiration was raised to set it aside'.[162] Keshab's authority was undermined by the same theory on which it was based, the missionaries became disorderly, and the practical activity of the organisation ground, at times, to a halt.

The inclusive and unsectarian rhetoric of Keshab's anniversary orations was undermined by the increasing hostility towards other faiths conveyed in the publications of the New Dispensation. The Cuch Bihar marriage, defended initially on the grounds that it would engender an expansion of the Brahmo fold through the extension of Brahmo influence into Cuch Bihar, came to be used as a justification for a necessary and Providentially sanctioned contraction in the New Dispensation's numbers. The *Sunday Indian Mirror* proclaimed that the 'winnowing fan' of Cuch Bihar 'has done, and is doing, immense good to the Brahmo Somaj by removing the chaff from its membership'.[163] Keshab's address in the *New Dispensation* 'To all our enemies' (in England and India, of all faiths and classes), demonstrates the extent to which an intense feeling of ostracism underlay his professions of brotherhood and solidarity.[164] In Bengali, the rhetoric was stronger still. The Sadharan Samaj Brahmos were 'monsters' who were 'stabbing the necks of our brothers and sisters', whilst 'indulging in luxury and adultery'.[165] Even Majumdar, when he challenged Keshab's doings, was denounced as a 'vicious wolf'.[166] Keshab's sense of isolation and frustration became painfully apparent in his prayers: 'Nobody likes me. If Hindus like me, Brahmos dislike me. If Brahmos like me, Hindus detest me... Now everybody dislikes me... But Lord, what I preach, are your words. I do not lie. People need to obey me'.[167]

The decreasing numbers of the New Dispensation, the increasing hostility of its publications to other religious groups, and the ever more rigid control exerted by Keshab over the activities of the Apostles, all indicate a contraction of the scale on which Keshab could realise, or desired to realise, his universalist ideals. Keshab's rhetoric of fraternalism and universalism came to jar not only with the political and social realities of Calcutta, but also with character of the New Dispensation itself. Keshab's statement in the *Indian Mirror* that 'I believe when the Brahmo Somaj [has] reached its ideal of perfection, there will, perhaps, be but two or three men in it' indicates that the organisation had ceased to be a project of national transformation, and had instead become a project of self-realisation.[168]

As we have seen, Keshab's extensive use of rituals constituted an attempt both to broaden the appeal of the New Dispensation and to combine different religious traditions in a universal synthesis that was nonetheless 'national' in its form of expression. However, considered from the perspective of the New Dispensation as a project of self-realisation, it may be advanced that rituals also allowed Keshab and his Apostles literally to 'perform' repeatedly a union of 'East' and 'West' which did not exist in the political and social reality of 1880s Calcutta. We can recall that Keshab defined the New Dispensation in the following way: 'It is subjective. It aims at synthesis and it aims at subjectivity. It endeavours to convert outward facts and characters into facts of consciousness'.[169] While this statement can be read as indicative of Keshab's 'aristocratic' approach to eclecticism, it can also be read as indicative of Keshab's tendency to view the problem of disharmony between 'East' and 'West' as one which could be solved at the level of subjectivity. To create harmony in the external world, one had simply to realise it in one's consciousness. In stating this, I do not intend to discount Keshab's efforts to bring about concrete social change in India. Rather, I mean to suggest that, by the 1880s, when his efforts were focused increasingly on a narrow band of Apostles, Keshab was effectively attempting to 'live out' an ideal of unity—to realise it subjectively, to 'become' it—when this unity did not exist in reality.

On the public-speaking platforms from which he delivered his anniversary orations, Keshab continued to represent himself much as he had done in Britain over a decade previously—as a man to be taken seriously, as a man who could both speak for 'India' and observe the 'world', and as engaged in a project of world-historical significance which had its origin in a Providential historical plan. However, the 'Keshab' who appeared before the public in January 1883 to deliver the 'message' of the whole of 'Asia' to the entirety of 'Europe' was very different to the 'Keshab' who appeared to the readers of the *New*

Dispensation, in the same year, delivering the following message to God: 'Shall I regard my life and mission as a failure? ...I have struggled constantly to pour oil over troubled waters and to reconcile differences. But in vain... The angry quarrels of those around me have pierced my heart and made it bleed profusely, and the multitudinous instances of revenge which I see before me torment my very bones'.[170] In his public orations, Keshab announced the inevitable (as Providentially sanctioned) success of the New Dispensation; in his public 'devotional' columns, he seems torturously aware that his universalist ideal was destined to fail.

Many of the contradictions and ambivalences of Keshab's position during the final years of his life are captured by what is surely the most intriguing self-image he constructed in the 1880s—that of the 'clownish juggler'. Keshab adopted the role of the 'clownish juggler' in a series of theatrical performances, which were intended to promote the ideas of the New Dispensation to a wider audience. An account of Keshab's performance as the 'clownish juggler' appeared in the *New Dispensation* of April 1883, and was subsequently disseminated widely in Unitarian circles in England through numerous reprints in *The Brahmo Year Book* and *The Inquirer*:

> The Juggler who appeared, on Tuesday last, in the last scene of the New Dispensation Drama, explained the deeper principles of the New Faith as they had never been explained before. There was the magician waving his magic wand, using his magical apparatus and performing wonderful conjuring tricks amid enthusiastic cheers. And yet there was a deep spirituality in every word that was said, in every magical feat that was performed. It was not a juggler playing tricks...but it was a teacher who taught wisdom through allegories and metaphors. Great prophets and seers have spoken in parables, but this clownish-looking Juggler of the New Dispensation enacted parables... The symbols of the various religions were then exhibited, such as the Christian's Cross, the Mahometan's Crescent, and the Vedic *Om*, the Saiva's Trident and the Vaishnava's *Khunti*. These stand aloof from each other in decided antagonism and never coalesce. Is it not possible to combine and amalgamate the truths which each represents? By dextrous shuffling these symbols were in an instant made into one... Eighteen centuries ago a sacred bird came down from heaven with glad tidings. It inspired, moved and sanctified thousands for a time, but it soon found a formidable foe in human Reason, at whose hands it eventually fell a victim. The general impression now is that the Holy Dove is dead, and there is no inspiration now. The juggler showed a dead

bird, and then to the astonishment of all present, and amid loud cheers, a living bird descended from above with a piece of paper tied round its neck, on which were inscribed the following words... 'Victory to the New Dispensation; harmony of all religions'.[171]

Through the performance, Keshab sought to demonstrate visually the ways in which the New Dispensation brought religions into harmony and injected sanctifying inspirational knowledge into human minds stultified by rationality. In one respect, Keshab's use of theatre to promote these ideas demonstrates a continuing concern with using popular idioms to convey his religious ideas to a wider public. As Timothy Dobe has shown, a variety of late nineteenth-century Indian ascetics, including Swami Rama Tirtha (1873–1906) and Sadhu Sundar Singh (1889–1929), reworked the performative registers of 'precolonial, vernacular holy men' within the modern public sphere in order to bring their teachings to a broader audience.[172] This 'republicizing of religiosity' has been interpreted by some historians as running counter to ideas of an Indian modernity created in the 'inner' domain of culture.[173] The use of theatre as a mode of religious instruction has, of course, a very long history in Bengal, but it was of particular importance in the last quarter of the nineteenth century, as Hindu revivalism created a renewed demand for plays that promoted religious devotion. A renewed emphasis on religious theatre was paralleled by the incorporation of anti-colonialist and nationalist themes into dramatic performances, which resulted in the systematic and extensive repression of theatrical performance in the late nineteenth and early twentieth centuries by the British authorities.[174] As Rakesh Solomon has noted, theatre incorporating nationalist themes enabled actors to 'perform' the 'idea of successful nationalist resistance and the idea of the end of imperial domination—on the public stage and thus, inevitably, on the political stage in colonial India'.[175]

Similarly, the medium of theatre enabled Keshab to 'perform' theatrically the idea of a successful union of 'East' and 'West' which had proved impossible to perform in reality. On the stage, Keshab had only to shuffle symbols to combine them as one. Reason and inspiration could be combined by magic. It might also be suggested that it was Keshab's acknowledgement that he was attempting to 'perform' an impossibility that led him to style himself as a clown. Only a 'clownish juggler' would attempt to 'juggle'—all at once—with the 'East' and the 'West', 'Asia' and 'Europe', the Cross, the Crescent, the *Om*, the Trident, the *Khunti*…or perhaps, as Keshab himself suggested, only a madman. Writing as 'The Pagal' (madman) in 1881, Keshab described all his 'movements and doings' as 'topsy-turvy', and claimed that 'My motives and reasoning, my philosophy and logic I myself comprehend not, how can others understand them? I am a puzzle to my ownself; to others a hopeless puzzle'.[176]

In a sense, the 'performance' of the unity of 'East' and 'West' was one that Keshab had been repeating, in different forms, throughout his life. In Britain in 1870, Keshab represented his own biography as an example in miniature of the union between 'East' and 'West' that would ultimately be effected on a world-historical scale. At the time, this representation was largely accepted by the English Unitarians, who regarded the Brahmo Samaj of India as an agent that would play a key role in extending the unity Keshab symbolised on a personal scale to the majority of Indian subjects. During the 1870s, Keshab attempted to construct a domestic environment which would enable him to 'perform' the roles of both an Anglicised gentleman and a Hindu ascetic. The acute difficulty of this attempt led Keshab to lead, in effect, a 'double life'. By the 1880s, Keshab had lost the support of his closest allies in Britain; the liberal reform schemes he proposed in Britain for mass education and Indian participation in the administration had not been adopted by the government; his convictions of the necessity of social reform in India and of the Providential nature of British rule had come into direct conflict through the Cuch Bihar marriage; and he was facing bitter opposition in India from both Sadharan and Adi Samaj Brahmos. He could no longer feel 'at home' in either Britain or India (as he did in both in 1870); he could no longer feel assured that the British public and government were in sympathy with his proposals for reform in India—a belief that he propounded regularly in the months following his return from his visit to Britain. By the 1880s, the liberal vision of Indian reform and eventual self-government under the tutelage of a benevolent imperialism had been revealed to be a charade, and a religious solution to political and social problems had been revealed to be inadequate. To continue to 'perform' the union of 'East' and 'West' in such a radically changed context, one was compelled to appear as a 'clown'. The figure of the clownish juggler can be read as symbolic of the impossible project of universalism in the context of colonialism.

Responses to the New Dispensation Abroad

The national and provincial press in Britain paid little attention to the New Dispensation; indeed, very few references to Keshab can be found outside the religious press in Britain during the 1880s. Activities such as the 'Pilgrimages to Saints', the ceremony of the Eucharist and the missionary tour were noted occasionally as curiosities, but Keshab's desire to publicise the New Dispensation as a religious development of world-historical significance was not realised.[177] His open letter of January 1883, in which he announced the coming of the New Dispensation, and which he intended to be published in all of the 'leading journals' across the globe, was only printed in one mainstream newspaper in Britain, in a highly abridged form.[178]

The lack of press interest in Britain may be explained, in part, by the simple fact that much of Keshab's immediate fame in Britain had rested on him being in the country—the longer he was absent, the less he warranted coverage. However, broader discursive and political shifts also rendered Keshab less appealing to British audiences in the 1880s than he had been a decade earlier. The Disraeli–Lytton partnership from 1876 had served to undermine liberal attitudes towards India with a new focus on 'Oriental' immutability; the combination of racial differentiation, peasant stabilisation and indirect rule which grounded Conservative policy in India served to construct a more rigid and hierarchical conception of the British right to govern.[179] The move away from constitutional notions of British rule in India towards a vision of the British monarchy as the dynastic successor of the Mughals was symbolised, above all, by Queen Victoria's assumption of the title of Empress of India in 1876, and the vast Delhi durbar of the following year.[180] Gladstone's return to power in 1880, and his appointment of Lord Ripon as Viceroy, served to reinvigorate briefly the liberal program of increasing the rights and roles of the Indian urban elite.[181] However, as the opposition to the Ilbert Bill would reveal, the Anglo-Indian community remained deeply hostile to any moves towards racial equality. As Metcalf has observed, the failure of Ripon's efforts revealed that his attempts to revive liberal government in India amounted to little more than 'a stormy interlude in the era of paternalism which had swept over India since the Mutiny'.[182] Liberal calls for greater Indian participation in government were frustrated by a growing perception that British paternalistic rule must be strengthened in the face of growing Indian national consciousness, lest the empire be placed in grave danger. As the Regius Professor of Modern History at Cambridge, J. R. Seeley, put it in 1881, 'if the feeling of a common nationality began to exist there [in India] only feebly…from that day almost our Empire would cease to exist'.[183]

Hierarchical and paternalistic conceptions of British imperial rule, bolstered by fears that Indian 'nationalism' could lead to the demise of empire, were paralleled by the emergence of more militaristic and patriotic popular conceptions of empire.[184] As McClelland and Rose have argued, from the 1880s the language of 'citizenship' in Britain began to be tied more closely to notions of national and imperial duties, and acquired a more distinctly militaristic and masculinist tone.[185] It was also from the 1880s that elementary state education in England began to acquire a more overtly imperialist slant, as teachers were encouraged to foster notions of good citizenship and patriotism in the classroom.[186] Emergent discourses of popular imperialism existed in tension with liberal Gladstonian rhetoric in the 1880s, and did not achieve a high degree of popular acceptance until the 1890s.[187] Nevertheless, Disraeli's more aggressive imperialism had certainly left an imprint on British attitudes to empire, and the need for a more muscular, conservative approach to people of other cultures was articulated in a variety of political, popular and academic arenas. It was in the 1880s that Max Müller's arch-rival at Oxford, Monier Monier-Williams, began to move away from his previously liberal position on 'Oriental' religions and to become increasingly critical of the 'limp-wristed comparative scholarship' exemplified by Müller's *Sacred Books*, a project which he denounced in 1887 as an 'unmanly' example of 'jelly-fish tolerance'.[188] In this context, Keshab's claims to have founded a new world religion that would rejuvenate morality in India and Britain were not regarded as worthy of serious attention.

Although Keshab did not feature in the national or provincial press in Britain in the 1880s, he did continue to receive sustained coverage within left-leaning Unitarian circles. While *The Inquirer* stated in May 1878 that it was 'entirely converted' to the views of Collet, and regarded the future of Brahmoism as lying in the hands of the Sadharan Brahmo Samaj, in practice the journal devoted far less space to the activities of the Sadharan Brahmo Samaj than it did to the activities of Keshab. Representations of Keshab in *The Inquirer* in the 1880s were influenced largely by the contrasting accounts of the New Dispensation promulgated by Collet and Majumdar. While Majumdar never wavered in his devotion to Keshab, his letters to Max Müller in the 1880s indicate that he was concerned by many of Keshab's innovations. As he admitted in a letter of August 1881, Keshab was 'becoming more and more metaphysical' to the point where 'he may completely elude popular understanding, and that is why I am the more anxious to explain him'.[189] Majumdar's desire to 'explain some of his [Keshab's] principles from a simple and rational theistic ground' took the form of a series of accounts of the New Dispensation sent to *The Inquirer* which presented a version of Keshab's teachings sanitised for English Unitarian audiences. Majumdar also promulgated a view of the New Dispensation as an expression of 'simple…Primitive Theism' in a series of lectures delivered during a visit to England in 1883.[190]

In response to one of Majumdar's accounts of the New Dispensation, a leading article in *The Inquirer* of December 1882 put forward the case that the teachings of the New Dispensation and of English Unitarianism were 'In some respects…identical, and in others the difference is in the form of expression, not in the actual thought'.[191] In blending together the leading conceptions of God, encouraging communion with God through revelation (communion of wisdom) and inspiration (communion of the soul), promoting a vivid conception of God's personality, and honouring the saints of other religions, Keshab was promoting 'our own sentiments'.[192] Other contributors to *The Inquirer* agreed that critics were mistaken in taking Keshab's 'bold imagery literally, or interpreting prosaically flights of poetry and metaphor'.[193] Broad religious minds should appreciate that 'the fairest way to judge others is to look at their beliefs from their own point of view', and recognise that 'Actions that are mountebankery in the eyes of Europeans are symbol language without any connection to the ridiculous in the eyes of Orientals'.[194]

However, Majumdar's limited success in retaining some credibility for Keshab in English Unitarian circles was undermined by Collet's persistent efforts to discredit him through the publication of accounts of his most objectionable practices. Collet focused in particular on Keshab's appearance as the 'clownish juggler' and his use of dance as a form of worship, which she claimed were indicative of his irrational and childish behaviour. Her accounts of the 'new dance' ceremony were published on numerous occasions in *The Inquirer*, which italicised the most objectionable elements: '*the shout and the gallop, and the joyous whirl round and round* went on, and it was quite a blessed sight to see so many boys and girls and men of mature years all dancing around'.[195] For Collet, the use of dance indicated a loss of self-control and a lack of propriety, and the participation of young boys and girls alongside men of mature years in such fervent displays of emotion threatened to lead to immorality. Collet reprinted accounts of the 'clownish juggler' in order to discredit Keshab further, dismissing the performance outright: 'Such is the New Dispensation in the hands of its founder. Let us thank God that he has ceased to lead the Theistic Church of India'.[196] As Majumdar complained to Müller, Collet's 'idolisation of Keshub was as singular, as her present violent and unreasoning antipathy'.[197] Having placed so much faith in Keshab in the 1870s, and having devoted so much energy to bringing his ideas to the attention of the British public, Collet clearly felt deeply betrayed, bemused and embarrassed by Keshab's refusal to adhere to her rational religious and social ideals. In the last editions of *The Brahmo Year Book*, she effectively wrote Keshab out of the history of Brahmoism, and constructed a new narrative of the development of Brahmo ideals from Ram Mohan to the Sadharan Samaj. It was no coincidence that Collet began compiling material for her biography of Ram Mohan when Unitarian antagonism towards Keshab was at its height.[198]

Collet's sense of disappointment and betrayal was echoed in *The Inquirer* in an editorial of September 1883. The author lamented, 'It is because we thought so highly of the Brahmo Somaj at one time, and hoped so much from it, that we regret so deeply its fall. At one time its religion was rational, spiritual, and sublime in its simplicity; now it has degenerated into mysticism, absurdity, and ceremonial folly'.[199] Readers were cautioned against responding enthusiastically to

Majumdar's lectures, which remained 'discreetly silent' on recent developments in Keshab's ideas and activities.[200] Keshab's former ally Bijoy Krishna Goswami had warned that Keshab's followers were hiding the 'original principle' of their 'warped doctrine' abroad, 'in order to be accepted by foreigners'.[201] *The Inquirer*, however, had gleaned its information from a close reading of Collet's *The Brahmo Year Book*, which had provided 'absolutely conclusive' evidence of Keshab's 'downward tendency…from Theism to superstition'.[202] The most damning evidence consisted of Keshab's claims to Divine authority, his 'extravagant' symbolism and asceticism, and his tendency to worship everything without any rational discrimination: 'The Trinity is worshipped, fire is worshipped, water is worshipped…the whole character of the institution…has been changed'.[203] To hammer the point home, readers were furnished with another reprint of Collet's accounts of the 'new dance' and the 'clownish juggler'.[204]

However, in spite of the general hostility to Keshab evident in *The Inquirer* in the 1880s, numerous articles continued to stress the value of particular elements of his ideas and practices. An anonymous article of August 1883 encouraged readers to 'leave off this practice of reproach against the Indian Christians'.[205] The desire for a 'New Dispensation' was understandable when one considered 'the hitherto slow, dreary, and imperfect religious influence of what is called the Old Dispensation'.[206] The author proposed that even the 'new dance' contained an important lesson: the use of 'natural impulses' in worship could provide an antidote to the English Unitarian tendency to 'freeze and petrify whatever they praise'.[207] Keshab's use of symbolism and ceremony was also occasionally held up for admiration—one editorial went so far as to admit that 'We confess to a weakness in this direction', and pointed to the power of rituals to act 'as a counterpoise to the tendency to dwell too exclusively upon the intellectual side of religion'.[208] While the English Unitarians were generally critical of the theology and practice of the followers of the New Dispensation, they continued to be impressed by their apparently 'natural' capacity for faith and devotion, a capacity which, as James Martineau lamented in a letter to a friend in 1885, Unitarians in England had lost: 'Whatever aspect of truth we may have saved from neglect, whatever spiritual resources we may have rendered more accessible, pass into other keeping and need another administration before they lay hold of the minds and hearts of men. It is the power of Faith that shall prevail. We have it not, except as a feeble residuum from the power of criticism'.[209]

It is somewhat surprising that the members of the Theosophical Society, which had been founded in New York in 1875, remained largely unaware of Keshabite Brahmoism until the 1880s, and, once they did take an interest, adopted an extremely negative view. The leader of the organisation, H. P. Blavatsky, published her major work *Isis Unveiled* in 1877. The Theosophical Society's emphasis on comparative religion, occultism and contemporary science, its opposition to dogmatic Christianity and its respect for Eastern and ancient religions seems to have had much in common with Keshab's universalism.[210] Blavatsky and her chief collaborator Henry Olcott moved in similar circles to Keshab. From the late 1870s, they corresponded with the founder of the Arya Samaj, Swami Dayananda Saraswati, and the Theosophical Society and the Arya Samaj became united for a time. Saraswati had met both Debendranath and Keshab and was sympathetic to the Brahmo cause, although he could not accept their rejection of the ultimate authority of the Vedas. Blavatsky and Olcott were also in contact with the Calcutta businessman Peary Chand Mitra (1814–83), a close associate of the Brahmos, who joined the Theosophical Society in 1877 and later became President of the Bengal Theosophical Society.[211] Considering these connections, it is surprising that an article on the Brahmo Samaj published in *The Theosophist* in March 1881 contains the Theosophists' first impressions of Brahmoism, gleaned from the *Sunday Indian Mirror*.[212]

While Blavatsky and her associates were impressed by Ram Mohan's erudition and religious universalism, they were appalled by what they heard of Keshab and the New Dispensation. Their negative view was shaped by a pamphlet they received from the Sadharan Brahmo Samaj leader Sivanath Sastri, which provided clear evidence of Keshab's 'personal leadership and reckless egoism'.[213] There was no doubt, Blavatsky opined, that the New Dispensation was a religion 'founded upon avatarism'.[214] Keshab was guilty of every 'extravagance of childish vanity' and even allowed himself to be bedecked in garlands and put in a swing, 'as though he were a divine being'.[215] In the view of Jocelyn Godwin, Blavatsky and Olcott's negative view of Keshab dissuaded them from making contact with Ramakrishna, a figure whom they may well have regarded as a genuine spiritual master.[216] The writers in *The Theosophist* refused to engage seriously with Keshab's ideas on any level, preferring instead to publish derisive accounts, gleaned from *Brahmo Public Opinion*, of his most eccentric activities, including a description of him appearing on stage wearing a sari and 'dancing as though for dear life', accompanied by a disciple wearing a 'necklace of old shoes'.[217] Keshab's poor reputation discouraged the Theosophists from entering into a dialogue with him, even though this dialogue may have been productive. The lack of Theosophical engagement with Keshabite Brahmoism demonstrates the depth of antipathy towards Keshab in the Calcutta press from the Cuch Bihar crisis onwards. To foreign observers encountering him for the first time, he appeared simply to be a clown.

Conclusion

The Cuch Bihar marriage certainly formed a turning point in Keshab's life. While the marriage was supported, in general, in the British press, it marked the end of the English Unitarians' admiration for Keshab, and resulted in the decline of Keshabite Brahmoism as a force for national transformation. By the 1880s, it had become clear in Calcutta that Keshab's universalist vision of harmony was belied by the realities of colonial oppression. In Britain, increasingly militaristic and paternalistic conceptions of empire, bolstered by growing fears of Indian nationalism, rendered British audiences less sympathetic to appeals from the colonial periphery. While the Unitarians continued to find elements to admire in Keshab's religious ideas and practices, their belief in the value of non-Western religions was shaken by Keshab's actions in later life, which seemed to represent the dangers posed, rather than the possibilities offered, by other cultures.

The numerous innovations Keshab introduced in the short history of the New Dispensation under his leadership were, in some respects, in keeping with ideas he had expressed previously. The 'Pilgrimages to Saints' constituted a renewed attempt to prove to the world that 'truth' was not 'European'. Keshab's attempts to present 'universal truths' in a 'national form' echoed his calls in England for Indian Christianity to assume an 'Oriental aspect'. However, Keshab's shift towards 'aristocratic' eclecticism constituted a definite break with the universalism of Ram Mohan and English Unitarianism, and served to privilege inspirational experience as opposed to reason as the standard by which the 'truth' of diverse religions could be judged. This epistemological shift demanded, in some respects, that Keshab assume a new role as a charismatic leader—while 'democratic' eclecticism required only 'reason' to arrive at its conclusions, 'aristocratic' eclecticism required a prophet.

Reflecting on Keshab's achievements through the New Dispensation, Majumdar lamented that Keshab 'was the truest and noblest result of his own religion. Outside himself the result was disappointing'.[218] In spite of its inclusionary rhetoric, the New Dispensation was characterised by the progressive exclusion of numerous religious 'enemies', who were imagined to have fallen victim to the Providential 'winnowing fan' of Cuch Bihar. While Keshab continued to regard himself as a figure of world-historical significance, he was troubled deeply by the thought that his universalist project was likely to fail. He focused increasingly on his personal communication with God in order to understand his place in a world that did not appear to be moving towards the holistic union for which he hoped. However, while the New Dispensation would never flourish into the world religion that Keshab had envisioned, aspects of Keshabite universalism would remain important to subsequent generations of Bengalis as they attempted to forge new understandings of India's place in the world, and the Unitarian dialogue with the Bengali elite would continue into the twentieth century.

7

CONCLUSION

UNIVERSALISM IN AN IMPERIAL WORLD

Ramakrishna paid his final visit to Keshab on 28 November 1883. It is recorded in the *Kathamrita* as follows:

> AT TWO O'CLOCK in the afternoon, M. was pacing the foot-path of the Circular Road in front of the Lily Cottage, where Keshab Chandra Sen lived. He was eagerly awaiting the arrival of Sri Ramakrishna. Keshab's illness had taken a serious turn, and there was very little chance of his recovery. Since the Master loved Keshab dearly, he was coming from Dakshineswar to pay him a visit...

> ...About five o'clock a carriage stopped in front of the Lily Cottage and Sri Ramakrishna got out with Lātu and several other devotees, including Rākhāl. He was received by Keshab's relatives, who led him and the devotees upstairs to the verandah south of the drawing-room. The Master seated himself on a couch...

> ...The Master was in a state of intense divine intoxication. In the well-lighted room the Brahmo devotees sat around the Master; Lātu, Rākhāl, and M. remained near him...Keshab entered the room. He came through the east door. Those who remembered the man who had preached in the Town Hall or the Brahmo Samaj temple were shocked to see this skeleton covered with skin. He could hardly stand. He walked holding to the wall for support. With great difficulty he sat down in front of the couch. In the mean time Sri Ramakrishna had got down from the couch and was sitting

on the floor. Keshab bowed low before the Master and remained in that position a long time, touching the Master's feet with his forehead. Then he sat up. Sri Ramakrishna was still in a state of ecstasy. He muttered to himself. He talked to the Divine Mother.[1]

Representations of Keshab in 1884

After a period of illness, Keshab died on 8 January 1884. Upon hearing the news, Ramakrishna became 'emotionally distraught', exclaiming that 'half of his life had gone away with Babu Keshab Sen's passing'.[2] Keshab's cremation was attended by many thousands of people, and obituaries were published in all of the leading newspapers in Calcutta and in Britain. The central importance of Keshab's role as charismatic leader in shaping the ideas and maintaining the unity of the New Dispensation is demonstrated by the fact that, following his death, the movement was split apart by factionalism and fell into decline.[3] Majumdar came to lead one of two main factions within the New Dispensation, and was successful in generating a degree of renewed international interest in Keshabite Brahmoism (albeit with the emphasis more firmly on the ethical teachings of Jesus) through his appearance at the World Parliament of Religions in 1893. However, Keshab's hope of establishing a new and popular world religion was never realised, and the New Dispensation failed to exert much social or religious influence or to attract a large number of followers.[4]

While Keshab had received little press coverage in Britain in the 1880s, his death resulted in the publication of numerous obituaries in the national and provincial press, many of which described Keshab as the 'well-known' or 'familiar' 'Indian Reformer', suggesting that there remained some degree of public consciousness of him.[5] The most widely circulated account of Keshab's life was provided by a Reuters telegram, which was reprinted in many of the leading British newspapers and journals.[6] This account was largely positive, presenting Keshab as the intellectual heir to Ram Mohan, and the New Dispensation as representative of an undifferentiated 'Brahmo Samaj', an organisation with which the 'greater part of the educated natives of Bengal sympathize more or less'.[7] Most of the positive accounts of Keshab's life focused largely on his visit to Britain, and stressed his gentlemanly manners, his command of the English language and his attempts to 'rescue' his countrymen from 'barbarous, debasing, and pernicious customs'.[8] Keshab's close relationship with Lord Lawrence was often noted, and the efforts of Brahmos to reform Indian religion were described as operating in tandem with the efforts of the British government.[9] Accounts of this kind continued to place Keshab squarely within a liberal imperialist narrative of progress.

However, this narrative was challenged by a different narrative of retrogression and failure. The obituary in *The Times* summed up many of the sentiments which appeared in less favourable accounts of Keshab's life in its comparison of the 'Keshab' of 1870 and the 'Keshab' of the 1880s: 'Had he died ten years ago, shortly after his return to India from that visit to England that seemed to promise the revelation of a new religion…he would have been handed down to posterity as the possible prophet and regenerator of his race and religion'.[10] However, back in India, Keshab had been unable to live up to his high ideals, which had 'either been disappointed or went unrealized', and it would not be long before the world witnessed 'the dissolution and disappearance' of Brahmoism.[11] Various explanations were sought for Keshab's failure to live up to the expectations he had raised in 1870. Chief among these was the injurious effect of Hinduism. *The Spectator*, which, in 1870, had held out high hopes that Keshab would not only elevate Indian religion, but would restore a purer Christianity to Britain, lamented that, in later years, he had 'degenerated', either 'from a positive degeneracy of the brain, or the sub-idea of Hindooism'.[12] Hinduism, according to this interpretation, was effectively equivalent to a mental disease—a parallel that was also drawn by the *Bristol Mercury and Daily Post*, which pointed to Keshab's mental retrogression into 'degenerate mysticism'.[13]

While Keshab's 'retrogression' was often blamed on the injurious influence of false religious systems, it was also linked to 'Oriental' predispositions towards despotic rule. In the last years of Keshab's life, Collet retreated to well-established tropes of Indian inferiority that were lodged deeply in Victorian racial thinking, and explained Keshab's pretensions to prophetic status in terms of the racial characteristics of Indians, observing that 'Nothing is easier to the Asiatic mind than the unquestioning submissive devotion to a heroic fellow-creature. That is the easy and pleasant duty of a child-like people'.[14] She contrasted

Keshab's authoritarian philosophy of 'reliance of the inferior on the superior' (a phase she termed 'childhood') with the Sadharan Samaj's commitment to a 'constitutional course' based on 'right relations between those who are virtually *equals*'.[15] The susceptibility of 'Oriental' minds to despotic rule was cited also by Monier-Williams as a factor in Keshab's fall from grace. As he cautioned in his article in the *Journal of the Royal Asiatic Society*, 'Nowhere is eminent ability worshipped with more fervour than in India...[Keshab] was the sole administrator of the affairs of the Society, and ruled it with the rod of an irresponsible dictator'.[16] At a time when Indians in London were beginning to make organised claims for greater representation, and to win the support of a limited number of Radical and Liberal MPs for raising questions in parliament concerning the reform of Indian government (John Bright approved the foundation of an informal Indian committee to secure combined parliamentary action in 1883), Keshab's 'irresponsible' rule of the New Dispensation stood as a cautionary tale of the misery that might ensue should Indians be allowed to govern themselves.[17]

In 1870, *The Inquirer* had championed Keshab as a 'prophet' who could bring into harmony the religious insights of 'East' and 'West'. Keshab's obituary in *The Inquirer* represented his life in very different terms. The narrative of a union of 'East' and 'West' was now replaced with a narrative that represented Keshab's life allegorically as a battle between the religious systems of Christianity and Hinduism.[18] Initially, Keshab 'discarded all the superstitious forms and idolatrous ceremonies so prominently associated with Hindoo religion...[and] imbued the old Hindooism with the spirit of Christianity'.[19] However, as time went on, 'The Hindoo element, with all its allied superstitions and childish ceremonies, superseded the simple rational Theism of former years'.[20] Keshab's gradual move away from the Theistic social gospel he had preached in England in 1870 was regarded as representative of the power of Hinduism to overwhelm the spread of pure and rational religion in India. Maintaining an appropriate balance between the intellectual and the emotional aspects of religion was an enterprise fraught with difficulty, and the potential perils were perceived to be far greater in India than in England. When Keshab visited England in 1870, the Unitarians saw in him a combination of 'Eastern' and 'Western' virtues held in perfect balance. By the time of his death, Keshab had become a symbol of the extreme difficulty of maintaining such a balance in India.

An alternative representation to these negative accounts of Keshab's life was provided by Max Müller, who maintained a correspondence with Keshab and Majumdar from 1880, after Keshab wrote to thank him for providing a defence of him in *The Times*.[21] Müller included a lengthy account of Keshab in his *Biographical Essays*, which appeared in 1884 and was widely reviewed.[22] In Müller's view, Keshab was a victim of 'envy', a deeply misunderstood man who had been treated as 'an idol, first worshipped and then broken'.[23] His claims to 'inspiration' referred to nothing 'miraculous', but to 'the real, natural, and only true inspiration which everyone knows who knows what truth is'; the marriage of his daughter when she was only a few months below marriageable age was entirely understandable, and to call the event 'a Child-marriage' was 'utterly unfair'.[24] Müller stated that he had continued to defend Keshab, even in his later years, as he feared that 'his physical, but his mental strength also, was in imminent danger'.[25] Indeed, Keshab's deteriorating mental health had made him 'not quite master of his thoughts', which explained his erratic behaviour and his authoritarian rule of the New Dispensation, which 'seemed too despotic even to Oriental minds'.[26]

Müller's defence of Keshab stemmed from a genuine sense of common endeavour between the German philologist and the Brahmo reformer, both of whom were committed, in principle, to the discovery of 'truth' in all of the religions of the world. In his letters to Majumdar, included in his *Biographical Essays*, Müller referred repeatedly to 'our' goals, and 'our antagonists', and assured Majumdar that 'though we may differ in the wording of our thoughts, our thoughts spring from the same source, and tend in their various ways towards the same distant goal'.[27] Müller's strong sense of the symbolic or ideal meaning hidden within religious practices and texts (the discovery of this meaning was essentially the purpose of his 'science of religion') lay behind his tolerant attitude towards Keshab's many innovations in the 1880s. Müller was not, as he informed Majumdar in a letter of 1881, 'fond' of Keshab's asceticism, singing, pilgrimages and shaving his head, but religion was always a 'compromise'.[28] Müller bemoaned that, because

Keshab 'carries a flag...he is accused of worshipping a flag'—whereas, in fact, 'there never has been and never will be a religion "without a flag"'.[29] In Müller's view, Collet's stern attitude towards Keshab's use of ritual and ceremony was neither pragmatic nor fair.[30] Keshab's followers in India and the 'ritualists' in Britain both required religious 'bread' as well as 'oxygen', and could be forgiven for their indulgences.[31] Such people may be regarded as 'Silly children, naughty children, if you like; but, for all of that, many of them very good boys'.[32]

However, the success of Müller's attempts to provide an alternative account of Keshab's life and work was limited by the fact that, by the time of Keshab's death, Müller's influence and popularity in academic circles was beginning to wane.[33] While his acceptance of the inaugural Hibbert Lectures in 1878 and the continued publication of the *Sacred Books* series enabled him to maintain his position as a well-known public intellectual, his reputation at Oxford was declining in the 1880s in the face of attacks from conservative and liberal quarters. Monier-Williams' increasing lack of sympathy with the 'effeminate' comparative project of the *Sacred Books* has been noted, but more powerful critiques of Müller's work were emerging from the new liberal ethnographic comparison associated with Edward Tylor and James Frazer.[34] Tylor's 1881 *Anthropology: An Introduction to the Study of Man and Civilization*, and his 1883 'Lectures on Anthropology', were highly influential in academic circles concerned with the evolution of societies and religions, and served to undermine Müller's monogenetic and idealist philosophy with a new polygenetic, atheistic and materialist belief in an evolution of human consciousness.[35] While, for Keshab, and, to some extent, for Müller, the Müllerian rational comparison of sacred texts and the Keshabite inspirational comparison of Divine attributes were two sides of the same coin (in the sense that they both attempted to find in diverse traditions expressions of the 'infinite'), this was a coin that was beginning to be devalued in the context of a progressively secularised and specialised academic environment.

Keshab's cremation in Calcutta attracted thousands of people, and praise for his contribution to Indian social and religious life was expressed in all of the leading Anglo-Indian and Bengali newspapers and journals, including those that had been particularly hostile towards him during his lifetime.[36] A large memorial meeting held in the

Calcutta Town Hall on 30 January 1884 was attended by many of the leading figures in the government and justice system in Bengal, as well as by representatives of the Hindu, Brahmo, Muslim and Christian communities.[37] The Britons who spoke at the meeting represented Keshab's life in the familiar terms of his emancipation from 'superstition' through the gift of English education. Sir William Hunter, who was responsible for the colossal statistical survey of British India (commissioned by Lord Mayo in 1869), and who, from 1882, presided over the commission on Indian education, laid great stress on the fact that it was with 'Western freedom of thought' that Keshab 'went forth as a young man on a campaign of his own'.[38] Keshab's life, in Hunter's view, was one of struggles, persecutions and renunciations, as he broke free from the traditions of his countrymen. While Hunter contended that Keshab 'represented, in a special manner, the fusion of European science with Indian thought', there was no doubt that the 'freedom of thought' that he attempted to extend to his countrymen was of 'Western' origin.[39]

Justice Cunningham, a Judge at the High Court of Calcutta, stressed similarly Keshab's debt to English education in breaking free from the 'surrounding ruins' of Indian society.[40] Cunningham began his address in a manner reminiscent of Keshab's own orations, by drawing attention to the conflict between 'modern thought' and 'old religious systems', and stressing the necessity of preserving the good qualities of both.[41] However, in Cunningham's version of history, the fundamental tension that existed was between a 'materialist' attitude and a 'superstitious' attitude.[42] He portrayed the 'clash' of the two 'branches of the great Aryan family' as a clash between 'science, art and critical analysis', on the one hand, and 'a vast structure of tradition, custom and primitive dogma' on the other.[43] If Keshab had, as Cunningham claimed, done a great service to humanity by ministering to 'man's spiritual wants', he had done so by drawing on traditions other than those of the 'Eastern' branch of the Aryan family.[44]

The Anglo-Indian press also drew attention to Keshab's debt to 'Western' civilisation. In the opinion of the *Englishman*, Keshab was 'no common Hindu'; rather, he was a 'self-made and self-cultured' man.[45] Evidence for Keshab's 'individuality' was to be found in his 'graceful manners', his 'refined address' and the 'Ciceronian finish' of his rhetoric; indeed, he was 'a fine model of the modern Bengali gentleman'.[46] The *Indian Daily News* echoed the *Englishman* and emphasised Keshab's gentlemanly manners and command of English, comparing his oratorical style to that of Gladstone and John Bright.[47] As Koditschek has observed, the early leaders of the Indian National Congress were aware of the central importance of English gentleman-liness to winning support from English liberals. This led them to place a premium on the skills of men like Dadabhai Naoroji and Surendranath Bannerjee, who 'embodied British manners and respectability to a fault'.[48] Antoinette Burton has shown that a micropolitics of gentlemanliness was crucial to Naoroji's eventual success in winning a seat in parliament in 1892.[49] The able performance of a micropolitics of English gentlemanliness was central, in the accounts of Keshab's life in the Anglo-Indian press, to the success of Keshab's endeavours, and allowed for his inclusion in a roll call of great Western orators.

Representations of Keshab propounded by the Anglo-Indian press and British government officials, which tended to erase his 'Indian-ness' by celebrating his English gentlemanliness and incorporating him into a tradition of great Western orators, appeared at a time when it was becoming quite clear that the Raj did not, in fact, regard Indian men as equal to their English counterparts. Keshab's death occurred at the height of the Ilbert Bill controversy, and only months after Surendranath Bannerjee's conviction and imprisonment for contempt of court. Anglo-Indian hostility to the prospect of being placed under the jurisdiction of Indian magistrates was expressed through a stream of vitriol in the Anglo-Indian press against the effeminate, inauthentic and ineffective *babu*. There is thus a notable contradiction in the fact that celebrations of Keshab's authentic English gentlemanliness appeared at precisely the moment when such gentlemanly behaviour among Indians was being derided as inauthentic and suspicious. The contradiction can be explained in part, it would seem, by the simple fact that Keshab had died.

Surendranath Bannerjee's newspaper the *Bengalee* printed a long eulogy to Keshab, which described him as the 'author of a great revival' and one of the 'greatest men of their [the Indian] race'.[50] Unlike the Anglo-Indian accounts, which placed Keshab in a tradition of great Britons, the *Bengalee* emphasised that Keshab held a place 'in the pantheon of our great men', forming part of a 'religious trinity of modern India', alongside Chaitanya and Ram Mohan.[51] The Sadharan Brahmo Samaj newspaper *Brahmo Public Opinion*—which had often expressed hostility to Keshab during his lifetime—stressed similarly Keshab's status as 'perhaps the greatest man in India', and emphasised the legacy he had left not only to India, but also to the world.[52] The *Indian Empire*, a newspaper aimed at the English-educated Hindu elite, provided a more forceful account of Keshab's 'Indian' heritage, claiming that he had attempted to 'conserve all that is good in Hindu philosophy and civilization, against a vigorous and organized attack of Christian civilization'.[53] England would 'shortly be called upon to consider' the 'difficult problem' of 'her Indian dependency'; Keshab had 'fully realised, what a majority of educated Indians have since realised, that while it is impossible to shut out the powerful influence of a Christian Government, India will not fare well by making an indiscriminate and wholesale surrender of her religious, political, and social institutions'.[54] While official and Anglo-Indian accounts of Keshab's life attempted to co-opt him into a history of the benefits of imperialism, accounts in the Bengali-owned press found in his life the beginnings of a critique of imperialism's shortcomings.

The Legacies of Keshabite Universalism

As C. A. Bayly has observed, British imperial rule in India made the problem of 'modernity' an Indian problem in the colonial era.[55] Modern Indian intellectual history 'attests to the virtuosity of Indian thinking' on the topic of 'modernity', and reminds us of the problems concepts of 'modernity' continue to pose in postcolonial times.[56] Postcolonial scholars in India have taken a leading role in theorising and deconstructing concepts of 'modernity'—through a critique of 'reason', through the displacement of the history of the 'West' as a metahistorical narrative, and through questioning the possibility of history being subsumed within a single system of representation. The problems of 'modernity', 'reason' and 'history' were problems with which Keshab also engaged and struggled, albeit in a different way and in a different context. His attempt to provincialise Europe stands as an important precursor to the project as pursued in the twentieth and twenty-first centuries.

As David Kopf has observed in his wide-ranging study of the Brahmo Samaj, every single Brahmo who joined the movement after 1860 was personally converted to the faith and community by Keshab.[57] As Kopf's study demonstrates, these converts moved in a variety of directions. Many, especially those who joined the Sadharan Brahmo Samaj, became involved in constitutional agitation to secure concessions for greater Indian participation in the government of India. Others became leading figures in Hindu 'revivalism', or went on to advocate *swaraj* through the *swadeshi* movement or more violent forms of opposition. Considering the range and extent of Keshab's influence on a variety of individuals, it is surprising that scholars have not paid more attention to his role in shaping Bengali social, political and religious ideas in the later nineteenth century.[58] Keshab's encounter with the 'West'—staged in Calcutta, in London and in the intertwined discourses which connected the two cities—provided a spectacular example of the possibilities, limits and contradictions of colonial subjectivity, which his contemporaries and subsequent generations in Bengal would have found difficult to ignore.

The task of assessing the importance of Keshab's influence on his contemporaries and subsequent generations cannot, of course, be one of simply identifying Keshab as the 'fountainhead' of particular ideas. Ideas emerge through a complex interaction of social, cultural, economic, political and discursive factors; their genesis cannot be traced solely to the mind of an individual. In any case, as Julius Lipner has pointed out, 'the cultural hothouse' of nineteenth-century Calcutta was characterised by 'a great deal of overlap and criss-crossing socially, religiously and/or intellectually'.[59] While it is beyond the scope of this book to explore Keshab's intellectual legacy in detail, I will suggest provisionally that his influence on his contemporaries and subsequent generations of Bengalis has been underestimated.

Keshab's universalist ideas certainly found echoes in the arguments advanced by Swami Vivekananda (1863–1902), who joined the *Naba Bidhan* in 1880, before becoming a disciple of Ramakrishna.[60] Indeed, Vivekananda played a role in Keshab's New Dispensation drama of September 1881.[61] While Vivekananda has often been portrayed as a representative of 'the high noon of a Hindu revival', his spiritual message, as Raychaudhuri has emphasised, was 'projected repeatedly as a universalistic faith'.[62] The arguments Vivekananda presented to the

World Parliament of Religions in Chicago in 1893, and in lectures across America, drew clearly on Keshab's notions of a mutual exchange between the 'spiritual' knowledge of the 'East' and the 'material' knowledge of the 'West'. Vivekananda's contention in New York that 'When the Oriental wants to learn about machine-making, he should sit at the feet of the Occidental... When the Occident wants to learn about the spirit, about God...he must sit at the feet of the Orient to learn', was influenced clearly by arguments Keshab had advanced to British audiences, and paraphrased directly a lecture Keshab had delivered in 1877.[63] Vivekananda's religious interpretation of evolution—from fungus, to plant, to animal, to man, and to God— drew on arguments Keshab had advanced.[64] The ideas he propounded in the 1890s concerning the 'Asiatic' origin of Christ were also prefigured by Keshab's pronouncements in the 1870s.[65]

Dermot Killingley has emphasised the extent to which Vivekananda's ideas were derived from 'Western' sources, and has contended that 'many of his distinctive ideas' were formed during his visit to the West from 1893 to 1896.[66] However, studies by Thomas Green and Elizabeth De Michelis have begun to give more weight to Keshab's influence on the development of his ideas.[67] Of course, it was Keshab who had popularised Ramakrishna in elite Calcutta society, so in this respect his indirect influence is indisputable. Green has suggested further that Vivekananda's approach to Ramakrishna was structured by the religious vocabulary of Keshab's Brahmo Samaj, which valued experience of the Divine as the ultimate source of religious authority.[68] De Michelis accords Keshab a central role in the genesis of the ideas Vivekananda espoused in his influential *Raja Yoga*, which in turn is treated as foundational to the conceptualisation and practice of yoga in the modern West.[69] Further research into these connections would prove productive in future studies of Vivekananda.

Keshab's universalism also found echoes in the ideas of the most studied of all the luminaries of Bengali culture, Rabindranath Tagore. While Tagore is often referred to in passing as a 'nationalist poet' or 'nationalist leader', most scholars have recognised universalism as a strong current in his thinking, particularly in the period following his disillusionment with and eventual rejection of 'nationalism' in the aftermath of the *swadeshi* movement.[70] In attempting to understand the genesis of Tagore's ideas, many historians have accorded great weight to Tagore's intellectual 'debts' to the 'West' (one biographer has claimed he 'admired the British character more than the Indian') and have suggested that his travels to the 'West' may have been motivated by a desire to gain a recognition abroad that he was lacking at home.[71] In contrast, Michael Collins has stressed the extent to which Tagorean 'anti-nationalism' was 'almost exclusively born out of Indian philosophical and theological traditions' (in particular, Tagore's reading of the *Upanishads*) and 'autochthonous historical experience'.[72] In my view, there are striking similarities between Tagore's post-nationalist conceptions of history and the historical ideas advanced by Keshab.

From the outset, we can draw attention to some clear differences in the worldviews of Keshab and Tagore. Most obviously, Tagore did not share Keshab's admiration for the British Raj, and Keshab's embrace of a figure such as Ramakrishna would have been anathema to Tagore and his Adi Brahmo heritage.[73] Nevertheless, Tagore's view of history shared important similarities with the views expressed by Keshab. Collins has contended that part of the 'distinctiveness of Tagore' can be found in his perspective on history, a perspective that revealed itself most powerfully in the years 1912–13:

> What is perhaps most interesting is that, like Hegel, Tagore saw World History as the steady unfolding of an idea. The marked distinction was that, unlike Hegel, he placed India at the centre of that process. In this regard, Tagore developed an alternative conception of modernity which saw the ideas, politics and technology of the West as only one aspect of a developing historical process, rather than its core movement.[74]

If we accept Collins' representation of Tagore's view of history, then we can also accept that Keshab's view of history—in which 'East' and 'West' played an equally vital role in a dialectical process which drove humanity and religion forward towards a unified ideal of 'perfection' or of 'God'—constituted an important precursor to it. Tagore's critique of imperialism rested, in part, on the argument that 'truth' was not the preserve of any particular group of human beings, and thus that the political and ideological domination of one society by another could never be justified. At times, he also expressed the view that truth, while universal, had been hitherto expressed most fully and clearly in Indian history.[75] Keshab, as we have seen, stressed repeatedly the superiority of an 'Eastern' form of inspirational 'truth' as a vehicle through which to establish the unity of 'East' and 'West', and he viewed this 'Eastern' mode of thought as existing in its purest state in India's past. If Tagore's ideas are to be placed, as Collins suggests they should be, in a genealogy of critiques of the 'liberating potential of Western modernity', then surely Keshab should also form part of this genealogy.[76]

It is not altogether surprising that scholars of Tagore have tended to neglect entirely his connection to Keshab.[77] Tagore seems to have distanced himself deliberately from Keshabite Brahmoism, as Keshab's reputation among religious universalists in the West had been so badly damaged in the later years of his life. William Radice has suggested that Tagore's lectures on *The Religion of Man* (delivered at the Unitarian Harris Manchester College in May 1930, and published in the following year) demonstrate his desire 'to reconnect with Unitarians and a wider circle of free-thinking, rationalist religious thinkers by carefully leaving Keshub, Ramakrishna, Vivekananda and Hindu revivalism out'.[78] Of course, Tagore's omission of such figures from his account of Indian religion would have stemmed, in part, from his opposition, in general, to revivalism, nationalism and Hindu chauvinism.[79] However, his lack of reference to Keshab when addressing British audiences may also have stemmed from an awareness that Keshab's innovations through the New Dispensation had given Bengali universalism in Britain a 'bad name'. In a lecture delivered in India in 1910, Tagore spoke enthusiastically about Keshab's commitment to universalist principles, and praised his attempts to find truth in all religions.[80] Tagore must have been aware that, when he delivered the spiritual message of 'Asia' to the 'West', he was following in the footsteps of a previous messenger.[81]

A striking aspect of Keshab's legacy is the diversity of directions in which his ideas were taken. While Vivekananda drew upon Keshab's rhetoric in order to argue for the superiority of 'Hinduism' to other religions, and Tagore echoed Keshab's ideas of history in his attempts to advance a universalist alternative to nationalism, other figures found in Keshab's ideas the basis for direct action against the British empire that Keshab so admired. It was Keshab's reception in the 'West', and the ideas he expressed there, which formed the basis of Bipin Chandra Pal's (1858–1932) assessment of him as a key figure in the history of the 'Battle of Swaraj' in India.[82] Pal, who joined the Brahmo Samaj in 1878, is most often remembered as a leader of the *swadeshi* movement, and as part of the so-called 'extremist' camp of nationalists that included figures such as Aurobindo Ghose and Brahmabandhab Upadhyay.[83] Pal's *Brahmo Samaj and the Battle for Swaraj*—a work that attempted to translate the radical elements of Brahmo social and spiritual thought into a political struggle for freedom—points to Keshab's lectures in England as 'one of the scriptures of our new cult of patriotism'.[84] While Keshab's religious message, in Pal's view, was 'little removed from Unitarian Christianity', his 'wonderful reception' in England, along with his 'intellectual' and 'moral' powers, 'relieved' English-educated Bengalis of their 'sense of the intellectual inferiority of their race', which 'was certainly by no means a negligible contribution to the birth and growth of the new Freedom Movement in India'.[85] In particular, Keshab's lecture in London, 'England's Duties to India', 'helped very materially to quicken a new national self-consciousness and a strong desire for political freedom in his own people'.[86] Pal, it seems, found in Keshab's universalist message to the 'West' the basis for a more overtly nationalist assertion of India's right to political freedom.

While Pal was frequently critical of Keshab's and Majumdar's Unitarian Theistic leanings, Brahmobandhab Upadhyay, who formally joined Majumdar's faction of the New Dispensation in 1887 (six years after becoming Keshab's disciple), may have found in them another route to the advocacy of *swaraj*.[87] As Lipner has observed in his biography of Upadhyay, Keshab's criticisms of the 'alienating character of Christianity' (in the sense that it had been presented by missionaries in India in a 'denationalised' form) were to 'loom large in Bhabani's [Upadhyay's] own understanding of his Christian commitment'.[88] Lipner draws attention also to Upadhyay's later use of Keshabite conceptions of 'idol worship' and the motherhood of God in his rehabilitation of Hinduism.[89] In August 1890, Upadhyay stated in the journal *The Harmony* that his attempts to harmonise religion stemmed directly from the 'great man' Keshab, whom 'God raised up'.[90] The subsequent development of Upadhyay's ideas and activities—his conversion to Roman Catholicism, his later embrace of *advaitic* (monistic) thought and his involvement in the anti-partition and *swadeshi* agitation—are too complex to trace here.[91] Nevertheless, it seems that Keshab's insistence on the need for 'Indianised' Christianity exerted a powerful influence on Upadhyay's attempts to remain culturally a Hindu in spite of being spiritually committed as a Christian.[92]

Subsequent generations of Bengalis largely discarded Keshab's idealist view of history, and constructed alternative historical narratives in order to propose political solutions to problems of inequality in India. Surendranath Bannerjee and his associates constructed historical narratives that drew India more closely into the constitutional history of Britain, and demanded that the liberal 'romance' of representative government this history embodied be extended to the Indian people.[93] While Keshab's holistic vision of progress subsumed the history of the 'West' within a broader dialectic, Bannerjee's perspective served to imbricate India's history firmly into the history of the 'West'. Dadabhai Naoroji and R. C. Dutt, who constructed economic histories that sought to understand the origins of Indian poverty through analyses that were focused rigorously on the material world, also departed from the idealist orientation of Keshab's historical narrative.[94] Alongside his economic critiques, Dutt wrote a *History of Civilization in Ancient India*, which, in contrast to Keshab's bifurcation of history into a 'spiritual' history of the 'East' and a 'material' history of the 'West', placed India squarely within the history of material civilisation, by emphasising the contribution made by Hindu civilisation to science as well as religion.[95] In Dutt's account, philosophy and science were not only characteristic of European Christian civilisation; rather, the history of the 'West' could also be found in the history of India.

There is little evidence to suggest that Keshab's ideas exerted any lasting influence on British audiences. Keshab's extensive Unitarian network of political, social, religious and familial connections had been crucial to his ability to gain influence in the British public sphere. When the Unitarians broke with Keshab in the aftermath of the Cuch Bihar controversy, his access to British audiences was diminished significantly. Furthermore, Unitarianism itself, by the time of Keshab's death, was declining in influence in Britain. In the last quarter of the nineteenth century, Unitarianism lost its ideological coherence as its members devoted their attention to a variety of causes—social service, socialism, the peace movement, temperance, vegetarianism and even Spiritualism.[96] The close familial and social ties that provided much of the basis for Unitarian influence were gradually undone by an increase in social mobility and intermarriage.[97] In addition, the continued Unitarian impetus towards social reform came to be grounded increasingly in a sociological, as opposed to a religious, understanding of social issues.[98] The Unitarians, like many of their contemporaries in Bengal, came to doubt the effectiveness of religious solutions to social and political problems.[99]

Keshab's vision of a mutual and equal exchange between 'East' and 'West' did not exert any significant influence on British policy in India. This is made abundantly clear by the increasingly aggressive turns imperialism took in India in the last quarter of the nineteenth century. Lord Dufferin (who replaced Lord Ripon as Viceroy in 1885) was sent out to India with explicit instructions to curb the progress of the reforms his predecessor had attempted to implement.[100] The end of Gladstone's third premiership in 1886 (precipitated by the defeat of the Irish Home Rule Bill, which split the Liberal party) inaugurated an era of Conservative government that, with the exception of a short Gladstonian interlude, would last until the twentieth century. Popular imperialism and more rigidly paternalistic conceptions of imperial rule grew in ideological force in the last quarter of the nineteenth century, as jingoistic Toryism and imperial expansionism reached their zenith.[101] As Britain's pre-eminent position among the world powers no longer appeared to be secure, a firmer hand in dealing with subject populations throughout the British empire was deemed to be necessary. Lord Salisbury had no doubt that self-government was only suitable for people of the 'Teutonic' race; the despotic actions of Lord Curzon, who pursued his plan for the partition of Bengal in 1905 with a flagrant disregard for public opposition in Calcutta, provided final confirmation that the British government in India were not willing to give a 'gift' of freedom and equality.[102] With the rise of more aggressive imperialism on the one hand, and nationalist extremism on the other, universalist ideals of mutual exchange and harmony ceased to provide a compelling lens through which to view Britain's relationship to empire.

Colonial Subjectivity: Possibilities, Limits and Contradictions

Keshab's visit to England enabled him to present his ideas to a considerable number of Britons, through the series of speeches he delivered to very large audiences, and through the extraordinary degree of national and provincial press coverage he received. The extensive network of Unitarian connections to which he had access enabled him to produce a considerable impact upon the British public sphere. His substantial degree of access to the highest levels of government, and, in particular, his connection with Lord Lawrence, ensured that his ideas were heard by people who were directly responsible for the administration in India. His success in securing British support for some of the reforms he advocated is demonstrated by the fact that the government provided financial support for a number of the initiatives conducted under the auspices of the Indian Reform Association, and supported his plans for the Marriage Act in 1872. Keshab felt 'at home' in the 'heart of the empire' in 1870, and was comfortable with his sense of identity as both an 'Indian' and a 'man of the world'. He was confident that he had the support of the British people and the British government for his program of religious and social reform, and the adulation he received from Unitarians bolstered his conviction that the Brahmo Samaj of India would engender a religious reformation in India, and would have a significant impact on religious progress in Britain.

The high degree of press interest Keshab generated in Britain, and the reports of the support he received which filtered back to the press in India, did much to cement his reputation in Calcutta as one of the pre-eminent religious and social reformers of his era. His visit to Britain was regarded generally in Calcutta as a 'triumph', and did much to secure increased support for the Brahmo Samaj of India. Keshab's confident presentation of the message of 'Asia' to the 'West' set an important precedent for subsequent visitors, including Swami Vivekananda and Rabindranath Tagore, and provided inspiration for later, more overtly nationalist, representations of Indian issues on the world stage.

However, Keshab's status as a colonial subject set strict limits to the meanings he could carry for British audiences. In 1870, the majority of British commentators interpreted Keshab's 'manliness' as resulting from the 'gift' of English education and Christian teaching, imparted through the civilising force of the British empire. The 'spectacle' of Keshab on the public platform provided evidence of the unquestionably beneficial effects of imperialism on colonial subjects. That Keshab's visit did little to undermine the widespread belief that the benefits of civilisation flowed in one direction—from metropole to colony—is demonstrated by the fact that, when Rabindranath Tagore came to London in the early twentieth century, his 'manliness' was interpreted similarly as engendered by the twin agencies of English education and Christian belief.[103] While Keshab was championed as an embodiment of the civilising achievements of the empire, he was also represented as half-civilised, as unworthy of occupying the position of teacher, and as an enemy to Christianity in Britain and India. While the Unitarians— and many others in Britain—found genuine value in Keshab's 'otherness', the 'gift' of his teaching was interpreted in a way that served to justify the continuance of imperial rule in India. At the time of Keshab's death, while some of the obituaries in the British press continued to portray him as symbolic of the transformative capacity of the imperial mission, his life was more often regarded as emblematic of the limits of the power of the civilising process. In 1870, Keshab was championed as a figure who, through an 'independence' conferred by the gift of English education, had achieved a measure of agency which had enabled him to progress beyond the 'superstitions' of his countrymen. By the 1880s, his activities and ideas signalled to British audiences the fundamental limits to agency in India imposed by 'Hinduism' and the 'Asiatic mind'.

While I have argued that a binary opposition of 'coloniser' and 'colonised' was fundamental to British interpretations of Keshab, the diversity of the ways in which Keshab was represented in Britain and in Calcutta demonstrates that neither side of the binary was homogenous. The genuine value the Unitarians ascribed to Keshab's 'otherness', and the extent to which they concurred with his conception of holistic historical progress, shows that imperial discourses were not structured entirely by a simple binary in which a rationalist, positivist 'West' constructed an image of a spiritual and ultimately backward 'East' in order to justify the continuance of imperial rule. An intellectual tension between the 'critical spirit' and the 'will to believe', and a desire to moderate the 'materialist' and 'rationalist' character of industrial and scientific modernity with 'spiritual' and religious insights, existed in both Britain and Bengal.

Keshabite Brahmos and English Unitarians were united in their attempts to spiritualise rationality and rationalise spirituality—to reconcile science and religion. Their attempts were informed by the intellectual and religious histories of Unitarianism and Brahmoism, and the traditions of Christianity and Hinduism on which they drew, and also by discourses of Romanticism, idealism and Transcendentalism, which exerted influence in both metropole and colony. These discourses did not travel uni-directionally from the metropole to the colony. Rather, they were interpreted creatively and selectively in multiple imperial sites, and were remade and reconfigured as they circulated across networks of empire.

Keshab's belief in historical progress constituted a point of continuity in his thought throughout his life. The evidence does not support David Kopf's contention that Keshab's lectures from the mid-1870s evince a 'total absence of any faith in social improvement or the idea of progress'.[104] In 1870, Keshab expounded two narratives of history— 'stadial' and 'holistic'—that expressed both the superior position occupied by Britain in the 'scale of nations' in the present, and the vital role that India would play in the furtherance of human progress in the future. His concept of 'madness' served to give epistemological substance to the perspective on 'truth' to which, he claimed, the 'East' had privileged access; the 'Pilgrimages to Saints' constituted an attempt to put the theory of 'madness' into practice. Keshab may have spiritualised his notion of progress, and emphasised increasingly its holistic and dialectical character, but he did not abandon it.

The narrative of progress that Keshab expounded aligned with hegemonic discourses of liberal imperialism in a number of important respects. It was a narrative that was predicated on a belief in the formal equality of all humans, and on an assumption that this formal equality would be realised through the extension of education, the increase in opportunities for self-government, the reduction in economic inequality and the spread of more tolerant attitudes towards religious belief, all of which would be furthered through the continuance of 'benevolent' imperial rule. However, Keshab reconfigured the liberal narrative of progress in holistic terms, and insisted that the distinctive 'national' qualities of Indians and people from the 'East' played a vital role in its unfolding. This provides evidence of the great extent to which liberal imperial narratives of progress could be transformed through their creative interpretation in the colonies.

It is possible to detect definite shifts in Keshab's thought in the 1870s and 1880s—a more spiritualised conception of femininity, a greater reliance on inspiration as a privileged mode of thought, an 'aristocratic' as opposed to 'democratic' approach to eclecticism, and a move away from free trade as a model for the circulation of ideas. However, it is difficult to subsume these shifts into a broader historical transition from 'liberalism' to 'culturalism'. While, in the course of the 1870s, Keshab laid greater emphasis on the subjective aspects of religion and stressed the importance of experience over reason, he went to great lengths to establish that his discourse of 'madness' was a 'rational' discourse, and insisted upon the necessity of balancing a focus on inner, subjective religious life with a commitment to reforming the external world. His spiritualisation of 'Indian' femininity and the domestic sphere occurred in tandem with his spiritualisation of Queen Victoria, the imperial family and the public sphere. Keshab's universalism attempted to hold together many of the divergent strands of thinking in Bengali intellectual culture.

In attempting to hold together so many divergent strands of thought, the universalism Keshab propounded assumed a complex and often contradictory character. Kopf has contended that Keshab's universalism offered a clear alternative to imperialism, on the one hand, and nationalism, on the other, and has argued that Keshab 'To the end of his life...offered harmony to both Indian nationalists and British imperialists'.[105] But what sort of harmony did Keshab offer?

While Keshab looked towards a future in which 'East' and 'West' would be united, he stressed repeatedly the fundamental differences between 'East' and 'West'. He thus contributed to the construction and reification of a difference between cultures that his universalism purported to transcend. His tendency to attempt both to eradicate and to preserve difference constituted an abiding tension within his universalism. Keshab's view of the Indian 'nation' was premised upon a belief that the people of 'India' were united by their innately spiritual nature—a nature that was elucidated through a series of comparisons with the characteristics of the 'Western other'. Keshab used the terms 'India', 'East' and 'Asia' interchangeably, suggesting that his concept of the Indian 'nation' was not geographically or temporally limited, but referred, rather, to the 'spiritual' characteristics of one half of the 'world'. While Keshab's valorisation of the spirituality of the 'East' provided a basis for his critique of 'Western' materialism, he had an abiding faith that the British empire constituted God's chief instrument in animating the historical dialectic between 'East' and 'West'. His idealist view of history led him to propose an idealist solution to the problem of inequality between 'East' and 'West'. He proposed primarily a spiritual alliance of 'Asia' and 'Europe', and did not, in general, make political demands. This ideal of spiritual unity did not resonate with the realities of an increasingly politically charged and racially divided India. Keshab's universalism did not, in fact, offer a clear alternative either to imperialism or to nationalism.

If Keshab's universalism was complex and often contradictory, then the same could be said of the universalism of the English Unitarians. In many respects, the inter-cultural dialogue between Keshabite Brahmoism and English Unitarianism demonstrates that religious discourses in an imperial context did not always take the form of an outright assertion of the superiority of British Christianity to other forms of religious faith. The religious dimensions of empire cannot be reduced to a missionary history of attempts to convert non-white peoples from 'heathen' religions to Christianity. The Unitarians shared Keshab's belief that the religious and social progress of humanity would be furthered greatly by a mutual exchange of ideas between 'East' and 'West'. Their vision of religious progress placed a high value on the religious beliefs of other cultures and civilisations.

However, while the English Unitarians engaged seriously in a dialogue with Keshabite Brahmoism that they hoped would enrich their own religious faith, their inclusionary attitude towards Keshab existed alongside a powerful exclusionary impulse. They welcomed Keshab with enthusiasm because the ideas he expressed appeared to confirm the truth of their own beliefs. They were wary of the numerous innovations Keshab introduced into the Brahmo Samaj of India and the New Dispensation in the 1870s and 1880s. While, even in the years following the Cuch Bihar marriage, they continued to find value in aspects of the religious practices of the New Dispensation, they never considered adopting any of these practices themselves.

The 'grammar of difference' through which the Unitarians interpreted Keshab in 1870 constructed him as an 'Eastern other' and attributed genuine value to his otherness. Keshab's 'racial' predisposition towards 'authentic' emotion and devotion imbued him with qualities that men and women in the 'West' lacked, but needed. However, the 'authentic' emotional immediacy of 'Indians' that rendered them worthy of admiration also defined them as people who were in need of protection and guidance. When Keshab appeared to have abandoned a 'rational' and Christian-orientated Theism in favour of an 'irrational' and Hindu-orientated mysticism, the 'racial' characteristics that had constituted a major part of his fascination for Unitarians were identified as a primary cause of his decline. A key basis for Keshab's inclusion—his 'racial' predisposition towards 'authentic' emotion and devotion—became a basis for his exclusion. The inclusionary impulse of English Unitarianism was structured by a grammar of racial difference that placed Keshab in a subordinate position whilst simultaneously valorising him. Albeit in less obvious, and perhaps in more insidious, ways, Unitarian universalism, like the theological absolutism of the traditional missionary enterprise, was predicated on an assumption that the religious beliefs of the Anglo-Saxon 'West' were, ultimately, superior to those of other cultures.

There can be no doubt that an exclusionary impulse also underlay the inclusionary rhetoric Keshab employed as leader of the New Dispensation. While Keshab insisted that the New Dispensation would unite all of humanity and all prior world religions into a common bond, he invoked the 'winnowing fan' of Cuch Bihar in order to make sense of his dwindling popularity in India and Britain. While he proclaimed Divine inspiration to be universal, in practice he aggregated to himself a special capacity to receive inspiration, and demanded that his religious strictures were observed. Keshab's belief in the importance of his own role in world history, and his conviction that he acted on the basis of Divine command, led him to adopt an increasingly hostile stance towards other religious groups that did not share his beliefs. The ever more rigid control he exerted over the diminishing number of followers of the New Dispensation suggests that the ideal of harmonious religious perfection towards which, in theory, all of human history progressed, would, in practice, be realised only within the limited apostolic community of a chosen few.

The activities of Keshab's apostolic community were characterised by attempts to 'perform' a unity between 'East' and 'West' that did not exist in reality. Throughout his life, Keshab actively, self-consciously and creatively sought to 'live out'—to experience and to 'perform'—the discourses to which he contributed and in terms of which he understood his place in the world. Historical accounts of Keshab that have interpreted his universalism solely through the lens of intellectual history or theology have failed to appreciate the significant, and often contradictory, ways in which he 'lived' the ideas he expressed. Keshab sought to unify discourses of a spiritual 'East' and a material 'West' not only by reconciling them intellectually and theologically, but also through embodying them in his own person, domesticating them in his own household, and subjectively realising them in his own consciousness. If the stage upon which Keshab appeared as the 'clownish juggler' constituted, literally, a theatre in which he could 'perform' the unity of 'East' and 'West', then this was a performance which he also staged, in various guises, in the theatre of the everyday—in his home, in his gardens, in his appearance. This book has served, I hope, to demonstrate the importance of the cultural and performative dimensions of Keshab's universalism.

As I have stressed throughout, the ways in which Keshab was constructed discursively were extraordinarily diverse—there was no single identity in terms of which he was interpreted. There was also no single identity in terms of which Keshab understood or represented himself. In Britain, he stressed his status as an 'Indian' and as a 'man of the world'; by portraying himself as an example in miniature of his holistic philosophy of progress, he represented himself as an embodiment of India's future; in his letters to his wife and friends, he emphasised his regional identity as 'Bengali'. In the 1870s, he attempted self-consciously to subjectively 'live out' a number of identities simultaneously: to perform the role of an English-educated and 'Westernised' 'native gentleman', and to perform the role of an ascetic guru with access to an authentically 'Eastern' inspirational knowledge—in this latter guise he appeared as an embodiment of an idealised notion of India's past. In the years leading up to the Cuch Bihar marriage, and more openly in the years following it, he represented himself as a 'great man' and a 'prophet', a figure of truly world-historical significance. However, this confident self-image existed alongside other, more troubled and fractured modes of self-representation: the 'clownish juggler', the madman and the 'puzzle'. His experience of colonial subjectivity was diverse, shifting and open-ended.

However, if the lived experience and discursive construction of colonial subjectivity was always mutable, it was also limited fundamentally by relations of power immanent in imperialism. It is significant that Keshab's final prayer, with which this book began, was addressed to his 'Mother'—that is, to God—whom he invoked as a source of strength in the face of the 'rebuke' he was receiving from critics in India and in Britain. Keshab's personal relationship with the Divine was, of course, of central importance to his sense of self. Throughout the 1870s and 1880s, Keshab turned increasingly to direct communion with his 'Mother' in order to make sense of his place in the world. His subjectivity came to be grounded in the direct experience of a Divine presence in which 'East' and 'West', self and other, and difference itself, might dissolve. However, even Keshab's relationship with this Divine presence was fractured by the imperial world in which he lived. Keshab continued to believe that his 'Mother', alongside her 'daughter' Victoria, held the British empire as her primary instrument for effecting the holistic union of 'East' and 'West'. The instrument in which Keshab placed his faith to engender the eradication of inequalities between 'East' and 'West' was an instrument that depended upon the construction and maintenance of grammars of difference in order to secure its existence. Keshab's universalist vision of harmony was predicated on the valorisation of a Providentially directed imperial system that produced and proliferated the inequalities he wished to transcend. While an 'Indian' and a 'man of the world', Keshab was always, inescapably, a colonial subject. The life he lived, and the meanings he carried, bear testament to the grandeur, ambition and idealism of a universalist dream that was impossible to realise in an imperial world.

NOTES

A NOTE ON TERMINOLOGY

1. Lipner, Julius J., *Hindus: Their Religious Beliefs and Practices* (2nd ed., London, New York: Routledge, 2010), pp. 37–75.

CHAPTER 1: INTRODUCTION

1. Mozoomdar, P. C., *The Life and Teachings of Keshub Chunder Sen* (3rd ed., Calcutta: Nababidhan Trust, 1931), p. 490 [Hereafter *PCM*]. *Dharmatattwa*, 23 Sep. 1884, pp. 195–6.
2. *PCM*, p. 501.
3. "The Pagal—V", in Sen, Keshub Chunder, *The New Dispensation or the Religion of Harmony, Compiled from Keshub Chunder Sen's Writings* (Calcutta: Bidhan Press, 1903), p. 248.
4. The most recent biographical study in English is Meredith Borthwick's, *Keshub Chunder Sen: A Search for Cultural Synthesis* (Calcutta: Minerva, 1977). Borthwick argues that Keshab spent his life trying to resolve his two heritages—'Indian' and 'English'—ultimately finding resolution in a vision of world harmony and religious synthesis institutionalised in the New Dispensation. Works discussing Keshab from a theological perspective include Damen, Frans, *Crisis and Religious Renewal in the Brahmo Samaj (1860–1884): A Documentary Study of the Emergence of the "New Dispensation" under Keshab Chandra Sen* (Belgium: Katholieke Universiteit Leuven, 1983); Boyd, R. H. S., *An Introduction to Indian Christian Theology* (Madras: ISPCK, 1969); Roy Pape, W., "Keshub Chunder Sen's Doctrine of Christ and the Trinity: A Rehabilitation", *The Indian Journal of Theology*, 25 (1976); Lavan, S., *Unitarians and India: A Study in Encounter and Response* (Boston: Skinner House, 1977); Thomas, M. M., *The Acknowledged Christ of the Indian Renaissance* (Bangalore: SCM Press, 1970). The classic Bengali

biography is Roy, G. G., *Acharya Keshavchandra* (3 vols, Calcutta, 1938). More recent literature that engages with Keshab's life and work is dealt with in the course of the book.

5.   Important works by apologists include those of P. C. Majumdar and P. K. Sen (see bibliography). The most influential dissenting accounts are Sastri, Sivanath, *History of the Brahmo Samaj* (2nd ed., Calcutta: Sadharan Brahmo Samaj, 1974)—first published in two volumes between 1911 and 1912—and Bose, Ram Chandra, *Brahmoism; or, History of Reformed Hinduism* (New York, London: Funk & Wagnalls, 1884). Accounts by Christian missionaries include Slater, T. E., *Keshab Chandra Sen and the Brahmo Samaj* (Madras, Calcutta, London: Society for Promoting Christian Knowledge, Thacker Spink & Co., James Clark & Co., 1884).

6.   Müller, Max, *Biographical Essays* (London: Longmans Green & Co., 1884), p. 72.

7.   "My Impressions of England", 12 September 1870, in Writers Workshop (eds.), *Keshub Chunder Sen in England: Diaries, Sermons, Addresses and Epistles* (4th ed., Calcutta: Writers Workshop, 1980) [Hereafter *WW*], p. 460.

8.   The literature is vast. See, for example, Hall, Catherine, *Civilising Subjects: Metropole and Colony in the English Imagination 1830–1867* (Cambridge: Polity, 2002); Midgley, Clare, Alison Twells and Julie Carlier (eds.), *Women in Transnational History. Connecting the Local and the Global* (Oxon: Routledge, 2016).

9.   Early attempts to bring domestic and imperial British history into a single analytic frame, many of which were inspired by Edward Said's seminal book *Orientalism*, often focused on 'binary oppositions' between coloniser and colonised. I agree with Catherine Hall that the 'framework of them/us, or what is absolutely the same versus what is absolutely other, will not do. It is not possible to make sense of empire either theoretically or empirically through a binary lens: we need the dislocation of that binary and more elaborate, cross-cutting ways of thinking'. Hall, *Civilising Subjects*, p. 16. Said, E. W., *Orientalism: Western Conceptions of the Orient* (London: Penguin, 1995); Said, E. W., *Culture and Imperialism* (London: Chatto & Windus, 1993).

10.   Ballantyne, Tony, *Entanglements of Empire. Missionaries, Māori, and the Question of the Body* (Durham, NC., Duke University Press, 2014), pp. 24–5.

11.   For an overview of recent trends in the writing of transnational and global history, see Moyn, Samuel and Andrew Sartori (eds.), *Global Intellectual History* (New York: Columbia University Press, 2013).

12.   The archival work of Rozina Visram has formed much of the basis for subsequent attempts to 're-write' South Asians back into British history. Visram, Rozina, *Asians in Britain: 400 Years of History* (London: Pluto Press, 2002); Visram, Rozina, *Ayahs, Lascars and Princes: Indians in Britain, 1700–1947* (London: Pluto Press, 1986).

13.   Kapila, Shruti, "Global Intellectual History and the Indian Political", in McMahon, Darrin M. and Samuel Moyn, *Rethinking Modern European Intellectual History* (New York: Oxford University Press, 2014), p. 254.

14.   Cooper, Frederick, *Colonialism in Question: Theory, Knowledge, History* (Berkeley: University of California Press, 2005), p. 26.

15. Stoler, Ann Laura and Frederick Cooper, "Between Metropole and Colony: Rethinking a Research Agenda", in Stoler, Ann Laura and Frederick Cooper (eds.), *Tensions of Empire: Colonial Cultures in a Bourgeois World* (Berkeley, Los Angeles, London: University of California Press, 1997), pp. 3–4.

16. Hall, *Civilising Subjects*, p. 16.

17. Burton, Antoinette, *Burdens of History: British Feminists, Indian Women and Imperial Culture*, 1865–1915 (Chapel Hill: University of North Carolina Press, 1994); Sinha, Mrinalini, *Colonial Masculinity: The 'Manly Englishman' and the 'Effeminate Bengali' in the Late Nineteenth Century* (Manchester: Manchester University Press, 1995); Stoler, Ann Laura, *Race and the Education of Desire: Foucault's 'History of Sexuality' and the Colonial Order of Things* (Durham, NC: Duke University Press, 1995); McClintock, Anne, *Imperial Leather: Race, Gender and Sexuality in the Colonial Context* (New York: Routledge, 1995); Midgley, Clare, *Women against Slavery: The British Campaigns, 1780–1870* (London: Routledge, 1992); Hall, Catherine and Leonore Davidoff, *Family Fortunes: Men and Women of the English Middle Class 1780–1850* (Oxon: Routledge, 2002).

18. This view of Keshab is advanced in Kopf, David, *The Brahmo Samaj and the Shaping of the Modern Indian Mind* (New Jersey: Princeton University Press, 1979), pp. 249–86. That the nineteenth-century Bengali elite suffered some form of 'identity crisis' has become almost a truism in the historiography.

19. Collins, Michael, *Rabindranath Tagore and the West: Nationalism, Empire and Inter-Cultural Dialogue, 1912–1941* (Unpublished PhD Thesis, University of Oxford, 2008), p. 77.

20. Bloch, Marc, *The Historian's Craft*, cited in Hall, Catherine, *Macaulay and Son. Architects of Imperial Britain* (New Haven and London: Yale University Press, 2012), p. xviii.

21. Ibid., pp. xviii–xix.

22. My approach is influenced by the methods of discourse analysis and the philosophy of Michel Foucault, and the various traditions of scholarship his work has inspired. The clearest exposition of Foucault's central insights concerning the relationship between power-knowledge and the 'production' of subjects can be found in Foucault, Michel, *Discipline and Punish: The Birth of the Prison* (London: Penguin, 1991). Foucault's later attempts to restore a measure of agency to subjects through the incorporation of notions of 'resistance' can be found in his series on sexuality: Foucault, Michel, *The Will to Knowledge: The History of Sexuality Volume I* (London: Penguin, 1998); Foucault, Michel, *The Use of Pleasure: The History of Sexuality Volume II* (London: Penguin, 1992); Foucault, Michel, *The Care of the Self: The History of Sexuality Volume III* (London: Penguin, 1990).

23. Venn, Couze, *The Postcolonial Challenge: Towards Alternative Worlds* (London: SAGE, 2006), p. 79. See also Blackman, Lisa, John Cromby, Derek Hook, Dimitris Papadopoulos and Valerie Walkerdine, "Creating Subjectivities", *Subjectivity* (2008).

24. Venn, *The Postcolonial Challenge*, p. 79.

25. Ibid.

26. Woodward, Kathryn, "Concepts of Identity and Difference", in Woodward, Kathryn (ed.), *Identity and Difference* (London: SAGE, 1997), p. 39.

27. See the introduction to Butler, Judith, *Bodies that Matter: On the Discursive Limits of "Sex"* (New York, London: Routledge, 1993).

28. Bayly, C. A., *Recovering Liberties: Indian Thought in the Age of Liberalism and Empire* (Cambridge: Cambridge University Press, 2012), p. 343.

29. Ballantyne, Tony and Antoinette Burton, "Introduction: Bodies, Empires, and World Histories", in Tony Ballantyne and Antoinette Burton (eds.), *Bodies in Contact: Rethinking Colonial Encounters in World History* (Durham, London: Duke University Press, 2005), p. 6.

30. Burton, Antoinette, "Making a Spectacle of Empire: Indian Travellers in Fin-de-Siècle London", *History Workshop Journal*, 42 (Autumn, 1996), pp. 126–46.

31. Dobe, Timothy S., *Hindu Christian Faqir. Modern Monks, Global Christianity and Indian Sainthood* (New York: Oxford University Press, 2015); Singleton, Mark, *Yoga Body. The Origins of Modern Posture Practice* (New York: Oxford University Press, 2010); Yelle, Robert A., *Semiotics of Religion. Signs of the Sacred in History* (London, Delhi, New York, Sydney: Bloomsbury, 2013).

32. Hall, *Macaulay and Son*, p. xviii.

33. Mantena, Karuna. *Alibis of Empire: Henry Maine and the Ends of Liberal Imperialism* (Princeton: Princeton University Press, 2010), pp. 1–20.

34. Chakrabarty, Dipesh, *Provincializing Europe: Postcolonial Thought and Historical Difference* (Princeton: Princeton University Press, 2000); Chatterjee, Partha, "Whose Imagined Community?", in Balakrishnan, Gopal (ed.), *Mapping the Nation* (London: Verso, 1996).

35. Mohr, Michel, *Buddhism, Unitarianism, and the Meiji Competition for Universality* (Cambridge MA: Harvard University Asia Center, 2014), pp. 247–8. Mohr identifies three types of universalism: empirical (relating to 'facts' that are claimed to be true irrespective of circumstances); epistemological (relating to mental processes); and ethical (relating to moral absolutes). While historians tend to accept the mutability of universalisms (plural), some philosophers continue to debate the epistemological foundations of 'universals'—see, for example, Strawson, P. F. and Arindam Chakrabarti (eds.), *Universals, Concepts, and Qualities: New Essays on the Meaning of Predicates* (Aldershot, England and Burlington, VT: Ashgate, 2006). For a theological approach, see Chandler, Daniel Ross, *Toward Universal Religion: Voices of American and Indian Spirituality* (Westport, CT: Greenwood Press, 1996).

36. Mohr, *Buddhism, Unitarianism*, p. 246.

37. Tsing, Anna Lowenhaupt, *Friction. An Ethnography of Global Connection* (Princeton and Oxford: Princeton University Press, 2005), p. 1.

38. Ibid., p. 9.

39. Bose, Sugata, "Different Universalisms, Colorful Cosmopolitanisms: The Global Imagination of the Colonized", in Bose, Sugata and Kris Manjapra (eds.), *Cosmopolitan Thought Zones. South Asia and the Global Circulation of Ideas* (Basingstoke: Palgrave Macmillan, 2010), p. 99.

40.   Bose, Sugata and Kris Manjapra (eds.), *Cosmopolitan Thought Zones. South Asia and the Global Circulation of Ideas* (Basingstoke: Palgrave Macmillan, 2010).

41.   Mohr, *Buddhism, Unitarianism*, p. 237.

42.   Jalal, Ayesha, *Self and Sovereignty: Individual and Community in South Asian Islam since 1850* (London: Routledge, 2000).

43.   Tsing, *Friction*, p. 9.

44.   Koditschek, Theodore, *Liberalism, Imperialism, and the Historical Imagination: Nineteenth-Century Visions of a Greater Britain* (Cambridge: Cambridge University Press, 2011), p. 6.

45.   Bose, "Different Universalisms", p. 109.

46.   Mohr, *Buddhism, Unitarianism*, p. 238.

47.   Koditschek, *Liberalism*, p. 1.

48.   Bayly, C. A., "Empires and Indian Liberals", in Hall, Catherine and Keith McClelland (eds.), *Race, Nation and Empire: Making Histories, 1750 to the Present* (Manchester: Manchester University Press, 2010), p. 74. Bayly expands upon these ideas in Bayly, *Recovering Liberties*.

49.   Mehta, Uday S., *Liberalism and Empire* (Chicago: University of Chicago Press, 1999), p. 192.

50.   Ibid., p. 193.

51.   Ibid., p. 191.

52.   Chakrabarty, *Provincializing Europe,* p. 8.

53.   Sartori, Andrew, *Liberalism in Empire. An Alternative History* (Oakland: University of California Press, 2014), p. 4.

54.   Ibid.

55.   For discussions of this ideological shift, see Mantena, *Alibis of Empire*; Pitts, Jennifer, *A Turn to Empire. The Rise of Imperial Liberalism in Britain and France* (Princeton and Oxford: Princeton University Press, 2005); Muthu, Sankar, *Enlightenment Against Empire* (Princeton: Princeton University Press, 2003).

56.   Chidester, David, *Empire of Religion. Imperialism and Comparative Religion* (Chicago and London: The University of Chicago Press, 2014); Dobe, *Hindu Christian Faqir*; Mandair, Arvind-Pal S., *Religion and the Specter of the West. Sikhism, India, Postcoloniality, and the Politics of Translation* (New York: Columbia University Press, 2009); Hall, *Civilising Subjects*; Thorne, Susan, *Congregational Missions and the Making of an Imperial Culture in Nineteenth-Century England* (Stanford: Stanford University Press, 1999); Comaroff, Jean and John Comaroff, *Of Revelation and Revolution. Christianity, Colonialism and Consciousness in South Africa* (Chicago: University of Chicago Press, 1991).

57.   Mandair, *Religion*. For a detailed discussion of the concept of 'religion' in nineteenth-century comparative religion, see Chidester, *Empire of Religion*, pp. 11–23.

58.   Chidester, *Empire of Religion*, p. 4.

59.   Ibid.

60.   For an overview of the historiography, see Gottschalk, Peter, *Religion, Science, and Empire. Classifying Hindu and Islam in British India* (New York: Oxford University Press, 2013).

61. For a fascinating account of these connections, see Gandhi, Leela, *Affective Communities. Anticolonial Thought, Fin-de-Siècle Radicalism, and the Politics of Friendship* (Durham, London: Duke University Press, 2006).

62. For an example of the 'politicisation of the Bengal Renaissance thesis', see Bose, N. S., *The Indian Awakening and Bengal* (3rd ed., Calcutta: Firma K. L. Mukhopadyay, 1969).

63. Joshi, V. C. (ed.), *Rammohun Roy and the Process of Modernization in India* (Delhi: Vikas Publishing House, 1975); De, Barun, "The Colonial Context of the Bengal Renaissance", in Philips, C. H. and M. D. Wainwright (eds.) *Indian Society and the Beginnings of Modernization* (London: School of Oriental and African Studies, 1976); Sen, Asok, *Iswar Chandra Vidyasagar and His Elusive Milestones* (Calcutta: Riddhi-India, 1977).

64. Seal, Anil, *The Emergence of Indian Nationalism: Competition and Collaboration in the Later Nineteenth Century* (Cambridge: Cambridge University Press, 1968); Gallagher, John, Gordon Johnson and Anil Seal, (eds.), *Locality, Province and Nation: Essays on Indian Politics 1870–1940,* (Cambridge: Cambridge University Press, 1973).

65. For an overview of the historiographical context within which subaltern studies emerged, see Ludden, David (ed.), *Reading Subaltern Studies: Critical History, Contested Meaning and the Globalization of South Asia* (London: Anthem Press, 2002).

66. This classic argument is made in Chatterjee, "Whose Imagined Community?". See also Chatterjee, Partha, *Nationalist Thought and the Colonial World: A Derivative Discourse* (Minneapolis: University of Minnesota Press, 1993) and Chatterjee, Partha, *The Nation and Its Fragments: Colonial and Postcolonial Histories* (Princeton: Princeton University Press, 1993). For a critique, see Sarkar, Sumit, "The Decline of the Subaltern in *Subaltern Studies*", in Chaturvedi, Vinayak, *Mapping Subaltern Studies and the Postcolonial* (London, New York: New Left Review, 2000).

67. Bayly, C. A., *The Birth of the Modern World 1780–1914: Global Connections and Comparisons* (Cambridge: University of Cambridge Press, 2004), p. 1.

68. Sartori, Andrew, *Bengal in Global Concept History: Culturalism in the Age of Capital* (Chicago: University of Chicago Press, 2008), p. 19. For a further elaboration of Sartori's position, see Moyn, Samuel and Andrew Sartori, "Approaches to Global Intellectual History", in Moyn and Sartori, *Global Intellectual History*. A more sceptical approach to the turn to the 'global' in history writing can be found in the same volume – see Cooper, Frederick, "How Global Do We Want Our Intellectual History to Be?", in Moyn and Sartori, *Global Intellectual History*.

69. *PCM*, p. 386.

70. This correspondence was edited by a relative of Keshab and published in Calcutta in 1941. Mahalanobis, Srimanika, *Brahhmananda Srikeshabchandrer Patrabali* (Calcutta, 1941).

71. Burton, Antoinette, "From Child Bride to "Hindoo Lady": Rukhmabai and the Debate on Sexual Respectability in Imperial Britain", *The American Historical Review*, 103, 4 (October, 1998), p. 1145.

72. Collet, Sophia Dobson (ed.), *Keshub Chunder Sen's English Visit* (London: Strahan and Co., 1871) [Hereafter *SDC*]. This was republished with additional material, including Keshab's diary in England, in *WW*. Collet, Sophia Dobson (ed.), *The Brahmo Year Book. Brief Records of Work and Life in the Theistic Churches of India* (7 vols, London, Edinburgh: Williams and Norgate, 1876–1883). Collet describes her collection on Keshab in England as 'a record of the principal occasions on which he met the British public, whether in the pulpit, on the platform, or at less formal social occasions'. Of course, Collet was not present on every occasion herself, rather, 'The reports have been taken from the most reliable sources, chiefly from the newspapers or magazines issued by the societies or localities concerned. Nearly all the addresses have been carefully revised by Mr. Sen', *SDC*, p. vi. Unfortunately, Collet does not list the newspapers and magazines from which the reports have been taken, and it is not always possible to determine the precise circumstances of locution, audience and performance. P. C. Majumdar's biography of Keshab is another valuable source—it reprints a great deal of contemporary material in full, and is one of the only sources to discuss Keshab's childhood. It is, of course, biased strongly in favour of Keshab, as Majumdar was his close friend and disciple. Keshab's autobiography covers only the later years of his life, and focuses on his spiritual development. Sen, Keshub Chunder, *Jeeban Veda or Life Scriptures (Autobiography) of Minister Keshub Chunder Sen*, trans. B. Mazoomdar (Calcutta: P. C. Mookerjee, 1915).

73. Marx, Karl, *The Eighteenth Brumaire of Louise Bonaparte,* https://www.marxists.org/archive/marx/works/1852/18th-brumaire/ch01.htm, last accessed 28 Jan. 2017.

CHAPTER 2: KESHAB IN THE CONTEXT OF NINETEENTH-CENTURY
BRITAIN AND BENGAL

1. Carpenter, Mary (ed.), *The Last Days in England of the Rajah Rammohun* Roy (London and Calcutta, 1860), p. 230.
2. Port, M. H., *Imperial London: Civil Government Building in London 1850–1915* (New Haven, London: Yale University Press, 1995), p. 5.
3. Porter, Roy, *London: A Social History* (London: Penguin, 2000), p. 229.
4. Auerbach, Jeffrey, *The Great Exhibition of 1851: A Nation on Display* (London: Yale University Press, 1999); Bennett, Tony, *The Birth of the Museum: History, Theory, Politics* (Oxon: Routledge, 1995), ch. 2; Kriegel, Lara, "The Pudding and the Palace: Labor, Print Culture, and Imperial Britain in 1851", in Burton, Antoinette (ed.), *After the Imperial Turn: Thinking With and Through the Nation* (Durham: Duke University Press, 2003).
5. Hochschild, Adam, *Bury the Chains: The British Struggle to Abolish Slavery* (London: Pan Macmillan, 2006); Dawson, Graham, *Soldier Heroes: British adventure, Empire and the Imagining of Masculinities* (Oxon: Routledge, 1994); Hall, Catherine, *White, Male and Middle Class: Explorations in Feminism and History* (Cambridge: Polity Press, 1992), ch. 10.

6.   Hall, Catherine and Sonya O. Rose (eds.), *At Home with the Empire: Metropolitan Culture and the Imperial World* (Cambridge: Cambridge University Press, 2006), p. 25.

7.   Porter, *London*, pp. 248–9.

8.   Ibid.

9.   Schneer, Jonathan, *London 1900: The Imperial Metropolis* (New Haven, London: Yale University Press, 1999), p. 7.

10.   Ibid.

11.   Visram, Rozina, *Ayahs, Lascars and Princes: Indians in Britain, 1700–1947* (London: Pluto Press, 1986).

12.   Porter, *London*, p. 367.

13.   Schneer, *London*, p. 7.

14.   Fryer, Peter, *Staying Power: The History of Black People in Britain* (Concord, MA: Pluto Press, 1984), p. 68.

15.   Burton, *At the Heart*, p. 27.

16.   For a study of the travel writings of Bengali visitors, see Sen, Simonti, *Travels to Europe: Self and Other in Bengali Travel Narratives, 1870–1910* (London: Sangam Books Limited, 2005). Inderpal Grewal, Antoinette Burton, Simonti Sen and Rozina Visram have all written studies of Indian visitors to London—the first three focused narrowly on a limited selection of visitors, while Visram set out to provide a comprehensive record of as many Indian visitors and residents as could be found in the archives. Grewal, Inderpal, *Home and Harem: Nation, Gender, Empire and Cultures of Travel* (London: Duke University Press, 1996); Burton, *At the Heart*; Visram, Rozina, *Asians in Britain: 400 Years of History* (London: Pluto Press, 2002). A vast literature exists on imperialism in the metropole by social and cultural historians, literary scholars and those engaged in critical colonial studies (for an overview, see, Hall and Rose, *At Home*). It is thus surprising that historians engaged in 'London History', as Jonathan Schneer has noted, 'have paid little more than lip service to the imperial theme'. Schneer, *London*, p. 12. See also Davis, John, "Modern London 1850–1930", *London Journal*, 20, 2 (1995), pp. 56–90.

17.   Schneer, *London*, p. 184.

18.   Ibid.

19.   Visram, *Asians*, p. 34.

20.   Ibid., pp. 64–6.

21.   Ibid.

22.   Burton, *At the Heart*, p. 26.

23.   Visram, *Asians*, pp. 86–8.

24.   For an analysis of Gandhi's experiences in London, see Hunt, James D., *Gandhi in London* (New Delhi: Promilla & Co., 1978).

25.   One of the earliest Indian associations in England was the British Indian Society, founded in 1839 by William Adam (a friend of Ram Mohan Roy) and George Thompson (an associate of Dwarkanath Tagore). The association was committed to improving the 'condition of the native population in India' and, what was regarded as a connected goal, 'advancing the prosperity of our own country [England]'. Visram, *Asians*, p. 123. See also Kaushik, Harish, *The Indian National*

Congress in England, 1885–1920 (New Delhi: Research Publications in Social Sciences, 1972); Majumdar, R. C., *History of the Freedom Movement in India* (Calcutta: Firma K. L. Mukhopadhyay, 1962); Mehrota, S. R., *The Emergence of Indian National Congress* (Delhi: Vikas Publications, 1971).

26. Schneer, *London*, p. 186.
27. Ibid.
28. Cumpston, Mary, "Some Early Indian Nationalists and their allies in the British Parliament, 1851–1906", *English Historical Review*, 76 (April, 1961).
29. Visram, *Asians*, p. 124.
30. Quoted in Schneer, *London*, p. 187.
31. Visram, *Asians*, p. 125.
32. Schneer, *London*, p. 294n.
33. Pratt, Mary Louise, "Arts of the Contact Zone", in Bartholomae, David and Petrosky, Anthony (eds.), *Ways of Reading* (Boston: Bedford/St. Martin's, 2002), p. 607.
34. Hall and Rose, *At Home*, p. 2.
35. Sinha, Pradip, "Calcutta and the Currents of History, 1690–1912", in Chaudhuri, Sukanta (ed.), *Calcutta: The Living City, Volume I* (New Delhi: Oxford University Press, 1990), p. 32.
36. Ibid.
37. Up to one third of estates changed hands in the twenty years following the Permanent Settlement. Zamindars were unable to meet the tax revenue demands of the British, which they were expected to collect from their tenants. They thus found their estates liable for sale. See Metcalf, Barbara D. and Thomas R. Metacalf, *A Concise History of India* (Cambridge: Cambridge University Press, 2002), pp. 76–9.
38. Sartori, *Bengal in Global Concept History*, p. 90. Blair Kling propounds the notion of an 'Age of Enterprise' in his biography of Dwarkanath—Kling, Blair, *Partner in Empire: Dwarkanath Tagore and the Age of Enterprise in Eastern India* (Calcutta: Firma KLM Private, 1981).
39. Sartori, *Bengal in Global Concept History*, pp. 95–101.
40. Ibid., p. 97.
41. Sinha, "Calcutta and the Currents of History", p. 33.
42. Chattopadhyay, Swati, "Blurring Boundaries: The Limits of "White Town" in Colonial Calcutta", *Journal of the Society of Architectural Historians*, 59, 2 (June, 2000), pp. 154–79.
43. For an overview of the Orientalist/Anglicist debates, see Kopf, David, *British Orientalism and the Bengal Renaissance: The Dynamics of Indian Modernization, 1773–1835* (Berkeley: University of California Press, 1969).
44. *PCM*, p. 42.
45. Ibid., pp. 42–3. On the family history of the Sens, see Ghose, L., *The Modern History of the Indian Chiefs* (2 vols, Calcutta, 1881).
46. *PCM*, p. 45.
47. Maunder, Samuel, *Biographical Treasury; A Dictionary of Universal Biography* (Harlow: Longman, Brown, Green and Longmans, 1845).

48. Borthwick, *Keshub*, p. 5.
49. Ram Kamal Sen had four sons. The eldest, Bansidhar, was keeper of the Calcutta Mint; Hari Mohan was next in line; then Piari Mohan (Keshab's father); then Murali Dhar, a distinguished attorney. The banking connections stretched across Ram Kamal Sen's nephews, who included the *Khazanchi* of the Agra Bank, the *Khazanchi* of the Bank of Bengal, and an employee of the Calcutta Branch of the Bank of Hindustan. Ibid., pp. 4–5.
50. Ibid., pp. 3–4.
51. *PCM*, p. 51.
52. Ibid., p. 54.
53. Hatcher, Brian, *Idioms of Improvement: Vidyasagar and Cultural Encounter in Bengal* (New Delhi: Oxford University Press, 1996), p. 31.
54. Ibid.
55. Borthwick, *Keshub*, p. 9.
56. *PCM*, p. 64.
57. Ibid., p. 63, p. 67.
58. "Address to Stanford Street Chapel", 28 Apr. 1870, *SDC*, pp. 86–7.
59. Ibid., p. 88.
60. For the anti-*sati* campaigns in India and Britain, see Mani, Lata, *Contentious Traditions: The Debate on Sati in Colonial India* (Berkeley: University of California, 1998).
61. Midgley, Clare, *Feminism and Empire: Women Activists in Imperial Britain, 1790–1865* (Oxon: Routledge, 2007), pp. 65–91.
62. Ram Mohan's 'catholicity' is held up for sustained praise by Keshab in his article "Rammohun and The Brahmo Samaj", *Indian Mirror*, 1 July 1865.
63. Ram Mohan's letter to Lord Amherst is reprinted in Collet, Sophia Dobson, *The Life and Letters of Raja Rammohun Roy* (4th ed., Calcutta: Sadharan Brahmo Samaj, 1988), pp. 421–5. For an analysis of Ram Mohan as an 'early liberal', see Bayly, *Recovering Liberties*, pp. 50–60. Bayly's perspective is critiqued in Chatterjee, Partha, *The Black Hole of Empire: History of a Global Practice of Power* (Princeton: Princeton University Press, 2012).
64. The former appeared in 1803–4 and was first translated into English under the auspices of the Adi Brahmo Samaj in 1884, with the title "A Gift to Deists". There is renewed controversy surrounding the publication of "Discussions on Various Religions", with some scholars now arguing that it never appeared in print. See Das, Asitabha (ed.), *Raja Rammohun Roy: Creator of the New India Age* (Calcutta: Readers Service, 2010), p. 458n.
65. Dermot Killingley emphasises Ram Mohan's Islamic heritage in Killingley, Dermot, *Rammohun Roy in Hindu and Christian Tradition: The Teape Lectures 1990* (Newcastle upon Tyne: Grevatt and Grevatt, 1993).
66. The press regulations were eventually relaxed again in the mid-1830s.
67. This argument is advanced in Mani, *Contentious Traditions*.
68. Hatcher, Brian, "Remembering Rammohan: An Essay on the (Re-)emergence of Modern Hinduism", *History of Religions*, 46, 1 (August, 2006).
69. Kopf, *The Brahmo Samaj*, p. 15.

70. For Debendranath's life, see Tagore, Satyendranath, and Indira Devi (eds.), *Autobiography of Debendranath Tagore* (Whitefish, MT: Kessinger, 2006).

71. Kopf, *The Brahmo Samaj*, p. 165.

72. For the genesis of this view among Orientalists, see Inden, Ronald, "Orientalist Constructions of India", *Modern Asian Studies*, 20, 3 (1986), pp. 401–46.

73. Kopf, *The Brahmo Samaj*, pp. 15–16.

74. Ibid., pp. 49–56.

75. See Hatcher, *Idioms of Improvement*; Sen, Asok, *Iswar Chandra Vidyasagar and His Elusive Milestones* (Calcutta: Riddhi-India, 1977).

76. For an analysis of Keshab's experiences in Ceylon, see Bayly, *Recovering Liberties*, p. 154. Keshab recorded his observations in Sen, Keshub Chunder, *The Book of Pilgrimages: Diaries and Reports of Missionary Expeditions* (Calcutta, 1940).

77. Keshab had two brothers and four sisters. Nothing is known about his sisters, but of the brothers: the eldest, Nabin Chandra, became Native Head Assistant of the Depositor's Department of the Bank of Bengal; next in line was Keshab; the youngest, Krishna Behari Sen, was the first sub-editor of the *Indian Mirror*, and later the editor of the *Sunday Indian Mirror* and rector of Albert College. Borthwick, *Keshub*, pp. 5–6.

78. Ibid., p. 27.

79. Ibid., p. 28. For a detailed account of Western influences on Keshab's intellectual development, see Piette, O. L., *Responses of Brahmo Samaj to Western Cultural Advances, 1855–1880: An Episode in India's Intellectual History* (Unpublished PhD Thesis, Syracuse University, 1974).

80. Kopf, *The Brahmo Samaj*, p. 249. These disagreements would continue in the 1870s. The Adi Brahmo Samaj was denigrated as 'a religion comprising a few moneyed aristocrats and people subservient to them' in *Dharmatattwa*, 20 Feb. 1871, pp. 306–7. Debendranath remained suspicious of Keshab's reverence for Christianity, stating in a lecture of 1871 that 'Christ was the reason why Europe was flooded with blood'. As reported by *Dharmatattwa*, 20 Feb. 1871, p. 306.

81. Kopf, *The Brahmo Samaj*, p. 184.

82. Debendranath's 'advert to banish' Keshab was placed in the *Tattwabodhini Patrika*, Jan. 1865, according to an article in *Dharmatattwa*, 20 Feb. 1871, p. 306.

83. For a list of Brahmo Samaj branches across India in 1872, see Kopf, *The Brahmo Samaj*, pp. 325–7. The establishment of a Brahmo Samaj typically involved the building of a Mandir (community prayer hall and meeting place), a girls' and boys' school, possibly a college, a discussion society for youth, a charitable hospital, printing press, a night school for peasants and workers, and a ladies' society. The best source for information on this period of Keshab's life is Damen, *Crisis*.

84. For example, *Pall Mall Gazette*, 8 Oct. 1869.

85. Bebbington, *The Nonconformist Conscience. Chapel and Politics, 1870–1914* (London: George Allen & Unwin, 1982).

86. Ibid., p. 2.

87. Ibid., p. ix.

88. Ibid., pp. 14–46.

89. Ibid.
90. Standard accounts of the history of Unitarianism include McLachlan, H., *The Unitarian Movement in the Religious Life of England: 1. Its Contribution to Thought and Learning 1700–1900* (London: George Allen & Unwin Ltd., 1934) and Wilbur, Earl Morse, *A History of Unitarianism* (2 vols, Cambridge, Mass.: Harvard University Press, 1946-1952).
91. A useful account of religious dissent in this period is Watts, Michael R., *The Dissenters* (2 vols, Oxford: Oxford University Press, 1978, 1996).
92. Watts, Ruth, *Gender, Power and the Unitarians in England 1760-1860* (London, New York: Longman, 1998), p. 3.
93. Webb, R. K., "The Unitarian Background", in Smith, Barbara (ed.), *Truth, Liberty, Religion: Essays Celebrating Two Hundred Years of Manchester College* (Manchester College Oxford, 1986), p. 19.
94. For a discussion of these academies, see Ibid., pp. 7–9.
95. Ibid., p. 9; Watts, *Gender, Power*, p. 3.
96. Webb, "The Unitarian Background", pp. 9–12; Watts, *Gender, Power*, p. x.
97. Fox, William J., "On the Character and Writing of the Rev. T. Belsham" (1830), quoted in Zastoupil, Lynn, *Rammohun Roy and the Making of Victorian Britain* (New York: Palgrave MacMillan, 2010), p. 10.
98. Zastoupil, *Rammohun Roy*, p. 10.
99. Unitarianism remained illegal under the Toleration Act until 1813, but the first avowedly Unitarian chapel was opened in 1774 in Essex Street, London, by Theophilus Lindsey. Webb, "The Unitarian Background", p. 14.
100. For a detailed discussion of Unitarian involvement in a range of reform issues, see Watts, *Gender, Power*.
101. Watts, *Gender, Power*; Gleadle, Kathryn, *The Early Feminists. Radical Unitarians and the Emergence of the Women's Rights Movement, 1831–51* (New York: Palgrave MacMillan, 1998); Watts, Ruth, "Rational Religion and Feminism: the Challenge of Unitarianism in the Nineteenth Century", in Morgan, Sue (ed.), *Women, Religion and Feminism in Britain, 1750–1900* (Basingstoke: Palgrave MacMillan, 2002).
102. For 'separate spheres' ideology, see Hall and Davidoff, *Family Fortunes*.
103. Martineau, Harriet, *Harriet Martineau's Autobiography* (3 vols, London: Smith, Elder & Co., 1877); Cobbe, Frances Power, *Essay on the Theory of Intuitive Morals* (London, 1855).
104. *Dharmatattwa*, 6 Apr. 1873, p. 70.
105. *Tattwa Koumudi*, 5 Feb. 1879, p. 200.
106. Webb, "The Unitarian Background", p. 18.
107. Watts, *Gender, Power*, p. 4.
108. Webb has gone so far as to suggest that 'Unitarian firms played a major role in the industrialization of England'. Webb, "The Unitarian Background", p. 16.
109. Watts, *Gender, Power*, p. 5.
110. Ibid., p. 106. For an analysis of the Unitarian chapel as a nexus of power relations, see Seed, John, "Theologies of Power: Unitarianism and the Social Relations of Religious Discourse, 1800–1850", in Morris, R. J. (ed.), *Class,*

Power and Social Structures in British Nineteenth Century Towns (Leicester: Leicester University Press, 1986).

111. Zastoupil, *Rammohun Roy*, p. 54; Bebbington, D. W., "Unitarian Members of Parliament in the Nineteenth Century, A Catalogue", *Transactions of the Unitarian Historical Society*, 23, 3 (April, 2009).

112. The Unitarian 'missionary history' is explored in Lavan, *Unitarians and India*.

113. Roy, Ram Mohan, "The Precepts of Jesus", in Nag and Burman (eds.), *The English Works of Rammohun Roy, Volume V* (Calcutta: Sadharan Brahmo Samaj, 1995), pp. 3–54. Early Unitarian interest in Ram Mohan is discussed in the opening chapters of Lavan, *Unitarians and India*.

114. A selection of these exchanges can be found in Nag and Burman, *The English Works*.

115. Bhattacharya, Subbhas, "Indigo Planters, Ram Mohan Roy and the 1833 Charter Act", *Social Scientist*, 4, 3 (October, 1975), pp. 59–60.

116. Ibid., pp. 59–60.

117. Stokes, E. T., "Bureaucracy and Ideology: Britain and India in the Nineteenth Century", *Transactions of the Royal Historical Society*, 30 (1980).

118. The most detailed recent account of Ram Mohan in Britain is Zastoupil, *Rammohun Roy*. Ram Mohan's correspondence with Jeremy Bentham and Robert Owen is included in Collet, *The Life and Letters* (1988), pp. 452–60.

119. On Vivekananda, see Radice, William (ed.), *Swami Vivekananda and the Modernization of Hinduism* (Delhi: Oxford University Press, 1997). Rabindranath's reception in London is the subject of Collins, Michael, "History and the Postcolonial: Rabindranath Tagore's Reception in London, 1912–1913", *International Journal of the Humanities*, 4, 9 (2007).

120. Carpenter, Mary, *The Last Days in England of Rajah Rammohun Roy* (London: Trübner & Co.; Calcutta, R. C. Lepage & Co., 1866). For a discussion of Mary Carpenter's efforts at social and educational reform, see Midgley, Clare, "Mary Carpenter and the Brahmo Samaj of India: a transnational perspective on social reform in the age of empire", *Women's History Review*, 22, 3 (2013), pp. 363–85.

121. See, for example, Carpenter, Dr Lant, *A Biographical Memoir of the late Rajah Rammohun Roy together with a series of extracts from his writings* (Calcutta: Asiatic Press, 1835).

122. On her deathbed, Collet sent a note to a friend imploring 'I am dying. I cannot finish my Life of Rammohun Roy. But when I enter the Unseen, I want to be able to tell Rammohun that his Life will be finished. Will you finish it for me?'. Reprinted in the "Editor's Note" to Collet, Sophia Dobson, *The Life and Letters of Raja Rammohun Roy* (2nd ed., Calcutta, 1914).

123. Harriet Martineau's hymn to Ram Mohan, composed for the occasion of his funeral, is reprinted in Carpenter, Mary, *Last Days in England of Rajah Rammohun Roy* (3rd ed., Calcutta: Ram Mohun Library & Free Reading Room, 1915), p. 205.

124. Hagiographies of Ram Mohan are too numerous to list. Examples include Majumdar, J. K., *Rammohun Roy and the World* (Calcutta: Sadharan Brahmo Samaj, 1975) and Singh, Iqbal, *Rammohun Roy* (3 vols, 2nd ed., Bombay, New Delhi,

1983). Singh presents Ram Mohan's life as a journey of self-emancipation from 'a narrow and stultifying social environment' into modernity. Singh, *Rammohun Roy*, p. 6.

125. Martineau, Harriet, "*Literary* Lionism", *London and Westminster Review*, 32 (April, 1839); Zastoupil, *Rammohun Roy*, p. 165.

126. From Sutherland's portrait in the *Indian Gazette* of 18 Feb. 1834. Reprinted in Collet, Sophia Dobson, *The Life and Letters of Raja Rammohun Roy* (London: Harold Collet, 1900), p. 129.

127. Ram Mohan's reputation as an 'enlightened Christian convert' was well-established before he arrived in Britain. Accounts of his 'conversion' were promoted through publications including the Church of England *Missionary Register*, and reprints of articles from the *Calcutta Journal*. William Roscoe gave Ram Mohan a letter to present to Lord Brougham by way of introduction; he is described therein as the 'celebrated and learned Rammohun Roy…of whom you must already have frequently heard as the illustrious convert from Hindooism to Christianity'. Carpenter, *Last Days* (1915), pp. 28–32, p. 59, pp. 84–5.

128. Roy, Rammohun, "Additional Queries respecting the Condition of India", Appendix 40, in vol. 5 of the Appendix to "Report from Select Committee on the Affairs of the East India Company", in *East India Company Volume 7: Reports from Committees* (1831); Roy, Rammohun, "Remarks by Rammohun Roy, on Settlement in India by Europeans, dated 14 July 1832", in the General Appendix, Section V, of vol. 8 of *Report from the Select Committee on the Affairs of the East India Company* (16th August 1832, House of Commons, London).

129. Hatcher, "Remembering Rammohan", p. 80.

130. Halbwachs, Maurice, *On Collective Memory*, trans. Lewis A. Coser (Chicago: University of Chicago Press, 1992), p. 119.

131. "The Inquirer: Its Aims and View", in *The Inquirer*, 2 Jan. 1858. An editorial in *The Inquirer* of 1876 recognised a distinction between the 'old' Unitarians on the 'right', who treated scriptures as the authority (if not a revelation) for all theological belief and regarded Christ as a mysterious being, and the 'new' Unitarians on the 'left', who treated scriptures as the fallible writings of fallible men, built their beliefs on the conclusions of conscience and reason, and denied the miracles of Christ but respected his character. *The Inquirer*, 26 Feb. 1876.

132. McLachlan, *The Unitarian Movement*, p. 186.

133. For the development of James Martineau's thought and his influence on Unitarianism, see Waller, Ralph, "James Martineau: the Development of his Thought", in Smith, Barbara (ed.), *Truth, Liberty, Religion: Essays celebrating Two Hundred Years of Manchester College* (Manchester College Oxford, 1986) and Waller, Ralph, "James Martineau's Influence on Unitarianism", in Hankinson, A. S. (ed.), *A James Martineau Miscellany* (Oxford, 2005).

134. *The Inquirer*, 12, 19 and 26 Feb. 1876; 15 Apr. 1876. See also Webb, Robert K., "The Background: English Unitarianism in the Nineteenth Century" in Smith, Leonard (ed.), *Unitarian to the Core: Unitarian College Manchester 1854–2004* (Manchester: Unitarian College, 2004); Peart, Ann, *Forgotten Prophets: The Lives of Unitarian Women, 1760–1904* (Unpublished PhD Thesis, University of

Newcastle, 2005), pp. 179–82; Webb, R. K., "The Limits of Religious Liberty: Theology and Criticism in Nineteenth-Century England" in Helmstadter, Richard (ed.), *Freedom and Religion in the Nineteenth Century* (Stanford: Stanford University Press, 1997), pp. 135–44.

135. *The Inquirer*, 26 Feb. 1876.

136. Kopf, *The Brahmo Samaj*, p. 31.

137. De Michelis, *A History*, p. 81. The Sadharan Samaj Brahmos described Theodore Parker and Francis Newman as the 'sun' and the 'moon' in 'the vast sky of Western Brahmoism' in *Tattwa Koumudi*, 6 May 1883, pp. 15–16.

138. Hanegraaf, W. J., *New Age Religion and Western Culture: Esotericism in the Mirror of Secular Thought* (Leiden: Brill, 1996), pp. 406–7.

139. Hanegraaf, W. J., "Empirical Method in the Study of Esotericism", *Method & Theory In the Study of Religion*, 7, 2 (1995), p. 404.

140. For a classic and wide-ranging study of mysticism in the Christian tradition, see Troeltsch, E. *The Social Teachings of the Christian Churches* (New York: Macmillan, 1931). For the Bengali context, see McDaniel, June, *The Madness of the Saints. Ecstatic Religion in Bengal* (Chicago and London: The University of Chicago Press, 1989).

141. These connections are explored in some detail in De Michelis, Elizabeth, *A History of Modern Yoga. Patañjali and Western Esotericism* (London, New York: Continuum, 2004).

142. For a nuanced account of these movements, see Gandhi, *Affective Communities*. A useful, comparative analysis of Theosophy can be found in Chidester, *Empire of Religion*, pp. 269–86.

143. The Tagore family supported Dr Esdaile's mesmeric hospital in the 1840s; Vivekananda became a freemason shortly after he joined Keshab's *Naba Bidhan*. Godwin, Joscelyn, *The Theosophical Enlightenment* (New York: State University of New York Press, 1994), p. 317; De Michelis, *A History*, pp. 99–100.

144. Metcalf, Thomas R., *The Aftermath of Revolt: India 1857–1870* (Princeton: Princeton University Press, 1965), p. 104.

145. Ibid., p. 108.

146. Dawson, *Soldier Heroes*, ch. 4.

147. According to Viceroy Mayo. Metcalf, *The Aftermath*, p. 98.

148. Gopal, S., *British Policy in India 1858–1905* (Cambridge: Cambridge University Press, 1965), p. 62, 122.

149. Metcalf, *The Aftermath*, p. 258.

150. Members of the covenanted ICS (so-called because its members had to sign a bond of loyalty and integrity) were recruited in England and held the highest posts. They were nominated by the Directors of the East India Company and chosen by competitive examination. Members of the uncovenanted ICS were recruited in India by local governments, and occupied subordinate positions in the administration. Ibid., p. 269.

151. Visram, *Asians*, p. 87.

152. Metcalf, *The Aftermath*, p. 273.

153. This paragraph draws extensively on Ibid., pp. 268–80.

154. Robb, Peter, *A History of India* (Hampshire, New York: Palgrave, 2002), p. 239. For an in-depth study of Vidyasagar's activities in the sphere of education, see Hatcher, *Idioms of Improvement*. On Mary Carpenter's activities in the sphere of Indian female education, see Burton, Antoinette, "Fearful Bodies into Disciplined Subjects: Pleasure, Romance and the Family Drama of Colonial Reform in Mary Carpenter's "Six Months in India"", *Signs*, 20, 3 (Spring, 1995).

CHAPTER 3: 'TRUTH IS NOT EUROPEAN': KESHAB ON HISTORY, EMPIRE, OTHER, SELF

1. "My Impressions of England", 12 Sep. 1870, *WW*, pp. 460–2.
2. *PCM*, p. 142.
3. Müller, *Biographical Essays*, p. 72.
4. The remaining three were Gopal Chandra Roy, Rakhal Das Roy and Krishna Dhan Ghosh.
5. Hoppen, K. Theodore, *The Mid-Victorian Generation 1846–1886* (Oxford: Clarendon Press, 1998), p. 457.
6. Keshab to his wife, London, 15 Apr. 1870, Mahalanobis, *Patrabali*, p. 136.
7. Arnold, David, *Science, Technology and Medicine in Colonial India* (Cambridge: Cambridge University Press, 2000), p. 4. As Amiya P. Sen has demonstrated, this narrative of history was also propounded by Ram Mohan and a range of Keshab's contemporaries in Bengal. Sen, Amiya P., *Hindu Revivalism in Bengal 1872–1905: Some Essays in Interpretation* (New Delhi: Oxford University Press, 1993), p. 60.
8. "Speech to the Philosophical Institution in Edinburgh", 19 Aug. 1870, *WW*, p. 374.
9. Keshab recounted this version of history on many occasions, for example, *WW*, p. 359, pp. 374–5; *SDC*, p. 299.
10. "Speech at the Welcome Soirée", delivered at the Hanover Square Rooms, London, 12 Apr. 1870, *SDC*, p. 27.
11. "Speech at the Farewell Soirée", London, 12 Sep. 1870, *WW*, pp. 448–9.
12. Keshab's "Parting Words at Southampton", 17 Sep. 1870, *WW*, p. 466.
13. Ibid., p. 467.
14. Ibid., p. 466.
15. Ibid.
16. Ibid.
17. Inden, "Orientalist Constructions", p. 442. For a study of the connections between German Indology, neo-Orientalism and British romanticism see Rabault-Feuerhahn, Pascale, *L'Archive des origines. Sanskrit, Philologie, anthropologie dans l'Allemagne du XIXe siècle* (Paris: Le Cerf, 2008).
18. Inden, "Orientalist Constructions", p. 442.
19. Chakrabarty, *Provincializing Europe*.
20. Said, *Orientalism*, pp. 92–3.
21. Mill, James, *The History of British India* (6 vols, 3rd ed., London: Baldwin, Cradock and Joy, 1826).

22. Mehta, "Liberal Strategies", pp. 73–5.

23. "Speech at the Welcome Soirée", pp. 37–8.

24. "Christ and Christianity", delivered at St James' Hall, 28 May 1870, *SDC*, p. 237.

25. "Hindu Theism", delivered at the Union Chapel Islington, 7 June 1870, *SDC*, p. 301.

26. "England's Duties to India", delivered at the Metropolitan Tabernacle, London, 24 May 1870, *SDC*, p. 197. The criticisms of British policy in India, and of British attitudes towards Indians, which Keshab made in this speech drew on arguments he had advanced in Calcutta in 1866 in his lecture "Jesus Christ: Europe and Asia". Because of its strongly critical stance towards British treatment of 'natives', this lecture caused outrage among the Anglo-Indian community in India. "Jesus Christ: Europe and Asia", Calcutta, 5 May 1866, in Sen, Keshab Chandra, *Keshub Chunder Sen's Lectures in India* (2nd ed., Calcutta: The Brahmo Tract Society, 1886), pp. 1–37.

27. "England's Duties", p. 197.

28. Ibid., p. 198.

29. "Speech in Leicester", 17 June 1870, *SDC*, p. 352.

30. "England's Duties", p. 211.

31. Ibid.

32. Ibid., p. 223.

33. Ibid., p. 225.

34. Ibid.

35. Ibid., pp. 224–5; Tagore, Rabindranath, *Gora* (Madras: MacMillan India, 1985).

36. "England's Duties", p. 224.

37. Ibid.

38. Ibid.

39. The Jamaica Committee launched a civil action on behalf of Alexander Phillips. The final decision in this case was issued by the Court of Exchequer Chamber on 23 June 1870. The court ruled that, due to legislation Eyre had passed prior to leaving Jamaica, Eyre's actions were found to be justifiable by the law in Jamaica and thus could not be actionable in England—a ruling which would leave a major imprint on English tort law for over a century. For the 1870 ruling, see Handford, Peter, "Edward John Eyre and the Conflict of Laws", *Melbourne University Law Review* (December, 2008) and Handcock, Moffatt, "Torts in the Conflict of Laws: The First Rule in Phillips v. Eyre", *The University of Toronto Law Journal*, 3, 2 (1940). The broader implications of the Eyre controversy are discussed in detail in Hall, *Civilising Subjects*.

40. Hall, Catherine, McClelland, Keith and Rendall, Jane, *Defining the Victorian Nation: Class, Race, Gender and the British Reform Act of 1867* (Cambridge: Cambridge University Press, 2000).

41. The Royal Commission reports contain many examples of witnesses who refer to the 'Mutiny'. See Hall, Catherine, "The Economy of Intellectual Prestige: Thomas Carlyle, John Stuart Mill, and the Case of Governor Eyre", *Cultural Critique*, 12 (Spring, 1989).

42. Ibid.
43. Ibid., p. 195.
44. Metcalf, *The Aftermath*, pp. 268–88.
45. Campbell, George, *India as it May Be; an Outline of a Proposed Government and Policy* (London: John Murray, 1853), p. 229.
46. Koditschek, *Liberalism*, p. 276.
47. "Women in India", delivered at the Victoria Discussion Society, London, 1 Aug. 1870, *WW*, p. 359.
48. Roy, Rammohun, "Brief Remarks Regarding Modern Encroachments on the Ancient Rights of Females, According to the Hindu Law of Inheritance" (1822), in Ghose, Jogendra Chunder (ed.), *The English Works of Raja Rammohun Roy, Volume II* (Calcutta: S. K. Lahiri & Co., 1901), pp. 193–208.
49. "England's Duties", p. 214.
50. Ibid., p. 217. As far as I am aware, Keshab never referred to his own wife in public in England, although he did present Queen Victoria with two portraits of her. I have found very few examples of Britons enquiring into Keshab's personal domestic arrangements.
51. Ibid., pp. 215–16.
52. Chatterjee, Partha, "Nationalism Resolves the Critical Question", in Sen, Amiya P., *Social and Religious Reform* (New Delhi: Oxford University Press, 2005), pp. 169–89; Sarkar, Tanika, *Hindu Wife, Hindu Nation. Community, Religion and Cultural Nationalism* (Indianapolis: Indiana University Press, 2001), pp. 250–67.
53. "Speech at the Farewell Soirée", p. 452.
54. "England's Duties", p. 220.
55. Ibid., p. 219.
56. Ibid., pp. 217–19.
57. Ibid., p. 219.
58. "Speech at Bath", 15 June 1870, *SDC*, p. 344.
59. "The Religious and Social Condition of India", Edinburgh, 19 Aug. 1870, *WW*, p. 377; also "The Liquor Traffic in India", delivered to the London Auxilliary of the United Kingdom Alliance, St James' Hall, 19 May 1870, *SDC*, p. 151.
60. "England's Duties", p. 119.
61. Ibid., pp. 206–8.
62. "Speech at the Welcome Soirée", pp. 30–1.
63. "The Religious and Social Condition of India", p. 377.
64. "Speech at the Welcome Soirée", pp. 27–31.
65. Ibid., pp. 31–2.
66. Ram Mohan spoke of Christ's 'Eastern' origins during his visit to England. Carpenter, *Last Days in England* (1915), pp. 99–100.
67. "Speech at the Welcome Soirée", pp. 41–2.
68. Ibid.
69. "Speech in Birmingham", 20 June 1870, *SDC*, p. 368.
70. "Christ and Christianity", p. 249.
71. "Speech at the Farewell Soirée", pp. 454–5.
72. "The Love of God", Unity Church, Islington, 1 May 1870, *SDC*, p. 104.

73. Ibid.
74. Keshab was a great admirer of Carlyle—he later devoted a 'Pilgrimages to Saints' to him.
75. "General Impressions of England and the English", in Basu, P. S., *Life and Works of Brahmananda Keshav* (2nd ed., Calcutta: Navavidhan Publication Committee, 1940), p. 272.
76. Ibid., p. 273.
77. "The Liquor Traffic", p. 151.
78. "Special Reception by the United Kingdom Alliance", Manchester, 25 June 1870, *SDC*, pp. 419–20.
79. "The Liquor Traffic", p. 153.
80. "Temperance Address in Shoreditch", 29 May 1870, *SDC*, p. 265.
81. Bayly, *The Birth of the Modern World*, p. 293.
82. "Speech at the Farewell Soirée", p. 451.
83. Ibid.
84. Ibid., p. 452.
85. "General Impressions", p. 272.
86. "Speech at the Farewell Soirée", p. 450.
87. "General Impressions", p. 274.
88. Keshab to his wife, London, 15 Apr. 1870, Mahalanobis, *Patrabali*, p. 136. I have translated the Bengali *magi* as 'wretched women'; other translations are possible.
89. Inden, "Orientalist Constructions"; Inden, Ronald, *Imagining India* (Bloomington, Indianapolis: Indiana University Press, 2000).
90. Dirks, Nicholas, *Castes of Mind: Colonialism and the Making of Modern India* (Princeton: Princeton University Press, 2001), p. 194.
91. Brun, Maria, "Institutions Collide: A Study of "Caste-Based" Collective Criminality and Female Infanticide in India, 1789–1871: A Critique of Nicholas Dirks Castes of Mind and the Making of Modern India", *LSE Working Paper Series* (March, 2010), p. 20.
92. "Speech at the Farewell Soirée", p. 449. Keshab employed an equally entertaining metaphor when addressing an audience in India: 'Would you like to eat and drink in the English way? I really think it is barbarous. The dining room appeared to be more like a zoological garden'. "General Impressions", p. 274.
93. Elias, Norbert, *The Civilizing Process* (Oxford: Blackwell, 2000).
94. C. A. Bayly has drawn attention to a variety of South and East Asian accounts of the 'ill-deportment' of Europeans, which served to challenge British missionary and anthropological critiques of 'native' manners and customs. Bayly, *Recovering Liberties*, p. 39, 156.
95. For the connection between beef, liberty and English Protestantism, see Rogers, Ben, *Beef and Liberty: Roast Beef, John Bull and the English Patriots* (London: Chatto & Windus, 2003).
96. "Speech at the Farewell Soirée", p. 460.
97. Writing from Calcutta in 1866, Mary Carpenter recounted an occasion on which Keshab accompanied her to two homes in Calcutta. In the 'native house', 'the rest of the so-called ladies appeared, but in a state of undress, many of

them, which showed that a Zenana was the only place fit for them....I was sorry to find that the young ones do not get any schooling in this family'; in the 'other house', 'Neatly-dressed young ladies came forward in a pleasing and very affectionate way to greet me, and led me into the well-carpeted little room, where the meeting was to be held.... This meeting is a wonderful advance, and the effect on the young ladies is very evident'. Letter from Mary Carpenter to Mrs Herbert Thomas, Calcutta, 25 Nov. 1866. Reprinted in Carpenter, J. Estlin, *The Life and Work of Mary Carpenter* (London: MacMillan & Co., 1879), pp. 331–3.

98.   "Diary in England", *WW*, p. 3, p. 40.

99.   Ibid., pp. 31–2, 48.

100.   Ibid., pp. 30, 43–4; Keshab to his wife, Bath, 16 June 1870, Mahalanobi, *Patrabali*, p. 146.

101.   Keshab to Aghor, London, 6 May 1870, Mahalanobi, *Patrabali*, p. 86.

102.   'Great men', in Keshab's view, were distinguished by their selflessness, sincerity and willingness to challenge the prevailing social and moral order. "Great Men", Calcutta, 28 Sep. 1866, in Sen, *Lectures in India* (1886), pp. 38–74.

103.   "Speech at the Welcome Soirée", p. 26.

104.   "Speech at Bath", p. 345.

105.   "England's Duties", pp. 197–8.

106.   Ibid., p. 198.

107.   "Speech at the Farewell Soirée", p. 452.

108.   "Address to Stamford Street Chapel", p. 84.

109.   "Speech at Bath", p. 344.

110.   "Speech at the Farewell Soirée", p. 453.

111.   Ibid., p. 460.

112.   For the importance of conceptions of financial and moral 'independence' in middle-class British ideology, see Hall and Davidoff, *Family Fortunes*.

113.   "Speech at Bath", pp. 342–3.

114.   "Address to Stamford Street Chapel", p. 86.

115.   "Christ and Christianity", p. 236.

116.   "Speech in Birmingham", p. 369.

117.   "Parting words at Southampton", p. 464; "My Impressions of England", p. 460.

118.   "Speech in Liverpool", June/July 1870, *SDC*, p. 441.

119.   "Speech in Birmingham", p. 379. However, Keshab was also critical of Ram Mohan for relying too heavily on the Vedas as a scriptural basis for the Brahmo Samaj.

120.   "Speech at the Farewell Soirée", p. 462.

121.   "Speech at the Welcome Soirée", p. 29.

122.   "Speech at the Farewell Soirée", p. 462; "Speech at the Annual Meeting of the British and Foreign Unitarian Association (BAFUA)", London, 8 June 1870, *SDC*, p. 310.

123.   Ibid., p. 314.

124.   Ibid.

125.   Ibid., p. 310.

126. Cobbe, Frances Power, *Life of Frances Power Cobbe as Told by Herself* (London, Swan Sonnenschein & Co., 1904), p. 451.

127. Gandhi landed at Southampton in 1888 wearing a white flannel suit. Ghose, Sankar, *Mahatma Gandhi* (New Delhi: Allied Publishers, 1991), p. 14.

128. Keshab to his wife, Glasgow, 25 Aug. 1870, Mahalanobi, *Patrabali*, p. 162.

129. Keshab to his wife, Liverpool, 7 July 1870, Mahalanobi, *Patrabali*, p. 151. *Bheto* does not literally mean 'a Bengali who eats rice *by hand*', but it refers to ordinary Bengalis eating ordinary food, and thus implies that the food is eaten by hand.

130. "Diary in England", p. 27.

131. Sen, *Jeeban Veda*, p. 65.

132. Ibid., p. 66.

133. Sen, P. K., *Biography of a New Faith, Volume Two* (Calcutta: Thacker Spink & Co., 1954), p. 27.

134. "Diary in England", p. 56.

CHAPTER 4: SPECTACLE, DIFFERENCE, FEAR AND FANTASY: REPRESENTATIONS OF KESHAB IN VICTORIAN ENGLAND

1. *The Graphic*, 25 June 1870.

2. Sastri, *History of the Brahmo Samaj*, p. 152.

3. *The Inquirer*, 2 July 1870.

4. *The Christian World*, 3 June 1870.

5. Reprinted in *The Inquirer*, 16 Apr. 1870.

6. Bebbington, *The Nonconformist*, p. 17.

7. Hall, Stuart, "The Spectacle of the 'Other'" in Hall, Stuart (ed.), *Representation: Cultural Representations and Signifying Practices* (The Open University, 1997), p. 231.

8. *Pall Mall Budget*, 23 Apr. 1870; *The Saturday Review*, 4 June 1870; *SDC*, p. 229.

9. Bradstock, Andrew, "'A Man of God is a Manly Man': Spurgeon, Luther and 'Holy Boldness'", in Bradstock, Gill and Morgan Hogan (eds.), *Masculinity and Spirituality in Victorian Culture* (Basingstoke: MacMillan Press, 2000), p. 213.

10. Singleton, *Yoga Body*, p. 95.

11. Frances Power Cobbe, reminiscing many years later, remembered Keshab's 'square face with powerful jaw' as a defining characteristic. Cobbe, *Life*, p. 492.

12. Bradstock, "A Man of God", p. 213.

13. Watts, *Gender, Power*, p. 101.

14. Bradstock, "A Man of God", p. 212.

15. *The Christian World*, 15 Apr. 1870; *The Record*, 11 May 1870; see also *The Graphic*, 2 July 1870.

16. *The Graphic*, 25 June 1870.

17. *Pall Mall Budget*, 23 Apr. 1870.

18. *The Saturday Review*, 4 June 1870.

19. Quoted in *The Inquirer*, 16 Apr. 1870.

20. *SDC*, p. 14.

21. Ibid., pp. 16–17.

22.   From the *English Independent*, reprinted in *The Inquirer*, 30 Apr. 1870.

23.   India Office Library John Lawrence Collection. MSS.Eur.F.90/31 (Letters to Secretary of State, vol. 3). No. 58 to Lord Cranborne. Calcutta. 19 Dec. 1866.

24.   *The Inquirer*, 2 July 1870; *Leeds Mercury*, 17 June 1870.

25.   Speaking at the Metropolitan Tabernacle, 24 May 1870, *SDC*, p. 226. The subject of Keshab's speech on this occasion was "England's Duties", which included considerable criticism of aspects of British rule in India.

26.   *The Saturday Review*, 4 June 1870.

27.   The allusion is to Marx, Karl, *Capital*, part 1, ch. 1, section 4, http://www.marxists.org/archive/marx/works/1867-c1/ch01.htm#S4, last accessed 30 Jan. 2017.

28.   Dean Stanley, speaking at the Hanover Square Rooms, London, 12 Apr. 1870, *SDC*, p. 5.

29.   *The Record (Supplement)*, 20 Apr. 1870.

30.   Speaking at a reception in Nottingham, 12 Jun. 1870, *SDC*, p. 384.

31.   Speaking at the Welcome Soirée, *SDC*, p. 7.

32.   *SDC*, p. 10.

33.   For example, *The Asiatic*, 10 Aug. 1870; *The Sporting Times*, 16 Apr. 1870; *Pall Mall Gazette*, 10 May 1870.

34.   *The Inquirer*, 27 Aug. 1870. How broadly this God was conceived could, however, vary—Cobbe herself had moved towards a position of universal Theism by this time.

35.   Cannadine, David, *Ornamentalism: How the British Saw Their Empire* (London: Allen Lane, 2001).

36.   From *Cassell's Magazine*, reprinted in *The Inquirer*, 27 Aug. 1870.

37.   *The Graphic*, 29 Oct. 1870.

38.   From Macaulay, Thomas Babington, "Minute of 2 February 1835 on Indian Education", in Young, G. M. (ed.), *Macaulay, Prose and Poetry* (Cambridge MA: Harvard University Press, 1957), p. 729.

39.   *Pall Mall Budget*, 23 Apr. 1870.

40.   Vance, Norman, *The Sinews of the Spirit: The Ideal of Christian Manliness in Victorian Literature and Religious Thought* (Cambridge: Cambridge University Press, 1985), p. 1.

41.   James Martineau to Rev. Charles Wicksteed, 5 May 1870, in Drummond, James and Upton, C. B., *The Life and Letters of James Martineau. Volume II* (London: James Nisbet & Co., 1902), p. 3.

42.   Reprinted in *The Inquirer*, 2 July 1870.

43.   *The Asiatic*, 13 Apr. 1870; *Pall Mall Gazette*, 10 May 1870.

44.   Reprinted in *The Inquirer*, 17 Sep. 1870.

45.   *The Asiatic*, 13 Apr. 1870; *The Inquirer*, 2 July 1870; *The Inquirer*, 27 Aug. 1870.

46.   *The Inquirer*, 27 Aug. 1870.

47.   Quoted in Houghton, Walter E., *The Victorian Frame of Mind: 1830–1870* (New Haven and London: Yale University Press, 1985), p. 125.

48.   Watts, *Gender, Power*, p. 112.

49. Carlyle as quoted in Houghton, *The Victorian*, pp. 97, 130. The second quotation is Houghton paraphrasing Carlyle.
50. *Pall Mall Budget*, 25 June 1870.
51. Mill, John Stuart, *The CollectedWorks of John Stuart Mill,Volume IX – An Examination of William Hamilton's Philosophy and of The Principal Philosophical Questions Discussed in his Writings*, ed. John M. Robson (Toronto: University of Toronto Press, London: Routledge and Kegan Paul, 1979).
52. Raeder, Linda C., *John Stuart Mill and the Religion of Humanity* (Columbia and London: University of Missouri Press, 2002), p. 148.
53. Ibid., pp. 146–7.
54. *Dharmatattwa*, 22 Mar. 1874, pp. 46–9.
55. For the broader context of these debates, and a detailed study of Anglican intuitionalism, see Gouldstone, Timothy Maxwell, *The Rise and Decline of Anglican Idealism in the Nineteenth Century* (Hampshire and NewYork: Palgrave Macmillan, 2005).
56. Houghton, *The Victorian*.
57. Ibid., pp. 106–7.
58. Bentham acknowledged that he borrowed the phrase 'the greatest happiness of the greatest number' from Priestley. Watts, *Gender, Power*, p. 111.
59. Ibid., pp. 100–1.
60. Quoted in Houghton, *TheVictorian*, p. 106. Ralph Waller identifies a tension between the 'critical spirit' and the 'will to believe' as central to James Martineau's thought: see Waller, Ralph, "The Critical Mind and the Will to Believe: James Martineau", *Transactions of the Unitarian Historical Society* (2002).
61. Reprinted in *The Inquirer*, 23 Apr. 1870.
62. Reprinted in *The Inquirer*, 30 Apr. 1870.
63. *The Asiatic*, 13 Apr. 1870.
64. *SDC*, p. 439.
65. Speaking at the Welcome Soirée, *SDC*, pp. 20–1.
66. Bebbington, *The Nonconformist*, p. 11.
67. Ibid., pp. 14-15.
68. *The Inquirer*, 2 July 1870.
69. Ibid.
70. *The Asiatic*, 22 June 1870.
71. Martineau speaking in Liverpool shortly after Keshab's departure, quoted in Sen, P. K., *Keshub Chunder Sen* (Calcutta: Art Press, 1938), p. 99.
72. From *Cassell's Magazine*, reprinted in *The Inquirer*, 27 Aug. 1870.
73. *The Inquirer*, 30 Apr. 1870.
74. Letter from Mary Carpenter to Keshab, Bristol, 15 Sep. 1870, Carpenter, *The Life and Work*, p. 383.
75. *PCM*, p. 144–5.
76. *The Record*, 6 June 1870.
77. *English Independent*, reprinted in *The Inquirer*, 30 Apr. 1870.
78. *Birmingham Daily Post*, 23 June 1870.

79. *Leeds Mercury*, 20 June 1870, 2 July 1870; *Birmingham Daily Post*, 2 June 1870, 8 June 1870.
80. *The Rock*, 3 May 1870.
81. Ibid.
82. *The Record*, 14 Apr. 1870, 20 Apr. 1870.
83. *The Record (Supplement)*, 20 Apr. 1870.
84. *The Record*, 20 Apr. 1870.
85. *The Record (Supplement)*, 17 June 1870; *The Record*, 18 June 1870.
86. *The Record (Supplement)*, 20 Apr. 1870; *The Inquirer*, 21 May 1870.
87. Thomson, John, *A Sermon on the nature of Theism; … protesting against the reception of Baboo Keshub Chunder Sen. Preached … July 3, 1870. To which is added an Essay on Sincerity, etc.* (London, Edinburgh, Aberdeen: Edward Howell, Simpkin, Marshall & Co., John Maclaren, A. & R. Milne, 1870), pp. 7, 41.
88. Ibid., pp. 45–6.
89. Ibid., p. 46.
90. Sinha, *Colonial Masculinity*.
91. In his *History of the Military Transactions of the British Nation in Indostan*, quoted in Ibid., p. 15.
92. Ibid., p. 15; India Office Library John Lawrence Collection. MSS. Eur.F.90/31(Letters to Secretary of State, vol. 3). No. 49 to Lord Cranborne. Delhi. 8 Nov. 1866.
93. Sinha, *Colonial Masculinity*, p. 17.
94. Burton, Antoinette, "Tongues untied: Lord Salisbury's "Black man" and the boundaries of imperial democracy", *Comparative Studies in Society and History*, 42, 3 (2000), pp. 632–61.
95. Ibid., p. 648.
96. Ibid.
97. Ibid.
98. *Birmingham Daily Post*, 27 June 1870.
99. Reprinted in *The Inquirer*, 11 June 1870
100. *The Christian World*, 3 June 1870.
101. *The Asiatic*, 20 July 1870.
102. Thomson, *A Sermon*, p. 36.
103. *The Rock*, 19 July 1870.
104. *The Saturday Review*, 11 June 1870.
105. *The Asiatic*, 20 Apr. 1870.
106. *The Asiatic*, 11 May 1870.
107. Reprinted in *The Inquirer*, 8 Oct. 1870.
108. *The Asiatic*, 29 June 1870.
109. Ibid.
110. Ibid.
111. *The Saturday Review*, 11 June 1870.
112. Ibid.
113. *Punch*, 16 Apr. 1870.
114. *The Asiatic*, 3 Aug. 1870.

115. See *The Christian World* (which includes articles from across the spectrum of the Nonconformist press), July–Sep. 1870.

116. *The Asiatic*, 29 June 1870, 13 Sep. 1870.

117. *The Record*, 8 June 1870.

118. *The Saturday Review*, 11 June 1870.

119. *Punch*, 24 Sep. 1870.

120. *The Asiatic*, 11 May 1870.

121. Thomson, *A Sermon*, p. 31.

122. Stallybrass, Peter and Allon White, *The Politics and Poetics of Transgression* (New York: Cornell University Press, 1986).

123. In this they follow Babcock, Stallybrass and White, *The Politics*, p. 17.

124. Quoted in Ibid., p. 5.

CHAPTER 5: TENSIONS AND TRANSITIONS: 1870–77

1.   As recorded in an account written by Swami Saradananda, quoted in Chatterjee, *The Nation*, p. 44. Majumdar dates the first meeting of Keshab and Ramakrishna to 1876, but scholars agree that this is inaccurate. See Chatterjee, *The Nation*, pp. 42–4. *Dharmatattwa* would later date the meeting to 1872, stating that the Belgharia garden house belonged to Joygopal Sen. It seems this first meeting will always be surrounded by a degree of mystery. *Dharmatattwa*, 23 Sep. 1886, pp. 194–6.

2.   "At The Star Theatre", 19 Sep. 1884, in Nikhilananda, Swami, *The Gospel of Sri Ramakrishna*, http://www.belurmath.org/gospel/chapter28.htm, last accessed 30 Jan. 2017, ch. 28, p. 12.

3.   See, for example, the article in *Dharmatattwa*, 22 May 1875, p. 99.

4.   *Dharmatattwa*, 7 Sep. 1886, p. 181.

5.   McDaniel, *The Madness*, p. 93.

6.   Ibid.

7.   Ramakrishna constitutes a field of academic study in his own right. For an interesting introduction to some of the scholarly controversies, and an overview of arguments concerning the ways in which Ramakrishna has been represented by the Ramakrishna Mission, see Hatcher, Brian, "Kālā's Problem Child: Another Look at Jeffrey Kripal's Study of Śrī Rāmakrsna", in *International Journal of Hindu Studies*, vol. 3, no. 2 (August, 1999), pp. 165–82.

8.   Neevel, Walter G., "The Transformation of Sri Ramakrishna", in Smith, Bardwell L., *Hinduism: New Essays in the History of Religions* (Leiden: E. J. Brill, 1976); Olson, Carl, *The Mysterious Play of Kālī: An Interpretative Study of Ramakrishna* (Atlanta: Scholars Press, 1990).

9.   McDaniel, *The Madness*, pp. 86–93.

10.   Ibid., pp. 95–6.

11.   Kripal, Jeffrey J., *Kālī's Child: The Mystical and the Erotic in the Life and Teachings of Ramakrishna* (2nd ed. London and Chicago: University of Chicago Press, 1998).

12.   Sartori, Andrew, "Beyond Culture-Contact and Colonial Discourse: 'Germanism' in Colonial Bengal", *Modern Intellectual History*, 4, 1 (2007), p. 84.

13. Dobe, *Hindu Christian Faqir.*
14. Sen, *Hindu Revivalism*, p. 308.
15. Ibid.
16. Kling, *Partner in Empire*; Sen, *Hindu Revivalism*; Sartori, *Bengal in Global Concept History*; Chatterjee, *The Nation*; Raychaudhuri, *Europe Reconsidered*; Murshid, Ghulam, *Reluctant Debutante: Response of Bengali Women to Modernization, 1849–1905* (Rajshahi: Rajshahi University Press, 1983).
17. Chatterjee, "Whose Imagined Community?", p. 217.
18. Ibid.
19. Chatterjee, *The Black Hole*, p. 157.
20. Bayly, *Recovering Liberties*.
21. Sartori, *Bengal in Global Concept History*.
22. "General Impressions", pp. 272–4.
23. Ibid.
24. Ibid., pp. 273–5.
25. Borthwick, *Keshub*, p. 135.
26. *Dharmatattwa*, 20 Feb. 1871, p. 312.
27. *PCM*, pp. 150–1.
28. Chatterjee, *The Nation*, p. 38. Keshab's disappointment with Christianity during his visit to England is noted in Lipner, Julius J., *Brahmobandhab Upadhyay: The Life and Thought of a Revolutionary* (New Delhi: Oxford University Press, 1999), p. 59.
29. *PCM*, p. 240; "General Impressions", p. 272.
30. *WW*, pp. 433–4.
31. "Annual Report of the Indian Reform Association 1870–71", reprinted in Sen, *Biography of a New Faith*, p. 276.
32. Ibid.
33. For some examples of articles in the *Sulabh Samachar*, see Gupta, J., *Keshabchandra O Sekaler Samaj* (Calcutta, 1949).
34. Kopf, *The Brahmo Samaj*, p. 18. Chatterjee provides a more conservative estimate—a peak circulation of 27,000 within the newspaper's first three months—but agrees that, in 1877, it was still the most widely-circulated Bengali-language newspaper. Chatterjee, *The Nation*, p. 44.
35. "Annual Report of the Indian Reform Association", pp. 279–80.
36. "Second Annual Report of the Indian Reform Association", reprinted in Sen, *Biography of a New Faith*, pp. 390–1.
37. Metcalf, *The Aftermath*, p. 116.
38. *Bristol Mercury*, 11 Mar. 1871.
39. Metcalf, *The Aftermath*, pp. 131-2.
40. Collet, *The Brahmo Year Book* (1876), pp. 49–50.
41. Ibid., p. 51.
42. *PCM*, pp. 245–6.
43. *The Friend of India*, 10 Aug. 1871.
44. *The Friend of India*, 26 Aug. 1871.
45. Letter from 'an Old Brahmo' to the *Indian Mirror*, reprinted in *The Friend of India*, 6 June 1872.

46. Ibid.
47. *The Times*, 5 Feb. 1872.
48. *The Times*, 11 Sep. 1871.
49. *Pall Mall Gazette* 4 Nov. 1871.
50. Ibid. *The Times* and *Pall Mall Gazette* were the principal sources of information on the marriage bill in the secular press in England, and their articles on the subject were reprinted widely (for example, *Birmingham Daily Post*, 23 Aug. 1871; *Leeds Mercury*, 22 Aug. 1871; *Glasgow Herald*, 8 Feb. 1872). In Calcutta, the bill was supported by the *Calcutta Review*, *The Friend of India*, *Pioneer*, *Englishman*, *Hindu Patriot* and *Indian Daily News*.
51. Keshab's efforts on behalf of women were written of approvingly in the *Englishwoman's Review*, 1 Apr. 1871. Frances Power Cobbe wrote in the *Pall Mall Gazette*, 6 May 1871, that Keshab was 'principally devoted...to the improvement of the condition of his countrywomen'. Keshab's letters to the Queen and his expressions of loyalty (for example, his sadness at the death of Lord Mayo) were widely reported - *The Graphic*, 23 Mar. 1872; *Birmingham Daily Post*, 3 Apr. 1872. His reputation as a social reformer even led to a series of advertisements in which he appeared as an endorsee of a treatise concerning the rationale of hygiene. *Manchester Times*, 29 Apr. 1871.
52. Sartori, *Bengal in Global Concept History*, p. 21.
53. "Primitive Faith and Modern Speculations", Calcutta, 23 Jan. 1872, in Sen, Keshub Chunder, *Lectures in India* (Calcutta: Navavidhan Publication Committee, 1954), p. 149.
54. "The Disease and the Remedy", Calcutta, 22 Jan. 1877, in Sen, *Lectures in India* (1954), p. 279.
55. Ibid., p. 290.
56. Sartori, *Bengal in Global Concept History*, p. 21.
57. Hatcher, Brian, *Bourgeois Hinduism, or the Faith of the Modern Vedantists. Rare Discourses from Early Colonial Bengal* (New York: Oxford University Press, 2008), p. 53.
58. *PCM*, p. 253.
59. Ibid., p. 252.
60. Sastri, *History*, p. 252.
61. Communal living was not, of course, common in England. The objective was to incorporate religion into daily life, and encourage certain 'English' virtues.
62. *PCM*, p. 270.
63. This description appeared in the *Indian Mirror* and is reprinted in Ibid., p. 274.
64. Damen, *Crisis*, pp. 173-4n. The efficacy of yoga as a route to 'transcendental experience' was emphasised in particular. *Dharmatattwa*, 24 May 1875, pp. 138–9.
65. "The Four Vedas", in the *Sunday Indian Mirror*, 5 Mar. 1876; Damen, *Crisis*, p. 173.
66. *PCM*, p. 277.
67. Damen claims that the content of Keshab's preaching differed significantly when he spoke in Bengali as opposed to English. His English orations presented a

Westernised form (tailored to European audiences) of teachings that were formulated originally in a distinctly Bengali idiom. P. C. Majumdar contradicts this, and states that Keshab devoted far more time to his English orations, which contain the fullest expositions of his teachings. In the present chapter, I have focused chiefly on Keshab's anniversary orations, delivered in English, as the objective is to relate Keshab's teachings to their representation and interpretation in England, and thus it makes sense to focus on the sermons to which English audiences would have been exposed. Damen, *Crisis*, pp. 7–9; *PCM*, p. 386.

68.   Reprinted in Chatterjee, *The Nation*, p. 45.

69.   Nikhilananda, Swami, *The Gospel of Sri Ramakrishna* (Chennai: Sri Ramakrishna Math, 1996), p. 137.

70.   Ibid.

71.   Ibid., p. 95.

72.   Ibid. These examples are from the 1880s, but there can be little doubt that the same issues would have arisen in discussion in the 1870s.

73.   *Dharmatattwa*, 6 May 1876, p. 96. The Lieutenant-Governor of Bengal, Sir Richard Temple, donated 5000 rupees towards the purchase of the building.

74.   *PCM*, p. 300.

75.   Ibid., p. 296.

76.   "Women in India", p. 365; "England's Duties", pp. 217–19.

77.   "England's Duties", pp. 199, 214; "Women in India", p. 359.

78.   *PCM*, p. 265.

79.   Ibid.

80.   Beveridge, Lord William Henry, *India Called Them* (London: George Allen & Unwin Ltd., 1947), pp. 83–6. Akroyd arrived in Calcutta in 1872. For the minutiae of the quarrel between Akroyd and Keshab, see Scherer, M. A., "A Cross-Cultural Conflict Reexamined: Annette Akroyd and Keshub Chunder Sen", *Journal of World History*, 7, 2 (1996).

81.   According to articles in *Sulabh Samachar*, 29 May 1873 and 2 July 1873.

82.   Sastri, Sivanath, *Atmacharit* (Calcutta, 1952), pp. 114–15.

83.   Keshab expressed his delight in 1876 that more women were becoming Theists, as it proved that the Brahmo faith was not bound by 'metaphysical dryness' but exhibited 'simplicity and sweetness' which appealed to 'the unsophisticated and untutored hearts of Indian women'. "Our Faith and Our Experiences", Calcutta, 22 Jan. 1876, in Sen, *Lectures in India* (1954), p. 264. Female education did continue to be promoted by the Brahmo Samaj of India and the New Dispensation—in 1882, the Indian Reform Association planned to establish an institution for the higher education of women. However, the institution was designed to provide an alternative to the overtly rational education provided by Calcutta University, which, Keshab's organisation claimed, 'tends to unsex them and is really a sort of degradation to them'. *The Friend of India*, 27 May 1882.

84.   Murshid, *Reluctant Debutante*.

85.   Sarkar, Sumit, "The Women's Question in Nineteenth Century Bengal", in Sangari, Kumkum and Sudesh Vaid (eds.), *Women and Culture* (Bombay: Research Centre for Women's Studies, 1985), pp. 157–72.

86. Chatterjee, *The Nation*, p. 132.

87. Ibid.

88. "Philosophy and Madness in Religion", Calcutta, 3 Mar. 1877, in Sen, *Lectures in India* (1954), pp. 322–3.

89. Ibid., p. 323.

90. The article is reprinted in *PCM*, pp. 445–7.

91. The extent to which Ramakrishna influenced Keshab, or vice versa, has been the subject of some controversy. See Chatterjee, *The Nation*, p. 47, for an overview. Keshab referred to inspiration in the years before he visited Britain, but he laid increasing emphasis on its value during the 1870s.

92. Nikhilananda, *The Gospel*, pp. 141–2.

93. Ibid., p. 142.

94. "Inspiration", Calcutta, 25 Jan. 1873, in Sen, *Lectures in India* (1954), p. 162.

95. Ibid., p. 164.

96. Ibid.

97. Ibid., p. 163.

98. Sartori, *Bengal in Global Concept History*, p. 108.

99. Ibid., p. 109.

100. For more nuanced analyses of Bankim, which stress continuity as well as change in his ideas, see Raychaudhuri, *Europe Reconsidered* and Lipner, Julius J., "Introduction", in Chatterji, Bankimchandra, *Anandamath or The Sacred Brotherhood*, trans. Julius J. Lipner (Oxford: Oxford University Press, 2005).

101. Sartori claims that Bankim was largely responsible for all of these innovations. Sartori, *Bengal in Global Concept History*, pp. 120–7. As far as I am aware, Sartori makes no mention of Keshab in any of his work.

102. Sartori, Andrew, "Emancipation as Heteronomy: The Crisis of Liberalism in Later Nineteenth-Century Bengal", *Journal of Historical Sociology*, 17, 1 (March, 2004), p. 80.

103. Sartori contends that schools of thought as diverse as British cultural criticism (represented pre-eminently by Matthew Arnold), Romanticism, a great variety of critiques of 'materialism', and also late-nineteenth century Bengali discourses of Indian 'spirituality' may all be placed under the broad rubric of 'culturalism'. They emerged, he argues, in response to the spread of global capitalism. Sartori, Andrew, "The Resonance of "Culture": Framing a Problem in Global Concept History", *Comparative Studies in Society and History*, 7, 4 (October, 2005).

104. "Inspiration", p. 162.

105. Ibid., p. 170.

106. Ibid., p. 186.

107. "Primitive Faith and Modern Speculations", p. 153.

108. Ibid., pp. 153, 155.

109. Ibid., p. 157.

110. "Philosophy and Madness", p. 293.

111. Ibid., p. 294.

112. Ibid., p. 293.

113. Ibid.

114. Ibid., p. 306.
115. Ibid., p. 312.
116. Ibid., p. 316.
117. Ibid.
118. Ibid.
119. Raina, Dhruv and S. Irfan Habib, "The Moral Legitimation of Modern Science: Bhadralok Reflections on Theories of Evolution", *Social Studies of Science*, 26, 1 (February, 1996), p. 32.
120. For example, the leading article in *The Inquirer*, 12 Aug. 1882, which claimed that Darwinism confirmed the existence of 'spiritual' laws. Darwin's family tradition was Unitarianism—his maternal grandfather Josiah Wedgwood was Unitarian, although his father and paternal grandfather were freethinkers and his boarding school was Anglican. Desmond, Adrian and James Moore, *Darwin: The Life of a Tormented Evolutionist* (London: Penguin, 1991), pp. 1–15. For a discussion of religious responses to Darwinism, see Moore, James, *The Post-Darwinian Controversies: A Study of the Protestant Struggle to Come to Terms with Darwin in Great Britain and America, 1870–1900* (Cambridge: Cambridge University Press, 1979).
121. *Dharmatattwa*, 8 Oct. 1874, pp. 206–7.
122. Bowler, Peter J., *The Eclipse of Darwinism: Anti-Darwinian Evolution Theories in the Decades around 1900* (Baltimore: John Hopkins University Press, 1983).
123. Koditschek, *Liberalism*, p. 211.
124. Ibid. See also Koditschek, Theodore, "Capitalism, Race and Evolution in Imperial Britain: 1850–1900", in Koditschek, Theodore, Sundiata Cha-Jua and Helen Neville (eds.), *Race Struggles* (University of Illinois Press, 2009), pp. 48–79.
125. Koditschek, *Liberalism*, p. 214.
126. For the increase in racism under Lytton's administration, see Bose, Nemai Sudhan, *Racism, Struggle for Equality, and Indian Nationalism* (Calcutta: South Asia Books, 1981), pp. 86–151.
127. McDaniel, *The Madness*, pp. 7–19.
128. Ibid., p. 287. See also De Michelis, *A History*.
129. McDaniel, *The Madness*, p. 8.
130. Ibid., pp. 8–9.
131. Chatterjee, *The Nation*, p. 55.
132. Ibid. Chatterjee is referring to a work of Mukhopadhyay entitled 'The history of India as revealed in a dream'.
133. Ibid.
134. "Philosophy and Madness", p. 322.
135. *The Friend of India*, 4 Sep. 1875.
136. *The Friend of India*, 18 Sep. 1875.
137. Ibid.
138. Reprinted in *The Friend of India*, 21 Mar. 1879.
139. Koditschek claims that Bankim's satire *Kamalakanta* may have been directed at Keshab, although he also suggests the target could be Bankim's own 'damaged alter ego'. Koditschek, *Liberalism*, pp. 281–2.

140. Sartori, "The Categorial Logic", p. 273.

141. Ibid., pp. 272–4.

142. The claim, made by the *Watchman* in May 1871, arose from a mix up with names, and was widely ridiculed in the Anglo-Indian press in Calcutta. British publications that carried the story included the *Pall Mall Gazette*, *Bristol Mercury*, *Bradford Observer*, *Liverpool Mercury*, *Hampshire Telegraph* and *Glasgow Herald*. Collet circulated letters pointing out the falsity of the claim.

143. *The Free Church of Scotland Monthly Record*, 1 Nov. 1873. Dall's entry into the Samaj was reported widely in the British press, but the ceremony's repudiation of the term 'Christian' was not noted outside the missionary press.

144. *Illustrated Missionary News*, 1 Sep. 1873.

145. Ibid.

146. *Missionary Herald*, 1 July 1873. *The Church Missionary Gleaner*, 1 July 1878, also took the view that, having once come so close to Christianity, evidence of Keshab's backsliding into Hinduism was overwhelming by the late 1870s.

147. *The Chronicle of the London Missionary Society*, 1 Aug. 1874 (from a report read before the General Missionary Conference, Allahabad, 1872–3).

148. Ibid.

149. Ibid.

150. Ibid.

151. Ibid.

152. Ibid. Ram Mohan did not believe that the New Testament was revealed; rather, he was impressed by the ethical principles of Jesus. "The Precepts of Jesus" brought him into conflict with the Serampore missionaries when it was published in the early 1820s.

153. On the history of the *Calcutta Review*, see Sen, Krishna and Debapriya Paul, "Archival Press Project: The Calcutta Review", *Victorian Periodicals Review*, 37, 2 (2004).

154. *Calcutta Review*, CIII, 1871.

155. Ibid.

156. Ibid.

157. Ibid.

158. Ibid.

159. *The Friend of India* was the most important newspaper of Eastern India, employing a combative style of journalism that was frequently critical of British imperial expansion. See Hirschmann, Edwin, "The Hidden Roots of a Great Newspaper: Calcutta's "Statesman"", *Victorian Periodicals Review*, 37, 2 (2004); Hirschmann, Edwin, *Robert Knight: Reforming Editor in Victorian India* (New Delhi: Oxford University Press, 2008). The name of the newspaper changed, in Jan. 1875, to *The Friend of India, in Which the Indian Observer is Incorporated*, and, in Jan. 1877, to *The Friend of India & Statesman*. I have used the abbreviated title throughout.

160. *The Friend of India*, 1 Feb. 1872. For support of the Indian Reform Association, see *The Friend of India*, 23 Oct. 1873.

161. *The Friend of India*, 11 May 1871.

162. Ibid.
163. *The Friend of India*, 6 June 1872. It transpired that the 'hymnicide' had been committed by Unitarians in Britain—they had sent the altered hymns to Keshab, who was unaware of their revisions. *The Friend of India*, 20 June 1872.
164. For example, the *Bradford Observer* mentioned Keshab without any background information in connection with vegetarianism, 16 Oct. 1875; no contextual information was provided for passing references to Keshab in *The Shield*, 1 Jan. 1876, or *The Examiner*, 27 Mar. 1875. Majumdar's visit to England in 1874 generated some publicity for the Brahmo Samaj of India—for example, *Manchester Times*, 10 Oct. 1874.
165. *The Friend of India*, 13 May 1876. For reprints in Britain, see, for example, *Pall Mall Gazette*, 7 June 1876; *Birmingham Daily Post*, 8 June 1876.
166. *The Friend of India*, 13 May 1876.
167. Ibid.
168. Ibid.
169. Ibid.
170. Ibid.
171. Ibid.
172. Ibid.
173. Collet, *The Brahmo Year Book* (1876), p. 17.
174. Ibid. (1877), p. 19.
175. Ibid. (1876), p. 25.
176. Ibid. (1877), pp. 22–3.
177. Letter from Keshab to Sophia Dobson Collet, 10 Dec. 1875, reprinted in Ibid.
178. Collet, writing in Ibid., p. 19.
179. Ibid., pp. 28–9.
180. Ibid.
181. *Contemporary Review*, January 1870.
182. On Parker's thought see Grodzins, Dean, *American Heretic: Theodore Parker and Transcendentalism* (Chapel Hill: University of North Carolina Press, 2002).
183. Writing in *The Examiner*, 26 Sep. 1874.
184. Ibid.
185. *The Inquirer*, 20 Jan. 1877.
186. Raychaudhuri, *Europe Reconsidered*, p. 344.
187. "Behold the Light of Heaven in India!", Calcutta, 23 Jan. 1875, in Sen, *Lectures in India* (1954), pp. 213–31.
188. Ibid.
189. Ibid., p. 232.
190. "Am I an Inspired Prophet?", Calcutta, Jan. 1879, in Sen, *Lectures in India* (1886), pp. 255–78.
191. Sen, *Hindu Revivalism*, pp. 57-60; Koditschek, *Liberalism*, p. 278; Borthwick, *Keshub*, p. 197.

CHAPTER 6: THE CUCH BIHAR CRISIS AND THE SEARCH FOR UNIVERSAL RELIGION

1. *Sunday Indian Mirror*, 20 Jan. 1878.
2. For a defence of Keshab's conduct, see *PCM*; for the viewpoint of the *Samadarshi* party, see Sastri, *History*; for reprints of documentary evidence, see Sen, *Biography of a New Faith*.
3. *PCM*, p. 321.
4. Kopf, *The Brahmo Samaj*, p. 327.
5. Koditschek, *Liberalism*, p. 278.
6. Majumdar, Rochona, *Marriage and Modernity: Family Values in Colonial Bengal* (Durham and London: Duke University Press, 2009), pp. 167–205.
7. Ramusack, Barbara N., *The Indian Princes and Their States* (Cambridge: Cambridge University Press, 2004); Ernst, W. and B. Pati (eds.), *India's Princely States: People, Princes and Colonialism* (London and New York: Routledge, 2007).
8. For Nripendra Narayan's lineage and a discussion of Suniti Devi's life, see Moore, Lucy, *Maharanis: The Lives and Times of Three Generations of Indian Princesses* (London: Viking, 2004), pp. 52–71.
9. Jhala, Angma Dey, *Courtly Indian Women in Late Imperial India* (London: Pickering and Chatto), 2008, p. 78.
10. Devee, Suniti, *The Autobiography of an Indian Princess* (London: John Murray, 1921), pp. 42–67.
11. *Sunday Indian Mirror*, 17 Mar. 1878.
12. Borthwick, *Keshub*, p. 192. These reports appeared in the *Sunday Indian Mirror*, 22 Dec. 1878. A copy of the first, signed by the Deputy Commissioner G. T. Dalton, in which it is stated that the marriage was a 'Hindu marriage' of '*perfect orthodoxy*', can be found in Müller, *Biographical Essays*, pp. 99–101.
13. For the focus on the sexual violence of white planters towards the enslaved, see Paton, Diana, "Decency, Dependence and the Lash: Gender and the British Debate over Slave Emancipation, 1830–34", *Slavery and Abolition*, 17, 3, (December, 1996) and Ferguson, Moira (ed.), *The History of Mary Prince, A West Indian Slave, Related by Herself* (Ann Arbor: University of Michigan Press, 1987).
14. Janaki Nair argues that nearly all of the imperial powers in the nineteenth century followed a strategy of foregrounding the position of women in order to denigrate politically and economically subjugated cultures. Nair, Janaki, *Women and Law in Colonial India: A Social History* (New Delhi: Kali for Women, 1996), pp. 51–2.
15. The legal point is made in Collet, *The Brahmo Year Book* (1878), p. 30.
16. Sturman, Rachel, *The Government of Social Life in Colonial India. Liberalism, Religious Law, and Women's Rights* (Cambridge: Cambridge University Press, 2012); Sharafi, M. *Law and Identity in Colonial South Asia. Parsi Legal Culture, 1772–1947* (Cambridge: Cambridge University Press, 2014); Chatterjee, Indrani, *Gender, Slavery and Law in Colonial India* (Delhi: Oxford University Press, 1999).
17. Sturman, *The Government*, p. 150.
18. *Pall Mall Gazette*, 11 Mar. 1878; *The Examiner*, 22 June 1878.

19. *Bristol Mercury*, 23 Mar. 1878.
20. See, for example, *Aberdeen Weekly Journal*, 4 Apr. 1878; *Hampshire Telegraph and Sussex Chronicle*, 6 Apr. 1878.
21. *Bristol Mercury*, 23 Mar. 1878. This account was reprinted in a number of provincial newspapers - for example, *The Blackburn Standard: Darwen Observer and North-East Lancashire Advertiser*, 23 Mar. 1878.
22. Burton, "From Child Bride", p. 1120. For the agitation leading to the Age of Consent Act, see also Forbes, Geraldine H., "Women and Modernity: The Issue of Child Marriage in India", *Women's Studies International Quarterly*, 2 (1979) and Heimsath, C. H., "The Origin and Enactment of the Indian Age of Consent Bill, 1891", *Journal of Asian Studies*, 21, 4 (1962).
23. The case is discussed in detail in Burton, "From Child Bride".
24. Ibid., p. 1120.
25. Ibid., p. 1122.
26. The quotations are from articles in the provincial press quoted in Ibid., p. 1136. Burton argues that metropolitan representations of Dadaji also reduced him to a 'coolie-like status'.
27. For a discussion of the "Maiden Tribute" series and an analysis of late-Victorian anxieties concerning the regulation of sexuality, see Walkowitz, Judith R., *City of Dreadful Delight: Narratives of Sexual Danger in Late-Victorian London* (Chicago: The University of Chicago Press, 1992); for campaigns against the Contagious Diseases Acts, see Walkowitz, Judith R., *Prostitution and Victorian Society: Women, Class and the State* (Cambridge: Cambridge University Press,, 1980).
28. Levine, Philippa, "Venereal Disease, Prostitution and the Politics and Empire: The Case of British India", *Journal of the History of Sexuality*, 4, 4 (1994); Levine, Philippa, *Prostitution, Race and Politics: Policing Venereal Disease in the British Empire* (New York: Routledge, 2003).
29. Forbes, "Women and Modernity", p. 407.
30. Carpenter, Mary, *Six Months in India* (2 vols, London: Longman, Green, 1868).
31. The principal themes of the text are discussed in Burton, "Fearful Bodies".
32. Ibid., p. 549.
33. Collet, *The Brahmo Year Book* (1878), p. 78.
34. Majumdar writing in the *Theistic Annual* for 1877, quoted in Ibid., p. 79.
35. Ibid., p. 79.
36. Ibid.
37. Ibid., p. 82.
38. Ibid. (1879), p. 5.
39. Ibid. (1878), p. 83.
40. Ibid.
41. *The Inquirer*, 18 May 1878. The concept of *adesh* had been described in *Dharmatattwa* in 1875 as 'a strange heavenly force' that 'helps one to attain the higher spiritual truth which is otherwise inaccessible through logic and rationality'. *Dharmatattwa*, 7 Aug. 1875, pp. 157–61.
42. *The Inquirer*, 18 May 1878.
43. *The Free Church of Scotland Monthly Record*, 2 Sep. 1878.

44. Ibid.
45. Ibid.
46. Forbes, "Women and Modernity", p. 408. For a discussion of child marriage in Hindu sacred texts see Kapadia, K. M., *Marriage and Family in India* (Calcutta: Oxford University Press, 1966), ch. 7.
47. Forbes, "Women and Modernity", p. 408. No age restrictions applied to marriage itself under this legislation, only consummation.
48. Burton, "From Child Bride", p. 1125.
49. Collet, *The Brahmo Year Book* (1878), p. 6.
50. *The Friend of India*, 12 Apr. 1878.
51. Devee, *Autobiography*, p. 63.
52. For a summary of articles, letters and petitions of protest, see Collet, *The Brahmo Year Book* (1878), pp. 9-77. Collet prints forty-four letters against the marriage, seven criticising the protesters, and two approving of the marriage. However, she was strongly biased in favour of the Sadharan Brahmo Samaj.
53. *Brahmo Public Opinion*, 6 June 1878, reprinted in Ibid., p. 77.
54. Ibid.
55. Ibid., p. 75.
56. Ibid.
57. *Tattwabodhini Patrika*, 23 Oct. 1879; *Tattwa Koumudi*, 7 Mar. 1879, pp. 218–19; *Tattwa Koumudi*, 7 Sep. 1879, p. 80.
58. This figure is claimed by *Brahmo Public Opinion*, 21 Mar. 1878. Damen, *Crisis*, p. 184.
59. *Tattwa Koumudi*, 5 Feb. 1879, p. 200.
60. *PCM*, pp. 333–5.
61. Ibid., p. 339.
62. Borthwick, *Keshub*, p. 197.
63. Nair, *Women and Law*, p. 72.
64. *PCM*, p. 329.
65. Keshab to Max Müller, 2 May 1881, reprinted in Müller, *Biographical Essays*, p. 114.
66. Keshab to Frances Power Cobbe, 29 Apr. 1878, reprinted in Sen, *Biography of a New Faith*, p. 192.
67. Devee, *Autobiography*, p. 47.
68. Ibid.
69. Letter from Mr Dalton to Keshab Chandra Sen, 27 Jan. 1878, reprinted in Devee, *Autobiography*, pp. 50–2.
70. Ibid., pp. 48–9.
71. Ibid., p. 49.
72. Jhala, *Courtly Indian Women*, p. 77.
73. Devee, *Autobiography*, p. 69.
74. Ibid., p. 42.
75. Ibid., p. 62.
76. Ibid., p. 63.
77. Ibid., p. 67.

78. Ibid.
79. Suniti Devi's memoir is discussed in some detail in Moore, *Maharanis*, pp. 52–71. The symbolic and literal role of women in royal marriages, including Suniti Devi, is a principal theme of Jhala, *Courtly Indian Women*. Sucharu Devi had waited fourteen years to marry the Maharajah of Mayurbhanj, after initial negotiations fell apart due to Keshab's reputation for radicalism. The Maharajah was killed in 1912 in a hunting accident. For details of her life, see Writers Workshop (eds.), *Sucharu Devi: Maharani of Mayurbhanj: A Biography* (Calcutta: Writers Workshop, 1979). In later generations, daughters of the Sen family would marry into the royal families of Kapurthala (Sikh) and the Chakma Raj (Buddhist). Suniti's granddaughter, Gayatri, married the Maharajah of Jaipur in 1940, and also wrote a memoir. Devi, Gayatri, *A Princess Remembers: The Memoirs of the Maharani of Jaipur* (Calcutta: South Asia Books, 1996).
80. Jhala, *Courtly Indian Women,* p. 97.
81. *Dharmatattwa*, 23 Aug. 1886, p. 174.
82. I use the term 'charisma' in the Weberian sense. Weber defines charisma as 'a certain quality of an individual personality by virtue of which he is considered extraordinary and treated as endowed with supernatural, superhuman, or at least specifically exceptional powers or qualities. These are such as are not accessible to the ordinary person, but are regarded as of divine origin or as exemplary, and on the basis of them the individual concerned is treated as a "leader"'. Weber, Max, *Economy and Society: An Outline of Interpretive Sociology, Volume One* (Berkeley, Los Angeles, London: University of California Press, 1978), p. 241.
83. For missionary loyalty, see Damen, *Crisis*, p. 184.
84. *PCM*, p. 395.
85. *Indian Mirror*, 19 Oct. 1879.
86. "Christ and Christianity", p. 257.
87. There are numerous studies of Keshab's theology. For a detailed account of doctrinal innovations and changes in the practical organisation of the New Dispensation, the reader is referred to the works of Frans Damen and Meredith Borthwick.
88. Majumdar claims that the New Dispensation was defined by these three main purposes. *PCM*, p. 350. His view is supported by Keshab's lectures of the period.
89. Keshab often emphasised the 'new-ness' of the New Dispensation. See, for example, "Is there any thing new in the New Dispensation?", in Sen, Keshub Chunder, *The New Dispensation or the Religion of Harmony, Compiled from Keshub Chunder Sen's Writings* (Calcutta: Bidhan Press, 1903), pp. 216–17. The answer to the question was that everything about it was 'new'.
90. "We Apostles of the New Dispensation", Calcutta, 22 Jan. 1881, in Sen, *Lectures in India* (1886), pp. 346–7.
91. Ibid., pp. 346–61.
92. "God-Vision in the Nineteenth Century", Calcutta, 24 Jan. 1880, in Sen, *Lectures in India* (1886), p. 341; "We Apostles", p. 380.

93. Versluis, Arthur, *American Transcendentalism and Asian Religions* (New York, Oxford: Oxford University Press, 1993), p. 307.

94. Cutler, Edward S., *Recovering the New: Transatlantic Roots of Modernism* (University of New Hampshire, 2003), p. 47.

95. "Footnotes to "The New Dispensation Dissected"", in *The Theosophist*, vol. III, no. I, October 1881, pp. 5–6.

96. Hatcher, Brian, *Eclecticism and Modern Hindu Discourse* (New York, Oxford: O.U.P., 1999), p. 8.

97. Lipner, Julius J., "Review Article: Brian A. Hatcher, *Eclecticism and Modern Hindu Discourse*", *International Journal of Hindu Studies*, 6, 1 (April, 2002), p. 79.

98. Hatcher, *Eclecticism*, p. 8.

99. For example, 'The new faith is absolutely synthetical...It loves unity above everything else', from his oration of January 1881, "We Apostles", p. 354.

100. Hatcher, *Eclecticism*, p. 118.

101. P. K. Sen differentiated Ram Mohan's universalism from Keshab's according to the distinction between 'subtraction' and 'addition'. Sen, *Biography of a New Faith*, p. 100.

102. Hatcher, *Eclecticism*, p. 97.

103. *The Inquirer*, 8 Sep. 1883.

104. Ibid.

105. *Sunday Indian Mirror*, 3 Oct. 1881, quoted in Ibid.

106. *SDC*, p. 242.

107. *Sunday Indian Mirror*, 1 Aug. 1880.

108. "The Trinity in Our Church, - An Historical Fact", in Sen, *The New Dispensation*, pp. 230–2. Keshab provided an alternative, theological account of the Trinity, which was similarly far removed from Christian Trinitarian orthodoxy, in his lecture "That Marvellous Mystery—The Trinity", 21 Jan. 1882, in Sen, *Lectures in India* (1886).

109. "Christian Baptism", pp. 20–1; "Baptism in the Vedas", pp. 85–6; "National Form of our Baptism", pp. 240–2, all in Sen, *The New Dispensation*.

110. "New Sacramental Ceremony", in Ibid., pp. 1–2.

111. "The Cross", in Ibid., pp. 4–6.

112. Keshab's desire to present the New Dispensation in a way that appealed to 'popular' sentiment is demonstrated further by the missionary tour undertaken in 1879 through Northern Bengal and Bihar, which was conducted in a military style inspired by the Salvation Army. The Salvation Army impressed Keshab and Majumdar with its ability to 'excite sympathy among the people' through 'humble, unaristocratic, popular ways of preaching'. Majumdar writing in *The Inquirer*, 27 Jan. 1883. The Salvation Army arrived in India in 1882. Keshab defended them publicly when they came under attack from the British authorities. See *The Friend of India*, 10 Oct. 1882.

113. Raychaudhuri, *Europe Reconsidered*, p. 235.

114. "Old and New", in Sen, *The New Dispensation*, pp. 207–8.

115. Damen, *Crisis*, p. 72.

116. Borthwick, *Keshub*, p. 220. On the work of Max Müller and nineteenth-century interest in comparative religion, see Girardot, N. J., "Max Müller's "Sacred Books" and the Nineteenth-Century Production of the Comparative Science of Religions", *History of Religions*, 41, 3 (February, 2002).

117. Ibid., p. 213.

118. Ibid., p. 222.

119. Ibid., pp. 218–20.

120. Ibid., p. 232.

121. Quoted in Ibid.

122. Quoted in Ibid. For further analysis of the ways in which concepts of 'religion' were affected by the 'comparative imaginary of the West', see Mandair, *Religion*.

123. Borthwick, *Keshub*, p. 214.

124. "We Apostles", p. 365.

125. Ibid., p. 366.

126. Ibid., p. 367.

127. Majumdar certainly expressed this view in a letter to Müller, writing that 'What you are doing as a philosopher and philologist we are trying to do as men of devotion and faith. It is the same universal recognition of all truths, and all prophets. I grant we are doing it in a Hindu style, perhaps in a Bengali style'. Majumdar to Max Müller, Calcutta, 14 Feb. 1881, reprinted in Müller, *Biographical Essays*, p. 150.

128. "Asia's Message to Europe", Calcutta, 20 Jan. 1883, in Sen, Keshub Chunder, *Keshub Chunder Sen's Lectures in India* (London, Paris, New York, Melbourne: Cassell and Company, 1904), p. 62.

129. Quoted in De Michelis, *A History*, p. 17.

130. *Dharmatattwa*, 7 Nov. 1882, p. 236. Sen, Keshub Chunder, *Yoga or Communion with God* (Calcutta: Brahmo Tract Society, 1885).

131. De Michelis, *A History*, p. 83.

132. Ibid.

133. Sen, *The New Dispensation*, p. 206.

134. "Asia's Message to Europe", pp. 49–51.

135. Ibid., pp. 51–6.

136. Ibid., pp. 67–9.

137. Ibid., pp. 69, 106.

138. Ibid., pp. 97, 106.

139. Ibid., pp. 117–18.

140. Arnold, *Science, Technology and Medicine*, p. 4. Amiya Sen notes that Bipin Chandra Pal wrote, as late as 1913, of Indian nationalist thought standing 'not only for the furtherance of the case of freedom in India….but also for the continuance of the British connection'. Sen, *Hindu Revivalism*, p. 60.

141. For the politics of the early Indian National Congress, see Mehrota, *The Emergence*, pp. 545–602.

142. Metcalf, *The Aftermath*, pp. 268–80.

143. Kopf, David, "The Universal Man and the Yellow Dog: The Orientalist Legacy and the Problem of Brahmo Identity", in Baumer, Rachel Van M. (ed.), *Aspects*

of Bengali History and Society (Honolulu: The University Press of Hawaii, 1975), p. 64.

144. The hardening of racial attitudes is noted by Sen, *Hindu Revivalism*, p. 58; Kopf "The Universal Man" and many others. For the details of the case against Bannerjee, see Bannerjee, S. N., *A Nation in Making* (Calcutta: Rupa, 1963), p. 69.

145. Hirschmann, Edwin, *White Mutiny: The Ilbert Bill Crisis in India and the Genesis of the Indian National Congress* (New Delhi: Heritage, 1980). As Sinha has demonstrated, opposition to the Bill led to the resurgence of the stereotype of the effeminate *babu*, with an emphasis on the *babu*'s cruel treatment of Indian and English women. Sinha, *Colonial Masculinity*, ch. 1.

146. Kopf, "The Universal Man", p. 64.

147. For a summary of Adi Brahmo Samaj critiques of Keshabite universalism, see Ibid., pp. 56–65.

148. Ibid., p. 64.

149. *Church Missionary Gleaner*, 1 July 1882; *The Friend of India*, 30 Jan. 1883.

150. *The Friend of India*, 23 Jan. 1882.

151. *PCM*, p. 445.

152. Quoted in *PCM*, pp. 426–7. The date and recipient of the letter are unclear.

153. For the decline in New Dispensation newspaper readership, see the figures quoted in the *Indian Mirror*, reprinted in Collet, *The Brahmo Year Book* (1882), p. 126. For the continuing attacks in the Sadharan Samaj's press, see *The Brahmo Year Book* (1879–1883), which reprints them exhaustively. The Calcutta liberal weekly the *Bengalee* includes numerous examples of attacks on Keshab's religion and person—for example, 21 Feb. 1880.

154. *Tattwa Koumudi*, 23 Oct. 1880, pp. 113–15.

155. *PCM*, pp. 400–2.

156. "We Apostles", p. 346.

157. *PCM*, p. 422, p. 424n.

158. Ibid., pp. 430–1.

159. Bijoy Krishna Goswami writing in a public letter from Dhaka to the Sadharan Brahmo Samaj. As reported in *Tattwa Koumudi*, 22 May 1879, pp. 285–6.

160. The accusation of 'theocracy' was made many times. See, for example, Collet, *The Brahmo Year Book* (1882), p. 7.

161. *PCM*, p. 437.

162. Ibid., p. 426.

163. Keshab writing in the 'devotional' column of the *Sunday Indian Mirror*, 19 Sep. 1880, reprinted in Collet, *The Brahmo Year Book* (1880), pp. 35–6.

164. Reprinted in *PCM*, pp. 441–2. The address continued, 'To all who hate us and abhor us for some reason or other, We send our fraternal love and good wishes'.

165. Keshab speaking in a private conversation in Bengali with Bijoy Krishna Goswami and a number of other preachers. Goswami reported Keshab's statements to the Sadharan Brahmo Samaj in a public letter from Dhaka, printed in *Tattwa Koumudi*, 22 May 1879, pp. 285–6.

166. Ibid.

167. *Dharmatattwa*, 22 June 1884, pp. 121–2.

168. *Indian Mirror*, 15 Feb. 1880.

169. "We Apostles", p. 365.

170. *New Dispensation*, 29 July 1883.

171. *New Dispensation*, Apr. 1883, reprinted in Collet, *The Brahmo Year Book* (1883), pp. 85–7.

172. Dobe, *Hindu Christian Faqir*, pp. 76–7.

173. See the critique of Partha Chatterjee in Joshi, Sanjay, "Republicizing Religiousity: Modernity, Religion and the Middle Class", in Peterson, Derek and Darren Walhof (eds.), *The Invention of Religion* (New Brunswick, NJ: Rutgers University Press, 2002), pp. 80–1.

174. Solomon, Rakesh H., "Culture, Imperialism, and Nationalist Resistance: Performance in Colonial India", *Theatre Journal*, 46, 3 (October, 1994), p. 323.

175. Ibid., p. 347.

176. "The Pagal – V", in Sen, *The New Dispensation*, p. 248.

177. The missionary tour was noted in the *Pall Mall Gazette*, 23 Dec. 1879 and the *Liverpool Mercury*, 29 Dec. 1879. The 'Pilgrimages to Saints' were mentioned in *The Graphic*, 10 Apr. 1880. The Eucharist ceremony was noted in the *Manchester Times*, 30 Apr. 1881 and *The Times*, 27 Apr. 1881.

178. *Pall Mall Gazette*, 31 Jan. 1883.

179. Koditschek, *Liberalism*, p. 319.

180. Cohn, Bernard S., "Representing Authority in British India", in Hobsbawm, E. and T. Rander (eds.), *The Invention of Tradition* (Cambridge: Cambridge University Press, 1983).

181. Koditschek, *Liberalism*, p. 321.

182. Metcalf, *The Aftermath*, p. 287.

183. Quoted in Mehrota, *The Emergence*, p. 208.

184. Kennedy, Dane, *Britain and Empire, 1880–1945* (London: Pearson, 2002); Cunningham, Hugh, "The Language of Patriotism, 1750–1914", *History Workshop Journal*, 12 (1981).

185. McClelland, Keith and Sonya Rose, "Citizenship and Empire, 1867-1928", in Hall and Rose, *At Home*, pp. 284–8.

186. McClelland and Rose, "Citizenship", p. 286; Heathorn, Stephen, *For Home, Country, and Race: Constructing Gender, Class and Englishness in the Elementary School, 1880–1914* (Toronto: University of Toronto Press, 2000).

187. Cunningham, "The Language of Patriotism".

188. Girardot, "Max Müller", p. 247. For the full text, see Monier-Williams, M., *The Holy Bible and the Sacred Books of the East, Four Addresses; To which is Added a Fifth Address On Zenana Missions* (London: Seeley & Co., 1887).

189. Majumdar to Max Müller, Simla, 20 Aug. 1881, in Müller, *Biographical Essays*, p. 154.

190. *The Inquirer*, 28 Apr. 1883; *The Inquirer*, 9 June 1883.

191. *The Inquirer*, 16 Dec. 1882.

192. Ibid.

193. *The Inquirer*, 15 Oct. 1881.

194. *The Inquirer*, 18 Aug. 1883.
195. *The Inquirer*, 11 Aug. 1883.
196. Collet, *The Brahmo Year Book* (1883), p. 87.
197. Majumdar to Max Müller, Calcutta, 14 Feb. 1881, in Müller, *Biographical Essays*, p. 149.
198. *The Inquirer*, 4 Nov. 1882.
199. *The Inquirer*, 8 Sep. 1883.
200. Ibid.
201. *Tattwa Koumudi*, 21 Apr. 1881, p. 263.
202. *The Inquirer*, 11 Aug. 1883.
203. Ibid.
204. Ibid.
205. *The Inquirer*, 18 Aug. 1883.
206. Ibid.
207. Ibid.
208. *The Inquirer*, 15 Oct. 1881.
209. Quoted in Webb, "The Unitarian Background", p. 26.
210. For an overview of Theosophy and a discussion of *Isis Unveiled*, see Godwin, *The Theosophical Enlightenment*.
211. Ibid., pp. 320–7.
212. "The Brahmo Samaj", in *The Theosophist*, vol. II, no. 6, Mar. 1881, pp. 131–2.
213. "Hindu Theism", in *The Theosophist,* vol. III, no. 9, June 1882, pp. 215–16.
214. "Footnotes to "The New Dispensation Dissected"", pp. 5–6.
215. "Hindu Theism", pp. 215–16.
216. Godwin, *The Theosophical Enlightenment*, p. 319.
217. "From Keshub Babu to Maestro Wagner via the Salvation Camp", in *The Theosophist*, vol. IV, no. 5, Feb. 1883, pp. 109–12.
218. *PCM*, p. 480.

CHAPTER 7: CONCLUSION:
UNIVERSALISM IN AN IMPERIAL WORLD

1. "Last Visit To Keshab", 28 Nov. 1883, in Nikhilananda, *The Gospel of Sri Ramakrishna*, ch. 15, pp. 1–2. http://www.belurmath.org/gospel/chapter15.htm, last accessed 30 Jan. 2017.
2. *Dharmatattwa*, 23 Sep. 1886, pp. 194–6.
3. The descent into factionalism occurred rapidly, as evidenced in *Dharmatattwa*, 23 Sep. 1884, pp. 195–6.
4. Kopf, *The Brahmo Samaj*, pp. 285–6. The Sadharan Brahmos expressed concerns that Brahmoism as a whole was in decline by the 1880s, with a total population in India of not more than 2000. *Tattwa Koumudi*, 5 Feb. 1884, p. 229.
5. *The Preston Guardian*, 12 Jan. 1884; *Leeds Mercury*, 9 Jan. 1884; *Daily News*, 9 Jan. 1884; *Birmingham Daily Post*, 9 Jan. 1884.
6. *Pall Mall Gazette*, 8 Jan. 1884; *The Preston Guardian*, 12 Jan. 1884; *The Newcastle Courant*, 11 Jan. 1884; *Birmingham Daily Post*, 9 Jan. 1884; *John Bull*, 12 Jan. 1884.

7. *Pall Mall Gazette*, 8 Jan. 1884.
8. *Glasgow Herald*, 18 Jan. 1884; *Daily News*, 9 Jan. 1884.
9. Ibid.
10. *The Times*, 10 Jan. 1884.
11. Ibid.
12. Obituary in *The Spectator*, reprinted in *The Inquirer*, 12 Jan. 1884.
13. *Bristol Mercury and Daily Post*, 15 Jan. 1884.
14. Collet, *The Brahmo Year Book* (1880), p. 18.
15. Ibid., p. 6.
16. Monier-Williams, M., "Indian Theistic Reformers", *Journal of the Royal Asiatic Society* (London: January, 1881).
17. Cumpston, "Some Early Indian Nationalists", p. 284.
18. *The Inquirer*, 12 Jan. 1884.
19. Ibid.
20. Ibid.
21. *The Times*, 24 Nov. 1880.
22. *Pall Mall Gazette*, 25 Oct. 1884; *The Times*, 4 Apr. 1885; *The Graphic*, 8 Nov. 1884.
23. Müller, *Biographical Essays*, pp. 67–79.
24. Ibid., pp. 70, 109–11.
25. Ibid., p. 82.
26. Ibid., pp. 78–9.
27. Max Müller to Majumdar, Oxford, 3 Aug. 1881, in Ibid., pp. 159, 166.
28. Ibid., p. 156.
29. Ibid., p. 157.
30. Max Müller to Keshab, no date, in Ibid., p. 106.
31. Max Müller to Majumdar, Oxford, 3 Aug. 1881, in Ibid., p. 157.
32. Ibid., p. 156.
33. Girardot, "Max Müller", pp. 243–50.
34. Ibid., p. 243.
35. Ibid., pp. 243–7. For a detailed account of the triumph of a more secularised anthropological school over Müller's theological and idealist approach, see Stocking, Jr., George W., *Victorian Anthropology* (New York: Free Press, 1987).
36. Majumdar reprints many obituaries, which he claims are 'from the most diverse sources, and are delivered from the most diverse points of view'. Not all of the obituaries he includes express unqualified admiration for Keshab. *PCM*, pp. 26–39.
37. According to the address of Sir William Hunter, Ibid., p. 28.
38. Ibid.
39. Ibid., pp. 28–9. Two years later, Hunter was appointed Vice Chancellor of the University of Calcutta.
40. Ibid., p. 30.
41. Ibid.
42. Ibid.
43. Ibid.

44. Ibid.
45. Reprinted in Ibid., p. 32.
46. Ibid.
47. Reprinted in Ibid., p. 33.
48. Koditschek, *Liberalism*, p. 290.
49. Burton, "Tongues untied".
50. Reprinted in *PCM*, p. 35.
51. Ibid.
52. Reprinted in Ibid.
53. Reprinted in Ibid., p. 34.
54. Ibid.
55. Bayly, C. A., "Afterword", *Modern Intellectual History*, 4, 1 (2007), p. 168.
56. Ibid.
57. Kopf, *The Brahmo Samaj*, p. xvi.
58. One recent study of the ideas and activities of elite Bengali figures from Ram Mohan Roy to Rabindranth Tagore, which gives particular weight to discourses of 'universalism', makes only one passing reference to Keshab. Dasgupta, Subrata, *The Bengal Renaissance. Identity and Creativity from Rammohun Roy to Rabindranath Tagore* (Delhi: Permanent Black, 2007).
59. Lipner, Julius J., "A Meeting of Ends? Swami Vivekananda and Brahmobandhab Upadhyay", in Radice, *Swami Vivekananda*, p. 66.
60. De Michelis, *A History*, p. 99. For a discussion of Keshab's close association with Vivekananda, see also pp. 108–10.
61. Priyanath Mallik—who became a follower of the New Dispensation—goes so far as to contend that both Brahmabandhab Upadhyay and, 'especially', Vivekananda, 'owed the beginnings of their spiritual culture to the pattern set by Keshab'. However, Mallik may have had a vested interest in magnifying Keshab's influence, and his claim should not be taken at face value. Quoted in Banerji, G. C., *Keshab Chandra and Ramakrishna* (Allahabad, 1931), p. 345.
62. Raychaudhuri, Tapan, "Swami Vivekananda's Construction of Hinduism", in Radice, *Swami Vivekananda*, pp. 1–10.
63. 'India…seems destined to sit at the feet of England for many long years, to learn Western art and science. And, on the other hand, behold England sits at the feet of hoary-headed India to study the ancient literature of this country'. "Philosophy and Madness", p. 325.
64. 'Starting as some fungus, some very minute, microscopic bubble, and all the time drawing from that infinite storehouse of energy, a form is changed slowly and steadily until in course of time it becomes a plant, then an animal, then man, ultimately God'. From Vivekananda's *Raja Yoga*, quoted in Killingley, Dermot, "Vivekananda's Western Message from the East", in Radice, *Swami Vivekananda*, p. 151.
65. Sen, *Hindu Revivalism*, pp. 363–401.
66. Killingley, Dermot, "Vivekananda's Western Message", p. 139.
67. Green, Thomas J., *Religion for a Secular Age. Max Müller, Swami Vivekananda and Vedānta* (London and New York: Routledge, 2016); De Michelis, A History.

68. Green, *Religion*, p. 40.
69. De Michelis, *A History*, pp. 74–140.
70. Edward Said refers to Tagore as an exponent of 'revolutionary nationalism' in Said, Edward, "Yeats and Decolonization", in Jameson, Frederick, Edward Said and Terry Eagleton (eds.), *Nationalism, Colonialism and Literature* (Minneapolis: University of Minnesota Press, 1990), p. 73. This simplistic characterisation is rejected by more detailed studies, such as Dutta, Krishna and Andrew Robinson, *Rabindranath Tagore. The Myriad-Minded Man* (London: Bloomsbury, 1995).
71. Kripalani, Krishna, *Rabindranath Tagore: A Biography* (Calcutta: Visra Bharati, 1980), p. 260; Dutta and Robinson, *Rabindranath Tagore*, p. 161.
72. Collins, Michael, "Rabindranath Tagore and Nationalism: An Interpretation", *Heidelberg Papers in South Asian and Comparative Politics*, 42 (October, 2008), p. 11; Collins, Michael, *Empire, Nationalism and the Postcolonial World: Rabindranath Tagore's Writings on History, Politics and Society* (London and New York: Routledge, 2012).
73. Radice, William, "Tagore's *The Religion of Man*", *Faith and Freedom*, 63, 2 (2010), pp. 104–12.
74. Collins, "Rabindranath Tagore and Nationalism", p. 3.
75. Ibid., pp. 21–9.
76. Ibid., pp. 25–9.
77. Dutta and Robinson make only two brief references to Keshab in their biography. Collins refers to Keshab as a 'highly formative' figure in Tagore's early life, but makes no mention of him with reference to Tagore's views on history. Collins, *Rabindranath Tagore and the West*, p. 74. Dasgupta makes only one passing reference to Keshab (giving his views on Ram Mohan) in Dasgupta, *Identity and Creativity*.
78. Radice, "Tagore's *The Religion of Man*", p. 105.
79. Radice notes that Tagore's voluminous writings contain no references to Ramakrishna, and very few to Vivekananda. Ibid.
80. Paul, Prasanta Kumar, *Rabindrajibani, Volume 6* (Calcutta: Ananda Publishers, 1993), pp. 117–18; Basu, Jharna, *Unish sataker bangala sahitya Keshabchandra* (1979), pp. 274–5.
81. Stephen Hay contends that 'the virtual identity of their [Tagore's and Keshab's] idea that Asia had a message for the West can scarcely be a coincidence', but does not expand further. Hay, Stephen N., *Asian Ideas of East and West: Tagore and His Critics in Japan, China and India* (Cambridge, MA., Harvard University Press, 1970), p. 23.
82. Pal, Bipinchandra, *Brahmo Samaj and the Battle of Swaraj in India* (Calcutta: Brahmo Mission Press, 1926).
83. Sen, *Hindu Revivalism*, p. 60; Kopf, *The Brahmo Samaj*, p. 227; Lipner, *Brahmabandhab*, p. 345; Bose, Sugata and Ayesha Jalal, *Modern South Asia: History, Culture, Political Economy* (London, New York: Routledge, 1999), p. 119.
84. Sen, *Hindu Revivalism*, p. 63; Pal, *Brahmo Samaj*, p. 56. For a study of Pal's politics, which neglects somewhat his religious views, see Mookerjee, Amalendu Prasad, *Social and Political Ideas of Bipin Chandra Pal* (Calcutta: Minerva Associates, 1974).

For an analysis of the relationship between his political and religious views, see Sartori, "The Categorial Logic".

85. Pal, *Brahmo Samaj*, pp. 55–9.

86. Ibid., p. 61.

87. Pal contrasts Keshab's and Majumdar's 'Unitarian Christianity' with the 'national religion' of Vivekananda in Pal, Bipin Chandra, *Memories of My Life and Times, Volume II (1886–1900)* (Calcutta: Yugayatri Prakashak Ltd., 1951), pp. 275–6.

88. Lipner, *Brahmobandhab*, p. 59.

89. Ibid., p. 63.

90. Quoted in Ibid., p. 82.

91. The reader is referred to Lipner, *Brahmobandhab*.

92. Lipner, "A Meeting of Ends?", p. 68.

93. Koditschek, *Liberalism*, pp. 286-93.

94. For a discussion of the life and work of Dutt, see Mukherjee, Meenakshi, *An Indian for All Seasons: The Many Lives of R. C. Dutt* (New Delhi: Penguin Books India, 2009).

95. Koditschek, *Liberalism*, pp. 293–310.

96. Webb, "The Unitarian Background", p. 26.

97. Ibid., p. 27.

98. Webb, "The Limits of Religious Liberty", p. 143.

99. The Unitarian connection with Bengal did not, of course, end with Keshab. Bipin Chandra Pal came to Britain on a scholarship provided by the British and Foreign Unitarian Association in 1898; Sivanath Sastri visited Britain in 1881 and maintained contact with English Unitarians. Pal, *Memories*, pp. 214–15. Tagore lectured to Unitarian audiences in the twentieth century. A small group of Brahmos continue to worship at the Unitarian church in Golders Green, London, to the present day.

100. Koditschek, *Liberalism*, p. 325.

101. Cunningham, "The Language of Patriotism"; McClelland and Rose, "Citizenship", pp. 284–8.

102. Koditschek, *Liberalism*, p. 333.

103. Collins, "History and the Postcolonial", pp. 75–6.

104. Kopf, *The Brahmo Samaj*, p. 24.

105. Ibid., p. 281.

BIBLIOGRAPHY

PRIMARY SOURCES

Abbreviations

PCM = Mozoomdar, P. C., *The Life and Teachings of Keshub Chunder Sen* (3rd ed., Calcutta: Nababidhan Trust, 1931).

SDC = Collet, Sophia Dobson (ed.), *Keshub Chunder Sen's English Visit* (London: Strahan and Co., 1871).

WW = Writers Workshop (eds.), *Keshub Chunder Sen in England: Diaries, Sermons, Addresses and Epistles* (4th ed., Calcutta: Writers Workshop, 1980).

Speeches and Works of Keshab Chandra Sen

"Address to Stanford Street Chapel", 28 Apr. 1870, *SDC*.

"Am I an Inspired Prophet?", Jan. 1879, in Sen, Keshab Chandra, *Keshub Chunder Sen's Lectures in India* (2nd ed., Calcutta: The Brahmo Tract Society, 1886).

"Asia's Message to Europe", 20 Jan. 1883, in Sen, Keshub Chunder, *Keshub Chunder Sen's Lectures in India* (London, Paris, New York, Melbourne: Cassell and Company, 1904).

"Behold the Light of Heaven in India!", 23 Jan. 1875, in Sen, Keshub Chunder, *Lectures in India* (Calcutta: Navavidhan Publication Committee, 1954).

"Christ and Christianity", 28 May 1870, *SDC*.

"Diary in England", *WW*.

"England's Duties to India", 24 May 1870, *SDC*.

"General Impressions of England and the English", in Basu, P. S., *Life and Works of Brahmananda Keshav* (2nd ed., Calcutta: Navavidhan Publication Committee, 1940).

"God-Vision in the Nineteenth Century", 24 Jan. 1880, in Sen, Keshab Chandra, *Keshub Chunder Sen's Lectures in India* (2nd ed., Calcutta: The Brahmo Tract Society, 1886) .

"Great Men", 28 Sep. 1866, in Sen, Keshab Chandra, *Keshub Chunder Sen's Lectures in India* (2nd ed., Calcutta: The Brahmo Tract Society, 1886).

"Hindu Theism", 7 June 1870, *SDC*.

"Inspiration", 25 Jan. 1873, in Sen, Keshub Chunder, *Lectures in India* (Calcutta: Navavidhan Publication Committee, 1954).

"Jesus Christ: Europe and Asia", 5 May 1866, in Sen, Keshab Chandra, *Keshub Chunder Sen's Lectures in India* (2nd ed., Calcutta: The Brahmo Tract Society, 1886).

"My Impressions of England", 12 Sep. 1870, *WW*.

"Our Faith and Our Experiences", 22 Jan. 1876, in Sen, Keshub Chunder, *Lectures in India* (Calcutta: Navavidhan Publication Committee, 1954).

"Parting Words at Southampton", 17 Sep. 1870, *WW*.

"Philosophy and Madness in Religion", 3 Mar. 1877, in Sen, Keshub Chunder, *Lectures in India* (Calcutta: Navavidhan Publication Committee, 1954).

"Primitive Faith and Modern Speculations", 23 Jan. 1872, in Sen, Keshub Chunder, *Lectures in India* (Calcutta: Navavidhan Publication Committee, 1954).

"Speech at Bath", 15 June 1870, *SDC*.

"Speech at the Annual Meeting of the British and Foreign Unitarian Association (BAFUA)", 8 June 1870, *SDC*.

"Speech at the Farewell Soirée", 12 Sep. 1870, *WW*.

"Speech at the Welcome Soirée", 12 Apr. 1870, *SDC*.

"Speech in Birmingham", 20 June 1870, *SDC*.

"Speech in Leicester", 17 June 1870, *SDC*.

"Speech in Liverpool", June/July 1870, *SDC*.

"Speech to the Philosophical Institution in Edinburgh", 19 Aug. 1870, *WW*.

"Special Reception by the United Kingdom Alliance", 25 Jun. 1870, *SDC*.

"That Marvellous Mystery—The Trinity", 21 Jan. 1882, in Sen, Keshab Chandra, *Keshub Chunder Sen's Lectures in India* (2nd ed., Calcutta: The Brahmo Tract Society, 1886).

"Temperance Address in Shoreditch", 29 May 1870, *SDC*.

"The Disease and the Remedy", 22 Jan. 1877, in Sen, Keshub Chunder, *Lectures in India* (Calcutta: Navavidhan Publication Committee, 1954).

"The Liquor Traffic in India", 19 May 1870, *SDC*.

"The Love of God", 1 May 1870, *SDC*.

"The Religious and Social Condition of India", 19 Aug. 1870, *WW*.

"We Apostles of the New Dispensation", 22 Jan. 1881, in Sen, Keshab Chandra, *Keshub Chunder Sen's Lectures in India* (2nd ed., Calcutta: The Brahmo Tract Society, 1886).

"Women in India", 1 Aug. 1870, *WW*.

Sen, Keshub Chunder, *Jeeban Veda or Life Scriptures (Autobiography) of Minister Keshub Chunder Sen*, trans. B. Mazoomdar (Calcutta: P. C. Mookerjee, 1915).

———, *The Book of Pilgrimages: Diaries and Reports of Missionary Expeditions* (Calcutta, 1940).

———, *The New Dispensation or the Religion of Harmony, Compiled from Keshub Chunder Sen's Writings* (Calcutta: Bidhan Press, 1903).

———, *Yoga or Communion with God* (Calcutta: Brahmo Tract Society, 1885).

BIBLIOGRAPHY

Newspapers, Journals and Manuscripts

Aberdeen Weekly Journal
Bengalee
Birmingham Daily Post
Bradford Observer
Bristol Mercury
Bristol Mercury and Daily Post
Calcutta Review
Christian Life
Church Missionary Gleaner
Contemporary Review
Daily News
Dharmatattwa
English Independent
Englishman
Englishwoman's Review
Glasgow Herald
Hampshire Telegraph
Hampshire Telegraph and Sussex Chronicle
Hindu Patriot
Illustrated Missionary News
Indian Daily News
Indian Mirror
John Bull
Leeds Mercury
Liverpool Mercury
Manchester Times
Missionary Herald
New Dispensation
Pall Mall Budget
Pall Mall Gazette
Pioneer
Punch
Sulabh Samachar
Sunday Indian Mirror
Tattwabodhini Patrika
Tattwa Koumudi
The Asiatic
The Blackburn Standard: Darwen Observer and North-East Lancashire Advertiser
The Christian World
The Chronicle of the London Missionary Society
The Examiner
The Free Church of Scotland Monthly Record
The Friend of India

The Graphic
The Inquirer
The Newcastle Courant
The Preston Guardian
The Record
The Record (Supplement)
The Rock
The Saturday Review
The Shield
The Spectator
The Sporting Times
The Theosophist
The Times

Roy, Rammohun, "Additional Queries respecting the Condition of India", Appendix 40, in vol. 5 of the Appendix to "Report from Select Committee on the Affairs of the East India Company", in *East India Company Volume 7: Reports from Committees* (1831).
———, "Remarks by Rammohun Roy, on Settlement in India by Europeans, dated 14 July 1832", in the General Appendix, Section V, of vol. 8 of *Report from the Select Committee on the Affairs of the East India Company* (16th August 1832, House of Commons, London).
India Office Library John Lawrence Collection. MSS.Eur.F.90/31.

Books, Pamphlets and Collections of Documents

Banerji, G. C., *Keshab Chandra and Ramakrishna* (Allahabad, 1931).
Bannerjee, S. N., *A Nation in Making* (Calcutta: Rupa, 1963).
Basu, P. S., *Life and Works of Brahmananda Keshav* (2nd ed., Calcutta: Navavidhan Publication Committee, 1940).
Beveridge, Lord William Henry, *India Called Them* (London: George Allen & Unwin Ltd., 1947).
Bose, Ram Chandra, *Brahmoism; or, History of Reformed Hinduism* (New York, London: Funk & Wagnalls, 1884).
Campbell, George, *India as it May Be; an Outline of a Proposed Government and Policy* (London: John Murray, 1853).
Carpenter, J. Estlin, *The Life and Work of Mary Carpenter* (London: MacMillan & Co., 1879).
Carpenter, Dr Lant, *A Biographical Memoir of the late Rajah Rammohun Roy together with a series of extracts from his writings* (Calcutta: Asiatic Press, 1835).
Carpenter, Mary, *Last Days in England of Rajah Rammohun Roy* (3rd ed., Calcutta: Ram Mohun Library & Free Reading Room, 1915).
———, *Six Months in India* (2 vols, London: Longman, Green, 1868).
———, *The Last Days in England of Rajah Rammohun Roy* (London, Calcutta: Trübner & Co., R. C. Lepage & Co., 1866).
Cobbe, Frances Power, *Essay on the Theory of Intuitive Morals* (London, 1855).

274

————, *Life of Frances Power Cobbe as Told by Herself* (London: Swan Sonnenschein & Co., 1904).

Collet, Sophia Dobson (ed.), *The Brahmo Year Book. Brief Records of Work and Life in the Theistic Churches of India* (7 vols, London, Edinburgh: Williams and Norgate, 1876-1883).

————, *The Life and Letters of Raja Rammohun Roy* (London: Harold Collet, 1900).

————, *The Life and Letters of Raja Rammohun Roy* (2ⁿᵈ ed., Calcutta, 1914).

————, *The Life and Letters of Raja Rammohun Roy* (4ᵗʰ ed., Calcutta: Sadharan Brahmo Samaj, 1988).

Devee, Suniti, *The Autobiography of an Indian Princess* (London: John Murray, 1921).

Devi, Gayatri, *A Princess Remembers: The Memoirs of the Maharani of Jaipur* (Calcutta: South Asia Books, 1996).

Drummond, James and C.B. Upton, *The Life and Letters of James Martineau. Volume II* (London: James Nisbet & Co., 1902).

Ghose, L., *The Modern History of the Indian Chiefs* (2 vols, Calcutta, 1881).

Gupta, J., *Keshabchandra O Sekaler Samaj* (Calcutta, 1949).

Macaulay, Thomas Babington, "Minute of 2 February 1835 on Indian Education", in Young, G. M. (ed.), *Macaulay, Prose and Poetry* (Cambridge MA: Harvard University Press, 1957).

Mahalanobis, Srimanika, *Brahhmananda Srikeshabchandrer Patrabali* (Calcutta, 1941).

Maunder, Samuel, *Biographical Treasury; A Dictionary of Universal Biography* (Harlow: Longman, Brown, Green and Longmans, 1845).

Martineau, Harriet, *Harriet Martineau's Autobiography* (3 vols, London: Smith, Elder & Co., 1877).

Martineau, Harriet, "Literary Lionism", *London and Westminster Review*, 32 (April, 1839).

Mill, James, *The History of British India* (6 vols, 3ʳᵈ ed., London: Baldwin, Cradock and Joy, 1826).

Mill, John Stuart, *The Collected Works of John Stuart Mill, Volume IX – An Examination of William Hamilton's Philosophy and of The Principal Philosophical Questions Discussed in his Writings*, ed. John M. Robson (Toronto: University of Toronto Press, London: Routledge and Kegan Paul, 1979).

Monier-Williams, M., "Indian Theistic Reformers", *Journal of the Royal Asiatic Society* (London: January, 1881).

————, *The Holy Bible and the Sacred Books of the East, Four Addresses; To which is Added a Fifth Address On Zenana Missions* (London: Seeley & Co., 1887).

Mozoomdar, P. C., *The Life and Teachings of Keshub Chunder Sen* (1st ed., Calcutta: Nababidhan Trust, 1887).

Müller, Max, *Biographical Essays* (London: Longmans Green & Co., 1884).

Nag and Burman (eds.), *The English Works of Rammohun Roy, Volume V* (Calcutta: Sadharan Brahmo Samaj, 1995).

Nikhilananda, Swami, *The Gospel of Sri Ramakrishna* (Chennai: Sri Ramakrishna Math, 1996).

————, *The Gospel of Sri Ramakrishna*, http://www.belurmath.org/gospel, last accessed 30 Jan. 2017.

Pal, Bipinchandra, *Brahmo Samaj and the Battle of Swaraj in India* (Calcutta: Brahmo Mission Press, 1926).

Pal, Bipin Chandra, *Memories of My Life and Times, Volume II (1886–1900)* (Calcutta: Yugayatri Prakashak Ltd., 1951).

Roy, Rammohun, "Brief Remarks Regarding Modern Encroachments on the Ancient Rights of Females, According to the Hindu Law of Inheritance" (1822), in Ghose, Jogendra Chunder (ed.), *The English Works of Raja Rammohun Roy, Volume II* (Calcutta: S. K. Lahiri & Co., 1901).

Roy, Ram Mohan, "The Precepts of Jesus", in Nag and Burman (eds.), *The English Works of Rammohun Roy, Volume V* (Calcutta: Sadharan Brahmo Samaj, 1995).

Sastri, Sivanath, *Atmacharit* (Calcutta, 1952).

———, *History of the Brahmo Samaj* (2nd ed., Calcutta: Sadharan Brahmo Samaj, 1974).

Sen, P. K., *Biography of a New Faith: Volume Two* (Calcutta: Thacker Spink & Co., 1954).

———, *Keshub Chunder Sen* (Calcutta: Art Press, 1938).

Slater, T. E., *Keshab Chandra Sen and the Brahmo Samaj* (Madras, Calcutta, London: Society for Promoting Christian Knowledge, Thacker Spink & Co., James Clark & Co., 1884).

Tagore, Rabindranath, *Gora* (Madras: MacMillan India, 1985).

Thomson, John, *A Sermon on the nature of Theism; … protesting against the reception of Baboo Keshub Chunder Sen. Preached … July 3, 1870. To which is added an Essay on Sincerity, etc.* (London, Edinburgh, Aberdeen: Edward Howell, Simpkin, Marshall & Co., John Maclaren, A. & R. Milne, 1870).

Secondary Literature

Arnold, David, *Science, Technology and Medicine in Colonial India* (Cambridge: Cambridge University Press, 2000).

Auerbach, Jeffrey, *The Great Exhibition of 1851: A Nation on Display* (London: Yale University Press, 1999).

Ballantyne, Tony, *Entanglements of Empire. Missionaries, Māori, and the Question of the Body* (Durham, NC., Duke University Press, 2014).

———, *Orientalism and Race: Aryanism in the British Empire* (Basingstoke: Palgrave Macmillan, 2002).

Ballantyne, Tony and Antoinette Burton (eds.), *Bodies in Contact: Rethinking Colonial Encounters in World History* (Durham, London: Duke University Press, 2005).

Ballantyne, Tony and Antoinette Burton, "Introduction: Bodies, Empires, and World Histories", in Tony Ballantyne and Antoinette Burton (eds.), *Bodies in Contact: Rethinking Colonial Encounters in World History* (Durham, London: Duke University Press, 2005).

——— (eds.), *Moving Subjects: Gender, Mobility, and Intimacy in an Age of Global Empire* (Urbana and Chicago: University of Illinois Press, 2009).

Basu, Jharna, *Unish sataker bangala sahitya Keshabchandra* (1979).

Bayly, C. A., "Afterword", *Modern Intellectual History*, 4, 1 (2007).

———, "Empires and Indian Liberals", in Catherine Hall and Keith McClelland (eds.), *Race, Nation and Empire: Making Histories, 1750 to the Present* (Manchester: Manchester University Press, 2010).

———, "Rallying Around the Subaltern", in Vinayak Chaturvedi (ed.), *Mapping Subaltern Studies and the Postcolonial* (London, New York: New Left Review, 2000).

———, *Recovering Liberties: Indian Thought in the Age of Liberalism and Empire* (Cambridge: Cambridge University Press, 2012).

———, *The Birth of the Modern World 1780–1914: Global Connections and Comparisons* (Cambridge: University of Cambridge Press, 2004).

Bebbington, D. W., *The Nonconformist Conscience. Chapel and Politics, 1870–1914* (London: George Allen & Unwin, 1982).

———, "Unitarian Members of Parliament in the Nineteenth Century, A Catalogue", *Transactions of the Unitarian Historical Society*, 23, 3 (April, 2009).

Bennett, Tony, *The Birth of the Museum: History, Theory, Politics* (Oxon: Routledge, 1995).

Bhattacharya, Subbhas, "Indigo Planters, Ram Mohan Roy and the 1833 Charter Act", *Social Scientist*, 4, 3 (October, 1975).

Blackman, Lisa, John Cromby, Derek Hook, Dimitris Papadopoulos and Valerie Walkerdine, "Creating Subjectivities", *Subjectivity* (2008).

Borthwick, Meredith, *Keshub Chunder Sen: A Search for Cultural Synthesis* (Calcutta: Minerva, 1977).

Bose, Nemai Sudhan, *Racism, Struggle for Equality, and Indian Nationalism* (Calcutta: South Asia Books, 1981).

Bose, N. S., *The Indian Awakening and Bengal* (3rd ed., Calcutta: Firma K. L. Mukhopadyay, 1969).

Bose, Sugata, "Different Universalisms, Colorful Cosmopolitanisms: The Global Imagination of the Colonized", in Sugata Bose and Kris Manjapra (eds.), *Cosmopolitan Thought Zones. South Asia and the Global Circulation of Ideas* (Basingstoke: Palgrave Macmillan, 2010).

Bose, Sugata and Kris Manjapra (eds.), *Cosmopolitan Thought Zones. South Asia and the Global Circulation of Ideas* (Basingstoke: Palgrave Macmillan, 2010).

Bose, Sugata and Ayesha Jalal, *Modern South Asia: History, Culture, Political Economy* (London, New York: Routledge, 1999).

Bowler, Peter J., *The Eclipse of Darwinism: Anti-Darwinian Evolution Theories in the Decades around 1900* (Baltimore: John Hopkins University Press, 1983).

Boyd, R. H. S., *An Introduction to Indian Christian Theology* (Madras: ISPCK, 1969).

Bradstock, Andrew, "'A Man of God is a Manly Man': Spurgeon, Luther and 'Holy Boldness'", in Gill Bradstock and Morgan Hogan (eds.), *Masculinity and Spirituality in Victorian Culture* (Basingstoke: MacMillan Press, 2000).

Brun, Maria, "Institutions Collide: A Study of "Caste-Based" Collective Criminality and Female Infanticide in India, 1789–1871: A Critique of Nicholas Dirks Castes of Mind and the Making of Modern India", *LSE Working Paper Series* (March, 2010).

Burton, Antoinette, *At the Heart of the Empire: Indians and the Colonial Encounter in Late-Victorian Britain* (Berkeley, Los Angeles, London: University of California Press, 1998).

———, *Burdens of History: British Feminists, Indian Women and Imperial Culture*, 1865–1915 (Chapel Hill: University of North Carolina Press, 1994).

———, "Fearful Bodies into Disciplined Subjects: Pleasure, Romance and the Family Drama of Colonial Reform in Mary Carpenter's "Six Months in India"", *Signs*, 20, 3 (Spring, 1995).

———, "From Child Bride to "Hindoo Lady": Rukhmabai and the Debate on Sexual Respectability in Imperial Britain", *The American Historical Review*, 103, 4 (October, 1998).

———, "Making a Spectacle of Empire: Indian Travellers in Fin-de- Siècle London", *History Workshop Journal*, 42 (Autumn, 1996).

———, "Tongues untied: Lord Salisbury's "Black man" and the boundaries of imperial democracy", *Comparative Studies in Society and History*, 42, 3 (2000).

Butler, Judith, *Bodies that Matter: On the Discursive Limits of "Sex"* (New York, London: Routledge, 1993).

Cannadine, David, *Ornamentalism: How the British Saw Their Empire* (London: Allen Lane, 2001).

Chakrabarty, Dipesh, *Provincializing Europe: Postcolonial Thought and Historical Difference* (Princeton: Princeton University Press, 2000).

Chandler, Daniel Ross, *Toward Universal Religion: Voices of American and Indian Spirituality* (Westport, CT: Greenwood Press, 1996).

Chatterjee, Indrani, *Gender, Slavery and Law in Colonial India* (Delhi: Oxford University Press, 1999).

Chatterjee, Partha, "Nationalism Resolves the Critical Question", in Amiya P. Sen, *Social and Religious Reform* (New Delhi: Oxford University Press, 2005).

———, *Nationalist Thought and the Colonial World: A Derivative Discourse* (Minneapolis: University of Minnesota Press, 1993).

———, *The Nation and Its Fragments: Colonial and Postcolonial Histories* (Princeton: Princeton University Press, 1993).

———, *The Black Hole of Empire: History of a Global Practice of Power* (Princeton: Princeton University Press, 2012).

———, "Whose Imagined Community?", in Gopal Balakrishnan (ed.), *Mapping the Nation* (London: Verso, 1996).

Chattopadhyay, Swati, "Blurring Boundaries: The Limits of "White Town" in Colonial Calcutta", *Journal of the Society of Architectural Historians*, 59, 2 (June, 2000).

Chidester, David, *Empire of Religion. Imperialism and Comparative Religion* (Chicago and London: The University of Chicago Press, 2014).

Cohn, Bernard S., "Representing Authority in British India", in E. Hobsbawm and T. Rander (eds.), *The Invention of Tradition* (Cambridge: Cambridge University Press, 1983).

Collins, Michael, *Empire, Nationalism and the Postcolonial World: Rabindranath Tagore's Writings on History, Politics and Society* (London and New York: Routledge, 2012).

———, "History and the Postcolonial: Rabindranath Tagore's Reception in London, 1912–1913", *International Journal of the Humanities*, 4, 9 (2007).

———, "Rabindranath Tagore and Nationalism: An Interpretation", *Heidelberg Papers in South Asian and Comparative Politics*, 42 (October, 2008).

————, *Rabindranath Tagore and the West: Nationalism, Empire and Inter- Cultural Dialogue, 1912–1941* (Unpublished PhD Thesis, University of Oxford, 2008).

Comaroff, Jean and John Comaroff, *Of Revelation and Revolution. Christianity, Colonialism and Consciousness in South Africa* (Chicago: University of Chicago Press, 1991).

Cooper, Frederick, *Colonialism in Question: Theory, Knowledge, History* (Berkeley: University of California Press, 2005).

Cumpston, Mary, "Some Early Indian Nationalists and their allies in the British Parliament, 1851-1906", *English Historical Review*, 76 (April, 1961).

Cunningham, Hugh, "The Language of Patriotism, 1750–1914", *History Workshop Journal*, 12 (1981).

Cutler, Edward S., *Recovering the New: Transatlantic Roots of Modernism* (University of New Hampshire, 2003).

Damen, Frans, *Crisis and Religious Renewal in the Brahmo Samaj (1860–1884): A Documentary Study of the Emergence of the "New Dispensation" under Keshab Chandra Sen* (Belgium: Katholieke Universiteit Leuven, 1983).

Das, Asitabha (ed.), *Raja Rammohun Roy: Creator of the New India Age* (Calcutta: Readers Service, 2010).

Dasgupta, Subrata, *The Bengal Renaissance. Identity and Creativity from Rammohun Roy to Rabindranath Tagore* (Delhi: Permanent Black, 2007).

Davis, John, "Modern London 1850–1930", *London Journal*, 20, 2 (1995).

Dawson, Graham, *Soldier Heroes: British adventure, Empire and the Imagining of Masculinities* (Oxon: Routledge, 1994).

De, Barun, "The Colonial Context of the Bengal Renaissance", in C. H. Philips and M. D. Wainwright (eds.) *Indian Society and the Beginnings of Modernization* (London: School of Oriental and African Studies, 1976).

De Michelis, Elizabeth, *A History of Modern Yoga. Patañjali and Western Esotericism* (London, New York: Continuum, 2004).

Desmond, Adrian and James Moore, *Darwin: The Life of a Tormented Evolutionist* (London: Penguin, 1991).

Dirks, Nicholas, *Castes of Mind: Colonialism and the Making of Modern India* (Princeton: Princeton University Press, 2001).

Dobe, Timothy S., *Hindu Christian Faqir. Modern Monks, Global Christianity and Indian Sainthood* (New York: Oxford University Press, 2015).

Dutta, Krishna and Andrew Robinson, *Rabindranath Tagore. The Myriad-Minded Man* (London: Bloomsbury, 1995).

Elias, Norbert, *The Civilizing Process* (Oxford: Blackwell, 2000).

Ernst, W. and B. Pati (eds.), *India's Princely States: People, Princes and Colonialism* (London and New York: Routledge, 2007).

Ferguson, Moira (ed.), *The History of Mary Prince, A West Indian Slave, Related by Herself* (Ann Arbor: University of Michigan Press, 1987).

Forbes, Geraldine H., "Women and Modernity: The Issue of Child Marriage in India", *Women's Studies International Quarterly*, 2 (1979).

Foucault, Michel, *Discipline and Punish: The Birth of the Prison* (London: Penguin, 1991).

————, *The Care of the Self: The History of Sexuality Volume III* (London: Penguin, 1990).

————, *The Use of Pleasure: The History of Sexuality Volume II* (London: Penguin, 1992).

————, *The Will to Knowledge: The History of Sexuality Volume I* (London: Penguin, 1998).

Fryer, Peter, *Staying Power: The History of Black People in Britain* (Concord, MA: Pluto Press, 1984).

Fuchs, Stephen, *Rebellious Prophets: A Study of Messianic Movements in Indian Religions* (Bombay, New York: Asia Publishing House, 1965).

Gallagher, John, Gordon Johnson and Anil Seal (eds.), *Locality, Province and Nation: Essays on Indian Politics 1870–1940,* (London: Cambridge University Press, 1973).

Gandhi, Leela, *Affective Communities. Anticolonial Thought, Fin-de-Siècle Radicalism, and the Politics of Friendship* (Durham, London: Duke University Press, 2006).

Ghose, Sankar, *Mahatma Gandhi* (New Delhi: Allied Publishers, 1991).

Gill, Sean, "*Ecce Homo*: Representations of Christ as the Model of Masculinity in Victorian Art and Lives of Jesus", in Gill Bradstock and Morgan Hogan (eds.), *Masculinity and Spirituality in Victorian Culture* (Basingstoke: MacMillan Press, 2000).

Girardot, N. J., "Max Müller's "Sacred Books" and the Nineteenth-Century Production of the Comparative Science of Religions", *History of Religions*, 41, 3 (February, 2002).

Gleadle, Kathryn, *The Early Feminists. Radical Unitarians and the Emergence of the Women's Rights Movement, 1831–51* (New York: Palgrave MacMillan, 1998).

Godwin, Joscelyn, *The Theosophical Enlightenment* (New York: State University of New York Press, 1994).

Gopal, S., *British Policy in India 1858–1905* (Cambridge: Cambridge University Press, 1965).

Gottschalk, Peter, *Religion, Science, and Empire. Classifying Hindu and Islam in British India* (New York: Oxford University Press, 2013).

Gouldstone, Timothy Maxwell, *The Rise and Decline of Anglican Idealism in the Nineteenth Century* (Hampshire and New York: Palgrave Macmillan, 2005).

Green, Thomas J., *Religion for a Secular Age. Max Müller, Swami Vivekananda and Vedānta* (London and New York: Routledge, 2016).

Grewal, Inderpal, *Home and Harem: Nation, Gender, Empire and Cultures of Travel* (London: Duke University Press, 1996).

Grodzins, Dean, *American Heretic: Theodore Parker and Transcendentalism* (Chapel Hill: University of North Carolina Press, 2002).

Guha, Ranajit, *Elementary Aspects of Peasant Insurgency in Colonial India* (Durham and London: Duke University Press, 1999).

————, "On Some Aspects of the Historiography of Colonial India", in Chaturvedi, Vinayak, *Mapping Subaltern Studies and the Postcolonial* (London, New York: New Left Review, 2000).

Halbwachs, Maurice, *On Collective Memory*, trans. Lewis A. Coser (Chicago: University of Chicago Press, 1992).

Hall, Catherine, "The Economy of Intellectual Prestige: Thomas Carlyle, John Stuart Mill, and the Case of Governor Eyre", *Cultural Critique*, 12 (Spring, 1989).

———, *White, Male and Middle Class: Explorations in Feminism and History* (Cambridge: Polity, 1992).

———, *Civilising Subjects: Metropole and Colony in the English Imagination 1830–1867* (Cambridge: Polity, 2002).

———, *Macaulay and Son. Architects of Imperial Britain* (New Haven and London: Yale University Press, 2012).

Hall, Catherine and Leonore Davidoff, *Family Fortunes: Men and Women of the English Middle Class 1780–1850* (Oxon: Routledge, 2002).

Hall, Catherine, Keith McClelland and Jane Rendall, *Defining the Victorian Nation: Class, Race, Gender and the British Reform Act of 1867* (Cambridge: Cambridge University Press, 2000).

Hall, Catherine and Sonya O. Rose (eds.), *At Home with the Empire: Metropolitan Culture and the Imperial World* (Cambridge: Cambridge University Press, 2006).

Hall, Stuart, "Introduction: Who needs 'Identity'?", in Hall, Stuart and Paul Du Gay (eds.), *Questions of Cultural Identity* (London: SAGE, 1996).

———, "The Spectacle of the 'Other'" in Stuart Hall (ed.), *Representation: Cultural Representations and Signifying Practices* (The Open University, 1997).

Handcock, Moffatt, "Torts in the Conflict of Laws: The First Rule in Phillips v. Eyre", *The University of Toronto Law Journal*, 3, 2 (1940).

Handford, Peter, "Edward John Eyre and the Conflict of Laws", *Melbourne University Law Review* (December, 2008).

Hanegraaf, W. J., "Empirical Method in the Study of Esotericism", *Method & Theory In the Study of Religion*, 7, 2 (1995)

———, *New Age Religion and Western Culture: Esotericism in the Mirror of Secular Thought* (Leiden: Brill, 1996).

Hatcher, Brian, *Bourgeois Hinduism, or the Faith of the Modern Vedantists. Rare Discourses from Early Colonial Bengal* (New York: Oxford University Press, 2008).

———, *Eclecticism and Modern Hindu Discourse* (New York, Oxford: O.U.P., 1999).

———, *Idioms of Improvement: Vidyasagar and Cultural Encounter in Bengal* (New Delhi: Oxford University Press, 1996).

Hatcher, Brian, "Kālī's Problem Child: Another Look at Jeffrey Kripal's Study of Śrī Rāmakṛṣṇa", in *International Journal of Hindu Studies*, vol. 3, no. 2 (August, 1999), pp. 165-82.

———, "Remembering Rammohan: An Essay on the (Re-)emergence of Modern Hinduism", *History of Religions*, 46, 1 (August, 2006).

Hay, Stephen N., *Asian Ideas of East and West: Tagore and His Critics in Japan, China and India* (Cambridge MA., Harvard University Press, 1970).

Heathorn, Stephen, *For Home, Country, and Race: Constructing Gender, Class and Englishness in the Elementary School, 1880-1914* (Toronto: University of Toronto Press, 2000).

Heimsath, C. H., "The Origin and Enactment of the Indian Age of Consent Bill, 1891", *Journal of Asian Studies*, 21, 4 (1962).

Hirschmann, Edwin, *Robert Knight: Reforming Editor in Victorian India* (New Delhi: Oxford University Press, 2008).

———, "The Hidden Roots of a Great Newspaper: Calcutta's "Statesman"", *Victorian Periodicals Review*, 37, 2 (2004).

———, *White Mutiny: The Ilbert Bill Crisis in India and the Genesis of the Indian National Congress* (New Delhi: Heritage, 1980).

Hochschild, Adam, *Bury the Chains: The British Struggle to Abolish Slavery* (London: Pan Macmillan, 2006).

Hoppen, K. Theodore, *The Mid-Victorian Generation 1846–1886* (Oxford: Clarendon Press, 1998).

Houghton, Walter E., *The Victorian Frame of Mind: 1830–1870* (New Haven and London: Yale University Press, 1985).

Hunt, James D., *Gandhi in London* (New Delhi: Promilla & Co., 1978).

Inden, Ronald, *Imagining India* (Bloomington, Indianapolis: Indiana University Press, 2000).

———, "Orientalist Constructions of India", *Modern Asian Studies*, 20, 3 (1986).

Jalal, Ayesha, *Self and Sovereignty: Individual and Community in South Asian Islam since 1850* (London: Routledge, 2000).

Jhala, Angma Dey, *Courtly Indian Women in Late Imperial India* (London: Pickering and Chatto), 2008.

Joshi, Sanjay, "Republicizing Religiousity: Modernity, Religion and the Middle Class", in Derek Peterson and Darren Walhof (eds.), *The Invention of Religion* (New Brunswick, NJ: Rutgers University Press, 2002).

Joshi, V. C. (ed.), *Rammohun Roy and the Process of Modernization in India* (Delhi: Vikas Publishing House, 1975).

Kapadia, K. M., *Marriage and Family in India* (Calcutta: Oxford University Press, 1966).

Kapila, Shruti, "Global Intellectual History and the Indian Political", in Darrin M. McMahon and Samuel Moyn, *Rethinking Modern European Intellectual History* (New York: Oxford University Press, 2014).

Kaushik, Harish, *The Indian National Congress in England, 1885–1920* (New Delhi: Research Publications in Social Sciences, 1972).

Kennedy, Dane, *Britain and Empire, 1880–1945* (London: Pearson, 2002).

Killingley, Dermot, *Rammohun Roy in Hindu and Christian Tradition: The Teape Lectures 1990* (Newcastle upon Tyne: Grevatt and Grevatt, 1993).

———, "Vivekananda's Western Message from the East", in Radice, William (ed.), *Swami Vivekananda and the Modernization of Hinduism* (Delhi: Oxford University Press, 1997).

Kling, Blair, *Partner in Empire: Dwarkanath Tagore and the Age of Enterprise in Eastern India* (Calcutta: Firma KLM Private, 1981).

Koditschek, Theodore, "Capitalism, Race and Evolution in Imperial Britain: 1850–1900", in Theodore Koditschek, Sundiata Cha-Jua and Helen Neville (eds.), *Race Struggles* (University of Illinois Press, 2009).

———, *Liberalism, Imperialism, and the Historical Imagination: Nineteenth-Century Visions of a Greater Britain* (Cambridge: Cambridge University Press, 2011).

Kopf, David, *British Orientalism and the Bengal Renaissance: The Dynamics of Indian Modernization, 1773–1835* (Berkeley: University of California Press, 1969).

————, *The Brahmo Samaj and the Shaping of the Modern Indian Mind* (New Jersey: Princeton University Press, 1979).

————, "The Universal Man and the Yellow Dog: The Orientalist Legacy and the Problem of Brahmo Identity", in Rachel Van M. Baumer (ed.), *Aspects of Bengali History and Society* (Honolulu: The University Press of Hawaii, 1975).

Kriegel, Lara, "The Pudding and the Palace: Labor, Print Culture, and Imperial Britain in 1851", in Antoinette Burton (ed.), *After the Imperial Turn: Thinking With and Through the Nation* (Durham: Duke University Press, 2003).

Kripal, Jeffrey J., *Kālī's Child: The Mystical and the Erotic in the Life and Teachings of Ramakrishna* (2nd ed. London and Chicago: University of Chicago Press, 1998).

Kripalani, Krishna, *Rabindranath Tagore: A Biography* (Calcutta: Visra Bharati, 1980).

Lavan, S., *Unitarians and India: A Study in Encounter and Response* (Boston: Skinner House, 1977).

Lester, Alan, *Imperial Networks: Creating Identities in Nineteenth-Century South Africa and Britain* (London: Routledge, 2001).

Levine, Philippa, *Prostitution, Race and Politics: Policing Venereal Disease in the British Empire* (New York: Routledge, 2003).

————, "Venereal Disease, Prostitution and the Politics and Empire: The Case of British India", *Journal of the History of Sexuality*, 4, 4 (1994).

Lipner, Julius J., "A Meeting of Ends? Swami Vivekananda and Brahmobandhab Upadhyay", in William Radice (ed.), *Swami Vivekananda and the Modernization of Hinduism* (Delhi: Oxford University Press, 1997).

————, *Brahmobandhab Upadhyay: The Life and Thought of a Revolutionary* (New Delhi: Oxford University Press, 1999).

————, *Hindus: Their Religious Beliefs and Practices* (2nd ed., London, New York: Routledge, 2010).

————, "Introduction", in Bankimchandra Chatterji, *Anandamath or The Sacred Brotherhood*, trans. Julius J. Lipner (Oxford: Oxford University Press, 2005).

————, "Review Article: Brian A. Hatcher, *Eclecticism and Modern Hindu Discourse*", *International Journal of Hindu Studies*, 6, 1 (April, 2002).

Ludden, David (ed.), *Reading Subaltern Studies: Critical History, Contested Meaning and the Globalization of South Asia* (London: Anthem Press, 2002).

Majumdar, J. K., *Rammohun Roy and the World* (Calcutta: Sadharan Brahmo Samaj, 1975).

Majumdar, R. C., *History of the Freedom Movement in India* (Calcutta: Firma K. L. Mukhopadhyay, 1962).

Majumdar, Rochona, *Marriage and Modernity: Family Values in Colonial Bengal* (Durham and London: Duke University Press, 2009).

Mandair, Arvind-Pal S., *Religion and the Specter of the West. Sikhism, India, Postcoloniality, and the Politics of Translation* (New York: Columbia University Press, 2009).

Mani, Lata, *Contentious Traditions: The Debate on Sati in Colonial India* (Berkeley: University of California, 1998).

BIBLIOGRAPHY

Mantena, Karuna. *Alibis of Empire: Henry Maine and the Ends of Liberal Imperialism* (Princeton: Princeton University Press, 2010).

Marx, Karl, *Capital*, http://www.marxists.org/archive/marx/works/1867, last accessed 30 Jan. 2017.

———, *The Eighteenth Brumaire of Louise Bonaparte,* https://www.marxists.org/archive/marx/works/1852/18th-brumaire, last accessed 28 Jan. 2017.

McClelland, Keith and Sonya Rose, "Citizenship and Empire, 1867–1928", in Catherine Hall and Sonya O. Rose (eds.), *At Home with the Empire: Metropolitan Culture and the Imperial World* (Cambridge: Cambridge University Press, 2006).

McClintock, Anne, *Imperial Leather: Race, Gender and Sexuality in the Colonial Context* (New York: Routledge, 1995).

McDaniel, June, *The Madness of the Saints. Ecstatic Religion in Bengal* (Chicago and London: The University of Chicago Press, 1989).

McLachlan, H., *The Unitarian Movement in the Religious Life of England: 1. Its Contribution to Thought and Learning 1700–1900* (London: George Allen & Unwin Ltd., 1934).

Mehrota, S. R., *The Emergence of Indian National Congress* (Delhi: Vikas Publications, 1971).

Mehta, Uday S., *Liberalism and Empire* (Chicago: University of Chicago Press, 1999).

———, "Liberal Strategies of Exclusion", in Ann Laura Stoler and Frederick Cooper (eds.), *Tensions of Empire: Colonial Cultures in a Bourgeois World* (Berkeley, Los Angeles, London: University of California Press, 1997).

Metcalf, Barbara D. and Thomas R. Metcalf, *A Concise History of India* (Cambridge: Cambridge University Press, 2002).

Metcalf, Thomas R., *The Aftermath of Revolt: India 1857–1870* (Princeton: Princeton University Press, 1965).

Midgley, Clare, *Feminism and Empire: Women Activists in Imperial Britain, 1790- 1865* (Oxon: Routledge, 2007).

———, "Mary Carpenter and the Brahmo Samaj of India: a transnational perspective on social reform in the age of empire", *Women's History Review*, 22, 3 (2013).

———, *Women against Slavery: The British Campaigns, 1780–1870* (London: Routledge, 1992).

Midgley, Clare, Alison Twells and Julie Carlier (eds.), *Women in Transnational History. Connecting the Local and the Global* (Routledge, 2016).

Mohr, Michel, *Buddhism, Unitarianism, and the Meiji Competition for Universality* (Cambridge MA: Harvard University Asia Center, 2014).

Mookerjee, Amalendu Prasad, *Social and Political Ideas of Bipin Chandra Pal* (Calcutta: Minerva Associates, 1974).

Moore, James, *The Post-Darwinian Controversies: A Study of the Protestant Struggle to Come to Terms with Darwin in Great Britain and America, 1870–1900* (Cambridge: Cambridge University Press, 1979).

Moore, Lucy, *Maharanis: The Lives and Times of Three Generations of Indian Princesses* (London: Viking, 2004).

Moyn, Samuel and Andrew Sartori (eds.), *Global Intellectual History* (New York: Columbia University Press, 2013).

Mukherjee, Meenakshi, *An Indian for All Seasons: The Many Lives of R. C. Dutt* (New Delhi: Penguin Books India, 2009).

Murshid, Ghulam, *Reluctant Debutante: Response of Bengali Women to Modernization, 1849–1905* (Rajshahi: Rajshahi University Press, 1983).

Muthu, Sankar, *Enlightenment Against Empire* (Princeton: Princeton University Press, 2003).

Nair, Janaki, *Women and Law in Colonial India: A Social History* (New Delhi: Kali for Women, 1996).

Neevel, Walter G., "The Transformation of Sri Ramakrishna", in Bardwell L. Smith, *Hinduism: New Essays in the History of Religions* (Leiden: E. J. Brill, 1976).

Olson, Carl, *The Mysterious Play of Kālī: An Interpretative Study of Ramakrishna* (Atlanta: Scholars Press, 1990).

Paton, Diana, "Decency, Dependence and the Lash: Gender and the British Debate over Slave Emancipation, 1830-34", *Slavery and Abolition*, 17, 3, (December, 1996).

Paul, Prasanta Kumar, *Rabindrajibani*, *Volume 6* (Calcutta: Ananda Publishers, 1993).

Peart, Ann, *Forgotten Prophets: The Lives of Unitarian Women, 1760-1904* (Unpublished PhD Thesis, University of Newcastle, 2005).

Piette, O. L., *Responses of Brahmo Samaj to Western Cultural Advances, 1855–1880: An Episode in India's Intellectual History* (Unpublished PhD Thesis, Syracuse University, 1974).

Pitts, Jennifer, *A Turn to Empire. The Rise of Imperial Liberalism in Britain and France* (Princeton and Oxford: Princeton University Press, 2005).

Port, M. H., *Imperial London: Civil Government Building in London 1850–1915* (New Haven, London: Yale University Press, 1995).

Porter, Roy, *London: A Social History* (London: Penguin, 2000).

Pratt, Mary Louise, "Arts of the Contact Zone", in David Bartholomae and Anthony Petrosky (eds.), *Ways of Reading* (Boston: Bedford/St. Martin's, 2002).

Rabault-Feuerhahn, Pascale, *L'Archive des origines. Sanskrit, Philologie, anthropologie dans l'Allemagne du XIXe siècle* (Paris: Le Cerf, 2008).

Radice, William (ed.), *Swami Vivekananda and the Modernization of Hinduism* (Delhi: Oxford University Press, 1997).

Radice, William, "Tagore's *The Religion of Man*", *Faith and Freedom*, 63, 2 (2010).

Raeder, Linda C., *John Stuart Mill and the Religion of Humanity* (Columbia and London: University of Missouri Press, 2002).

Raina, Dhruv and S. Irfan Habib, "The Moral Legitimation of Modern Science: Bhadralok Reflections on Theories of Evolution", *Social Studies of Science*, 26, 1 (February, 1996).

Ramusack, Barbara N., *The Indian Princes and Their States* (Cambridge: Cambridge University Press, 2004).

Raychaudhuri, Tapan, *Europe Reconsidered: Perceptions of the West in Nineteenth- Century Bengal* (New Delhi: Oxford University Press, 2002).

———, "Swami Vivekananda's Construction of Hinduism", in William Radice (ed.), *Swami Vivekananda and the Modernization of Hinduism* (Delhi: Oxford University Press, 1997).

Robb, Peter, *A History of India* (Hampshire, New York: Palgrave, 2002).

Rogers, Ben, *Beef and Liberty: Roast Beef, John Bull and the English Patriots* (London: Chatto & Windus, 2003).

Roy, G. G., *Acharya Keshavchandra* (3 vols, Calcutta, 1938).

Roy Pape, W., "Keshub Chunder Sen's Doctrine of Christ and the Trinity: A Rehabilitation", *The Indian Journal of Theology*, 25 (1976).

Said, E. W., *Culture and Imperialism* (London: Chatto & Windus, 1993).

———, *Orientalism: Western Conceptions of the Orient* (London: Penguin, 1995).

———, "Yeats and Decolonization", in Frederick Jameson, Edward Said and Terry Eagleton (eds.), *Nationalism, Colonialism and Literature* (Minneapolis: University of Minnesota Press, 1990).

Sarkar, Sumit, "Calcutta and the 'Bengal Renaissance'", in Sukanta Chaudhuri (ed.), *Calcutta: The Living City, Volume 1* (New Delhi: Oxford University Press, 1990).

———, "The Decline of the Subaltern in *Subaltern Studies*", in Chaturvedi, Vinayak, *Mapping Subaltern Studies and the Postcolonial* (London, New York: New Left Review, 2000).

———, "The Women's Question in Nineteenth Century Bengal", in Kumkum Sangari and Sudesh Vaid (eds.), *Women and Culture* (Bombay: Research Centre for Women's Studies, 1985).

Sarkar, Tanika, *Hindu Wife, Hindu Nation. Community, Religion and Cultural Nationalism* (Indianapolis: Indiana University Press, 2001).

Sartori, Andrew, *Bengal in Global Concept History: Culturalism in the Age of Capital* (Chicago: University of Chicago Press, 2008).

———, "Beyond Culture-Contact and Colonial Discourse: "Germanism" in Colonial Bengal", *Modern Intellectual History*, 4, 1 (2007).

———, "Emancipation as Heteronomy: The Crisis of Liberalism in Later Nineteenth-Century Bengal", *Journal of Historical Sociology*, 17, 1 (March, 2004).

———, *Liberalism in Empire. An Alternative History* (Berkeley: University of California Press, 2014).

———, "The Categorial Logic of a Colonial Nationalism: Swadeshi Bengal, 1904–1908", *Comparative Studies of South Asia, Africa and the Middle East*, 23, 1&2 (2003).

———, "The Resonance of "Culture": Framing a Problem in Global Concept History", *Comparative Studies in Society and History*, 7, 4 (October, 2005).

Scherer, M. A., "A Cross-Cultural Conflict Reexamined: Annette Akroyd and Keshub Chunder Sen", *Journal of World History*, 7, 2 (1996).

Schneer, Jonathan, *London 1900: The Imperial Metropolis* (New Haven, London: Yale University Press, 1999).

Scott, David, *Refashioning Futures: Criticism after Postcoloniality* (Princeton: Princeton University Press, 1999).

Seal, Anil, *The Emergence of Indian Nationalism: Competition and Collaboration in the Later Nineteenth Century* (Cambridge: Cambridge University Press, 1968).

Seed, John, "Theologies of Power: Unitarianism and the Social Relations of Religious Discourse, 1800–1850", in R. J. Morris (ed.), *Class, Power and Social Structures in British Nineteenth Century Towns* (University of Leicester Press: Leicester, 1986).

Sen, Amiya P., *Hindu Revivalism in Bengal 1872–1905: Some Essays in Interpretation* (New Delhi: Oxford University Press, 1993).

————, *Social and Religious Reform: The Hindus of British India* (New Delhi: Oxford University Press, 2003).

Sen, Asok, *Iswar Chandra Vidyasagar and His Elusive Milestones* (Calcutta: Riddhi- India, 1977).

Sen, Krishna and Debapriya Paul, "Archival Press Project: The Calcutta Review", *Victorian Periodicals Review*, 37, 2 (2004).

Sen, Simonti, *Travels to Europe: Self and Other in Bengali Travel Narratives, 1870– 1910* (London: Sangam Books Limited, 2005).

Sharafi, M. *Law and Identity in Colonial South Asia. Parsi Legal Culture, 1772–1947* (Cambridge: Cambridge University Press, 2014).

Singh, Iqbal, *Rammohun Roy* (3 vols, 2nd ed., Bombay, New Delhi, 1983).

Singleton, Mark, *Yoga Body. The Origins of Modern Posture Practice.* (New York: Oxford University Press, 2010).

Sinha, Mrinalini, *Colonial Masculinity: The 'Manly Englishman' and the 'Effeminate Bengali' in the Late Nineteenth Century* (Manchester: Manchester University Press, 1995).

Sinha, Pradip, "Calcutta and the Currents of History, 1690–1912", in Sukanta Chaudhuri (ed.), *Calcutta: The Living City, Volume I* (New Delhi: Oxford University Press, 1990).

Solomon, Rakesh H., "Culture, Imperialism, and Nationalist Resistance: Performance in Colonial India", *Theatre Journal*, 46, 3 (October, 1994).

Stallybrass, Peter and Allon White, *The Politics and Poetics of Transgression* (New York: Cornell University Press, 1986).

Stocking, Jr., George W., *Victorian Anthropology* (New York: Free Press, 1987).

Stokes, E. T., "Bureaucracy and Ideology: Britain and India in the Nineteenth Century", *Transactions of the Royal Historical Society*, 30 (1980).

Stoler, Ann Laura, "Carnal Knowledge and Imperial Power: Gender, Race and Morality in Colonial Asia", in di Leonargo, Micaela (ed.), *Gender at the Crossroads of Knowledge: Feminist Anthropology in a Postmodern Era* (Berkeley: University of California Press, 1991).

Stoler, Ann Laura and Frederick Cooper, "Between Metropole and Colony: Rethinking a Research Agenda", in Ann Laura Stoler and Frederick Cooper (eds.), *Tensions of Empire: Colonial Cultures in a Bourgeois World* (Berkeley, Los Angeles, London: University of California Press, 1997).

———— (ed.), *Haunted by Empire: Geographies of Intimacy in North American History* (Durham, London: Duke University Press, 2006).

————, *Race and the Education of Desire: Foucault's 'History of Sexuality' and the Colonial Order of Things* (Durham, NC: Duke University Press, 1995).

Strawson, P. F. and Arindam Chakrabarti (eds.), *Universals, Concepts, and Qualities: New Essays on the Meaning of Predicates* (Aldershot, England and Burlington, VT: Ashgate, 2006).

Sturman, Rachel, *The Government of Social Life in Colonial India. Liberalism, Religious Law, and Women's Rights* (Cambridge: Cambridge University Press, 2012).

Tagore, Satyendranath, and Indira Devi (eds.), *Autobiography of Debendranath Tagore* (Whitefish, MT: Kessinger, 2006).

Thomas, M. M., *The Acknowledged Christ of the Indian Renaissance* (Bangalore: SCM Press, 1970).

Thompson, James, "Modern Britain and the New Imperial History", *History Compass*, 5 (2007).

Thorne, Susan, *Congregational Missions and the Making of an Imperial Culture in Nineteenth-Century England* (Stanford: Stanford University Press, 1999).

Troeltsch, E. *The Social Teachings of the Christian Churches* (New York: Macmillan, 1931).

Tsing, Anna Lowenhaupt, *Friction. An Ethnography of Global Connection* (Princeton and Oxford: Princeton University Press, 2005),

Vance, Norman, *The Sinews of the Spirit: The Ideal of Christian Manliness in Victorian Literature and Religious Thought* (Cambridge: Cambridge University Press, 1985).

Venn, Couze, *The Postcolonial Challenge: Towards Alternative Worlds* (London: SAGE, 2006).

Versluis, Arthur, *American Transcendentalism and Asian Religions* (New York, Oxford: Oxford University Press, 1993).

Visram, Rozina, *Asians in Britain: 400 Years of History* (London: Pluto Press, 2002).

——, *Ayahs, Lascars and Princes: Indians in Britain, 1700–1947* (London: Pluto Press, 1986).

Walkowitz, Judith R., *City of Dreadful Delight: Narratives of Sexual Danger in Late-Victorian London* (Chicago: The University of Chicago Press, 1992).

——, *Prostitution and Victorian Society, Women, Class and the State* (Cambridge: Cambridge University Press, 1980).

Waller, Ralph, "James Martineau's Influence on Unitarianism", in A.S. Hankinson (ed.), *A James Martineau Miscellany* (Oxford, 2005).

——, "James Martineau: the Development of his Thought", in Barbara Smith (ed.), *Truth, Liberty, Religion: Essays celebrating Two Hundred Years of Manchester College* (Manchester College Oxford, 1986).

——, "The Critical Mind and the Will to Believe: James Martineau", *Transactions of the Unitarian Historical Society* (2002).

Watts, Michael R., *The Dissenters* (2 vols, Oxford: 1978, 1996).

Watts, Ruth, *Gender, Power and the Unitarians in England 1760–1860* (London, New York: Longman, 1998).

——, "Rational Religion and Feminism: the Challenge of Unitarianism in the Nineteenth Century", in Sue Morgan (ed.), *Women, Religion and Feminism in Britain, 1750–1900* (Basingstoke: Palgrave MacMillan, 2002).

Webb, Robert K., "The Background: English Unitarianism in the Nineteenth Century" in Leonard Smith (ed.), *Unitarian to the Core: Unitarian College Manchester 1854–2004* (Manchester: Unitarian College, 2004).

——, "The Limits of Religious Liberty: Theology and Criticism in Nineteenth-Century England" in Richard Helmstadter (ed.), *Freedom and Religion in the Nineteenth Century* (Stanford: Stanford University Press, 1997).

————, "The Unitarian Background", in Barbara Smith (ed.), *Truth, Liberty, Religion: Essays celebrating Two Hundred Years of Manchester College* (Manchester College Oxford, 1986).

Weber, Max, *Economy and Society: An Outline of Interpretive Sociology, Volume One* (Berkeley, Los Angeles, London: University of California Press, 1978).

Wilbur, Earl Morse, *A History of Unitarianism* (2 vols, Cambridge, MA.: Harvard University Press, 1946-1952).

Woodward, Kathryn, "Concepts of Identity and Difference", in Kathryn Woodward (ed.), *Identity and Difference* (London: Sage, 1997).

Writers Workshop (eds.), *Sucharu Devi: Maharani of Mayurbhanj: A Biography* (Calcutta: Writers Workshop, 1979).

Yelle, Robert A., *Semiotics of Religion. Signs of the Sacred in History* (London, Delhi, New York, Sydney: Bloomsbury, 2013).

Zastoupil, Lynn, *Rammohun Roy and the Making of Victorian Britain* (New York: Palgrave MacMillan, 2010).

INDEX

Abercrombie, John, 38
Adam, William, 234
adesh, 150, 153, 163, 164–5, 169, 264
Adi Brahmo Samaj, 18, 39, 69, 124,
    177, 185–7, 193, 213, 236, 237
advaitic thought, 215
Age of Consent Act (1891), 159
Age of Culture, 119
Age of Enterprise, 25
Age of Liberalism, 119
Agricultural and Horticultural Society,
    Calcutta, 28
Akroyd, Annette, 133
Albert Hall, Calcutta, 132
alcohol, 41, 71, 121, 122, 123, 216
'Am I an Inspired Prophet?' (Sen), 162,
    187
American Unitarian Mission, 30
Amherst, William Pitt, 32
Ancillon, Johann Peter Friedrich, 38
Anglicanism, 27, 40, 84, 88, 89, 92,
    97, 104, 106
Anglo-Indians, 18, 24, 124–5, 145,
    147, 185–6, 194, 207–10
Anthropology (Tylor), 207
Apostle of India, 93
Apostle of the East, 57
Apostles of the New Dispensation, 1,
    187–90, 188

apostolical religion, 173, 186–200
Arabic, 32, 33
Arabs, 22, 157
architecture, *39*, 40
Aristotle, 38
Arnold, David, 58, 184
Arnold, Matthew, 49, 97, 258
Arya Samaj, 199
asceticism, 40, 118, 128–32, 138, 145,
    149–50, 163, 206
'Asia's Message to Europe' (Sen),
    182–3, 190–91
Asiatic Society, 28, 186
Asiatic, The, 95, 98, 108, 109, 110
Aspland, Robert, 48–9
atheism, 36, 44, 146
Austin, John Langshaw, 8
Australia, 22
authoritarianism, 38, 147, 151, 153,
    165, 172, 187, 204–5
autocracy, spiritual, 162–3
avatars, 3
ayahs, 23
Ayurveda, 143

babus, 107, 118, 145, 209, 268
Bakhtin, Mikhail, 111
Ballantyne, Tony, 5, 9

INDEX

Indian Reform Association, 121–6,
148, 218
Industrial School, 122
journalism, 33, 200
Keshab's cremation (1884), 207–8
Lily Cottage, 1, 132, 172, 202
M. G. Road, 2
Medical Education Committee, 28
Metropolitan College, 29
Mint, 28, 236
Normal School for Ladies, 122, 123,
125, 162
Parental Academic Institution, 28
poverty, 73, 122
racial divisions, 26
Sadhan Kanan, 129
Sanskrit College, 28, 32, 36
School Book Society, 28
Tattwabodhini School, 35
Union Bank, 25–6, 119
White Town, 26
Working Man's Institution, 122
Calcutta Review, 147
Calvin, John, 89
Calvinism, 35, 89
Cambridge University, 23, 24, 195
Campbell, George, 66
Canada, 22
Cannadine, David, 93
Canning, Charles, 52
capitalism, 10, 12, 71–2, 137–8, 258
Carey, William, 28, 31
Carlyle, Thomas, 3, 65, 66, 70, 96,
180
'Carnival', 111, 113
Carpenter, Lant, 46, 98, 99
Carpenter, Mary, 46, 54, 75, 98, 99,
103, 122, 161–2, 247
caste, 27–31, 58, 67–9, 72–3, 77, 84,
92, 125
Catholicism, 12, 41, 43, 84, 92, 215
Ceylon, 36
Chaitanya Mahaprabhu, 3, 104–5, 143,
180, 188, 210
Chakrabarty, Dipesh, 12, 60

Channing, William Ellery, 49, 88, 97,
99, 174
'character', 63–8
charity, 121
Charter Act
of 1813: 31
of 1833: 45, 52
Chatterjee, Bankimchandra, 119, 137,
144, 145, 152, 184, 259
Chatterjee, Partha, 67, 118, 119, 134,
143
Chicago, Illinois, 46
Chidester, David, 14
child marriage, 18, 58, 67, 69, 125,
150, 153, 154–73
child prostitution, 161
China, 22, 45, 157
choga, 145
Chowringhee, Calcutta, 26
Christ, *see* Jesus
Christian Life, 49, 168
Christian Reformer, The, 48, 49
Christian World, The, 41, 87, 89, 104, 108
Christianity
Anglicanism, 27, 40, 84, 88, 89, 92,
97, 104, 106
baptism, 177
Baptists, 31, 40, 57, 63, 89, 146, 148
Bible, 30, 37, 42, 69, 82, 89, 96, 97,
180, 260
Calvinism, 35, 89
Catholicism, 12, 41, 43, 84, 92, 215
civilisation, 13, 47, 70
Clapham Sect, 31
Congregationalism, 40, 44
conversion, 13, 22, 32, 35, 47, 92,
96, 222
crucifixion, 178, 191, 193
Eastern Orthodox, 143
'essential spirit', 93, 98, 103
Eucharist, 177, 178, 194
evangelicalism, 13, 22, 31, 41, 45,
96, 98
Jesus, *see* Jesus
Keshab, *see* Christianity and Keshab

liberal, 11, 13
and madness, 143
and masculinity, 94
Methodism, 40, 44, 145–6
missionaries, *see* missionaries
monotheism, 177
muscular, 70, 88
and New Dispensation, 172, 174,
   175, 177–8, 180, 188, 191, 204,
   205
Nonconformists, 20, 40–41, 87, 89,
   97, 100, 104, 110, 161, 168
Oriental aspect, 61, 69, 92, 200,
   212, 215–16
and politics, 100
Presbyterianism, 40, 104, 106, 110
Protestantism, 41, 106
Quakers, 40, 41, 174
and rationality, 140
rational dissenters, 42
Roy, 47
sectarianism, 70, 95, 121
and slavery, 41, 100
Teutonic, 92
Trinity, 35, 42, 43, 45, 177
Unitarianism, *see* Unitarians
universalism, 13, 38, 40
Christianity and British India, 3, 13,
   31–2, 35, 69, 82, 92–3, 210
and Brahmoism, 31
Charter Act (1813), 31
Oriental aspect, 61, 69–70, 92, 200,
   212, 215–16
Queen's Proclamation (1858), 51,
   157
and Roy, 47
see also missionaires
Christianity and Keshab, 38, 222
Bible, 69, 82
criticism, 69, 86, 92, 103–14
English Christianity, 70, 120–21
'essential spirit', 93, 98, 103
idolatry, 77
India, spread in, 3, 69–70, 82, 92,
   124, 210, 215–16

introduction to, 30
and New Dispensation, 172, 174,
   175, 177–8, 180, 188, 191, 204,
   205
and primitive faith, 145–9
Oriental aspect, 61, 69–70, 92, 200,
   212, 215–16
sectarianism, 70, 121
spiritual v material, 98, 100–103
Church Missionary Intelligencer, 108
Church Missionary Society, 30, 105
citation, 8
citizenship, 195
City of London, 21
Civil Service, 23, 52–3, 57, 65, 184, 242
civilisation, 6, 13, 47, 53–4, 59–62,
   65–6, 70, 82, 89, 93, 140
'character', 63–8
and Christianity, 13, 47, 70, 105
decline of, 35, 58
and education, 53–4, 65, 68, 70, 81,
   89–90, 91
and evolution, 142
exchange, 59–60
and materialism, 70, 71
and native dress, 74–5
spiritual health, 101
and table manners, 74
women, 54, 68, 156, 159, 160
Civilizing Process, The (Elias), 74
Clapham Sect, 31
class, 93
clitoridectomy, 157
Clive, Robert, 99, 100
'clownish juggler', 191–4, 197, 198,
   224–5
Cobbe, Frances Power, 38, 43, 79,
   93–5, 103, 108, 112, 151, 167–8
Coleridge, Samuel Taylor, 38
collective memory, 48
Collet, Sophia Dobson, 19, 43–4, 162,
   232–3
and asceticism, 150
and authoritarianism, 204–5
and 'clownish juggler', 197, 198